The Sovietization of Eastern Europe

Published and Forthcoming by New Academia Publishing

History and Culture (Russia / Eastern Europe)

THE INNER ADVERSARY: The Struggle against Philistinism as the Moral Mission of the Russian Intelligentsia, by Timo Vihavainen

RUSSIAN FUTURISM: A History, by Vladimir Markov

WORDS IN REVOLUTION: Russian Futurist Manifestoes 1912-1928, A. Lawton and H. Eagle, eds., trs.

IMAGING RUSSIA 2000: Film and Facts, by Anna Lawton

BEFORE THE FALL: Soviet Cinema in the Gorbachev Years, by Anna Lawton

RED ATTACK WHITE RESISTANCE: Civil War in South Russia, 1918, by Peter Kenez

RED ADVANCE WHITE DEFEAT: Civil War in South Russia, 1919-1920, by Peter Kenez

ASPECTS OF BALKAN CULTURE, by Jelena Milojković-Djurić

SLAVIC THINKERS OR THE CREATION OF POLITIES, by Josette Baers

REMEMBERING UTOPIA: The Culture of Everyday Life in Socialist Yugoslavia Breda Luthar and Marusa Pušnik, eds.

History / International Affairs

TURKEY'S MODERNIZATION: Refugees from Nazism and Atatürk's Vision by Arnold Reisman

GOD, GREED, AND GENOCIDE: The Holocaust through the Centuries by Arthur Grenke

NATIONALISM, HISTORIOGRAPHY AND THE (RE)CONSTRUCTION OF THE PAST, Edited by Claire Norton

AN ARCHITECT OF DEMOCRACY: Building a Mosaic of Peace by James Robert Huntley, Foreword by Brent Scowcroft. (Memoirs and Occasional Papers, Association for Diplomatic Studies and Training)

Scarith Books (fiction / memoirs)

THROUGH DARK DAYS AND WHITE NIGHTS: Four Decades Observing a Changing Russia, by Naomi F. Collins

ON THE WAY TO RED SQUARE, by Julieta Almeida Rodrigues

FROM WARSAW TO WHEREVER, by Zygmunt Nagorski

JOURNEYS THROUGH VANISHING WORLDS, by Abraham Brumberg

PETS OF THE GREAT DICTATORS & Other Works, by Sabrina P. Ramet

To read an excerpt, visit: www.newacademia.com

The Sovietization of Eastern Europe

New Perspectives on the Postwar Period

edited by
Balázs Apor, Péter Apor and E. A. Rees

New Academia Publishing
Washington, DC

New Academia Publishing, 2008

Printed in the United States of America

Library of Congress Control Number: 2008922326
ISBN 978-0-9800814-6-6 paperback (alk. paper)

New Academia Publishing
P.O. Box 27420, Washington, DC 20038-7420
info@newacademia.com - www.newacademia.com

Contents

Illustrations

Figures

Tables

Foreword

This volume is based on a joint workshop on 'New Perspectives on Sovietization and Modernity in Central and Eastern Europe 1945-1964' held at the European University Institute in San Domenico, Florence on 26-27 May 2005, and at the Central European University in Budapest on 17-18 June 2005. The editors wish to acknowledge the support provided by the European University Institute, the Central European University and the Higher Educational Support Program of the Open Society Institute in the framework of the Regional Seminar in Recent History in funding the workshop and in hosting it. The editors also wish to acknowledge the assistance of Mr. Chris Engert in preparing the papers for publication.

Part I

Theories of Sovietization

Introduction

The Sovietization of Eastern Europe

E. A. Rees

The sovietization of Eastern Europe involved the transplantation of institutions and methods developed in the USSR into the very different environments provided by the states of Eastern Europe after 1945. This volume examines these processes. Sovietization was shaped both by Soviet ideology and by deeper Russian cultural values and assumptions. Whereas modernization in the Russian Empire had been equated with westernization and western civilization, after 1917, the Bolsheviks equated modernization with sovietization, which was collectivist and anti-capitalist, based upon state intervention in the ordering of economic and social life as part of a messianic project of creating a new Soviet civilization.[1] The Soviet regime lasted over seventy years, reaching its apogee in the Brezhnev era (1964-1981). Throughout this period, the Soviet model underwent significant internal transformations, which reflected, in part, the changes in the wider world.

The term sovietization implies the creation of a specific Soviet system with its own institutional structures and practices, comprising economic, political, social and cultural sub-systems, characterized by particular means of system integration, and distinguished by particular methods of rule. As such, it can be analyzed in terms of its capacities and potentialities, its structural limitations, and the factors that might lead to its breakdown or failure.

Sovietization had a dual aspect, firstly, as part of the Soviet imperial project in Eastern Europe in the decades after 1945, and secondly, as part of a Soviet socialist strategy of modernization. These two aspects of the sovietization project were held in tension, which shaped the model's development and ultimate demise. The volume examines how this transference of ideas and practices was effected, and the way in which these ideas and practices were absorbed, adapted and resisted by the societies into which they were implanted. Sovietization involved a radical re-conceptualization of the past, the present and the future. It was related to a strategy of indoctrination, which aspired to make the official ideology an integral part of the life of the individual, through the transformation of all aspects of human experience and the fundamental refounding of cultural life. This is explored in terms of the transformation of the structures of power and authority within society, and, linked to it, a fundamental new conception of the way in which the economic life of the society, and its engagement with developing technology, could be transformed. The study of this transplantation process will seek to bring out how far the cultures, traditions and practices of the various countries of Eastern Europe proved receptive or resistant.

Sovietization, as a term, has both an analytical dimension, which explains the nature of the inner workings of the Soviet system of rule, and a normative dimension, which carries either a positive or a negative evaluation. It was first used in the Soviet Union itself, as a term that carried very positive connotations regarding the establishment of a new superior system for the organizing of human affairs. However, it came to be widely used in a pejorative sense in the 1940s and 1950s by critics of Soviet rule over Eastern Europe. Thereafter, the term, both in the USSR and in the West, fell into disuse. Since 1989, its use has been revived by East European and western scholars, and, in this volume, we argue for its analytical value.

Soviet leaders used the term 'sovietization' (*sovietizatsia*) amongst themselves, as shown by Lenin's correspondence concerning the consolidation of control over the Transcaucasus and over the Baltic states in 1918-21.[2] It was rarely, if ever, used by these leaders in public, but it appeared in press articles and even in party and state documents. This is one instance in which there was a certain distinction between private and public discourse. As sovietization was often done by stealth, it was impolitic to speak of it too explicitly.

We have no well authenticated use by Stalin of the term sovietization. It has been asserted that in a speech to the Politburo on 19 August 1939, on the terms of the Nazi-Soviet pact, Stalin offered a survey of the provisions of the treaty that would establish Soviet control over the Baltic states and Eastern Poland, and extend the Soviet sphere of influence to Romania, Bulgaria and Hungary. In this speech he is purported to have discussed the possibility of establishing a Soviet regime in Germany in the event of her being defeated in war, and to have also speculated on the 'sovietization' of France. The contents of this speech were published in a French journal already in 1939. They were published in Russia in 1994. The document's authenticity is strongly contested by some specialists, and the probability is that it is a forgery.[3]

In reality the extension of the Soviet sphere of influence over Central and Eastern Europe after 1945 involved regulating inter-state relations, delimiting the borders of these states, determining their ethnic composition through expulsions and population transfers, fixing their constitutions, and deciding on the compositions of their governments. This served as the prelude to the sovietization of these countries. Sovietization involved the adaptation of the original model to the very distinctive circumstances of the individual countries of the region. Over time the model was further modified to take account of new and changing circumstances.

Communization or Sovietization?

The first countries to be sovietized were those which had made up the former Russian Empire. After the October Revolution, sovietization was first imposed upon Russia itself, then upon Ukraine[4] and Byelorussia.[5] With the Bolshevik victory in the Civil War, it was extended over the White and nationalist controlled areas of Siberia, North Caucasus, and then into the Transcaucasus and Central Asia.[6] The sovietization of most of these regions was a concomitant of their conquest by military force. The establishment of political control also involved breaking peasant and working class opposition.

In the 1920s, sovietization took a new form, and was accompanied by a policy of fostering non-Russian languages and cultures (Ukrainization, Byelorussianization) and indigenization (*korenizatsiya*), as part of a process of state and nation building, whereby traditions were invented and adapted. In Stalin's memorable phrase, the aim was to create policies 'national in form, socialist in content'. After 1929, these policies were modified with a new emphasis on Russification. It was also reflected in the exportation of the Revolution, and the sovietization of conquered territories – initially in 1939 over the Baltic republics[7] and eastern Poland,[8] and again, in 1945, with the incorporation of these territories, as well as Moldova and Ruthenia, within the USSR.

Sovietization in the USSR went through phases that are well-known: War Communism 1918-1921, the New Economic Policy 1921-1928, and the Command Administrative Economy from 1928/9 onwards. Each phase constituted a specific variant of the Soviet model, and was intimately connected with wider aspects of the unfolding strategies of the Bolshevik regime; its policies towards the peasantry, the working class, the intelligentsia; its policies towards the Russians and non-Russian peoples; and its policies towards women. Sovietization created new structures of government, and established new relationships between the state and these disparate social groups. It was crucially connected to the way in which identities were ascribed to different groups and social classes.

Sovietization was an all-embracing, transforming conception of politics. At the temporal level, it involved the adoption of a new calendar, punctuated by public rituals, and the creation of a particular notion of historical time. Spatially, sovietization was reflected in the renaming of towns, streets, schools, farms and factories, in the new architecture, monuments and sculptures. It was reflected in the remaking of the countryside, the remolding of the non-Russian regions, in the conquest of the remote, inaccessible regions of the USSR, including the Arctic.[9] Stalin's plan for the transformation of nature in the late 1940s reflected another aspect of the visionary aspiration of sovietization to reshape geographic space.

The sovietization of the public and the private sphere was reflected in the intensification of indoctrination, the creation of new behavioral patterns, new communication codes, which sought to instill new disciplinary norms and to nurture an affective relationship between the individual and the state, embodied by its leader.[10] The new Soviet civilization was informed by a strong utopian, revolutionary, iconoclastic impulse, which, in the 1930s, was subsumed by the priorities of political control, and by the state direction of all aspects of development.[11]

The early Soviet regime enforced a program of social leveling, the restructuring of society, and the proletarianization of the party and state apparatus. Proletarianization was also reflected in manners, dress and habits of speech. After the Revolution, the cities were proletarianized, with the disappearance of the high-class shopping areas, the financial districts, and exclusive residential quarters. Industrial development combined a strategy of implanting proletarian centers to ensure control of rural areas and national regions. Modernization involved the eradication of all that was conceived as being non-proletarian and non-socialist.

Sovietization was allied to the development of specific organizational principles, especially those embodied by the Party, in terms of democratic centralism. This was termed—at the time—as Bolshevization.[12] During the Stalin era, Bolshevik organizational principles were extended to all other institutions in the USSR.[13] In the 1920s, the communist parties in the Communist International were purged, re-organized and effectively Bolshevized.

At the outset, a distinction needs to be drawn between communization and sovietization. 'Communism' was always an on-going project, part of an ideological aspiration, many of whose utopian pretensions were modified or jettisoned. The Soviet system, in contrast, was constituted by concrete institutional structures and practices, established by the end of the 1920s, which proved extremely durable and which survived in a more or less modified form until 1985, although some of these structures and practices were adapted over time in order to cope with new tasks.

The political structures of this system were established early on, with the Communist Party occupying the central position within the one party state, buttressed by the state bureaucracy, the secret police and the military. The Party conceived of itself as an élitist, militant vanguard party. Its militarized conception of politics was shaped by the ideology of class warfare, and by the experience of the underground and of Civil War. In the mass organizations, such as the soviets, youth organizations acted as surrogates of the Party, whilst the trade unions, in Lenin's phrase, acted as 'transmission belts' which connected the political leadership with society. Soviet administrative practices were, in large measure, derived from military models which, in the 1920s, were already being criticized as primitive and at variance with the practices of the most advanced Western countries.[14]

Sovietization involved the politicization and ideologization of all aspects of life, which effectively negated politics as the free exchange of opinion, negotiation and the open articulation of demands.[15] The political sphere was monopolized by the party, and was neither constrained by any countervailing power nor checked by the rule of law. The dominance of the political regime severely limited the autonomy of the social, economic, and cultural sub-systems. The manipulative and coercive aspect of political power was highly pronounced, whilst the prevalence of systems of control and surveillance created opacity with regard to political and social processes.

The Stalinist system attempted to create a new culture, which encompassed the life of the individual in its diversity.[16] It aspired to the fundamental restructuring of society and culture, whereby class membership was ascribed by the regime, identities were remolded, and a particular Soviet conception of *kulturnost'*, which aimed at creating the new Soviet man and woman, was propagated.[17] Through the sovietization of the system of education (*obrazovanie*) and upbringing (*vospitanie*), the regime sought to restructure social consciousness, to inculcate socialist values, to foster Soviet patriotism, whilst subverting traditional thoughts and practices, in part through an unprecedented assault on organized religion.[18] The life experiences of people were transformed; through the sovietization of the family, childhood, gender identities and relations,[19] through the transformation of workplace relations, recreation and leisure.

All fields of knowledge (textbooks, encyclopedias, dictionaries, manuals, maps) were restructured as part of the creation of a wholly new Soviet *weltanschauung.*[20] It was associated with the propagation of a 'consequentialist' conception of ethics and a new Soviet morality.[21] The regime sought to create its own language, its own concepts, its own value system, and its own discourses.[22] Stephen Kotkin coined the term 'speaking Bolshevik' to illustrate the extent to which the state achieved a remolding of mass consciousness and the internalization of the official value system in the 1930s.[23] But the official language could be subverted.[24]

Sovietization aimed at the transformation of mass culture; through education and censorship, and the development of artistic policies shaped by the ideals of 'socialist realism'. This represented a shift away from a narrowly conceived 'proletarian' conception of art of the early revolutionary era, and sought to establish something, more universal, more classical, and more related to the Russian realist cultural tradition.[25] Socialist realism encapsulated three basic principles: *narodnost* (the spirit of the people), *klassovost* (spirit of the class) and *partiinost* (party mindedness).[26] In this, Stalin envisaged writers as 'engineers of humans' souls'. This also involved a commitment to the promotion of high culture, as well as to popular culture, with its sentimentalized, folkloric celebration of the people (*narod*) and their past.[27]

The closure of the public sphere in the Stalin era was associated with a profound change in political rhetoric, in a new language that defined the relations between the state and its subjects more rigidly. Stalin spoke of the Soviet state as a 'monolith' with every person acting as a cog (*vintik*) in a great machine,[28] exemplifying what Engels had characterized as 'barracks socialism' with its *étatisme,* regimentation, and uniformity. The Soviet model borrowed from traditional Russian practices, and drew inspiration from socialist ideas. The regime fostered a collective consciousness which aimed at creating a new *Homo Sovieticus.*[29]

In terms of economic organization, sovietization involved the socialization of the economy and the eradication of private property following the dissolution of the New Economic Policy in 1928/9. It combined the program of forced industrialization through successive Five-Year Plans, based upon state ownership and planning, which accorded priority to heavy industry. Through collectivization and de-kulakization, agriculture was restructured, and the private sector virtually abolished, although the small peasant plots and the collective farm *(kolkhoz)* market remained important to the economy. The labor market continued to operate to some extent, although labor conscription and severe labor laws were introduced during the Second World War. Money, notwithstanding the official ideology, which sought its abolition, remained a vital medium of exchange.

The power of the state was reinforced by the legal system, with its notion of class justice, and the criminalization of behavior based on the demarcation between those defined as the fiends and those defined as the enemies of the new socialist order. In areas such as Central Asia, with its Muslim population, the notion of crimes of daily life (*bytovye prestuplenia*), related to polygamy, child brides, *etc.*, was introduced. From 1930 onwards, the system of forced labor of the Gulag became a central aspect of the economic system, and was used with the aim of reforging (*perekovka*) the mentalities and behavior of criminals and political offenders.

Under Soviet socialism, the state, which was supposed to wither away, became the dominant force, the instrument whereby socialism and communism was to be built. Socialism, which was to liberate the individual, severely circumscribed individual rights, imposing duties and obligations that counter-balanced the new 'right' and freedoms that were offered. The economic model introduced in 1929 was defined as 'socialist', but it allowed workers no control over the productive process. The system of industrial management was hierarchical, with the role of managers constrained by the needs to meet plan targets. The forms of labor participation that were allowed took the forms of 'initiatives' such as shock-work, *Stakhanovism,* and socialist emulation campaigns.[30]

Notwithstanding Soviet communism's autarkic aspirations, it also borrowed and adapted ideas, technologies and practices from the West. Already under Lenin, the Soviet regime embraced Taylorist methods of labor organization and Fordist methods of mass production.[31] Lenin summarized his technocratic image of modernization in a memorable phrase concerning the famous Goelro project: 'Communism is Soviet power plus the electrification of the whole country'. Bolshevik enchantment with American civilization was summarized in Stalin's assertion that they aimed to combine 'American efficiency and Bolshevik sweep.'

In the 1920s and 1930s, the Soviet government signed contracts with companies such as Ford and International Harvester, for the building of western model of cars and tractors. Foreign planes were also built under patent. The USSR borrowed a wide diversity of technologies and production system from Germany, the USA and Japan.[32] Agricultural collectivization was partly inspired by N.M. Tulaikov's studies of modern agriculture in the USA.[33] Whole sectors of industry—metallurgy, oil, and rail transport—were based upon the adaptation of ideas from the West. The Moscow metro drew on the experience of the building of the London and Berlin undergrounds. The restructuring of Moscow was based upon the study of western urban models. In 1936, a commission, headed by Anastas Mikoyan, studied the development of retail networks and department stores in the USA to see what could be applied in the USSR.[34]

Soviet socialism aspired to become a new technological-based civilization.[35] The Soviet economic system demonstrated a formidable capacity for the mobilization of manpower and resources. Its modernization strategy aimed to catch up speedily and overtake the advanced capitalist countries. Projects were developed with the aim of creating what was bigger and better, for reasons of efficiency and prestige, and to demonstrate the superiority of the Soviet model. In industry large units, with large scale production volumes, dominated. The adverse side of this were the problems of 'gigantomania' and poor co-ordination.

In the field of military technology, the USSR was compelled to adapt itself, like all other states, to the needs and requirement of modern warfare; in terms of productive capacity, the development of new weapons system, and in the training of manpower. The primacy of defense considerations profoundly shaped industrial development, and created a dual economy, with the emergence of the closed cities and limited access regions.

In the field of science, the USSR sought to seize the lead in promoting the policy of the mass training of scientific cadres and the application of planning and direction to scientific research and development. It adopted science and technology from the capitalist world in the confident belief that socialism could ensure the fullest exploitation of their potentialities.

Marxism-Leninism, as an ideology, provided only limited guidelines as to what policies the Soviet government should pursue. The state's security priorities dictated in large measure the decision to follow the course of forced industrialization and agricultural collectivization. In the development of the Soviet state, the recourse to older more authoritarian and coercive methods of government, of control and regimentation, and of mass mobilization, profoundly shaped the way in which the model evolved.

The Soviet regime underwent significant changes under Stalin, through an extraordinary ritualization of politics, the sacralization of politics, which was reflected in the leader cult, the language of political communication, and the practices of denunciations and informing.[36] It was marked by a reliance on state repression, and a turn to more conservative social policies with regard to the family, divorce, abortion, and education.[37] The era of experimentation gave way to an era of uniformity and discipline, in which the fragile remnants of democratic practices were crushed, and a new emphasis was placed on social discipline and hierarchy. Soviet development was characterized by huge rural-urban migration, and by high levels of upward social mobility. Moshe Lewin famously characterized the paradoxical processes of the 'ruralization' of the towns, the 'peasantization' of the working class and the transfer of traditional attitudes into the new society.[38]

The Second World War provided a basis for rebuilding the regime's legitimacy on the basis of its military victory and its status as the leading communist world power.[39] Soviet patriotism was allied to the notion of

Soviet power as the continuation and culmination of the progressive trends in Russian history.[40] The post-war years were less marked by the mass mobilization and political upheavals that had characterized the inter-war decades. They also saw the rise of official xenophobia, anti-westernism and anti-Semitism as devices deployed to control public moods and attitudes.

During the Stalin era, egalitarianism was repudiated and emphasis was placed on social hierarchy, on respectability, culture and civility.[41] Within this society, the distribution of power, status and wealth was largely determined by the ruling authorities. The social hierarchy was shaped by the official *nomenklatura,* and the provision of rewards, services and access to scare goods and resources.[42] Status and honor were dispensed through titles, awards and prizes. Access to those with power was closely regulated, but the system of *blat,* of connections, favoritism and nepotism was an integral and pervasive part of the system.

Social control was maintained in other less subtle ways. The public discourse reflected the class ideology of the Party, and the intrusion of Marxism-Leninism into all public, intellectual and artistic spheres. The discourse reflected a preoccupation with both internal and external enemies. Social control was exercised through the Party, the youth organizations, the trade unions; through the system of committees set up in work places and in residential blocks; through the system of internal passports and residence permit; through work books; as well as the more obvious system of police surveillance.

Sovietization and Modernity

Stephen Kotkin coined the term 'Stalinist civilization' as a realization of the ideals of the eighteenth century Enlightenment in the USSR, with Stalin as a kind of enlightened despot, using state power to transform a recalcitrant, backward and primitive society into one that was modern, scientific and rational.[43]

The British philosopher Bertrand Russell, in *The Theory and Practice of Bolshevism,* published in 1920, announced the failure of the Bolshevik's experiment in Communism.[44] The communist project as an ideological goal, Russell believed, had already lost its energizing force, and he predicted that the regime would substitute the goal of attaining communism with the goal of the industrial transformation of the country and the creation of a powerful state. Russell also recognized a central duality within Bolshevism – its commitment to a certain conception of modernization, and its commitment to an ideological world view, which, in many ways, was unmodern, shaped by ideological zeal and intolerance of other world views, which was a denial of the Enlightenment commitment to rational discourse. It was, he asserted, a regime that had the capacity to produce its own Inquisition. This duality provides a key to understanding the metamorphosis of Leninism into Stalinism, which was shaped by the regime's internal logic and by the objective difficulties with which it was confronted.

How far the Soviet regime might be considered to be a modernizing regime is itself problematical. Alongside its economic, social and cultural achievements, the Soviet regime was, in many senses, profoundly anti-modern—the restriction of civil society, the impingement on any sense of citizenship, the impediments to free communications, the restriction on individual freedom and free expression.[45] These negative features of the Soviet model cannot be dismissed as part of a general equation of plus and minuses. There is a real sense in which these negative aspects seriously restricted development in all other spheres, and indicate how far the Soviet regime profoundly misunderstood the nature of modernity.

The Sovietization of Eastern Europe

Whilst the Soviet leadership's attitude towards Eastern Europe predisposed them towards a policy of sovietization, the full implementation of the Soviet model in these countries was not inevitable. In 1945, Stalin considered the possibility of placing priority on the continuation of the wartime alliance with the USA and the UK. However, the tensions within the alliance and the growing distrust, undoubtedly heightened by Soviet measures to consolidate its power in the East European states, resulted in the adoption of a policy of full sovietization after 1947.

Stalin intended to turn Eastern Europe into a buffer zone that would guarantee Soviet security. From this zone, he intended to exact reparation payments for the war damage caused by the Germans. In Soviet propaganda, it was presented as the liberation of these countries from Nazi tyranny. The sovietization process was intimately connected with the onset of the Cold War, the creation of NATO and the Warsaw Pact, and the partition of Germany.

Sovietization proceeded through distinct stages in most of the East European countries. From 1945 to 1947/8, the local Communist Parties ruled in alliance with other left of center and peasant parties. In this initial period, the government introduced reforms, particularly land redistribution, as well as limited nationalization of industry. From 1947/8 to 1953, it was the Stalinist model of sovietization that was enforced in its most intense way, through consolidation of the one party state, collectivization of agriculture, and the nationalization of industry and the rapid development of heavy industry.

After 1945, the USSR extended its control over Eastern Europe, as a border region and buffer zone. Control over the states of Eastern Europe was established by the Red Army, the security police, the governmental and party bodies of the USSR, and through their close links with the institutions of each individual country. Sovietization, however, was not solely a matter of military subjugation. The USSR withdrew the Red Army from Czechoslovakia in 1945 and Bulgaria in 1947. But the Red Army retained bases in East Germany, Poland, Romania and Hungary, ostensibly to maintain communication lines. Under the Warsaw Pact, the retention of Soviet bases in the East European states was purportedly on the basis of mutual agreement.

The first institutions to be sovietized were the armed forces and the security apparatus. The security agencies were modeled on those of the USSR:, in Romania – the *Securitate;* in Bulgaria – the Committee of State Security; in Hungary – the State Protection Authority (*ÁVH*); in Poland – the State Security (*SB*); in Czechoslovakia – the State Security (*St.B*), and in the GDR – the *Stasi.*

Sovietization was carried through by cadres who were Moscow trained, who had spent long periods in exile in the USSR, and who were themselves thoroughly sovietized. The leaders of the post-war People's Democracies – Walter Ulbricht, Mátyás Rákosi, Josip Broz Tito, Enver Hoxha, Georgi Dimitrov, Gheorghe Gheorghiu-Dej, Bolesław Bierut and Klement Gottwald represented a distinct generation of Marxist-Leninists, schooled in the Stalinist tradition and molded by the anti-fascist struggle. These states of the 'peoples' democracies' were viewed as following the Soviet model of development, albeit at a lower level. The rapid imposition of sovietization meant that the developments in the USSR were telescoped. The term sovietization came into general currency after 1945, to describe the process of transformation imposed on the Soviet occupied countries of Eastern and Central Europe.[46] It was a term used before the term 'totalitarianism' was widely applied to these states.

The imposition of the Soviet model transformed the intellectual and cultural life of the satellite states, wherein the USSR was seen as the embodiment of the future. It was a conception of modernity that was non-capitalist which seemingly offered the prospect of rapid advance. It was a model which, in 1945, was thought to have demonstrated its strength and viability through its defeat of Nazi Germany, and by the transformation of the USSR into a super-power, and the undisputed leader of the world communist movement. It was based upon a radical critique of western individualism, and posited the view of a modern, dynamic society based on collectivist principles. In this, communism was projected as the embodiment of a new form of politics, based upon the realization of a conception of a new planned order of human society, in which those who wielded power were not politicians in the conventional sense, but were also socialist philosophers, who sought to combine the practicalities of the political management of society with the realization of the longer term philosophical goals of remolding society and the individual.

The social base of the new people's democracies varied considerably as between states. Czechoslovakia was the one country in Central and Eastern Europe where the establishment of socialism commanded broad public support. The wartime persecution of communists in Czechoslovakia provided a major legitimating force for the communist regime after 1945.[47] In Poland and Hungary, the support was small. In Yugoslavia and Albania, the generation of wartime partisans dominated the political life of both countries for the next 30 years. In Yugoslavia, the Tito government attempted the sovietization of the system in its full Stalinist variant early on, but, after the break with Stalin in 1948, it drew increasingly away from the Stalinist model, and adapted the Soviet model, primarily through its experiments in worker self-management. Albania, on account of its break with Yugoslavia, clung more stubbornly to the Stalinist model the longest. The people's democracies emulated the Soviet model, but also drew on the authoritarian methods of rule of the pre-communist era in their own countries, and adapted, in part, to the political cultures of their own countries.[48]

The internal developments within the peoples' democracies were shaped by the wider international context: the Soviet triumph over Nazi Germany, and the discrediting of pro-Nazi regimes and movements in Eastern Europe, which created an extraordinary imbalance in the domestic politics of these states. The imposition of sovietization in 1948-53 was associated with intensified repression, with the show trials of alleged enemies of the regimes in Czechoslovakia and Hungary, although not in Poland. Although the period of 'terror' and 'High Stalinism' in most East European countries was relatively short, its impact was immense.

By 1953, the countries of Eastern Europe had, to a large extent, been successfully sovietized. Thereafter, the transplantation of cultural and social practices to these countries became part of a more ambitious project to remake Eastern Europe in the image of the USSR. The reforging of Eastern Europe was conceived in terms of applying the Soviet model of modernization, and the application of specific Soviet notions of modernity, which were socialist and collectivist, and which accorded the state the central role as the agency of modernization. In Czechoslovakia, with its developed industrial culture, the imposition of the Soviet model of modernity encountered considerable difficulties, notwithstanding broad popular support for the communist government in 1948.

Sovietization and Empire

The founding of the Soviet imperia also involved elements of self-sovietization by local communist élites, operating under Soviet tutelage. Sovietization as an imperial project, and as the negation and antithesis of western imperialism, was inseparable from the projection of Soviet civilization as being superior both in its capacities and in its moral claims. Sovietization, in terms of relations between states, and between states and regions, should also be seen as part of an imperialistic conception, whereby a system of domination and subjugation was effected and rationalized, and whereby a subaltern identity was ascribed to the subjected peoples.[49] In the 1930s, official Soviet spokesmen vehemently denied that the relationship between the central authorities and the non-Russian republics was one of colonial exploitation.[50]

Soviet imperialism, including cultural imperialism, drew its inspiration, in part, from the experience of the Russian Empire, even though Soviet hegemony over Eastern Europe purported to be based on socialist principles, and on the fraternal relations between socialist states.[51] The project advanced in the USSR in the 1920s, that the future new socialist states in Central and Eastern Europe would become republics within the USSR, was never attempted. This would have provoked an international outcry, and would have generated intense opposition within these states, and creating potentially unmanageable tensions within an enlarged USSR. Whilst the new people's democracies were granted nominal sovereignty, they were bound to the USSR by treaties of friendship and mutual co-operation.

In his Memoirs, Khrushchev refers explicitly to the 'sovietizing' in 1944-45 of the annexed Baltic states of Estonia, Latvia and Lithuania, western Byelorussia and western Ukraine.[52] This re-established the frontiers of the former Russian Empire. The incorporation of the Baltic states was 'approved' by referenda. The annexation of the Byelorussian and Ukrainian territories was justified as part of projects of national unification.

Sovietization combined both 'hard' controls and 'soft' controls – the cultivation of identification with the dominant power, in terms of values and aspirations. In the emerging bi-polar world of the Cold War, with its designated spheres of influence, the *Pax Americana* confronted the *Pax Sovietica*. Both the sovietization of Eastern Europe after 1945 and the Americanization of Western Europe involved significant differences in the way that, and the extent to which, economic and military hegemony was exercised, as well as through the importation of ideas, managerial methods, mass culture and consumption models as auxiliary methods of influence.[53]

The sovietization of Eastern Europe was effected with the help of Soviet advisers and specialists, who offered advice both of a technical and of a political kind. In some cases, it was more than simply advice: the Soviet Marshall K. Rokossowski became the Polish Minister of Defence. Sovietization required the adaptation of the model to local circumstances, in order to root the model in local traditions, values and practices. Notwithstanding these qualifications, the Soviet model aspired to great uniformity and homogeneity across cultures.

The Soviet model, in its Stalinist variant, was based upon an extensive model of development which drew upon a large supply of labor and material resources, and tended to be wasteful of these resources. It functioned at a lower level of efficiency than capitalist enterprises operating within a competitive market economy, in which consumer preference remained important. The Stalin model of industrialization showed a low regard for social costs in development, and little concern for environmental degradation. This system of forced development, with taut planning, reinforced the difficulties of resource management and low consumption levels in this shortage economy. Consequently, the adaptation of the system to a pattern of more intensive development in the post-Stalin era incurred serious difficulties.

Soviet hegemonic rule over Eastern Europe was driven primarily by military, security, and ideological considerations. Economic motivations, in terms of gaining access to markets, raw material supplies or providing outlets for investment, did not figure strongly. Economically, it might be argued that the Soviet bloc was, for most of its existence, always a financial burden to the USSR, through subsidized defense expenditure and subsidized fuel and gas supplies. Soviet domination of Eastern Europe did not involve large-scale colonization by citizens of the USSR. Only in Estonia, Latvia and Lithuania was there such an influx of Russians, Ukrainians and other Soviet citizens.

The Empire was bound together institutionally, economically and culturally. The main binding force linking these countries together was provided by their ruling parties, and by their links at the very highest level with the Communist Party of the Soviet Union. After the Yugoslav break with the USSR, the Cominform (Communist Information Bureau) was established to ensure that the other East European communist states and non-ruling communist parties in Western Europe were kept in line. The links between leaders and parties, and their relative ranking were a central component of this system of relations between states. Party congresses in the satellite states were periods of intense contact, with the attendance by fraternal delegates from the other bloc parties, with a special place of honor always reserved for the Soviet delegation. In periods of crisis, these contacts assumed central importance.

With sovietization, the East European economies were incorporated into an enlarged Soviet dominated economic space. Long-established trade links between these countries and other western countries were abruptly severed, and all foreign-owned assets were nationalized. The industrialization of many of the backward countries of Eastern Europe based upon the Soviet model involved the creation of heavy industry, an urbanized population with a large industrial working class, and the acculturation of a peasant population into urban and industrial life. Sovietization meant state ownership and planning, but in the East European countries, especially in Poland and Hungary, the private sector in agriculture, in manufacturing and the retail sector was tolerated to a much greater degree than in the USSR.

The countries of the Soviet bloc shared the same symbols and rituals; the most important events such as May Day, the October Revolution anniversary, and Victory Day were celebrated as part of a common experience. They shared the same revered texts, and looked to the same founding fathers. They shared a similar socialist iconography, as well as the same heroic conception of workers, women and soldiers. The renaming of towns, streets, squares, factories, and collective farms created the same image of the advancing socialist revolution, of states which followed a common destiny and were being drawn ever closer together. The transplantation of the bombastic architectural style of 'High Stalinism' to Eastern Europe, as with the Palace of Culture in Warsaw as a gift to the Poles, a copy of the Stalin towers in Moscow, illustrated a similar drive towards cultural integration.

Sovietization Domesticated

With Stalin's death in 1953, this intense phase of sovietization was eased with the adoption of the 'New Course', political repression was relaxed, and the policy of forced industrial development moderated. By this time, the sovietization of the satellite states had been effectively completed. Thereafter, policies were adapted to domesticate the Soviet model, to adapt and adjust it to local conditions, as a way of building support. This allowed a certain diversity in the interpretation and application of the Soviet model.

The Soviet system of rule, as Terry Martin argues, combined both hard and soft controls.[54] War Communism relied on hard controls, the New Economic Policy (NEP) relied more on a system of social management, whilst the Command Economy of the Stalin era was heavily reliant on hard controls. De-Stalinization after 1953 marked a conscious shift from hard control to a system based upon the management of social and economic problems, but with hard controls as an auxiliary, always on call. In the East European satellites, de-Stalinization required an adaptation of the sovietization process, now tempered by a new emphasis on consumerism, and new self-sovietizing strategies.

Sovietization was advanced as the creation of a new 'civilization' that claimed universal relevance. The Soviet model shared, in exaggerated form, many of the assumptions regarding modernity that were held in the capitalist West in the post-war decades; the belief in the efficacy of social planning and of state intervention for promoting social improvement. The Soviet model was to be profoundly affected by economic and technological changes, and changes in patterns of welfare provision, consumption and leisure that were already being developed in the West.

Each of these regimes endeavoured to mobilize broad public support, behind a program of post-war reconstruction, and to offer the prospect for a more dynamic modernizing economy and society, in which the state would be the central vehicle of modernization, to which individual and group interests would be subordinated, and by which a new sense of social justice and fairness would be established. These regimes appealed to idealism, to the elevation of collective interests above individual interests, in which the party-state sought to present itself as an embodiment of the common good, and as an instrument that was able to resolve long-standing and deep-seated problems of national development.

Sovietization and Regime Legitimation

The existence of the USSR as a 'guarantor' of Soviet power in Eastern Europe placed the domestic regimes in a position of duality, as they were caught between the demands of their own people, and the demands of their Soviet masters. This itself posed a danger to legitimization strategies, where regimes claimed to embody the interests of the nation and people, as a means of building popular allegiance and consensus. The paradox of these strategies of political mobilization was that their actual purpose was to secure the political de-mobilization of the population and their effective exclusion from the political sphere.

The new regimes in Eastern Europe, as indeed the USSR itself, sought to base themselves upon a new notion of 'legitimacy'. In the Weberian sense, these regimes did not attempt to base their claim to legitimacy upon 'tradition', 'rational-legal' authority, or upon 'charisma', although each of these three elements was drawn upon. Instead, these regimes were 'self-legitimizing', basing their claims to legitimacy upon past, present and future achievements.[55] It was based upon a claim to a superior, scientific understanding of history. In this, they sought to construct legitimacy around the symbols, the trappings of communist power, in the conviction that, in time, the regimes would become more strongly rooted in society.

The question of legitimacy was related to other crucial aspects of the regime. The restriction of the public sphere through tight control of communication effectively destroyed public opinion, which requires the existence of alternative sources of information, and alternative sources of interpretation. Where these are absent there exist only public moods and public attitudes, which the communist regimes all showed a keen interest in tracking and manipulating, by playing on insecurities, and upon the themes of the internal and external enemy. Public attitudes varied from outright opposition to full support, with an immense range of complex responses in between, of compliance, conformity and resistance.[56]

The restriction of the public sphere encouraged a retreat into the private sphere, the life of the self, the family, friends and the *dacha*, whilst it eroded any sense of civic consciousness.[57] It reflected attempts to use the existing circumstances for personal advantage, a sense of powerlessness, and a resigned acceptance of the realities of the political sphere, albeit without any necessary willingness to accept the demands made upon them by the state, but to advance counter demands.[58]

The restriction of the public sphere had profound implications in the shaping of individual and group identities, with the regime ascribing roles for individuals and groups, and prescribing and proscribing attitudes, beliefs and behavior. The regime's insistence on its right to define the accepted conception of the present, and the vision of the future was also connected with the rewriting of public memory in accordance with the regime's conception of the past.

Sovietization involved not only the construction of notions of legitimacy, based upon past, present and future achievements, but also sought to forge affective relations between the people and the state and its leader. Within this system, great importance was assumed by the symbolism of power, the aura attached to institutions, personalities, past events, and to the ideology itself. Much of the authority of these regimes was bound up in this investment in symbolic capital, which underpinned the relations between the state and its subjects. The fragility of these processes of 'self-legitimation' became visible in moments of crisis. Sovietization was also seen as an alien imposition. In the East European countries, the attempt to equate sovietization with proletarianization was unsuccessful, with industrial workers often being the most vocal critics of the very regimes which claimed to rule in their name.

The successive crises in the Soviet bloc were associated with the failure of these regimes to control the public sphere. The protests in 1953 in East Germany and Czechoslovakia (Pilsen) were prompted by the changes inaugurated following Stalin's death. The 1956 Uprising in Hungary and the protests in Poland were influenced by Khrushchev's attack on Stalin at the Twentieth Party Congress. The 1968 crisis in Czechoslovakia stemmed from attempts to carry through domestic reform. These crises were followed by efforts to 're-sovietize' or 'normalize' these countries, through the closure of the public sphere.[59] Soviet military intervention on these occasions, served to de-legitimize these governments, and exposed the shallow nature of their claims to autonomy and sovereignty. The reliance on hard control compromised attempts to foster more subtle forms of soft control.

The attempt by the USSR to project a positive and benign image of itself encountered the strong historical antipathy towards the Russians, notably in Poland, Hungary and Romania. Its role as a guarantor of the frontiers of the Easter European states and as an advocate of greater national homogeneity could not overcome its image as a hegemonic power and the sponsors of regimes that lacked the basis of popular sovereignty.

Here, sovietization involved an attempt to occupy the high moral ground. The Soviet victory was depicted as the triumph of Soviet civilization over Nazi barbarism, and the discredited governments of Eastern Europe that had been its allies. The Soviet war memorials that were erected across Eastern Europe were intended as tangible symbols of Soviet wartime sacrifices. This constructed a taboo against questioning the sovietization process or the benign role of the USSR in the transformation.[60] The constraints imposed by the Cold War, and of East-West rivalry, with the closing of the Iron Curtain imposed their own logic upon the official discourse.

The extent to which ordinary citizens could disengage from the demands of the state was limited. The state was the direct employer of the great majority of its citizens, including many who served in the police, the security forces, and the armed forces. In the GDR and Czechoslovakia, many people were required to act as informers on their fellow citizens. A high proportion of the adult population were party members, and a high percentage of young people and children belonged to youth and children's organizations. The educational system and the mass media were used to disseminate the regime's ideology.[61] With foreign travel severely restricted, the mass media closely controlled, and almost all external sources of information and opinion excluded, these were very much closed societies.

Whilst the public sphere was tightly regulated, the private sphere remained an area which remained, to some degree, isolated from outside regulation. There was always a tension between what the authorities desired and what the public expected. In the process of 'self-legitimization', the authorities were keen to demonstrate their ability to deliver, not only in terms of goods and services, but also in terms of symbolic capital that served to create a sense of public satisfaction, pride and well-being. At a basic level, there was the need for the authorities to demonstrate a basic competence in the provision of public, municipal services, as well as in dealing with the larger questions of domestic and international relations.

The conception of the public good advanced by the governments of the people's democracies was heavily colored by socialist ideology which informed all aspects of public policy. It reflected a specific approach to basic, existentialist questions. It elevated the collective above the individual, and highlighted the provision of public goods and services as opposed to private provision. It saw the goal of the good society as the full development of the individual within the framework of a socialist order. The value placed upon self-enrichment, property, and status based upon lifestyle was largely negative. A high value was placed upon self-improvement, and the attainment of excellence in fields such as learning, the arts and sport. The notion of individual rights was heavily counter-balanced by the obligations laid upon socialist citizens to the party-state. The people's democracies, like the USSR, but to a less extreme extent, were characterized by the lack of pluralism, the weakness of civil society, and by the absence of countervailing forces to balance the power of a highly-centralized party-state apparatus. The gap between the protestations of the government, and the experience of ordinary citizens, and their perceptions of the motives and aims of their government, could be very great. 'Self-legitimation' was often perceived as a hypocritical mask that concealed the self-interest of those in power.

De-Stalinization and Adaptations of the Soviet Model

Stalin's death in 1953 led to major modifications of the Soviet model as it had developed after 1928/9. Terror as a system of political control was abandoned, and the system of forced labor was wound down. With Khrushchev's 'Secret Speech' at the Twentieth Party Congress in 1956 the excesses of the 'cult of personality' were denounced, with the erasure of Stalin's name and the removal of his statues and images from public buildings and places. Khrushchev sought to cleanse the Soviet model of the excrescences of the 'cult of personality' and its criminal distortions. With de-Stalinization, the mature Soviet model emerged, whose operational codes and practices differed significantly from that of the original model in its phase of establishment. The relations between the party-state and society underwent significant changes, with a new emphasis on mediation through soft controls, inducements and strategies of incorporation. But the monopolistic structures of party-state rule and of economic management remained fundamentally unchanged.

Khrushchev's speech inaugurated the systematic dismantling of the Stalin-cult in the USSR and in the East European states. The political culture of Poland, Czechoslovakia, Hungary and the GDR did not provide a propitious soil in which the notion of a leader cult could grow. The situation was different in Yugoslavia, Albania, and Bulgaria, where the substantial cults of Tito, Hoxha, and Dimitrov, and later, in the 1970s and 1980s in Romania, the cult of Ceauşescu, were central components of these political systems and their strategies of legitimation.[62]

The attack on Stalin dealt a major blow to the Soviet regime's credibility and moral authority. It hastened the internal division of the communist bloc, into polycentrism, with Moscow, Beijing and Belgrade as rival centers. But this allowed a new emphasis to be placed upon socialist legality and socialist humanism, and a limited revival of civil society, represented by the 'Thaw' in the arts. In place of the system of control, coercion and exhortation, new emphasis was placed upon material incentives and, with this, the development of a consumerist strategy. Khrushchev's prediction that the USSR would out-produce the USA in twenty years was the basis of the claim that communism would be established. A more managerialist, technocratic style of government emerged, reflected in the new generation of leaders, Kádár in Hungary, Gierek in Poland, Honecker in the GDR, and Zhivkov in Bulgaria.

The confident belief was that state ownership and planning provided the basis for a more fully-rounded policy of economic development, by shifting more resources into agriculture and light industry, and by the development of the Soviet welfare state with the extension of its provisions to the collective farm workers. It was believed that this system could be adapted to allow the full development of new economic sectors, which reflected the changing patterns of industrial development to cope with the growing demand for mass consumer goods. Moreover, it was believed that this system would provide the underpinning of political stability, shifting from a system that relied on controls, coercion and ideological exhortation, to one that relied increasingly upon economic self-interest, and the benefits provided by the state.

In the 1960s, the Soviet model attempted to adjust itself to the modern world by incorporating western technologies and adapting to the consumer goods revolution through the supply of televisions sets, refrigerators, and more modern furniture. The signing of a contract with FIAT to build a giant car plant at Togliatti in 1961 for volume car production in the USSR marked an important turning point. The FIAT car, the *Zhiguli* (*Lada*), stood in contrast to its simpler, more basic Soviet models such as the *Volga* and *Moskvich,* or the GDR's *Trabant,* and Czechoslovak's *Škoda.* Nevertheless, the transport priorities of the regime placed emphasis upon public rather than private provision for both ideological and economic reasons.

The Brezhnev era attained a new degree of development, with major urban conurbations boasting the achievements of modern technology, functioning public utilities, the provisions of shops, theatres, cinemas and entertainment centers. The urban landscape adopted an international style: as witnessed by the modern boulevard with skyscraper blocks of Moscow's Prospekt Kalinina (now Novy Arbat) in contrast to the post-war, heavy ornate buildings of Gorky Street (now Tverskaya), the Ostankino television tower built in 1967, the new suburban tower blocks, office blocks, hotels, and the new stations of the metro with their cleaner modern lines in contrast to the classic designs of socialist realism from the Stalin era. The increased presence of tourist and foreign students in centers such as Moscow imparted a new atmosphere to urban life. For foreign students from Third World countries, institutions such as the Patrice Lumumba University provided training for future cadres of sovietization.

Soviet consumer culture, despite attempts to develop advertising and market research, was plagued by low quality, lack of diversity, lack of innovation in design, and unresponsiveness to changing needs.[63] Soviet department stores and public catering in restaurants, cafes (such as the ubiquitous *stolovaya*) imparted a basic, utilitarian, functionalist character to consumption. The exclusion of western products, clothing – especially denim jeans and music, *etc.*, invested these rare goods with an exotic character, which could only be procured through personal contacts. The lack of diversity in the spheres of production and distribution was reflected in banal design, low quality, and standardization of mass products which reflected the sovereignty of the supplier rather than that of the consumer. This imparted a grey, monotonous quality to much of urban life. The communist regimes were also obliged to address important social changes, the gradual emergence of a new youth culture,[64] and the changing role of women in society.[65]

The adaptation of the Soviet model to the more flexible, more complex, multi-varied output of a modern economy was impeded by the rigidities in the centrally-planned economy. This prompted extensive debate. In the USSR, E.G. Liebermann promoted the ideas of the use of computers to cope with the growing complexity. In Czechoslovakia, Ota Šik advanced the idea of combining elements of the market and the plan. In Hungary, the New Economic Mechanism, developed from the early 1960s onwards, represented the most ambitious attempt to introduce market reforms within the communist system.[66] The Council of Mutual Economic Development (COMECON) established in 1949, became the agency coordinating economic links between the countries of the Eastern bloc, encouraging a division of labor and specialization between states, reflecting their own traditions and expertise. *Škoda* cars from Czechoslovakia, *Ikarus* buses from Hungary, and Bulgarian wine. The communist regimes were obliged to address new questions: the development of consumer culture, the growth of the mass media, and the question of leisure.

These developments within the communist bloc prompted criticisms from more ideologically driven regimes, such as Communist China's denunciation of Hungarian 'goulash socialism'. In the West, however, it prompted debate as to the capacity of communist planned economies to catch up and overtake the West, and led some commentators to speculate as to whether communist and capitalist systems were not converging on a common model, shaped by the priorities that regulate the organization of all industrial societies.[67]

Sovietization in Eastern Europe saw the adaptation of many of the public policies developed in the USSR: full employment, and the drawing in of a larger proportion of the female population into public employment; the provision of public housing to cope with rapid urbanization; the development of the socialist welfare state: maternity rights; sickness benefits, pensions; the extension of educational provision via pre-school nurseries, primary and secondary schools, and the expansion of higher and technical education, aimed at increasing educational provisions especially for workers and peasants as part of an active policy of positive discrimination.

The subsidizing of housing, transport and foodstuffs, and the provision of basic necessities on a mass scale, reflected the priorities of state socialist paternalism. This precluded production of more exclusive, select products that were, nonetheless, disparagingly dismissed by the official ideology as the trappings of Western consumerism. Western capitalism's preoccupation with consumption, the commercialization of human relations, and the satisfaction of egotistical needs, was seen as a mark of its decadence, in contrast to the original, Spartan, egalitarian ideals of socialism.

The public provision of services was central to the strategy of 'self legitimization' of the people's democracies. Whilst the Soviet model was able to create a reasonably educated, well-housed, well-fed, healthy, labor force, the policies of social leveling, restrictions on wage differentials, the uniformity in the provision of social amenities, and the limited development of the consumer sector served to de-moralize and de-motivate workers.

East European societies were restructured on the model of the USSR. The large-property owning classes, in industry and agriculture, saw their property nationalized by the state. In time, the relative standing of the professional classes was eroded. Those classified as skilled manual workers tended to benefit, whilst routine clerical, white collar professions saw their position weakened. The higher administrative, managerial strata, including those in the armed forces, saw an increase in their status, their political influence and their economic privileges.

At the highest intellectual level, sovietization was reflected in the commandeering of science, through the academies and universities, and their effective subordination to a Soviet model, whereby the primacy of Soviet science was celebrated, and direct links were forged with Soviet research institutes and universities, whilst links with western centers of learning were severed or closely regulated. As in the USSR, the party occupied a central role in directing science and harnessing it to the socialist project. Whilst the physical sciences were accorded priority, the humanities and the social sciences tended to be neglected.

The sovietization of the educational process in schools, universities and institutes drew them close to the Soviet model.[68] The most significant trend was the incorporation of political education and military training as a required part of the curriculum. The sovietization of curricula and of textbooks reflected the new ideological line with regard to history, literature, and the social sciences, with a new emphasis on 'patriotic' themes, and the cultivation of collectivist values. The fostering of educational, cultural, tourist and sporting interchanges between the USSR and the other member states of the bloc were part of the process.

Alongside the role of the educational system in instilling political values into youth, note should also be made of the impact of the sovietization of the armed forces, and, with this, the key role of these bodies, as in the USSR, in instilling political and patriotic values into a generation of youth subject to conscription. The conspicuous role of the armed forces within the wider society, in sports, in mass displays, and as a focus of national pride, was a hallmark of these regimes. The tension between the armed forces as bearers of non-communist values from the past, and as institutions that were subject to political control and sovietization early on, by their subordination to the Soviet armed forces through the Warsaw Pact alliance, demonstrates the multi-layered process at which these influences operated.

Economic development was linked to urban development, and technological progress, encapsulated in the grandiose projects of industrialization, such as the new giant steel towns, based on Magnitogorsk, that were developed in Poland at Nowa Huta, and in the GDR at Eisenhüttenstadt. Magnitogorsk was modeled on Gary, Indiana; hence an American model of modernity was first sovietized in the USSR, and then exported to Eastern Europe. These two projects, based upon Soviet iron ore supplies, represented, in a very direct way, the integration of these economies into the Soviet economy. These prestige state projects, embodied the Soviet conception of modernity. These towns were envisaged as microcosms of the future socialist order and were intended to rival and surpass the equivalent steel towns of the capitalist West.

In terms of urban planning and development, the countries of the people's democracies borrowed from both the USSR and from the West.[69] The Soviet model itself adapted itself to international trends in architecture. In place of the communal apartments (*kommunalka*) of the Stalin era, were built the individual apartments of the Khrushchev era (later labeled as *khrushchoby*). House building from the 1960s was based upon high density complexes, of prefabricated concrete apartment units. Model housing estates, co-existed alongside the more typical cheap, utilitarian, grey housing suburban complexes, which stood in stark contrast to the grandeur of capitals such as Prague and Budapest.

The difficulties of transplanting Soviet models of industrial organization and technology to the countries of Eastern Europe which already possessed developed industrial cultures was pronounced. Alongside the plant director, the head of the trade union, and the secretary of the party cell, acted as two auxiliaries, who were intended to assist in promoting production. The focus on production, the creation of a sense of allegiance to the work-place, represented a new development, highlighted by the introduction of Soviet conceptions of 'Taylorism', 'norm setting' and the widespread use of wage norms based upon piece rates. These devices, which served to keep the labor force internally divided, were transplanted to Eastern Europe.[70]

In some areas of life, the model offered by the USSR was not well-suited for implantation in Eastern Europe. Where the Soviet model was deemed less sophisticated, the people's democracies sought to develop their own style and to innovate in ways that might be later introduced into the USSR. After the grim austerity of the post-war years, an increasing concern with design and style was in evidence in the socialist states.[71] The emergence of a burgeoning middle-class was reflected in a tendency towards a certain *embourgeoisement* of attitudes with regard to material culture and life-style.[72] Historically, East Germany, Poland, Czechoslovakia and Hungary had a more sophisticated consumer culture and the socialist system was judged by its ability to meet the expectations of its people.[73]

The transplanted Soviet model was poorly attuned to the national sensitivities and political cultures of many of these states. In terms of cultural provision, the need to meet the expectations of a well-educated public with sophisticated tastes, posed the question of how strictly censorship could be applied. In film, TV and radio, and in books and the publishing medias generally, the operation of a restrictive censorship tended to alienate audiences.

The organization of many social, cultural and sporting activities around the work-place, common in many big capitalist companies, was widely used in the socialist states. Communist regimes allowed competitive sports, but restricted the commercial exploitation of sport, and laid more emphasis on mass participation, rather than on passive watching, but also sought to extract the maximum capital from international sporting success.[74] The work-place also increasingly became a focus of political activity as organized by the party and the trade unions.

Sovietization was not exclusively a one-way process. The Soviet model implanted in the satellite state acquired, in some cases, a life of its own. The most conspicuous success was the GDR, whose consumer culture and mass media was more sophisticated than those in the USSR, shaped in large measure by the need to compete with the FRG. In the GDR, socialist realism in art tended to reflect native German realist traditions. The pioneering in the GDR of the industrial combine modeled on Western corporations, as a way of achieving greater integration, and allowing a de-centralization of planning decisions, was adopted into the industrial system of the USSR in the 1970s as the combine (*obedinenie*).[75] The collectivized agricultural sector in Hungary was more efficient than its Soviet parent system.

Aspects of Sovietization

In this volume, we explore various aspects of the sovietization processes. Tarik Amar studies the utilization of the concept of sovietization and its elaboration as part of a Soviet imperial project, and part of a Soviet civilizing mission in Eastern Europe.

The clash between Soviet conceptions of modernity and the more established models in the Eastern European countries was pronounced.

Valentina Fava examines the specific case of the *Škoda* motor works in Czechoslovakia as a concrete illustration of what sovietization meant in terms of managerial methods, labor organization, the use of technology and planning methods in a key industrial enterprise.

The extension of Soviet hegemony over Eastern Europe was reflected in the enormous imbalance in military and economic power between the USSR and its satellites. The Soviet Union's dominance of the Warsaw Pact was reflected in its monopolization of control on military technology and strategic planning. Matthias Uhl examines the case of the missile-ization of the Warsaw Pact forces from 1958 to 1965, which reflected the problem of maintaining control over the satellites whilst guaranteeing the primacy of Soviet strategic interests.

In the field of consumption the people's democracies were expected to develop more sophisticated provisions to meet the expectations of their peoples.[76] Marcello Anselmo explores the efforts to develop techniques of market research in the GDR, and the structural and ideological rigidities that constrained such initiatives. In the field of leisure, the people's democracies developed their own strategies independently of the Soviet model by drawing upon domestic traditions. This process is examined in David Crowley's study of the Polish film societies. Sybille Mohrmann analyzes the reception of Soviet films in East Germany in 1945 and explores the problems of meeting audience expectations, whilst satisfying the Soviet authorities' aspiration to instill correct ideological values and to impart a positive image of the USSR.

The implantation of Soviet style rituals in the people's democracies involved attempts to regulate the use of public space, to organize the lives of people and to remold public consciousness as part of a new system of regime legitimation. Roman Krakovsky examines the way the May Day parades in Czechoslovakia were developed as public rituals as a concrete manifestation of sovietization. Balázs Apor examines the spatial dimension of the cult of Mátyás Rákosi in Hungary, and the efforts made to link this with earlier cults in Hungarian history. Petr Roubal examines the Czechoslovak *Spartakiada* with its mass sporting displays, which, like the political rituals, symbolized the integration of the individual into the collective.

As part of the establishment of ideological control over the people's democracies, the cultivation of positive images of the USSR occupied a place of priority, as examined by Mohrmann. Jan C. Behrends explores the role performed in this field by the creation of friendship societies, such as the *League for Polish-Soviet Friendship*.

In the early phase of sovietization, the ideological struggle against religion was backed up with severe repression. The studies by Anca Maria

Şincan and Mateja Režek of religious policy in Romania, and Slovenia and Yugoslavia illustrate the intensity of these anti-religious campaigns, and the forms of resistance that they encountered, and provide insight into how far the local communist authorities drew lessons from the even more intensified assaults on religion in the USSR.

Sovietization involved the construction of new meta-narratives of national history in the East European countries, involving adaptation of the Soviet narrative that highlighted the 'progressive' trends in history, as part of a teleological vision that led to the triumph of communism. The studies by Árpád von Klimó, Maciej Górny and Péter Apor examine how far independent Marxist traditions in historiography survived in Hungary, East Germany, Poland and Czechoslovakia.

1

Sovietization as a Civilizing Mission in the West

Tarik Cyril Amar

This essay looks at sovietization as part of a wider conceptualization of the Soviet project and the way it was transplanted into the USSR's immediate neighboring territories, which were annexed under the terms of the Nazi-Soviet Pact of August 1939. It explores sovietization as both an analytical and a normative category that was used to explain the objectives of Soviet policy and to rationalize them. It takes as its subject the western Ukrainian city of Lviv, formerly eastern Polish Lwów, which underwent sovietization twice, after Soviet forces conquered it in autumn 1939, and after they re-conquered it in the summer of 1944 along with the area of inter-war Poland, which the Soviet conquerors regarded as Western Ukraine. Thus, Western Ukraine, as well as Lviv, experienced two closely-related sovietizations.[1] Soviet control, socio-political organization, official and everyday culture, and massive state violence directed against the city's population were first introduced between the end of 1939 and the summer of 1941, when the Soviet Union was expanding westwards as a consequence of its *de facto* alliance with Nazi Germany. After a devastating German occupation between 1941 and the summer of 1944, Soviet power and sovietization returned when the Soviet Union again took control over Lviv.

Lviv, typical of a broad swathe of territory from the Baltic to the Black Sea, where states and societies underwent Soviet conquest twice, was annexed to the Soviet Union to form what then became known as the Soviet West, which, though sovietized, has been less prominent in studies of sovietization than the territories further west, where Soviet control was established not through direct annexation but through the establishment of sovereign client states. An exception can be found in the work of David Marples treating the area of post-1939 Soviet expansion – satellite as well as direct annexation – as a strongly interdependent whole.[2] However, in the main, comparatively few scholars have systematically analyzed the Soviet western occupations between the autumn of 1939 and the summer of 1941 within the sovietization paradigm, while post-Soviet Union publications from the Baltic states and Poland have used it more frequently to describe the experience of their societies not only at the end of and after the Second World War, *i.e.*, under their second Soviet occupation, but also in the initial phase of the war. Yet, while a relationship between the first sovietization and the second one is regularly hinted at or explicitly asserted in such works, it has frequently not been the focus of interpretation.[3] Recently, this continuity, however, seems to be attracting more attention.[4]

Traditionally, at any rate, the western historiography of sovietization has mainly been concerned with the period of Stalin's post-war years and with an area between, from west to east, the Soviet zone of occupation in Germany and the post-war western borders of the Soviet Union and, from north to south, the Baltic coast of post-war Poland and the southern border of Bulgaria, with Yugoslavia and Albania forming special cases or exceptions.[5]

The principal interpretative themes of this sovietization historiography have developed around two closely-related problems. The first can be summarized under the heading of uniformity versus diversity, the second under the title of outside imposition versus indigenous development.[6] While the term 'sovietization' has not been used by all the authors writing about this region's post-war history, in general, all the terminologies employed mainly refer to the processes of significantly compelled subordination to the interests and control of the Soviet Union, as well as to a strong emulation of its 'way of life', in conjunction with the establishment of authoritarian or totalitarian political systems that were ideologically committed to Socialism and/or Communism. It is this minimum consensus, which has variously been described as the 'imposition of communist-controlled government' or of a 'Stalinist blueprint', as 'Stalinization', 'Communist take-over', 'Satellization', the 'introduction of Soviet totalitarianism into Eastern Europe', 'Communization', or 'Marxization'.[7]

At the same time, the term 'sovietization', like the much less frequently used term 'Bolshevization', occupies a special position, since it is clearly and directly derived from contemporary usage.[8] Moreover, like the term 'Bolshevization', the sovietizers themselves applied the term 'sovietization' as a positive self-description. Such a relationship between the language used by the historians and their objects calls for a full *Begriffsgeschichte,* which this essay cannot provide. At any rate, the 'sovietization' terminology seems not to have been subjected to rigorous post-linguistic-turn analysis, which cannot be attributed to its relatively recent origin.

'Totalitarianism' and its cognates are of about the same age and have long had their proper *Begriffsgeschichte*.[9]

Thus, in the case of the term 'sovietization', it is still difficult to say precisely when it came to be employed. It is, however, clear that it emerged soon after the collapse of the tsarist empire and the Bolshevik seizure of power in 1917.[10] By the time of the Soviet Union's participation in the Second World War, at any rate, 'sovietization' was already registered in Soviet dictionaries as a specialized neologism. The 1940 fourth volume of the general Russian dictionary, compiled under chief editor D. Ushakov, had short entries for '*sovietizatsia*,' '*sovietizirovat*', and '*sovietizirovatsia*', qualifying the terms as new and part of the lexicon of politics and explaining that something (*chto*) could be sovietized as well as somebody (*chto-kovo*). The two meanings given were to 'organize ... Soviet power somewhere' and 'to inculcate [*vnedrit*] Soviet ideology, world view and understanding of the practical tasks of Soviet power'.[11] In 1963, a dictionary of *literary* Russian featured the terms. Notably, although explicit reference was made to Ushakov's definitions of 1940, the 1963 version was shorter and left out the ideology, the world view, and the inculcating, reducing sovietization to a more bland sense of making and becoming Soviet.[12] By 1984, a four-volume general dictionary had no entry for sovietization.[13] According to Olaf Mertelsmann, the term went out of usage in the Soviet bloc in the 1950s.[14]

This short survey of Soviet lexicography supports scholars who have long argued that the history of sovietization should be written with reference to a longer period which began several years before Soviet troops (re-) entered formerly non-Soviet Eastern and Central European areas in 1944.[15] It would, however, be useful to put the phenomenon of sovietization into an even larger context by locating it in a complex tradition of Soviet and Russian imperialism, and of the tense, as well as productive, Russian and Soviet reflection on the West as their Other. This approach differs principally from that of, for instance, Michal Reiman, who noted that the concept of sovietization entered historiography from the vocabulary of politics and referred to inter-war Soviet aspirations, but also argued that the meaning of sovietization 'changed fundamentally after the Second World War', restricting his interpretation of sovietization to the post-war years.[16]

While a significant change of meaning did occur, continuities and the historical conditions and effects of simultaneous change seem to have been little explored. In other words, the simple assumption here is that the contemporary usage of the same word of 'sovietization' for phenomena in the pre-war Soviet Union and post-war Eastern and Central Europe calls for an explanation rather than an arguably anachronistic analytical *a priori* division. The territories and populations, which were first sovietized between 1939 and 1941, form a 'missing link', worth special attention because they offer the best opportunity for reconstructing the shorter and longer continuities of sovietization, as well as their limits.

Such an approach should not be confused with the accusations of imperialism, leveled against the post-1939 sovietization. Independently of their great plausibility, they were indeed part of contemporary politics. In the case of the Soviet westwards expansion from 1939, 'imperialism' has been used nearly exclusively to designate and rightly condemn the fact that the Soviet leadership imposed foreign rule and satellite regimes by force and deception on a region, whose peoples were—in their majority—opposed to this conquest. This condemnation rhetorically exploited the circumstance that the Bolsheviks continued phrasing the ultimate goal of 'world revolution' as a near-synonym of the destruction of Western 'imperialism'.[17]

In only a superficially-different vein, authors of the Left, be they Western, Soviet dissident or post-Soviet, have identified 'empire' and 'imperialism' as a part of the Soviet Union's fall from true Socialist and/or Communist grace. In their perspective, too, there is decidedly no room for a Soviet imperialism which is not imagined *a priori* as an antithesis or fundamental perversion of Communism/Socialism.[18] In both perspectives, the specific question of the relationship between Second World War Soviet expansion and pre-war, as well as pre-Soviet, paradigms of Russian and Soviet imperialism was reduced to a label, accusatory on one side, apologetic or at least mitigating on the other.

Yet, in spite of the terminological-ideological interference, for the historian, the continuities, discontinuities of the unprecedentedly successful 1939 western turn of the Russian/Soviet imperialist tradition are too important to be dismissed as either trivial or polemical.

At the same time, as authors such as Francine Hirsch and Timofei Agarin have recently pointed out, there has long been a historical literature, which has interpreted the Russian empire as well as the Soviet Union in terms of colonialism. However, this approach, while oriented towards scientific conceptualization, has also tended, in Agarin's words, to focus upon a 'specific point of view, which regards the Tsarist empire as well as Bolshevik socialism as *mere* variations of *traditional* colonial powers'.[19] More importantly, it has usually not explored continuities between the pre-war Soviet Union and its wartime expansion, but merely stressed the differences and categorical divisions between, for instance, Soviet pre-war policies in Central Asia and sovietization in Eastern and Central Europe. Recently, scholars such as Jörg Baberowski, Francine Hirsch, Yuri Slezkine and Terry Martin have revised and revived an imperial approach to Soviet history. Importantly, however, their work has not included the Soviet western expansion from 1939.[20]

Independently, however, from the old politics of the 'imperialism' terminology, the categories of the longer-existing colonial approach, or the fresh research and interpretations provided by the recent discussion of Soviet empire, there can be little doubt that, as Ewa Thompson has shown, Soviet expansionism in the West from 1939 has not usually been interpreted as a form of imperialism, to which the categories and concepts of post-colonial theory should be applied.[21] Specifically, historians of the Soviet Union have usually not interpreted the expansion of 1939-1941 – 'the most successful colonial expansion in the entire history of Russia' – in, as Thompson writes, 'nationalist-colonial' terms.[22] The question between Thompson's criticism and the historians that she criticizes is not what Soviet expansion in Central Europe was, but what it has, or has not, been perceived as and why. Clearly, this question leads us back to the first reactions of participants and contemporaries.

In order to concentrate on what sovietization in Europe meant for the Sovietizers, we need to look at where Soviet society came from when it started going west. It expanded into Central Europe at a particular moment in its own rapid, and often violent, development. While much of sovietization occurred only at the end of, and after, the Soviet-German war, during the initial phase of the Cold War, the Soviet expansion in, and sovietization of, Central Europe began before these two conflicts. What took place between the Soviet mode of life and the Western Other, on which Soviet discourse had come to bestow a vital measure of cathexis, was an encounter, charged with symbolic meaning for both sides.

The Conquerors' Background: The Struggle against Backwardness

Not only the conquered interpreted their meeting with the conquerors as an encounter between different 'cultures', 'civilizations', or even 'worlds'. The Soviet conquerors, too, depended upon such categories. For them, the potential meanings of the encounter with the West as a highly significant, even self-constitutive, Other was derived from a long Russian-imperialist tradition as well as from a specifically Soviet contemporary context. Concerning the former, as Martin Malia and Boris Groys have argued, modern Russia's relationship to its Western Other was crucial for its identity. While Groys has emphasized that Russia's identity was neither included in the narratives of the West, nor situated clearly outside it, Malia has focused on the peculiar inversion made possible by the assimilation of Marxism.

For Groys, 'Russian thought since Chaadaev' – or since Russia's encounter with the West through the Napoleonic Wars – had answered the increasingly urgent question of national identity by 'interpreting Russia as a space where Western discourse about the Other was to be realized or materialized'.[23] Simplifying Groys' argument, Russian intellectuals throughout the nineteenth century contrasted a West, identified with a changing, but continuing, tradition of Enlightenment and Universalism, with a Russia whose acknowledged inferior performance at universalist reason was to be compensated by a superior ability to unite reason and 'life', *i.e.*, those areas of individual and social existence which the discourses of the West were increasingly locating beyond the reach of universalist reason. Thus, Russia's self-perception as the West's Other was as much based upon Western categories as Russia's image of the West itself. Importantly, in this imagination an 'authentic Russia', as opposed to its current appearance, was 'situated either in the pre-historic past, or in the utopian perspective, which were both modeled according to a pattern of corresponding Western theories of the Other...'[24]

Tracing the emergence of this fundamental part of Russian identity further back and juxtaposing it with the complementary evolution of Russia's image in the West, Martin Malia has made a similar argument and emphasized the sudden inversion of the pattern, which was made possible by the Bolshevik seizure of power in the Russian Empire in the name of Marxism. Russia, according to Malia, 'ceased to be Europe's laggard Eastern train; she now embodied or claimed to embody, Europe's most advanced ideal, Socialism'.[25] In Malia's view, the combination of Marxist Socialism and Russia's particular kind of Otherness was rendered more probable and influential by a principal affinity between these two imaginary complexes.

Marxist Socialism was built on the radical negation of what it defined as capitalism. Rejecting private property and the market, as well as the assignment, through them, of social status, individual welfare and, ultimately, happiness, Marxist Socialism was realizable only as 'non-capitalism'. Such non-capitalism, construed as fulfilling and overcoming the historical necessities of capitalism needed its imaginary opposite, capitalism, as much as the idea of Russia needed the reverse and complement of the imagined West. At the same time, the adoption of Marxism offered the opportunity not merely to confront capitalism with a putatively better version of modernity, but to overtake it in world-historical development so that the universality of this frame of reference enabled Russia to be not only better than the West, but also to occupy a place which the West still had to reach. Thus, young Marx's initial search for a way to overcome what he perceived as the mid-nineteenth century backwardness of Germany may, in part, explain how 'a theory devised to overcome the backwardness of the first, German plateau of the West-East cultural gradient was finally put into practice on the last and lowest level of the European system, Russia'.[26]

Malia, however, ends his account of the four stages of the making and consolidation of the Soviet system with the purges of 1936 to 1938, and interprets the years of the Second World War chiefly in terms of a comparison of fascism and Communism, an analysis of international diplomacy and alliance-making as well as the West's changing perceptions of the Soviet Union. His argument does not, however, include an examination of the effects of the Soviet westward expansion from the autumn of 1939 on Soviet identity.[27] This expansion was the first moment in Soviet history in which the Bolshevik reversal of the West-East gradient, was successfully, if by force, imposed in practice. As David Brandenberger has shown, the beginnings of the shift from a more 'internationalist' idea of being Soviet to a more Russo-centric one clearly preceded the attack on Poland.[28] Within official Soviet discourse, as well as general reception, the traditions of Russian imperialism were being re-integrated into Soviet self-understanding precisely at the time when the Soviet Union was about to begin a major wave of westwards expansion.

At the same time, Soviet reactions to their own empire were made more complex by the fact that Soviet thinking and feeling remained tied to a long tradition of what Jörg Baberowski has called 'self-orientalization'. As David Joravsky has pointed out, the Bolsheviks were continuing a long Russian-imperialist struggle pitting a modernizing state against its own society in 'the premier backward country, that is, the first to call itself backward, to begin the struggle to overtake and surpass the world leaders in modernization'.[29] Stalin's public declaration of 1931, describing Russia as the continuously beaten, because eternally backward, victim of more advanced aggressors is famous, not least for his call to overcome this backwardness within ten years or be crushed.[30]

In fact, considerable and significant parts of Western reflection on the Soviet Union have been guided by a related paradigm. Mirroring Bolshevik self-perceptions as the equivalent of a medieval crusading – and Teutonic – '*Schwertbrüderorden*' (Stalin 1921), as élite 'Samurai', (Trotsky 1919), their ambivalent critics sometimes recognized a 'new anthropological type'. (Berdiaiev 1923) in them.[31] Some western historiography after the Second World War once more inverted outcomes and exchanged hope for pessimism by arguing that Socialism's progressive potential had been drowned in the sea, or rather mud, of backward peasant Russia.[32] Other Western authors adopted and perpetuated Soviet party-state ideology and declared that the catching-up and surmounting backwardness was a real achievement of the Soviet regime.[33] The dismantling of substantial parts of the regime and most of its empire from above in the second half of the 1980s was accompanied by Soviet admissions that this optimism was mistaken.[34]

Thus, for the making, as well as the unmaking, of the Soviet Union, its critics as well as its apologists, backwardness and the ability or inability to overcome it remained crucial. At the same time, during the post-1939 Soviet expansions, assigning backwardness to the conquered new subjects and purportedly eliminating it were key components of Soviet discourse about their version of a 'civilizing mission'. As Soviet author M. Bril wrote in 1940 in a book dedicated to the first anniversary of the 'liberation' of Western Ukraine, the latter as well as Western Belarus had been 'backward economically and culturally' and in a state 'even worse than under the tsarist regime [sic]'. The liquidation of this backwardness was in full swing, with soviet Baku oil workers teaching their 'liberated Ukrainian brothers' to work efficiently and on a Bolshevik scale at a speed which exceeded what the latter could even have dreamed of under Poland.[35]

One of the most prominent and public Soviet discourses about the elimination of backwardness before 1939, centered on a notion of culture articulated and re-shaped through the concept of *kulturnost'*. While the Soviet Union claimed a revolutionary legitimacy and, especially in the post-1939 Soviet West, returned occasionally to the slogans and practices of 'cultural revolution', official Soviet discourse had, by 1939, long signaled a willingness to challenge the West precisely by outdoing it in a specific variant of a seemingly more traditional culture. In early Bolshevik discourse, Lenin's exploitatively conservative attitude had reliably prevailed over 'Scythian' as well as 'modernist' experimentation. He had summed up his position before the Party in March 1919 on the 'Successes and Difficulties of Soviet Power', reminding his party comrades and followers that, 'You won't have enough to eat from smashing capitalism. We must take all culture, which capitalism has left behind and build socialism from it'.[36] This disposition was the basis – distinct from the final product – of the post-revolutionary concept of *kulturnost'* and its later rise to dominance in Soviet discourse on culture. In public Bolshevik discourse, its opposite and alternative, a 'specifically proletarian' culture, was 'abandoned after 1932'.[37]

While the crucial Soviet concept of *kulturnost'* achieved new prominence and power between 1935 and 1939, arguably, it marked neither a retreat to these early arguments – which had mainly aimed at a pragmatic exploitation of professionals and academics, *i.e.*, 'specialists' – nor a mere reaction to the 'cultural revolution' of the early 1930s. While the concept's imaginative power was enhanced by the fact that, as Catriona Kelly and

Vadim Volkov have pointed out, it was 'never clearly defined', it stood for a more innovative and aggressive approach,[38] stressing the issue of what needed to be done to acquire *kulturnost'*.[39]

Moreover, where Lenin's position had virtually amounted to neatly separating capitalist politics and economics from capitalist culture, and instructing the Party and the proletariat to appropriate the latter from a position of political dominance, the rise of *kulturnost'* was a signal that this process had been completed to such an extent that it was now possible to challenge in the field of culture the capitalist world that still remained. This capitalist world had a specific site. As Michael David-Fox has pointed out, the history of *kulturnost'*, although usually associated with the interpretations of the 'Great Retreat' or the 'Big Deal', which have stressed domestic Soviet developments, was, from the beginning, strongly tied to Soviet constructions of, and self-delineations against, the West.[40]

The importance and pervasiveness of the Soviet need for self-identification in opposition to a West, admired, feared, emulated and despised at the same time, was—arguably at least—as constitutive as the codification of an economistic variant of late left Hegelianism, plus commentaries, into binding scripture, while the reliance on an obligatory canon and a rejection of a radically externalized Other were not mutually exclusive. As noted by Michael David-Fox, the more *kulturnost'* dominated, the more the private or traditional realms of life were 'linked either to bourgeois individualism *or* to backwardness'.[41] The expansion from 1939 marked the point at which this dialectic collapsed into a new imperialist synthesis. Appearing in the old world as missionaries of the new Stalinist civilization, the Bolsheviks took the logical next step and fused the bourgeois *with* the backward.

When the Soviet authorities lamented and fought the 'survival' of 'capitalism' in the minds of their new Western subjects, they used the same word for this survival as for that which Soviet anthropologists identified as the chief obstacle to progress with tribal societies in the East – *perezhitki*.[42] At the same time, the mental 'survival' of capitalism, which was to be removed by further education, was declared to be the chief target and problem of the further 'Building of Socialism' among the Soviet population in general. Moreover, we should take seriously *Pravda's* pre-war insistence that the drive for *kulturnost* was going to be not merely a temporary campaign but a long, systematic self-education effort.[43] In other words, when the Soviet Union began to go West, *kulturnost'* kept having effects not in terms of the results of a temporary campaign but as a generalized aspiration.

The Conquerors' Experience of Conquest: Public Description

In retrospect, the continuity between the Soviet westward expansion in autumn 1939 and the general Soviet context of the time was highlighted by the September 1939 issue of *Bilshovik Ukrainy*, the 'theoretical and political monthly' of the Central Committee of the Ukrainian Soviet Republic. Its first part was taken up by V. Molotov's speech to the Supreme Soviet of the USSR on the treaty with Germany. It was followed by a long programmatic article under the title 'The Manifesto of Victorious Communism', which was a panegyric to Marx and Engels, as the founding fathers of Communism, but also asserted the significant further development added by Lenin and Stalin. With the Stalin Constitution in place – here, as elsewhere, called the Stalin Constitution of Socialism, not, *nota bene*, merely of the Soviet Union – and 'socialism built in its foundations', the aim now was to 'catch up and overtake' the capitalist countries of Europe and the USA. These, however, were certain to be defeated because 'no forces of the old world would be able to resist the advantages of the Soviet system. A 'new epoch of world history' was about to begin and the pre-eminent task was to 'overcome the survival of capitalism' in people's minds so that they would all become 'cultured, educated, highly conscious builders of socialism'.

All of this taken together meant that, whereas ninety years previously, Communism had been the 'specter' of the Communist Manifesto, now it had become a real force embodied in the Soviet Union's power, which heralded the advance towards 'the triumph of Communism in the whole world'.[44] The force of the article, at any rate, lay in juxtaposition: celebrating the origins of Socialism/Communism as well as a recent 'epochal' advance in its history, it followed Molotov's announcement of an agreement with Germany printed in the same issue. The rest of the world outside the triumphantly progressive Soviet Union was an 'old world', while the new Constitution adopted within the Soviet Union belonged not only to the Soviet Union, but potentially the entire world, being the Constitution of 'socialism' as such.

The relegation of this 'old world' was pursued further in the very next article of the same issue of *Bilshovik Ukrainy*, on 'Socialist Humanism'. Its gist was not merely the praise of its subject matter, a socialist humanism built upon the absence of private property of the means of production which was to result in 'a real rebirth of humanity' through superior work, culture, education and political participation. It also offered a pronounced comparison with the dated, as well as fraudulent, humanism of capitalism born in an earlier Renaissance, but forever incomplete and flawed. Importantly, the article also stressed Lenin's assertion that the new socialist humanism was exceptional because it was capable of building the new world with 'those people, who [have been] raised by capitalism, spoiled by it, corrupted by it, but exactly by this also hardened for the struggle'. Molotov featured prominently in this article, too. He emphasized the need to overcome the mental 'survival of capitalism' as the central task in the incipient transition from Socialism to Communism under the conditions of 'capitalist encirclement'.[45]

The September issue of *Bilshovik Ukrainy* was ambiguous. Its choice of articles, their content and language were clearly open to interpretation as an aggressive manifesto of future victories over the 'old world' and there was no reason to exclude military ones. At the same time, the latter were not discussed openly, and the issue's key note was also set by what was formally a non-aggression agreement with Nazi Germany, and Molotov's reminder that Soviet life took place within capitalist encirclement. What, in retrospect, made the September issue so resonant of the conquests about to follow was, in fact, the October issue, which opened, again, with a speech by Molotov – this time, his radio announcement of the Soviet campaign into Poland on 17 September. The second item of the journal was the unsigned editorial 'Liberation from the Lordly Yoke'. Its first sentence declared that the Soviet Union's intervention was nothing other than an 'act of great socialist humanism', thus clearly establishing an important link between core Soviet aims at home and the current military move. Claiming that the Soviet conquerors were liberating Western Belarus and Western Ukraine from age-old Polish oppression as well as backwardness, the article asserted that the liberated population was now going to follow Soviet examples. The then First Secretary of Soviet Ukraine, Nikita Khrushchev, was cited, implying very strongly that only Socialism, brought by revolution or 'liberation', could make full human beings out of subjects. Speaking rather confusedly about the experience of *pre*-1939 Soviet Ukraine, once it had been liberated from the 'Polish landowners', Khrushchev celebrated the manner in which 'from these landless poor, from these slaves of the Polish lord people arose, raised themselves up materially and spiritually [*... z tsykh batrakiv, z tsykh rabiv polskoho pana pidnialysia liudy, nidnialysia materialno i dukhovno*]'. Now, the inhabitants of the newly 'liberated' eastern territories of a Poland, described as a 'prison of peoples ... just like tsarist Russia', were confidently expected to advance in the same manner to full humanity and thereby confirm the Soviet self-image as a superiorly progressive and humane civilization.[46]

Over the following months, *Bilshovik Ukrainy* kept spreading the same message. The 22nd anniversary of the *Great October Revolution* was an occasion to express special pride in the Red Army's recent glory and the fact that the Revolution had begun the 'liberation' of all mankind. With 'liberation' having just taken on a concrete, military-expansionist meaning, the statement offered the opportunity to link the western conquest and the teleological mission of Soviet socialism.[47] Stalin's sixtieth birthday inspired Khrushchev to point out that the 'liberation' and 'unification' of Western Ukraine and Western Belarus as well as the current Soviet 'assistance to the Finnish people' were a vindication of Stalin's nationality policy and a confirmation of the fact that the Soviet Union was now not only capable of providing a 'free existence' to its own population, but also of 'influencing the international situation' so that 'even our enemies' had to reckon with it.[48]

The Bolshevik cadres sent westwards to administer and develop the new territories and populations featured as 'that glorious detachment', gaining a 'new world-historic victory'.[49] For the first anniversary of the Soviet conquest of eastern Poland, in September 1940, *Bilshovik Ukrainy*, reporting on the 15th Congress of the Communist Party of Ukraine, summarized 'A Year of Social Reconstruction of the Political and Economic Life in the Western Oblasts of Ukraine' by Stalin's teaching on the essential link between backwardness and the national question as the basis for policies in Western Ukraine:

> The essence of the national question ... lies in liquidating that backwardness (economic, political, cultural) of the nationalities, which [*i.e.*, backwardness] we have inherited from the past, [in] giving the backward peoples the opportunity to catch up with central Russia in state, cultural and economic respects.

One year after the annexation of Western Ukraine, an article in *Bilshovik Ukrainy* stressed that overcoming the region's backwardness required the commitment of the backward themselves since 'Socialism cannot be obtained as a present [but] must be built'.[50]

Thus, *Bilshovik Ukrainy*, on the whole, did not stress Soviet claims of having preserved their kind of peace by their agreement with Germany, nor was the 'liberation' of the ethnic minorities of eastern Poland the exclusive reason for the Soviet triumph. Soviet discourse about the march westwards was more closely integrated into the general Soviet discourse of the period. The conquest of Western Ukraine offered a field for practicing and demonstrating the claims of 'socialist humanism', the superiority of Soviet nationality policy and thus modernization, with the latter being the key to the former.

The Conquerors' Experience of Conquest: Non-public Discourses

Thus, the conquest and re-conquest of Western Ukraine in 1939 and 1944 offered an opportunity to assign backwardness to the conquered populations and, explicitly as well as implicitly, progressive superiority to the conquerors. This conquest encounter, however, was also rife with contradictions, when the conquerors imagined their conquest and their role in it. These difficulties, as will be seen below, clearly stood in the tradition of Russian, then Soviet 'self-orientalization'. They also stemmed from the encounter with the Other referred to variously as simply 'Europe', 'western Europe,' or the 'West', which, in parallel to the grandiose discourse of Soviet superiority, constantly provoked feelings of insecurity and, indeed, of inferiority.

Thus, while *Bilshovik Ukrainy* wrote of a 'glorious detachment' of Sovietizers going west in a way reminiscent of R. Kipling's idea of men going east to shoulder another advanced man's burden, the first Lviv province (*oblast*) party conference in 1940 was a setting for drawing a rounder picture of the 'liberators'. In general, speakers presented Lviv as an 'outpost [*forpost*]' of the 'blossoming Soviet fatherland' and first *oblast* secretary Hryshchuk was proud of the 'great honor' shown to the sovietizers by their assignment, and insisted that, in the main, they were worthy of it.

The scourge of Soviet officialdom made itself felt in the form of 'moral failure', *i.e.*, alcoholism and lethal shoot-outs in the center of Lviv. During one of them, a bystander, Dr Goldberg had been killed when trying to intervene. Plunder and embezzlement were rife. Finally, there were 'many cases' of male Communists engaging in illicit, possibly forced, sexual relationships with local women. A local worker had commented on a speech by a district party committee (*raikom*) secretary on the Paris Commune that, 'it's good that he gives a speech, but that he comes to our women, that's bad'. The sense of superiority had been too much for at least one factory director, who claimed that locals were generally unable to work. Intriguingly, a speaker for the Communist youth organization *Komsomol* also regarded it as an instance of 'moral decay' when 'some' *Komsomol* activists from the East got married 'a few days after arrival' in Lviv.[51]

Soviet self-doubt about living up to the self-imposed ideal of progressive 'liberators' and enlighteners was also articulated as a fear of what other colonizers would have called 'going native'. A recurrent Soviet anxiety over the allegedly ethically corrupting influence of the locals was highlighted in a province party committee (*obkom*) report to the Ukrainian Central Committee after the second Soviet conquest of Lviv in 1944. The report dealt with the corruption of the Soviet military draft officers – the '*Voienkomat*' structure – and attributed their failings to their going native in an environment contaminated not only by recent German occupation, but also by its whole pre-socialist past:

> The toilers of Lviv *oblast*, before 1939, as well as during the rule of the German occupiers, have been trained in patterns of bribery for bureaucrats, pleasing them in order to escape state obligations and, first of all, to free themselves from military service.

This 'strong temptation' was often too much for the 'badly educated, inferior-quality individual' staff of the '*Voienkomat*' offices.[52]

In 1947, the case of Lviv University professor Mikhail Popov caused significant excitement at the University, the city and regional party authorities. Popov, ethnically Russian and having come to Lviv from Russia, was accused of siding with the pre-Soviet Ukrainian intelligentsia of the city, and, once on a slippery slope, arguing openly in favor of objective, non-politicized science as well as the 'Nordic theory' of the emergence of ancient Rus', for which he was expelled from the University. At a meeting dedicated to his humiliation, a speaker warned that Popov's case had wider significance. It was darkly connected to the struggle for collectivization in Western Ukraine and demonstrated once more that:

> ...we are working in ... circumstances, where not long ago, not long ago at all, the old world was [still there]. We understand that here the mental traditions of the old generation, the dying generation, are having their effects on the minds of our professors.[53]

While the conquered thus made it possible to interpret even the inferiority of the individual Soviet official or the, in fact, ubiquitous Soviet phenomena of corruption and 'speculation', as well as the heterodoxies and dissent of Soviet scholars as an ultimate sign of the superiority of the Soviet order, successful conquest and even military victory in the 'Great Fatherland War' was not always enough to alleviate the deeply-rooted complex of Soviet self-orientalization, which retained its power to set insecure and cruel Soviet élites against Soviet subalterns. According to a report by the Lviv *obkom* of 1947, a military hospital in the city was the site of what amounted to an absurd, but striking, performance of the persistence of self-humiliation in victory.

The hospital was no exception among the majority of Soviet institutions in that it treated its population of 200 veterans with a mixture of inefficiency, corruption and brutality.[54] Political education was collapsing, the invalids were, in effect, starving, while the staff embezzled their food and told them that 'ration is ration'. Alcoholism, beatings, including beatings of nurses, and sex which was considered to be illicit rounded off the picture.

What was special about this report was the particular attention that the *obkom* paid to the treatment of a mentally impaired invalid called '*Bakir*' by the staff. He had been discharged without any further care and was sleeping on the ground outside the hospital. Feeding on the refuse [*otbroski*] of the hospital, he was regularly kicked and beaten by its staff to drive him away. The *obkom* made a special point of the fact that German POWs, who were kept as a work-force at the hospital, witnessed these scenes and 'shrieked with laughter' at this treatment of *Bakir*, whom they had nicknamed '*Vanka*', the diminutive of 'Ivan', the German colloquial generic term for Russians, Eastern Slavs or inhabitants of the Soviet Union in general. At the same time, it is likely that '*Vanka*' was also a reference to the name of a traditional Russian toy, the '*Vanka-Stanka*,' a small doll with a low center of gravity and a half-round lower part making it tilt up again when pushed over.[55] '*Bakir*', driven by hunger, kept returning for more abuse. In view of the good knowledge of Russian that would have been required for the German POWs to compare '*Bakir*' and the toy, one wonders again whether the '*Vanka*' nickname was not produced by them and the hospital's staff together.

Moreover, the *obkom* maintained that the German POWs had better conditions than the sick and were the favorites of the head of the hospital, who allegedly told his patients that they would 'croak from hunger' if it were not for the Germans, one of whom 'works better than three of you. Our people don't want to work'.[56] The hospital staff, led by the director, managed to stage a perverse reversal of any sense of triumph that the victory over Germany may have engendered in the veteran patients: even demonstratively defeated and captive Germans were held up by Soviet authority as better and more disciplined workers than victorious, but invalid, Soviet soldiers, and were permitted to laugh openly at the sadism with which the representatives of Soviet authority treated a signally 'backward' patient, who had been re-named into an epitome of Russian identity.[57]

The episode demonstrated the persistence of the self-abuse, which was a constitutive element of the Russian/Soviet identity as a backward, catching-up, and overtaking society. As Joravsky, and, more recently, Esther Kingston-Mann have emphasized, this struggle for and against a 'true West', which was—by necessity—self-defeating to the extent that it was self-overcoming, was accompanied by self-hatred as well as messianism. The Bolsheviks, who were, in some ways, not just compelled to follow, but embodied this tradition, were insecure as well as highly aggressive.

Their Marxism-Leninism, enhanced by Stalin's cultic leadership, as well as his recent exceptionalist assurance that it could lead the way in '*one* country taken separately', offered a superior self-image.[58] However, their special relationship with the West as an object of envy and fear meant that this self-image remained fragile. Clearly, both insecurity and fragility are just as likely to lead to aggression as to submission. It is not possible to understand the meaning that sovietization had for the sovietizers without grasping the place of this developmental project in their evolving identity as Soviet '*kulturtreger*', *i.e.*, conquering carriers of a teleologically superior Soviet socialist culture to those classified as modern but significantly less developed.

Conclusion

This essay has made three main points. Firstly, sovietization – understood as Soviet expansion into Eastern and Central Europe from autumn 1939 – belongs to a long perspective of the formation of Russian identities in the context and under the influence of Russian imperialism, as well as in the context of the West as a defining Other. This was a complex process, involving different parts of Russian society in different ways at different times with different intensity.

Secondly, sovietization also belongs to a more immediate Soviet-Stalinist context. In order to understand the meaning of sovietization for the sovietizers and to exploit the phenomenon of sovietization as much as possible in order to enhance our understanding of the Soviet phenomenon as a whole, we should pay particular attention to the soviet point of departure for westward expansion. In this regard, recent research, in particular, has brought out ever more distinctly that there were three major ideational shifts in the second half of the 1930s – the development of a new Soviet formula for Russian national supremacy in the 'Friendship of the Peoples' model, as shown by Terry Martin, the parallel and related move towards a Russian National Bolshevism as detailed and located in the pre-war period by David Brandenberger, and the making of a *kulturnost'* that was neither conservative nor domestic. Laden with xenophobia, it was also about claiming superiority over the Other outside. Generally, the Soviet Union was celebrating its self-invention as a supremely progressive society.

Yet, the real confrontation with the West had deeply ambiguous results from the beginning. While it has often been pointed out that, on the whole, the satellites of Eastern and Central Europe as well as some of the annexed territories were, in fact, in many respects, more modern than the

Soviet core, the Western conquests in general immediately triggered a discourse of assigning backwardness, which was marked by obsessive intensity. At the same time, looking at non-published discourse, we see that they also kept causing great insecurity within the Soviet hierarchies. The Soviet Union's turn westwards was a triumph of military power, force, and highly opportunistic diplomacy, but it also indicated that the tensions inherent in the Soviet relationship with its Western Other could not be resolved by the application of a Soviet civilizing mission.

2

Between American Fordism and 'Soviet Fordism': Czechoslovak Way towards Mass Production

Valentina Fava

The Czechoslovak motor industry of the inter-war period was technically sophisticated, albeit fragmented and craft based. With the advent of communist power in Czechoslovakia, which was consolidated in 1948, and the establishment of the Soviet type economic system based upon the principles of state ownership and central planning, the motor industry was subjected to radical re-organization. Through the prism of the motor industry, we can see the contending visions of American modernity in contrast to a Soviet model of modernity, and the difficulties encountered in applying these alternative models, which were developed in quite different circumstances, to the economic environment of Czechoslovakia, with its very different industrial culture, with its distinctive practices of management and work-place relations. The Czechoslovak automobile industry in the early 1950s illustrates the contradictions of Soviet modernization and the modalities of its transfer to the satellite countries. The examination of the economic planning process at various levels sheds light on the forms of productive 'rationalization' implemented in those five years and the resulting 'clash of perceptions' regarding industrial modernity. Škoda, as the country's leading car manufacturer, presents a good example for an analysis of the effect of the transfer of the Soviet system of industrial administration and management to Czechoslovakia, underscoring the differences between the development of the Czechoslovak automobile industry and the Soviet one, as well as those between the Czechoslovak understanding and application of Fordist methods and the Soviet experience.

The First Five-Year Plan (1949-1953) saw the implementation of the Soviet system of industrial administration and model of management in Czechoslovakia.[1] The plan, which became law in October 1948 and was subsequently modified in 1950-51, marked a significant break with the 'socializing democracy' principles of the Two-Year Plan (1947-1948). Balanced development was now considered secondary to increased growth and investments, to be achieved through structural transformation with priority given to heavy industry. The years between 1949 and 1953 witnessed a strong move towards rationalization, industrial concentration and the creation of large, multi-facility enterprises. At the same time, the decision-making process was gradually centralized, and the existing enterprises were turned into production units, devoid of any authority concerning products, processes, salaries, customers and suppliers.[2]

Soviet Model and Modernity: the Perspective of the Automotive Industry

The American model of mass production – 'the high volume manufacture of standardized goods using special-purpose machinery and predominantly unskilled labor—together with the host of systematic management techniques, organizational structures, and research and marketing services developed for its efficient administration and effective exploitation'—was considered the paragon of industrial modernity for much of the twentieth century.[3]

For more than three decades, American car manufacturers were the object of 'industrial pilgrimages' by engineers and entrepreneurs from the rest of the world. In the 1950s, with the Marshall Plan and productivity missions, the production techniques and management methods developed in Detroit were transferred and adapted to the various European institutional contexts, sometimes leading to the hybridization of the original model.[4]

In the early 1930s, even the Soviet authorities benefited from American technical expertise: collaboration with Ford led to the construction of the Gorky plant for assembling model A cars, and Soviet engineers went to the United States to learn how to organize production.[5] The Soviet approach to the 'gospel of productivity' of the twentieth century has been referred to as a 'cult of Fordism'.[6] However, until the 1950s and beyond, according to Yves Cohen, the implementation of Fordism in Soviet automotive factories was characterized by an apparent lack of comprehension of its basic principles. Technicians, managers and workers did not go beyond the 'most external face' of the functioning of the assembly line. A fixation on quantity led them to overlook fundamental aspects of the 'American model', such as 'interchangeability', or the fact that—in mass production—a small problem could have massive repercussions on the entire cycle. The same can be said for minimizing manual labor and replacing it with machines and the importance of the quality of the materials used. This unique hybridization of Fordism took root in the 1930s, but its consequences characterized Soviet factories until the 1960s and beyond.[7]

As late as the 1950s, Soviet industry was still based upon a caricature of the original version of Fordism, rather than on the American mass production which had developed along with the changing American market and demand. This was partly due to the nature of the relationship between Soviet and American industry, which peaked in the 1930s and diminished steadily in the subsequent decades. Moreover, the Taylorist and Fordist techniques hybridized with the formal and informal aspects of the Soviet system of industrial administration.

In the 1950s, the Soviet automobile industry was composed of a few enormous multi-facility enterprises—ZIS in Moscow and ZIM in Gorky—with diversified production programs. The same enterprise produced cars, trucks and buses, sometimes even bicycles and refrigerators. These enterprises were vertically integrated: most of the mechanical parts and semi-finished materials were manufactured in-house, and only a few electrical components were produced outside by smaller enterprises with specialized production programs.[8]

The autarchy of the giant enterprises was, in part, a response to one of the principal problems faced by Soviet industry: the unreliability of the supply of materials and machinery. These were specified by the planners and were not controlled by the enterprises, which could take no action against ineffective or slow suppliers. The resulting unpredictability of supplies led to both chronic disruptions in work and the so-called 'storming'. This meant that work proceeded slowly during the first part of each production period, followed by a mad rush at the end in order to fulfill the plan as soon as the supplies became available. Independence from outside suppliers was the most efficient method for ensuring adequate reserves for meeting the targets. Other possible solutions were informal organizational arrangements, such as the creation of clientele relationships, informal supply networks, reliance on the expediters and the bargaining both between firms and between the various administrative levels.[9]

Each enterprise had its place in the complex Soviet economic bureaucracy: they were controlled by the Ministry of Automobile and Tractor Industry, which, in turn, was divided into central administrations, organized both according to their products and according to their functional role. Co-ordinating the various levels and structures of the economic bureaucracy was quite complicated, and contributed to the chronic shortages in materials, manpower and machinery that hampered the system. Paul Gregory has described in detail how the Soviet bureaucracy experienced principal-agent problems, due to the information asymmetry that characterized relations between central authorities (ministries) and local institutions (the local Party, Union chapters and enterprises). The literature also sheds light on the opportunistic behavior of enterprise managers, who over-demanded input and sacrificed quality for physical output targets, thereby avoiding new technology.[10]

The main Soviet motor vehicle enterprises shared a highly centralized and hierarchical organization: they were divided into departments according to functions and operations. There were sources of conflict also within the enterprises: along with the enterprise director, who—theoretically—was the one-man boss, there was also a kind of 'technical wizard', the chief engineer. He was second-in-command after the director of the firm, and was responsible for the technical operation of the enterprise, the machinery, plant maintenance, product design and so forth.[11] In addition, the plant Party secretary and the trade union chairman were also responsible for performance. The latter two, along with the enterprise director, formed the so-called '*troika*' of the Soviet enterprise.

The introduction of scientific management was another controversial issue in the development of the Soviet enterprise. Despite numerous attempts, the literature appears to confirm that Taylorist practices were rarely implemented in the Soviet factories, at least until the advent of the Second World War. According to Lewis Siegelbaum, the Stakhanovist movement of the 1930s and other forms of socialist competition symbolized the rejection of Taylor's technocratic utopia, in so far as they abolished the 'distinction between managers' conceptualization of work tasks and workers' execution of them'.[12] This also resulted in irrationalities: the misuse of machinery, disproportions in production, and tension between workers. Furthermore, on the shopfloor, foremen, who had suffered most from the introduction of scientific management elsewhere, retained an important role in the USSR in that they had:

> to match job tasks to available workers, ensure that the appropriate equipment was in working order and that supplies of power, tools, spare parts and raw and semi-finished materials were adequate, understand technical processes sufficiently to impart his knowledge to new workers and evaluate the performance of his charges and mete out sanctions to workers who violated labor discipline and rewards to those who over-fulfilled their quotas.[13]

Finally, as Donald Filtzer notes,

> while the Soviet regime struggled throughout its entire existence to impose so-called technically-based norms, that is, norms calculated on the assumption that equipment would be used at

its optimal technological capacity, the overwhelming majority of norms continued to be set 'empirically', that is, calculated on the basis of actual equipment utilization within the given enterprise and taking account of all of the ordinary disruptions to work rhythms.[14]

Škoda and the 'Sovětský řizení'

In the years between the two wars, the Czechoslovak car industry was characterized by a low degree of concentration as well as the use of craftsman-like production methods, appropriate for producing automobiles in relatively small series. Even Škoda, one of the manufacturers most inclined towards mass-production, had neither the equipment nor the production volumes to compete with the major European 'Americanized' companies.[15] The Czechoslovak technicians who visited US plants in the 1920s had not principally been interested in the grandiose quantitative results of American industry, such as the huge assembly plants, but had been more interested in the organization and production of machine tools and components.[16]

After the war, Škoda was nationalized, and became the only car producer in the country: AZNP (Automobilové Závody, Národní Podnik). In any case, the Czechoslovak approach to the American model of mass-production had very little in common with the Soviet 'cult of Fordism'.

During the Two-Year Plan (1947-1948), an engineer from General Motors, Alexander Taub, was given the task of drawing up a plan to rationalize the Czechoslovak car industry.[17] According to Taub, the car manufacturing sector could have become the 'driver' behind Czechoslovakian re-construction: the key was to reach the minimum threshold of 200 cars-per-day for each plant, in order to exploit the advantages of economies of scale. This would lead to the production of a small, inexpensive car, a 'people's car' that would expand the still restricted domestic market. The key conditions for this development were the rationalization of the mining industry and land reform, which would provide raw materials and low-cost labor, respectively. Finally, it was essential to mechanize and automate production.

The American model was not only imitated in terms of layout and plant organization, but also in terms of enterprise structure. The company of reference in this case was not Ford, but General Motors, a sort of 'mosaic composed of small and medium-sized companies' that were supported by specialized component producers, which, in turn, functioned as 'central plants'. The nature and origin of the AZNP, a collection of nationalized plants, was well suited to this type of organizational structure, and the insistence on co-ordinating production in separate and geographically distant units coincided with the desire to create a balanced national economy, providing a possible solution to the problem of industrialization in Slovakia.

The new Czechoslovakia was to be based not only upon the principles of 'Socialist Democracy' that underlay the Košice Treaty, but, above all, on the modernity and efficiency of its industry, which was to be brought up-to-date in accordance with the latest criteria of efficiency utilized by the American car industry.[18]

After February 1948, this plan was abandoned: Taub fled back to the United States, and the rationalization, which remained a priority for the planners, proceeded along lines that were completely different from those previously envisaged.

However, the Czechoslovak technicians who had worked with Taub on the plan's design and had visited leading American factories in 1947 had developed a critical and up-to-date view of the American model. Their reports illustrated how the war had accelerated technological advances in some processes, under-scored the development of American industry, and confirmed that Ford, which, with its famous 'any color you want as long as it's black' philosophy, had for some time been overtaken by General Motors, which was instead guided by principles of 'flexible mass-production' and 'mass-marketing'.[19] Furthermore, they were clearly aware of the enormous differences between Czechoslovak and American production and market conditions, and emphasized the need for 'piecemeal borrowing', a selective adaptation of American modernity to Czechoslovak reality.[20]

This special knowledge and the awareness of the need to adapt it to local conditions, albeit transformed, remained a benchmark for comparisons made by the Czechoslovak technicians in evaluating the principles and practical application of the Soviet Model.

The ČZAL and its Plans: from National Rationalization to the International Division of Labor

According to the Five-Year Plan, the mass-production of cars was not a priority and car production was marginalised.[21] The documents produced by the ČZAL – the Central Directorate in Charge of Motor vehicle and Aeronautic Production – between 1949 and 1951 reveal a progressively widening gap between the expectations of the Czechoslovak technicians involved in the re-organization of the sector and the actual results of the rationalization itself. In 1949, in fact, there was disagreement between the directors of the ČZAL, the plant managers and the central functionaries of the Communist Party with regard to the development of the car industry and the country's motorization.[22]

ČZAL technicians immediately reported both the contradictions and the risks involved in the marginalization of the car manufacturing industry, which was justified by the tense political climate in Europe, and predicted the problems that would arise, firstly, in the exportation of Czechoslovak vehicles into dollar markets, and, secondly, in the country's motorization. While generally in agreement with the plan's directives, they under-scored how important it was to continue to pursue research and development that would result in a new model of car which could, when the time came, satisfy the population's demand for a 'people's car'.[23]

In 1949, the ČZAL developed a project designed to increase car production, which was, in effect, an elaboration of Taub's plan in the light of the 'new situation' resulting from the First Five-Year Plan. In fact, it was believed that it would be possible to enjoy some of the benefits of modern mass-production by intervening solely on the organizational aspects outlined by Taub, given that they were unable to modernize in terms of plants and equipment. This amounted to further centralization of the sector through the rationalization and standardization of production, and the improvement of worker productivity. The first step was to facilitate and assist the process of 'natural selection' that had resulted everywhere in the success of companies with more 'financial resources and technical experience', and to concentrate all of the country's car production in a single plant.[24] The model of reference was still the United States, to which Great Britain increasingly adhered by 1949. In the former country, the market appeared to have been dominated by large companies for some time; in the latter country, the sixty-three pre-war auto-manufacturers had, by the end of the war, merged into six groups, which accounted for 90% of the cars produced in Great Britain.[25]

The goal was to arrive, at the end of the First Five-Year Plan, with a single national development plan for motor vehicles, which would permit the production of two models – built using shared and interchangeable components and pre-assembled units – in order to satisfy the various types of existing demand (including defense and export) in terms of cost, power and load capacity.

The rationalization was also intended to be applied to the production of components: every component was to be standardized and concentrated in one specialized plant. Only in this way, as the American example of General Motors showed, would it be possible to produce high volumes using modern methods. Finally, the ČZAL aimed to do away with the semi-autonomous structure of the individual motor vehicle plants, which still relied on in-house production, by choosing the most modern plant for each component and concentrating large-scale production there.

This plan was part of a larger design involving the international division of labor envisioned by the CMEA (or COMECON – the Council of Mutual Economic Co-operation), which was just being formed at the time.[26] In January 1949, representatives of the Czechoslovak government backed the idea of making it an international organization which, with integration and specialization as its guiding principles, would eliminate industrial autarchy and investment duplication in the Eastern European bloc countries.[27]

There was an urgent need to organize a division of production programs among the people's democratic republics, which meant, according to the ČZAL, that the establishment of car manufacturing plants in each country would become redundant. There were political and strategic reasons to discourage this hypothesis: the armed forces needed a standardized industry whose production could be quickly converted to making military vehicles in large numbers if the need should arise. Production specialization was even envisioned for components. The plan was to create a single, super-specialized facility for each component, leading to a 'mosaic-style production' that would include the entire CMEA area.

For the ČZAL, the stakes for the extension of rationalization to all of the plants in Eastern Europe were high: producing for the entire Eastern bloc would have meant having a 'market' large enough to absorb the volume of production, which would justify the increased investment and the purchase of the machinery required for mass-production in Czechoslovakia. If the enormous potential of the CMEA could be utilized, an economy of scale over a vast area would become a reality, and the Czechoslovak car industry, considered the oldest and most advanced, would play a leading role.[28]

However, in 1951, the ČZAL was dismantled, motor vehicle production became a branch of the Ministry of Heavy Industry, and these plans were shelved.

With regard to the plans to rationalize the sector at national level, the same ČZAL technicians noted that there was increasingly evident friction between the planners and the managers of the production units, and sometimes even between the local party officials. Four years had passed since the nationalization of the key enterprises. Although the old *conzerns* had been dismantled, the 'localism' of the former private firms and factories still remained as the principal obstacle to the rationalization of the sector.

To the technicians at the ČZAL, this seemed to be the principal factor acting as a deterrent to Czechoslovak industry from achieving the organizational efficiency of a large American corporation or of the British 'Big Six', whose strength lay in the willingness of the single private producers to delegate authority to a central headquarters. The technicians realized the importance of this obstacle, and they proposed the creation of a centralized Research and Development department (already proposed by Taub) which would perform the critical function of mediating between producers, designers and planners.[29]

There was, however, a fundamental misunderstanding: the technicians were basing their ideas on the organization of large American corporations, which were founded on the delegation of authority from the central executive branch to the divisions, which was true to an even greater extent for the British 'Big Six'. In Czechoslovakia, however, the rationalization of production was proceeding through the progressive centralization of strategic decision-making, from the periphery towards the center, without any delegation of authority to the units on the periphery, which were charged with merely overseeing production.

Instead of easing the problems, the friction between production and planning increased in the early 1950s, aggravating one of the typical co-ordination problems of the political economy of communism, the lack of a correct upward flow of information, with the consequent difficulties of co-ordinating the operations of the various planning centers and production units.[30]

With the disbanding of the ČZAL, development was entrusted to a research center for motor vehicles (UVMV, *Ústav pro výzkum motorových vozidl*), similar to the Soviet NAMI (*Nauchnyi Auto Motornyi Institut – the Scientific Auto-Motors Institute*), totally dedicated to research, and devoid of any managerial or co-ordinating function or power.[31]

The problems underscored by the ČZAL remained largely unresolved even when new investments in the car industry became possible and it was decided to build a new plant (1957-1963); the supply problems caused by the planning and the continual shortages of plastic and raw materials, as well as the inadequacy of the equipment, slowed down construction and favored in-house production. In this way, the Czechoslovak automobile industry maintained a high degree of verticalization until the 1970s: most of the mechanical units were produced in series, corresponding to the number of vehicles that the same enterprise intended to produce.[32]

The Czechoslovak Automobile Industry and the 'Cult of Fordism': Industrial Pilgrimages to the Soviet Union and Soviet Advisers

In 1949, the ČZAL technicians justified their continuing reference to the capitalist automotive industry by citing the development of the Czechoslovak industry, which posed problems that were foreign to the Soviet experience. In fact, Soviet industry—they wrote—had not developed, as the American and European industries had, through a process of 'natural selection', which had led to a concentration of the sector. The concentration had instead been imposed by the state comparatively recently, and production had always been organized and regulated by the plan. As a result, it did not have to face – or so the technicians at the ČZAL believed —the co-ordination problems arising from the centrifugal tendencies of the various production units.[33]

In analyzing the ČZAL documents, however, what strikes the reader is the absence of concrete notions of what Soviet industrial modernity consisted of, counter-balanced by a fairly accurate knowledge of Western production processes. In 1949, the Czechoslovak technicians had not yet had the opportunity to examine Soviet plants after the war, and had only a vague notion of how production was organized in the factories.[34] The first visits by Czechoslovak automotive technicians to the USSR occurred only in February-April 1951: six engineers and the directors of some important mechanical enterprises visited the Ministry of Transport Vehicles and Tractors, the Moscow Stalin plant (ZIS), the Molotov plant in Gorky (ZIM), the ATE-1 plant in Moscow for electrical equipment, and the museum of the Moscow Polytechnic.[35]

During the same weeks, the Czechoslovak government accepted, after considerable resistance, the COMECON Bureau's recommendation to invite 'Soviet advisers'. They presided not only over the transfer of Soviet technical and organizational know-how to Czechoslovakia, but also over its application, as well as the transformation of what had begun as a co-operative project into what swiftly became a one-way street, which involved the 'dissemination of Soviet science'.[36]

Not only did the Soviet advisers organize the reform of the planning authorities (SÚP), the transformation of the general directorates into central administrations within the Ministries and the reinforcement of the Ministry of Heavy Industry, they also convinced local planners that Czechoslovakia possessed material and human resources of which it had so far failed to take advantage. In all sectors, therefore, it became necessary to eliminate new investments, utilize existing resources through rationalization, and apply the Soviet rule of 'maximum planning'. But, first and foremost, they attempted to instill discipline, co-operation and order in the plants. The reform of planning methods and of industrial management meant, for the car manufacturing industry, the abolition of the ČZAL, the complete militarization of the sector and the collapse of Czechoslovak car production.

The Introduction of the Soviet Model of Management and the Automobile Industry

After 1951, the effects of sovietization on Czechoslovak industry can best be observed from the standpoint of the production unit, specifically the Škoda-AZNP Mladá Boleslav factory. The intervention of Soviet advisers and the dismantling of the ČZAL had important repercussions on the productive plants. On the one hand, the attempt to standardize production and make only one model of automobile in the country made it necessary to alter production plans; on the other, the need to 'exploit existing resources' opened the doors for the introduction of Soviet methods of work organization into Czechoslovak plants. This attempt met with various forms of resistance among workers and technicians, and was, in the end, suspended, at least in part, following the deaths of Stalin and Gottwald and the strikes in Germany and Poland in 1953-54.[37]

With regard to the production plans, unlike the AZNP, the Soviet advisers encouraged the transfer of the production of the Tatra 600 – a medium-sized car formerly produced at the Kopřivnice Plant, which had been converted to military production in 1951—to Škoda's Mladá Boleslav plant, which almost brought production to a complete halt. As a result, the number of cars produced in Czechoslovakia in 1953 dropped to the lowest level ever recorded: 6,300 vehicles.[38]

With the First Five-Year Plan the methods of work organization developed for the Soviet context and designed to manage the stage of forced industrialization (1929-1937) were transferred to AZNP.[39] Discipline, piecework and socialist competition became the keywords of the campaigns for the promotion of the efficiency of the plants. Their effect on Škoda production becomes clear if we examine the situation of the Mladá Boleslav factory just before the implementation of the plan.

In terms of production technology, Mladá Boleslav was basically 15-20 years behind the times. The machinery was old, there was much manual labor employed and the introduction of new organizational methods ran into predictable bottlenecks on the shopfloor, caused by unaffordable equipment and scarce manpower. The Škoda management had been requesting more modern equipment since 1949, but the requests had been ignored.[40]

At Mladá Boleslav, work was still organized along pre-Taylorist lines, with a high demand for skilled workers, little mechanization, few technically-skilled middle-managers and an abundance of auxiliaries. In addition, there was frequent recourse to manual labor, procedures were long and time-consuming, and 61% of workers were paid through a simple piecework formula. While there were professionals who operated according to the tenets of scientific management, focusing on time-and-motion studies, their roles in the factory were not yet well-defined and their number was decidedly low.[41]

In a situation like this, Soviet rationalization consolidated an old system of work, a pre-Taylorist one, ideal for small-scale, high-quality production, because, in the face of scarce mechanization, it imposed quantitative goals that could be achieved only through the extensive application of the scarce workforce available and the informal, *de facto* self-management of the workshops. On the other hand, by giving rise to systems of control and administration, it fostered the hierarchies, bureaucracies and rationalization typical of the scientific management model.

The push towards 'rationalization' became more insistent in the last two years of the Five-Year Plan, and coincided with the first political trials in Czechoslovakia. There were two main methods used: persuasion and ideological encouragement on the one hand, under the form of socialist competition, and harsher discipline on the other. In the latter sense, the sequence of directives issued by the government and implemented ran as follows:

> Disciplinary procedures against overtime, absenteeism and high labor turnover;
> Rigid definition of production norms and standardization (1951-1952);
> Introduction of the Dispatching System, *khozraschet* (profit and loss accounting) (1952) and technical control over production (OTK).

These measures could have represented a step forward towards a form of systematic management that was suited to the mass-production of cars, but, due to the coercive methods and the absence of the process and product technology that were fundamental requirements of mass-production, they were transformed into expressions of a power that became increasingly 'administrative', and which were far removed from the interests and needs of production and incomprehensible on the shop-floor. It was a power which, as Yves Cohen has shown for the Soviet Union, often used these 'administrative procedures', borrowed from scientific management, to notify the working class of the Party's will.[42]

In fact, the common element in most of the actions taken by the Czechoslovak government in these years was the attempt to assign clear-cut responsibilities and to concretize, formally and on paper, every decision relating to an aspect of the production process, no matter how minor, punishing every violation with strict penal measures.

These measures were often counter-productive: instead of resolving production problems, they made them worse, by increasing the gap between working practices and the scientific methods defined by laws and technical norms. Moreover, they increased the tension between the production unit and the central planners.[43]

One of the government's first measures implemented in April 1953, concerned the question of defective parts and the low quality of Czechoslovak products.[44] According to the government, Czechoslovak factories lacked technological discipline due to the fact that workers and technicians ignored correct procedures, modified signs and altered technological processes subject to their individual preferences, permitted tasks to exceed the programmed times, and exercised inadequate quality-control at every level.

Furthermore, the Mladá Boleslav plant was forced to undergo constant changes in production planning, and lacked raw materials, machinery and an adequate workforce, which made it impossible to adhere to technical norms and standards. Any acceleration in working times could only result in an increase in the number of defective parts and a drop in the quality of the final product. Observance of the time-limits would inevitably have conflicted with technological requirements and worker safety. If these were respected, the norms could not be met. Inevitably, the empirical methods prevailed, and such an inflexible and harsh intervention could only make the situation worse.

The gap between dictates and reality can also be seen as an indication of how political and technological rules can work together to deprive workers of a professional status which is incompatible with 'strict discipline during working hours and the absolute submission of all work to the will of one man, the Soviet manager'. However, the ideal 'socialist worker' was closer to the Russian farmer-factory worker of the 1930s, than the Czechoslovak skilled metalworker, not to mention the technicians, who were averse to passively accepting a factory regime that showed little respect for their experience and know-how.

The introduction of the technical control department (OTK) and the Dispatching System had the same effect.[45] The first was an independent department whose purpose was to verify that the products met 'national standards, norms, technical specifications, design specifications and technological processes' at each stage of production, from fuel and raw materials to the finished product. Nothing could leave the factory without a document issued by this department, which was also charged with writing down, codifying and registering every procedure.

The *dispečerská služba,* or dispatching system, was a technique for allocating and co-ordinating tasks, invented in the United States at the end of the 19th century for application in the electrical and railway sectors. The Bolsheviks had been attracted by the fact that the system had been designed to co-ordinate efforts to achieve a goal and had tried to implement it in the early 1930s. It involved an analysis of the various operations and their sub-division, in terms of duration, manpower and production subunits, according to the departments and machinery available. It included communications centers connected to the production lines via telephone and served to maintain a steady flow of production inside the company, to prevent and resolve production bottlenecks and, above all, to mitigate the consequences of irregular supply.[46]

In fact, it was the introduction of the dispatching system in Soviet industry in the 1930s, considered to be one of the maximum indicators of Stalin's 'totalitarian intentions', which Yves Cohen cited in order to demonstrate the political value of administrative practices '*dans leur materialité*'.[47] What had begun as a mere '*technique*' in American industry had been transformed into an instrument for the elimination of '*le commandement latéral des ateliers*' and to impose a '*subordination clairement verticale: les ordres tombent en cascade et la discipline est heureusement renforcé*'.[48]

At Škoda, the first company to introduce the dispatching system into Czechoslovakia, the production units were not receptive and the system was a source of conflict between co-ordinators and technical personnel. The conflict with the technical managers and the hostility with which 'conservative' directors viewed the new department can be seen from the intervention made, in October 1952 by the director of the AZNP, to clarify the separate roles and powers of the production and the co-ordination personnel, and to ensure that the latter did not interfere excessively in the sphere of the former.[49] Nevertheless, the measure introduced a formal distinction between executive and managerial organs: the dispatchers, those responsible for the plan's fulfillment, could, in fact, interrupt production and give categorical orders to the departments.

There were other signs of resistance by the technical staff documented in June 1953. The technicians of Mladá Boleslav, while lauding the new system, which seemed to reduce production-line time and result in a continuous flow of production, could not deny that there were difficulties in overcoming the diffidence of workers and foremen, as well as the co-ordination personnel themselves, some of whom refused to be transferred from production to do a job that required the skills of a telephone operator. On the same occasion, in the enterprise's organizational chart the names positions were changed, with the introduction, according to the Soviet dictates, of the 'chief engineer', 'chief mechanic' and so forth.[50]

Increasingly, the company's records show both the surprise and the disapproval of the factory personnel at the swelling of the bureaucratic apparatus, with the consequent proliferation of paperwork, and with the simultaneous introduction of the *khozraschet*, a 'truly socialist system of organization of labor', which consisted of the calculation of the profits and losses for each work-unit. The adoption of a matching accounting system, which was intended to make each worker feel responsible for the overall success of production, was translated into a means for pressuring each unit to increase savings in terms of costs and more control over the strict application of the norms.[51]

Tensions in the factory and in the country finally came to a head following the currency reform of 1 June 1953. Two weeks before the events in Germany, the elimination of the ration card system in Czechoslovakia provoked spontaneous demonstrations, with workers taking to the streets in protest over the reforms, demanding that the government guarantee their salaries.[52]

Škoda and the New Course: New Prospects for the Car Industry

Following the July protests, Jaromír Dolanský and Viliam Široký compiled the 'August Thesis'. This document presented an accurate analysis of the state of the Czechoslovak economy, coupled with a critique of Party policies. Although it was decided not to discuss the thesis in public, and although, on Moscow's advice, the harsher parts were 'smoothed out', especially the references to the political context, the thesis set off a period of discussion within the Communist Party, concerning economic and organizational principles, which reached its high point with Antonín Novotný's speech at the Party's Tenth Convention, in June 1954.

At the AZNP, the period from 1954 to 1964, including the Second Five-Year Plan and part of the Third, was characterized by the planning and construction of a new facility and contains considerable ambiguity.

In the autumn of 1953, under pressure from the Ministry of Industry, a secret document was prepared which exposed all the shortcomings of the previous management. The judgement was harsh: 'short-sighted management', reduced to a strictly normative function, had caused the production unit more problems than it had solved.[53] The document emphasized the need to de-centralize decision-making and to define new modalities for managing the relationship between the production unit and the central administration.

In addition, albeit only indirectly and very prudently, the problem of transferring the 'Soviet experience' to Czechoslovak industry was also raised, with the recommendation that it be adopted more intelligently and with greater respect for local tradition and for the existing productive practices.

The principal target of criticism was the series of re-organizations of the Czechoslovak car industry that had failed to establish 'direct contact' between enterprises and the government apparatus that they were intended to provide. There were innumerable instances of lack of co-ordination between industries, of an abundance of contradictory orders, general confusion and a dearth of clearly-defined priorities among the various branches of the ministry. The lack of a shared vision by each single department of the ministry was evident in the disastrous management of the supply system.

According to the AZNP, instead of creating efficient 'co-ordination' and internal 'organization', the ministry had simply given 'orders'. Furthermore, the multiplicity of norms had been used by many offices as an excuse for not taking any responsibility and for not making any independent decisions. In fact, another complaint was that there was an over-abundance of paperwork: it seemed necessary to dismantle the 'paper directorships' and return to the real problems of production and technology.

Not even the regulations regarding piecework were calculated properly: wages for manual workers were too low, and to obtain a liveable salary, it was necessary to work overtime. Finally, the incompetence of a few had caused growing dissatisfaction, on the part of the workers, with the planned economy, which had to be remedied as soon as possible: the principles and values of socialist organization, evidently betrayed in the previous years, had to be urgently restored. Stalin's view, as explained in *Problems of Leninism*, was invoked, which advocated a return to a genuine 'Soviet management'.[54]

There was a clear vision of the problems involved in the management of the car manufacturing enterprise and of the shortcomings of the First Five-Year Plan. However, it was balanced by the Stalinist overtones and the difficulty inherent in transforming a critique of 'misapplication' into a broader and more politically-based analysis. In fact, the 'Soviet model of management' was not under attack here, only its mistaken implementation in Czechoslovak.

The real extent of the Czechoslovak 'New Course' should not be overestimated. In fact, it was basically a re-orientation of the economic policy, within the confines of the planned economy, whose principles and institutions were not even remotely challenged. However, the fact that the authorities recognized the need to re-balance the country's industrial development and to pay some attention to the needs of its citizenry, particularly in terms of living standards, put an end to the intensive militarization of the Czechoslovak economy.

This meant new investments for the country's largest car-maker, which could be dedicated to mechanizing and automating production processes. In 1955, again following the Soviet example, the car industry was removed from the control of the Ministry of Heavy Industry and a separate Ministry of Automobile and Tractor Industry was formed.[55]

Finally, on 30-31 March 1956, Mladá Boleslav hosted the first Czechoslovak conference of automotive experts, with the mission of setting the guidelines for the subsequent development of the sector. The plant was the focus of the planners' interest, and they finally seemed to be seriously considering some of the proposals made by the AZNP nearly a decade earlier. In fact, most of the reports delivered at the 1956 conference were inspired by the old reports of the Taub affair and of the accounts of the technicians who went to America in 1947. Although not referred to directly, the Taub plan was 'rediscovered'.[56]

In 1957, work began on a new plant, very similar to the one designed by Taub. Work also began on the design of a 'socialist people's car', the Škoda 1000 MB, which was to have gone into production in 1963.[57]

The new investments resolved the imbalance between technology, business organization and systems of control which had increasingly hampered post-war growth, and seemed to create the conditions that would finally allow Škoda to become part of the 'Soviet model of management' and begin mass-production of cars. However, by the 1960s, the problems of the 'shortage' economy had become routine and – albeit in a different way – planners and, on the shop-floor, technicians, when searching for solutions to the problems that continued to arise in co-ordinating plans and the production process, kept laying the groundwork for a possible hybridization of the Soviet model of management: in fact, while at planning level, there began to be a formal and well-studied movement in favor of a far-reaching ideological revisions, and the introduction of market mechanisms which ultimately culminated in the Prague Spring, while, at plant level, the old daily practices kept governing the life of the factory far more intimately than the directives issued by the planners.

Conclusions

The Škoda case illustrates a clash that not only involves two views on how to build a car, but also (and more importantly) on how to transfer and apply an industrial model. The Czechoslovak technicians had a profoundly ambivalent reaction to the measures applied on the occasion of the First Five-Year Plan. On the one hand, they had misgivings and voiced important criticism, on the other, they professed admiration for the Soviet Union and its economic and social model. The Soviet model of mass-production was 'exaggerated Fordism', characterized by a profoundly ideological interpretation of the original Fordist principles and their hybridization into the context of a 'shortage' economy. The Czechoslovak technicians knew very well how mass-production was organized in the U.S. auto-plants, but they had no idea how it was implemented in the Soviet Union. In the post-war years, in order to modernize the car industry, they had thought of transferring some of the techniques learned in the U.S. to Czechoslovakia, with a clear understanding of the need to adapt them to the different economic, social and political context.

In fact, with the First Five-Year Plan, modernization of the Czechoslovak car industry was first delayed and then only partly realized. In any case, the Soviet methods of work organization were transferred to the factories without any attempt to adapt them to the local conditions of production, the nature of the local workforce or their technical capabilities. The dysfunctions that this generated in the system, typical of the 'shortage' economy, were recognized by the Czechoslovak technicians, who continued to seek solutions using the knowledge acquired in the years before and after the Second World War. The continual re-emergence of the awareness of a heritage of technical skills and know-how and the demand for greater autonomy in production and freedom from political decision-making reflect the resistance of the 'Czechoslovak road'.

The imposition of the Soviet model on the Czechoslovak motor industry involved a radical alteration of the industrial structure of a country, which, in terms of size, geographical location and industrial history, had almost nothing in common with it. The results were disastrous, and in the early 1960s, Czechoslovakia found itself facing a serious economic crisis. The inadequacy of the Soviet model was soon evident, and the fight against the bureaucratization of the economy became a priority for the Economic Commission of the Central Committee of the Communist Party (*Ekonomická komise ÚV KSČ*).[58] But well before the liberalized political climate could result in critiques and proposals for reform, some technicians had already expressed serious misgivings concerning the suitability of the measures that had been adopted to modernize Czechoslovak industry.

3

Sovietization and Missile-ization of the Warsaw Pact, 1958-1965

Matthias Uhl

At the end of the 1940s, Soviet military strategy was re-oriented towards the new enemy, the USA and the European NATO countries. Initially, the Soviet Union counterposed its conventional superiority to the nuclear superiority of the USA. Although the first Soviet atomic-bomb test had already been carried out in 1949, nuclear weapons became available to military units on a large scale only much later. The Soviet air force took delivery of its first atomic bombs in 1954, the land forces and navy did not obtain nuclear warheads until the end of the 1950s, and the air defense forces received theirs even later.[1]

After the foundation of the Warsaw Treaty Organization in May 1955 and the formation of the Unified Armed Forces of the Warsaw Pact with the Joint High Command at its head, the military-political confrontation between the USSR and the USA developed into a confrontation between NATO and the Warsaw Pact military bloc. Starting in the mid-1950s, this conflict was determined primarily by the rapid development of military technology. The most important goal was the creation and development of strategic nuclear forces. For this purpose, the USSR came to depend primarily on strategic missile forces. At the same time, a new military strategy, the strategy of all-out nuclear-missile warfare, was developed. As a result, the Soviet views about the conditions, the nature, the course, and the outcome of armed conflict changed radically.[2]

The build-up of the Soviet Strategic Missile Forces, first established in 1959, led to heated discussions about the priority of the various types of forces and their roles in a future war. Numerous Soviet army commanders and military theorists, including many military district commanders, held to the view that the land forces would remain the most important branch of the armed forces, even in a nuclear war, since a war in Europe, they believed, could only be brought to a conclusion through the occupation of the enemy's territory. By contrast, Nikita Khrushchev and the leadership of the Soviet General Staff were convinced that the strategic missile forces would play the leading role in a future war, particularly in accomplishing the main strategic mission. Khrushchev and the leadership of the Ministry of Defense around Marshal Rodion Ia. Malinovskii were ultimately able to prevail over the conservative officers in the armed forces, and their strategic concept became the official military doctrine of the USSR. As a result, the Soviet military were equipped with various types of missiles, which were to be used primarily as carriers for nuclear warheads. Among these weapons, intercontinental ballistic missiles (ICBMs) and intermediate-range ballistic missiles (IRBMs) played a key strategic role.[3]

With the introduction of nuclear missiles, a revolutionary development took place in the Soviet forces, which led to a complete change in the existing war scenario, and the relationship between strategy, operations, and tactics changed fundamentally.

First, in connection with the development of the Strategic Missile Forces, the role of strategic weapons grew. Soviet military think-tanks believed the Strategic Missile Forces would be able to have an immediate effect on the course of a war, and would achieve decisive results. There was a high probability that the primary military and political goals of a war could be reached with strategic weapons. If this were the case, the operational level would expand upon the success of the strategic level, and the tactical level would realize the results obtained by operational art.[4] Second, the existing time-frames for the strategic actions of the forces changed. It now appeared possible to achieve the envisaged war aims in a single operation or even with a single strike. Accordingly, previous assumptions that war was a more or less lengthy period of a continuation of politics by violent means were overthrown. There was an increasing tendency to see the path to war as an instantaneous act. Third, strategic operations acquired a greater spatial range in comparison to their role during Second World War. The ranges of weapons now included all continents and oceans. The distinction between the front and the hinterland was definitively abolished:

> From the outset, the conduct of combat operations extends deep into the hinterland of the combatant countries, and there is no strategic space that is not already exposed to attack within the first minutes of the war.[5]

Hence, Soviet military strategy, like that of the USA, became directly dependent upon the use of strategic nuclear weapons. The main goals of Soviet-planned military operations in an 'all-out nuclear war' were, to take out the USA by massive nuclear strikes and to conquer all Western Europe with the troops of the Warsaw Pact. Even for the second aim, in the eyes of the Soviet General Staff, there was no alternative to the use of massive atomic attacks on military and civilian targets in Western Europe.

Khrushchev's public presentation at the 4th Session of the Supreme Soviet in January 1960 of the strategy of all-out nuclear missile war as the new military doctrine of the USSR shows that, by the beginning of the 1960s, the strategic use of exclusively conventional forces was no longer considered a real option. Missiles and nuclear weapons had altered the operational capability of military forces too radically. Atomic firepower had reached a new dimension, which made it possible 'to deliver a crushing defeat to any aggressor on his own territory'.[6] At the beginning of the 1960s, the only 'defense' doctrine of the Warsaw Pact was a sweeping strategic attack, which would destroy the forces of potential enemies on their own territory:

> Only by means of a determined attack on several fronts in a strategic operation can the results of nuclear strikes be exploited most effectively in the theater of war and can the opponent be crushed completely and his territory occupied within a short time.[7]

But it was clear to the Soviet General Staff and the Joint High Command of the Unified Forces that not only the Soviet Army, but also the forces of its allies, would have to re-orient themselves to the conditions of 'all-out nuclear war'. The Joint High Command had established the important foundations for this 'sovietization' and 'missile-ization' of the Warsaw Pact by 1961.[8]

During the 1960s, the authors of Soviet military doctrine, strategy, and operational planning thought that the Warsaw Pact was fully prepared to destroy the European NATO forces in fast, deep operations with a daily attack speed of 80-100 km and the conquest of the territory up to the Atlantic within 12 to 16 days. At the beginning of the 1960s, Soviet military strategy recognized only one form of use for nuclear weapons: the massive strategic nuclear strike, executed by the joint use of nuclear weapons at all order-of-battle levels. This nuclear strike was to be directed simultaneously against targets in the strategic and continental spheres, and also at those in the theatre of war and on the battlefield. The attack by superior conventional forces in Europe that was to follow immediately was to destroy the available NATO forces in Europe completely with the use of further nuclear weapons. The Soviet General Staff seemed to count on an overwhelming success of the Warsaw Pact forces in the Western European theatre of war in a war with the United States and NATO. At the same time, the military leadership of the Unified Armed Forces maintained that, notwithstanding the increased significance of missiles, strong conventional forces were still required to implement its offensive strategy. Consequently, Marshal Malinovskii emphasized at the XXII Party Congress of the CPSU at the end of October 1961 that, 'definite victory can be obtained against the aggressor only by the unified action of all types of forces'.[9]

In the summer of 1965, a study carried out by the US intelligence service, the CIA, came to the conclusion that, in just a few years, the Warsaw Pact had been transformed from an organization that only existed on paper into an important element of Soviet security and military policy. Moreover, the report showed that, from the beginning of the 1960s, the USSR had been engaged in a successful program to boost the military potential of its Eastern European allies and had turned the Warsaw Pact into an effective military structure.[10]

The most important foundations for the radical transformation of the Warsaw Pact were laid at the meeting of the Political Consultative Committee (PCC) in Moscow on 28 and 29 March 1961. At this meeting, Nikita Khrushchev, Walter Ulbricht, and the other communist bloc party leaders and heads of government, discussing the increasingly acute crisis in Berlin, also decided to implement a comprehensive program to re-arm and modernize the armies of the Eastern European member states of the Warsaw Pact.[11]

The goal was to bring the armed forces of the USSR's European allies into line with the new military strategy of the Soviet Union. Since the mid-1950s, there had been dramatic changes in Soviet defense research, primarily due to extremely rapid developments in atomic and missile technology.[12]

This is why, at the end of the 1950s, the Soviet Union began the first steps to change the structure of the Warsaw Pact military forces fundamentally, with the aim of harnessing Eastern European armies for war. The 'Alliance on hold' was on the way to becoming an active element of Soviet military plans for a possibile nuclear war in Europe.[13] To prepare the Warsaw Pact troops for the new Soviet offensive concept, it was necessary for them to know Soviet military configurations and tactics. The first step in this direction was the transition of the obsolete East German, Polish, Czechoslovak and Hungarian rifle and mechanized divisons into modern motorized rifle divisions. In addition, some former rifle divisions were converted into tank divisions. With these new types of divisions, it was now possibile to build up Soviet-type combined-arms armies. A combined-arms army of a Warsaw Pact member at the beginning of 1960s normally included three motorized rifle divisions and an armored division, with a total of 14 launchers for guided operational-tactical surface-to-surface missiles (SCUD) and unguided tactical rockets (FROG), more than 1,000 tanks, about 1,300 APCs (armored personal carriers), and 350 artillery pieces and mortars. With the aid of the nuclear weapons at their disposal, they were independently able to destroy large enemy troop concentrations, and to 'sweep away everything in their way that might offer resistance to their advance or hinder them'.[14]

While the military leadership of the Warsaw Pact planned for the combined-arms armies to be able to seize operational objectives as far as 400 km away, the Soviet tank armies had the capability of seizing strategic objectives in operations that deeply penetrated the entire front. The order of battle of a tank army at that time included three armored divisions and one motorized rifle division. It boasted 12–14 launchers for SCUD and FROG missiles, 1,300 tanks, 850 APCs, and 210 artillery pieces. The tank armies were regarded as the most important assault force for the fronts. In the eyes of the Soviet military leadership, they had great power, high mobility, and low vulnerability to enemy nuclear weapons. After the first nuclear strike, they were to act as an armored fist, penetrating deeply into the operational structure of the enemy, tearing up the enemy's strategic front, and destroying NATO's capability for further organized resistance. With an average attack speed of 100 km per day, the tank armies of the Warsaw Pact were to deliver deep and devastating strikes against the NATO defense system. The goal, as stated above, was to reach the Atlantic coast quickly.

The planners in the Soviet Army General Staff assumed that the crucial factor in a war, envisaged as a world conflict involving the mass use of nuclear weapons, would be the initial phase. Accordingly, the level of combat readiness of the Warsaw Pact armed forces, and their access to the latest technology and weapons, had to be such that the 'imperialist enemy' would be unable to achieve any decisive initial advantage through a sudden attack using nuclear weapons and missiles. Instead, the Pact's own troops would carry out '*Blitzkrieg-fast*' operations to destroy the enemy's nuclear weapons and immediately go onto the offensive. This meant preparing not only the Soviet army, but also the Warsaw Pact forces, 'for offensive actions to crush the enemy as quickly as possible on its own territory'.[15] However, to achieve this goal, it would be necessary to modernize the armies of the USSR's allies and equip them with the most recent Soviet advances in armaments.

To this end, between 1962 and 1965, the armed forces of the GDR, Czechoslovakia, Bulgaria, Romania, Poland, and Hungary were to be provided with the following: more than 880 fighter aircraft, 555 helicopters, 6,075 tanks, 17,312 armored vehicles, 554 radar stations, 41,440 radio sets, and a large amount of other equipment. At the same time, on instructions from the USSR, a start was made to equip the armies of these countries with state-of-the-art missiles for the first time. This was to involve supplying them with 3,112 S-75 Dvina/SA-2 Guideline AA missiles, 4,320 3M6 Shmel/AT-1 Snapper anti-tank missiles, 120 S-2 Sopka/SSC-2b Samlet coastal defense missiles, 3,966 K-13/AA-2 Atoll air-to-air missiles, and 301 P-15 Termit/SS-N-2 Styx ship-to-ship missiles.[16]

In total, the armies of the USSR's European allies were to use these weapons to establish the following new units equipped with guided missiles by the end of 1965: 104 AA (anti-aircraft) missile units, 84 anti-tank missile batteries, and five coastal defense missile batteries. At the same time, the navies of Poland, Bulgaria, Romania, and East Germany received a total of 28 missile patrol-boats from the 205/OSA-1 project, which served as delivery systems for the P-15 Termit/SS-N-2 Styx sea-target missile. The total value of these pre-dominantly Soviet arms deliveries to the Warsaw Pact nations between 1962 and 1965 has been estimated at over 2.8 billion rubles.[17] To place this figure in context, in 1961, the USSR State Planning Committee estimated the value of the total Soviet arms production for that year at 4.1 billion rubles.[18]

In spite of this major expenditure, these planned arms deliveries fell far short of the requirements determined by the Warsaw Pact Joint High Command, which believed that an expenditure of over 4.4 billion rubles between 1961 and 1965 would be required for the re-armament and modernization of the armed forces. With that sum, the Soviet military heads of the Warsaw Pact aimed to supply more than 2,334 fighter aircraft, 880 helicopters, 9,040 tanks, and 22,017 APCs to the armed forces of the USSR's alliance partners.

To purchase these armaments was beyond the economic and financial capacity of the Warsaw Pact member states. Accordingly, the Armaments Commission of COMECON met in Moscow on 17 March 1961 with leading officials from the State Planning Commissions and the Chiefs of Staff of the Warsaw Pact nations to discuss arms deliveries between 1962 and 1965. At the end of the meeting, the participants had agreed on the above-mentioned figure of 2.8 billion rubles and had formulated a draft resolution for the meeting of the PCC scheduled for late March, which was then duly approved by the committee.[19]

The presumption that this historic decision represented an attempt by the political and military leadership of the Warsaw Pact to make significant changes and improvements to the military potential of the Eastern alliance, which was regarded as inadequate at that time, is confirmed by further documents from the Russian State Archives of the Economy. These documents show that the measures implemented by the Soviet General

Staff and Joint High Command to boost the capacity of the Warsaw Pact armies were not restricted to conventional weapons. In its resolution of 29 March 1961, the PCC also stated that, for the first time, the armed forces of the Soviet Union's alliance partners would be equipped with theater and tactical nuclear weapon carriers.[20]

This significantly increased the military strike power of the Alliance. More importantly, however, the Soviet military leadership was in this way bringing the Warsaw Pact armed forces into line with the new military doctrine of the USSR as announced by Head of Government and Party Secretary Nikita Khrushchev in early 1960. This doctrine was based on the extensive use of strategic, theater, and tactical nuclear missiles. The Soviet General Staff believed that a war between the blocs would be an intercontinental conflict, and also a war between coalitions. In their view, the principal weapons in the conflict would be nuclear weapons, with missiles as the main delivery system. To implement the strategy of a 'comprehensive, all-out nuclear war', it was necessary to change the military structure of the Warsaw Pact and forge the armies of its member states into an effective combat force in the context of the use of nuclear weapons. Accordingly, the forces of the USSR's European allies under the Joint Supreme Command were equipped with tactical and theater nuclear weapon delivery systems, on instructions from the political and military leadership of the USSR.[21]

To ensure the nuclear combat capability of all Warsaw Pact forces, the resolution of 29 March 1961 of the PCC provided for 14 R-11/SCUD missile brigades and 40 Luna/FROG missile units to be made available to the Warsaw Pact member states. Each R-11/SCUD brigade had a total of six launching pads from which missiles could be fired, with the capacity of carrying nuclear warheads with an explosive force of up to 40 kilotons over a distance of 200 kilometers. Hungary and East Germany were each to receive one such brigade (costing 4.8 million rubles); Romania and Bulgaria were to receive two, and Poland and Czechoslovakia four.

Whereas the purpose of the R-11/SCUD was to deliver nuclear weapons at army command level, the Luna/FROG missile complex was intended for delivery at divisional level. Soviet planning allocated one Luna/FROG missile unit to each Warsaw Pact division. Each unit would have two launch pads and would cost 190,000 rubles. The USSR charged its allies 18,000 rubles per missile. The launching devices shot unguided missiles capable of carrying nuclear warheads with an explosive force of up to 20 kilotons over a range of 40 km. Since the USSR clearly had supply problems, given the higher priority of equipping its own forces, it was initially possible to equip fully only the six East German divisions with the missile complex. In the other Warsaw Pact countries, the numbers of weapon systems delivered were initially insufficient to equip all the units under the Joint High Command. In Poland, for example, which, according to the protocol, had 14 divisions under Warsaw Pact command, only eight Luna missiles units were allocated, and Romania received only five of the required eight units.[22]

The apparent preferential treatment of East Germany in the supply of nuclear missile delivery systems was clearly associated with its particularly important position within the alliance. This can also be discerned in the area of theater missiles. As early as the beginning of December 1960, the Joint High Command informed the EGA (East German Army) leadership at a joint meeting that East Germany would be receiving R-11 missiles and launching systems in 1962. Special training in the USSR for the officers and troops began as early as February 1961, that is, before the relevant resolution had been adopted by the PCC. At the beginning of 1963, the 'Independent Artillery Brigade 2' missile unit had already been included in the group of EGA units placed under the command of the Joint High Command of the Warsaw Pact.[23]

The supply of delivery systems for tactical nuclear warheads for the EGA proceeded even more rapidly. The process of establishing the first Luna/FROG missile unit, in the guise of 'Independent Artillery Unit 9,' began in May 1962, and was completed after the delivery of Soviet hardware on 30 September 1962. Just a few weeks later, during the Cuban Missile Crisis, the unit was already in 'heightened combat readiness' and was among the EGA troops under the command of the Warsaw Pact Joint High Command.[24] By the end of 1962, two more tactical missile units had become operational, and by May 1963, all six of the active EGA divisions were fully equipped with the Luna weapon system.[25] The reason for the prompt delivery of the missiles may have been an exchange of letters to this effect between Ulbricht and Khrushchev, in which the East German Head of Government and Party Secretary, immediately after the meeting of the Armaments Committee of COMECON held on 17 March, requested that priority should be given to the missile deliveries.[26]

In contrast to the GDR, most of the other Warsaw Pact member states did not get approval from the Soviet Union for the supply of theater and tactical nuclear missile delivery systems until 1962. However, the supply of nuclear weapon delivery systems required not only a resolution by the PCC, but also a further two resolutions from the USSR Council of Ministers and the relevant bilateral government-to-government agreements.[27] The Soviet Head of Government and Party Secretary then notified the First Secretaries of each of the 'fraternal states' of the Warsaw Pact in writing of the forthcoming delivery.[28]

However, while this meant that the Warsaw Pact countries had acquired nuclear weapon carriers, decisions on the use of atomic warheads remained the sole preserve of the USSR. In the early 1960s, Soviet Defense Ministry plans envisaged the following scenario for the use of nuclear weapons by the Warsaw Pact allies: in a period of tension, the nuclear warheads – until then stored in the Soviet Union – would be taken by Soviet special commando units to the various countries and would be distributed to the missile units of the allied forces. Specialists from the USSR would then supervise the loading of the warheads in the missiles and clear their use in combat. Thus, the nuclear weapons of the Warsaw Pact armies would remain under Soviet control at all times, right up to the moment of launch.[29] The decision on the initial use of nuclear weapons was the exclusive responsibility of the commander-in-chief of the Soviet armed forces, namely, the General-Secretary of the Communist Party of the Soviet Union (CPSU); detailed operational planning for tactical and theater/tactical atomic weapons was carried out by the national command structures of the Warsaw Pact member states in consultation with Soviet commanders and advisers.[30]

The documents of the Armaments Commission of COMECON for the meeting of the Political Advisory Committee in March 1961 also provide some interesting insights into the situation within the Warsaw Pact at that time. Generally, the most surprising aspect concerns the wide discrepancies in the defense spending levels of the member states of the Warsaw Pact. In 1959, the GDR spent the least amount on military purposes of any country in the Alliance, at a *per capita* equivalent of 15 rubles, while Czechoslovakia spent the most, at 56 rubles *per capita*. This put Czechoslovakia's defense spending at a level significantly higher than even that of the USSR, which, in 1960, had a *per capita* expenditure of approximately 45 rubles.[31] Accordingly, it is little wonder that the GDR had the highest debts to the USSR of any of the Eastern Alliance partners for the purchase of defense equipment. By 1960, this debt had already reached over 183 million rubles, as compared with Czechoslovakia's debt for arms supplies at that time of just 4.5 million rubles.[32] On the one hand, these figures show that the individual members of the Warsaw Pact Alliance did not enjoy equal status. In the eyes of the USSR, favorable strategic and political goodwill could justify preferential treatment of certain member states, and if those states also had major economic problems, the Soviet Union would take measures to reduce the financial and economic burdens resulting from its membership to the Alliance. However, the example of Czechoslovakia also shows that the other Alliance partners had to compensate for the effects of this Soviet policy in the form of increased military spending.

The most striking feature of the comparisons between NATO and the Warsaw Pact, in terms of combat capability and weapons potential, as submitted to the Political Advisory Committee in March 1961, was the drastic over-estimation of the capacity of the Western military alliance. The intention was presumably to increase the pressure on the Warsaw Pact member states to boost their level of commitment to the building up of the Alliance. In so doing, the USSR was endeavoring to release badly needed resources for the re-inforcement and modernization of its own armed forces. Notwithstanding all its efforts to increase the combat capability of the Warsaw Pact through sovietization and missile-ization, equipping its own troops still remained the highest priority.

In 1963, the USSR Defense Ministry's procurement budget, at over 5,866 billion rubles, was already twice the total arms and modernization program for the Warsaw Pact for 1962 to 1965.[33] The aim of this spending was to equip the Soviet armed forces, within one year, with over 200 intercontinental missiles, 320 medium-range missiles, 375 theater/tactical missiles, and 900 tactical missiles. Other procurement plans included the purchase of 2,320 tanks, 855 fighters and fighter-bombers, 95 strategic bombers, 160 transport aircraft, 465 helicopters and 9 nuclear submarines.[34]

This shows quite conclusively that, in spite of increased efforts to giving increased prominence to the Warsaw Pact from the beginning of the 1960s, the Soviet Union relied on its own forces and resources when it came to military and security issues. The political and military leadership of the USSR saw the 'sovietization' and 'missile-ization' of its Eastern Alliance as merely an additional instrument of its own military and security policy.[35]

Part III

Consumerism and Leisure

4

'Der werktätige Verbraucher': Defining the Socialist Consumer. Market Research in the GDR, 1960s/'70s.

Marcello Anselmo

Consumption and Political Agreement

> The quality of consumer experience, or the quality of life experience in general, could easily reflect on the quality of labor experience.[1]

Thus, Albert Hirschmann described the influence that consumer disillusionment had upon the solidity of both the economy and the political system of the German Democratic Republic (GDR). In the divided Germany after the Second World War, the 'battlefield' of consumerism was one arena in which two models of development competed. On one side, there was the capitalistic society and its glittering well-being which sprang from North American culture, on the other side, there was 'real socialism' with the ideal of the supremacy of labor, which was of Soviet origin. Both sought to manage and to organize industrial mass-society by guaranteeing high standards of living and sought to adjust life-styles that were in constant transformation.

The events of 17 June 1953 underlined the urgency to develop a device to measure the consumer-demand integrated within the 'real socialist' political context of the GDR. The uprising of the Berlin building-workers and the ensuing repression, carried out with tanks by the Soviet occupation forces, underlined the political necessity of constructing popular consent, based primarily upon the raising of both the standard of living and consumerism. The SED (*Sozialistische Einheitspartei Deutschlands*), the Socialist Unity Party of Germany, having adopted Soviet policies and models, began a process of economic development directed at improving the material conditions of the population, and, above all, at rationalizing the relationship between the productive structures and the supply of goods to the population.[2]

From the mid-1950s, complex economic measures were instituted, including the special plan to increase output of 'goods for daily requirements' (*Waren des Täglichen Bedarfs - WtB*), which aimed to guarantee the population a widespread distribution of staple commodities, and the opening of shops entitled 'a thousand small things' (*1000 kleinen Dinge*), which sold a wide range of manufactured goods at very low prices. At the same time, initiatives which aimed at winning over the working masses, such as the '*Hau-Ruck-Aktion*', for example, were launched, which were public conferences organized by party functionaries at which the most urgent necessities and needs were discussed with the population.[3]

The factory and service workers had to be freed from their 'primary needs', and enabled to benefit from the growth of both the economy and socialist society through consumer activity; in other words, the figure of the socialist consumer emerged upon the scene. The 'liberation from primary needs' had to be planned through the continuous forecasting of the material needs of society, in such a way as to bring 'needs into agreement with production'.[4] In this historical period, the consumer was not yet considered to be a central figure in the economic system, while the figure of the worker-producer as an active subject (*Werktätig*) was very much emphasized. Although primacy was assigned to work as the foundation of 'real socialist' society, the task of the 'mobilization of the popular masses' in order to fulfill the plan of 'building of socialism' through inducements and incentives assigned a growing role to the consumer.

The developments in the direction of promoting a consumer culture in the GDR reflected a pattern that was followed in varying degrees in the USSR and the other Eastern bloc countries. In the case of the GDR, it was carried through under the direction of the first party secretary, Walter Ulbricht (1950-1971), who was noted, in other regards, as being ideologically conservative, and an advocate of tight party control over society. The innovation in terms of producing a new socialist consumer-society coincided with the sealing of the GDR's borders with the FRG (Federal Republic of Germany), and the building of the Berlin wall in 1961. The GDR's promotion of consumer culture was fostered by the need to compete with the FRG, and to meet the high expectations of East German consumers. It was also fostered by the crucial geo-political position of the GDR as a frontline state confronting the capitalist West. The resources that the state devoted to satisfying consumer demand was also in part facilitated by the low expenditure of the GDR on defense, which was partly subsidized by the USSR. The GDR was the state which pioneered the most radical innovations in developing a socialist consumer culture. In this, it offered a modification which was within the limits of the Soviet model, and acted as an experimental field for the other people's democracies.[5]

The problem examined in this text is whether the figure of the consumer was in some way considered to be a part of the discourse in the constructing of socialist society, and also whether, and to what extent, the consumer succeeded in advancing his or her own demands. In addition, the methods used to observe and study the consumer and to determine his or her 'consumption needs' will be investigated. Did specific institutions exist to study the behavior and habits of the consumers? According to what parameters was the investigation of the market of individual and collective needs and desires carried out in a 'real socialist' society directed by a regimen of economic planning? And finally, is it possible to establish whether an independent and original system of consumption, elaborated in the Fordist economy of Soviet roots, actually existed?

Observing the Consumers: Institutional Practices and Social Activities

In the GDR, the New Economic System (*Neues Ökonomisches System*, or *NÖS*) was introduced between 1963 and 1967, with the aim of adapting the system of economic planning, and of rationalizing and modernizing the productive and industrial machinery. The Socialist Economic System (*Ökonomischen System des Sozialismus*, or *ÖSS*) was developed from 1967 to 1970, and was directed mainly at increasing the income of the population. The economic planning, programming and drafting system was articulated through three layers: the State Planning Commission (*Staatliche Plankommission*, or *SPK*), which acted at state level; and the *Bezirksplankommission* (BPK) and the *Kreisplankommission* (KPK), which were responsible for registering and controlling the implementation of planning directives at territorial level.

In economic planning, a constant gap between the productive system and the reality of social needs persisted. This, in part, reflected state priorities and rigidities in the planning and production system, but it also reflected the fact that 'information about the needs' of the society was lacking. To remedy this defect, the Institute of Research on Requirements (*Institut für Bedarfsforschung - IfBF*) had been founded already in 1961. In 1966, it was renamed the Institute for Market Research (*Institut für Marktforschung - IfMF*), with its main office in the city of Leipzig.[6] The change of name reflected a new recognition of the market as a place of production and social exchange, acknowledged by society and the systems of a planned economy of 'real socialism', but it was also, as we shall see, the sign of an analytical transformation of surveying the techniques and languages used for investigating both the market and consumer patterns.

The staff that ran the Institute was recruited from the university faculties of economics and the social sciences and from the higher educational institutes involved in the programs of economic planning. In its thirty years of activity, the staff remained relatively small. The Institute was circumscribed by its contradictory position between a vanguard function – as it planned the material developments of the socialist-developed society – and a marginal position, due to the fact that its work was not seriously taken into consideration by the commissioning institutions. According to the historian Ina Merkel, 'the results of the Institute's research never had particular influence on the economic policies of the GDR'.[7] The surveying of consumers, and the analysis of distribution efficiency/inefficiency and of the other forms of socialist consumption had little bearing on economic policy; they produced few concrete measures to transform, correct or re-adapt the productive mechanism. The results of the research were published every four months in the magazine *Mitteilungen des Institutes für Marktforschung*, which represents, together with the research material held in the German federal archives, the sources for this study. The magazine was diffused mainly among the workers of the economic planning agency, although it was also available to a wider public in the public libraries.

The *IfMF*'s task was the 'observation of the market and of consumer behavior', plus the professionalization of the social surveying and study methods of the GDR.[8] It had to provide data on both the real amount and the quality of the consumer goods that were required by the population, and, through the transmission of data to the productive structures, to influence production directly, which, in turn, affected the work and contributed to the establishing of priorities.

However, from the beginning, the experts researching the requirements of the socialist market studied the traditional surveying methods adopted by capitalist economies, in order to elaborate an investigatory model that could fit socialist society and its social diversifications. The adoption of such techniques posed difficulties from the outset, given that consumers in Western societies operated in quite different circumstances to those of socialist consumers, who were constrained by the lack of social and political competition. In East Germany, the mechanisms of social status and social differentiation connected to consumerism found their manifestation in less recognized and visible forms.

The *IfMF* worked on state assignments that were commissioned by the Ministry for Trade and Supply (*Ministerium für Handel und Versorgung*) and the State Planning Commission (*SPK*). The research undertaken consisted of studying consumer behavior and opinions through surveys carried out on selected samples of the population, which represented the constitutive social groups of 'real socialist' society: white collar employees, workers, farmers and members of the intelligentsia. From the mid-1960s, the criteria used were refined by including distinctive categories, such as gender, generation and place of residence in the analysis.

The surveys explored the relationship between supply and demand, and, moreover, studied the actual levels and aspirations with regard to living standards (*Lebenstandard*) and the way of life (*Lebensweise*). These two aspects were, in reality, directed at finding and affirming a socialist way of life (*Lebensstil*) through the fostering of social habits that were supported by socialist moral values that could nurture social activity which was compatible with the aspirations of real socialism. The main aim of the survey was to 'involve the population in the management and planning of the people's economy'.[9] The use of social surveys to study the market aimed to isolate behavior that was still grounded in capitalist economic culture, in order to stimulate action and behavior that would affirm socialist ideals and support the government's social plans; the observation and control of the consumers was considered to be a necessary condition to *persuade* them of the validity of the 'real socialist' alternative.[10]

The individual consumer had to be freed from primary needs through education in socialist consumption, which was substantially different from the device of individual enrichment typical of that of 'value consumption' (*Geltungskonsum*), which was perceived to be the driving force of capitalist consumption systems. The aim was to construct models of consumerism, which were based not upon individual wealth accumulation, but upon the propagation of a common social wealth: individual fulfillment had, in this way, to be subordinated to a general collective fulfillment.

From this point of view, consumerism was interpreted as a part of the more generic social needs. This approach was modified with the transformation of the Institute's aims in 1966, when it was entrusted with the task of investigating the entire 'socialist market', and not exclusively the 'requirements' of the population.[11]

The Institute's focus was switched from the observation of the transformation of social needs to the observation of the new economic context, the market and its clearance mechanisms, a field of economic and social life that both consumers and the productive structure contributed to territorialize conceptually.[12] The recognition of the market as an economic space within socialism can be interpreted as the transformation of the position of consumerism within the dynamics of economic production and social reproduction under 'real socialism'.

During the 1960s, the whole of society in the GDR experienced a marked improvement in material living-conditions due to the completion of the post-war reconstruction and the commencement of socio-economic modernization, which was also stimulated by the stabilization of the international political situation.[13] Within this context of general improvement, consumerism as a strategy did not aim at the improvement of profits in the productive structure, or at developing commerce and socialist distribution, but, instead, aimed at the affirmation of social behavioral models which were compatible with the ideological representation of the society. These models, however, increasingly came into contradiction with the new needs and subjectivities that the Institute's research described and mapped. This tendency contributed to the modification of research methodology to compensate for the incompatibility between the ideal and the reality. The Institute was commissioned to examine the planning strategies of the social needs and the education of consumers in the economic and value relations of socialism.

By 1965, the figure of the 'active consumer' (*Werktätige Verbraucher*) came into semantic and conceptual use for analyzing socialism. The aim of consumer goods market-research (*Konsumgütermarktforschung*) was defined as 'the more and more effective liberation from material and intellectual needs'.[14] This involved developing 'methods and applications that perfectly allowed the active consumer's conscience, psyche, thought, feelings, will and wants to be acknowledged'.[15] His or her positive or negative, active or passive market behavior (*Marktverhalten*) had to be identified, be it expressed as 'buyer, consumer or demand element' (*Nachfrager*).[16] In other words, it dealt with the understanding of the 'consumer's psyche and ideology', in order to 'improve the cultural and educational function of retail commerce in the socialist conscience of the active consumers'.[17]

The empirical surveys began to turn to observations 'in the field' of consumer behavior relating to the acceptance, the purchasing rhythms and the turnover of consumer goods. Within the research, the idea that both property and access to consumer goods were perceived as the manifestation of 'social prestige' began to emerge; in other words, the symptoms of the formative and grounding processes of socialist consumption society had been met.

A concrete example emerges from a study on the purchase and accumulation of valuable domestic linen. Such goods constituted, even under 'real socialism', the dowry or the *trousseaux* for the daughters of the family. It was mainly traditional goods that socialist consumers preferred, despite the possibilities created by the productive structures and attempts to foster new tastes, and these continued to be regulated by popular conventions. According to data provided by research, 74% of those interviewed declared that they considered domestic linen the best present for weddings and honeymoons.[18] Socialist consumers, in other words, still used traditional symbols and modalities of accumulation and prestige.

In 1967, the *IfMF* conducted a study aimed at defining socialist market research; it took into consideration the relationship existing between market conditions (supply and demand), consumption levels, and the effects caused by the adoption and actualization of the New Economic System (*NÖS*).[19] The cultural, economic and social transformation that came after the development of the 'new economic planning system' implied, for socialist analysts, a re-formulation of the economic strategies in order to improve the living conditions of active consumers further. Several key industries in the productive cycle were now 'economically obligated to turn their attention to the market more than ever', and were thus required to accord 'to the market its real importance within the realization of the economic objects already present in the productive plans'.[20]

This new importance accorded to the market implied attention to the productive structure, and to the behavior, choices and desires of consumers. It dealt with an activity that should have allowed 'the industries, the *Kombinate* and the several production co-operatives, to outline the features of a developing and active market policy (*Marktpolitik*)', to attain 'a fundamental transformation in the economy of several industries, in gathering data and in elaborating productive parameters (*Leistungsentscheidungen*), and to effect and control market processes'.[21] The object was to investigate the transformation of the consumer structure not only with regard to 'food products, textiles and clothing, consumer durables and services of different sorts', but also with regard to 'the field of free-time (*Freizeit*) and living conditions'.[22]

Thus, as a long term objective, the market survey established the forecasting and development of market predictions which took account of the changing social and economic variables generated by increased disposable income, changes in working hours and the re-organization of the social life of consumers in the GDR. Moreover, the emergence of different fields of consumer goods which went beyond primary needs began to be recognized: social needs, for example, were extended to encompass the immaterial consumption sphere (leisure, recreation, sport and the arts). Socialist society was required to address complex questions posed by a tangible advance in the living conditions of the population, and was required to deal concretely with the growing demand for consumer durables of a 'modern' character and of high value, such as 'cars, refrigerators, washing machines, but also synthetic clothes of new production'.[23]

The emergent demand for more modern and differentiated goods obliged the economic authorities to elaborate strategies to ensure an adequate supply, which the same analysts clearly considered to be insufficient. To deal with this situation, measures were advanced not only to remedy market shortages, but also to push socialist consumers towards a relationship with goods and personal property that was quite different from the practice of monetary and symbolic capital accumulation. The *IfMF* was called upon to develop 'sociological and psychological surveys of the consumers', which were to cast light upon the 'purchase motivation, the consumption behavior patterns and habits as well as the effects of advertising'. In other words, a 'real market investigation' had to be undertaken.[24]

In these years, the socialist market acquired a more concrete and conceptual form, with the building of large scale industrial plants and new purchase modality services. The market center (*Kaufhalleverband)* and the department store (*Warenhäus)* were among the first territorial signs of the irreducibility of consumerism in a 'developed real socialist society'.[25] In this, the GDR was compelled to develop patterns of consumer culture through direct comparison with the FRG. Whilst this development was pursued within the structure of a socialist economy, it represented the most advanced development of retail structures in any of the Eastern bloc countries.

The theoretical and interpretative inlay of *IfMF* researchers was based upon a primary assumption: 'the primacy of production over consumption'.[26] This priority rendered the socialist consumer a producer, above all, whose activity led to the enrichment of both social production and consumerism, and established a particular 'proletarian *Habitus*' which was related to consumer taste and habits.[27] Nonetheless, 'the managing of the social system's development', should have transformed 'not only the dimension and the structure of socialist production, but, at the same time, also the dimensions and structure of individual consumption'.[28]

Finally, a strategic value was ascribed to the socialist consumer from the moment that the transformation of the purchase modality which was internal to the working of 'real socialist' economic and social equilibria was considered to be inevitable by the market researcher. This recognition became direct with the affirmation that 'the consumerism of the individual is an objective base and a condition for production'.[29] In other words, the productive system had to consider the necessities and needs expressed by individuals through paying greater attention to the social reproduction process.

It was necessary, then, to interpret social needs in order to develop the productive, commercial and distribution dimensions of real socialism; however, at the same time, it was also necessary to consider that 'the consumerism of the individual is remarkably bound to extra-economic factors and processes'.[30] The recognition of such factors was the basis of the socialist market surveys, and influenced research workers and analysts 'to adopt pluralistic investigation methods (*Methodenpluralimus*), which allowed them to comprehend the real laws that regulate the consumer field in all its complexity and totality, considering reasons, conditions and development factors in their objective-subjective-material-ideal-economic and psychological components'.[31] Through the development of socialist motivational research, the hidden factors of individual and social action which shaped socialist consumer behavior in relation to the purchase decisions about particular products could be determined.

The acknowledgement of the factors that influenced consumer choice enabled the 'real socialist' economy to maximize the success of the commercial launching of new products, and, in the same way, gave it the possibility of pre-determining certain behavior through education in consumption so as to reach a 'rationalization of needs and desires'. This last aspect was one of the objects of socialist market research, whose data were used not only to correct and adjust production plans, but also contributed to define a 'real socialist' (ethic and aesthetic) way of life. The motivational research applied to socialist market research sought to explore the unknown territories that regulated the 'creative' activity of the consumer;[32] in other words, the moments when the actions performed and repeated by individuals affected the general economic determination of the market.

In an economic and social context which, in spite of all appearances, was susceptible to certain impulses of modernization and transformation of material conditions, this entailed an increasing necessity not only to prevent the emergence of needs, but also to bring to account a demand – which certainly referred to different goods – that often changed in a way that was hardly compatible with the mechanism of prognosis and economic planning. It dealt with re-constructing the behavioral genealogy of the socialist consumer, and also considered the habits supplanted (*Überlebter*) by the non-socialist context.

The researchers then embarked upon a path through which they wished to outline the position of an individual in a typology of society characterized by 'non-antagonistic contradictions' (*nicht antagonistischen Widersprüche*) between binary socio-economic determination, such as 'production and consumption, demand and supply, social and individual interests, social and individual conscience'.[33] The relationship between consumers and goods was set within a complex social situation in which an intense activity of exchange took place between individual factors and other factors bound to the transformation of the political class-consciousness 'of the goods he receives, in which the consumer's perception is based upon an inter-play between these goods and past experience in terms of the memories that influenced him'.[34] According to the analysts, the socialist consumer brought his personal memory with himself, through his behavior and daily relationship with the goods. This involved a whole set of irrational elements that came in relationship with complex factors linked to the process of the formation of social consciousness.

The basis of the consumer's behavior was the 'need/requirement' and its configuration process. The need, as a historically-defined social category, was characterized both as a condition from which the individual and the society had to be freed, as well as a basis upon which to construct the action of planned production and overall economic strategies. The 'liberation from needs' entailed, then, not only a neutral fulfillment of primary needs, but also a refinement of consumer aspirations; thus, 'man does not seek mere food, rather particular drinks and foods, he does not need just to cover himself (*bekleiden*), he dresses (*kleidet sich*), he does not want simply a roof, rather a housing culture and comforts (*Wohnkultur und Wohnkomfort*)'.[35] The condition of need was interpreted as an individual condition of complex fulfillment, which had 'consequences for the goods supply structure', and an equivalent standard of living for society. This remained an unsolved problem, which related not so much to the quantitative supply of production capacity, as to the essence of production without specific objects in the market; as a consequence, the investigation of socialist consumer behavior should have contributed to the understanding of the absence of co-ordination between material production and the individual/collective satisfaction of socialist consumers.

Modernity, Needs and Desires

In the socialist market, the distribution of goods and their circulation in a difficult social web had, as its main task, the satisfying of social and individual needs, while the gain for the sale of an individual good lay only in the fact of having it sold. The functioning of the socialist consumer cycle was based upon a 'dialectic relationship' between social and individual needs; the way of fulfilling the former should have allowed the launching of 'consumer goods for the liberation of the individual from his or her needs, so that the permanent need for new products remained 'constantly present in the society'.[36]

Socialist consumption was connected to the generation of demand through the development of what was defined as 'productive consumption' (*produktive Konsumtion*), which was supposed to establish the subordinate nature of the consumer in relation to the 'producer', to make their relationship reveal a continuous and constant factor for the economic growth of the whole socialist economy. In short, the motivational market research in socialism tried to elaborate a market strategy that allowed it to create the conditions for a 'permanent demand' for new products which ran parallel to an increase in productivity. Thus, the consumption of goods became, even in the socialist context, the mainspring of the functioning of the economic cycle.

The automatism that should have linked social needs to individual needs clashed with the different nature of the formation of needs, for 'social needs bring forth objective features, while individual needs bring forth subjective features'.[37] Both characteristics belonged to the idea of need considered as a psychic category, as well as an economic one, for individual goods became different not in the collective plan, but rather 'in the consumer's imagination'.[38] The socialist consumer was recognized as performing a particular function: that of the selection and formation of a criterion of individual distinction that the market and the planned productive structure could no longer ignore, especially with regard to the formulation of long-term planning directives. Consumer preferences had a dynamic significance, since 'a consumer good cannot only satisfy a specific need, but also provoke a new one'.[39]

The definition of an automatism in needs production had to be faced again, which, this time, should have been regulated by a kind of social fulfillment, before that of individual fulfillment, and should not be mediated by the property of a good, but instead by the functionality or usefulness that this entailed for the liberation of the individual from needs. This was a dynamic that resulted from the 'double feature' assigned to goods through Marxist theory, which, on the one hand, characterized labor and, on the other, consumerism; but if, in the first case, production defined the value relation which defined the real use value, in the second case, the evaluation of an individual consumer towards the exchangeable value and social significance came into play, which was an assessment which, if shared by others, provided the social value of a good.[40]

Even maintaining the need as a primary category of investigation, the socialist market survey began to ask how and why the survey results displayed social and individual desires, and how these were transformed into 'consumer consciousness' that acted critically with regard to the goods that the consumers had access to. In this sense, they wanted to explore the transformation of the need (*Bedürfnis*) with regard to requirement (*Bedarf*), and to understand how, once the latter had been fulfilled, the psychological and irrational element of desire (*Wunsch*) interacted. In concrete terms, the relationship that defined the demand had to be searched for here, not so much about food products, but about 'televisions or camping equipment',[41] thus bringing into question the legitimacy of the requirement of these luxury consumer goods, which were linked to the sphere of secondary unfulfilled needs, and material extensions of the manifest desire of 'modernity' in daily life.

This displayed, in a contradictory way, the necessity of a socialist consumer system within which 'the objects for the liberation from goods have the feature of goods that before being consumed must be bought'.[42] Thus, the real economic motive had to be nothing other than 'a certain quantity of money in the hands of the population'.[43] Money was to be used for the purchase of goods, an activity which was, in its turn, subjected to the influence of the subjective elements of the consumers: 'the taste, the fantasy, the emotional state (*Laune*), the sensitivity, the *Spleen*, but was susceptible to the variable of easy prices that defined the advantage of the purchase'.[44]

It was not only the price, but also a linked aesthetic that was aimed at shocking the sensitivity and the acceptance of the socialist consumer, which, with the improvement of living conditions that developed '[...] complex material and spiritual needs', which, in their turn, stimulated 'an increase in the demand for high value technical goods and for modern and fashionable products (*modischen*)'.[45]

According to the analysts, by the end of the 1960s, the socialist consumer was technically 'free from primary needs', but demanded the introduction of complex and valuable consumer goods, bound to individual perception of social advancement. The socialist consumer should have been 'persuaded' in the choice of the products not only by the utility value, but also by the 'color, shape and surface as well as by the packaging of the goods', and by 'modern commercial techniques, for example, the introduction of new selling techniques, or the change of the shop's opening hours'.[46] As the *IfMF* indicated, it was necessary to 'verify the rational core that exists in the concept, abused in the West, of "image" (*image*) united to the "personification of goods", since 'to possess or not to possess certain goods, objectively increases the esteem and the prestige of the owner'.[47] In 'real socialism', the goods displayed 'the success and the result that the consumer derived from being a producer'.[48] Moreover, the socialist consumer was destined to see his own preferences and choices modulated 'through an advertisement shown in many communication media which, in addition to promoting certain goods, a particular brand and the peculiar qualities of a product', worked also as a 'spur to its utilization field (*Verwendungsbereitschaft*), supporting a way of behavior (*Verhaltensweisen*) that weakened outdated (*überholte*) ideas and shaped the *new*'.[49]

The consumer had to be observed in the physical places of the socialist market: in retail shops, street-traders' stalls, shopping centers (*Warenhaus*), bookstalls, hotels, bars; in short, the places where 'the consumer approaches directly as a customer and a direct observation of his behavior becomes possible'.[50]

The practices of observation proceeded through the direct interrogation of the single consumer using pre-arranged question-grids aimed at obtaining data about the choices and the economic premises that guided the personal and social activity of the individual consumer. The questions addressed to the consumer could be both direct and indirect, but they assumed that the consumer was 'fully conscious of the reason of his purchase and consumption (*Kauf-und Konsummotive*), and [...] ready to describe them properly without misunderstandings'.[51] From the mid-1960s onwards, the consumer recognized an effective role of his or her participation in a complex social fact within which he or she displayed a multiple activity composed of economic, cultural and social elements that affected the modality of the inter-relationship between individuals and their life context.

The inevitability of the consumer mechanism had been recognized as a structural factor in the 'real socialist' society so that market-research workers defined a theoretical model of socialist consumerism in which, in the absence of modern and differentiated goods, the compensation goods that defined the originality of the 'real socialist' device were the guaranteed provision of public goods and services. These were provided through loans and economic public support via, what was called, the social fund (*gesellschaftlichen Fond*) which covered the allocations to assure free services to the population in important sectors of social life: health care, education, housing, culture and sport facilities. This social consumerism, which aimed at the strengthening of 'the consumer' in order to increase the value of 'the producer', was the real mainstay of the socialist economic device, and, in order to increase the cycle of social reproduction and fulfillment, it was this, albeit lame, device, which allowed the 'real socialist' political power to perpetuate itself for a half century.

From this point of view, it is easy to understand why socialist market motivational research deduced, by the end of the sixties, that housing conditions were the most significant indicator of the living-standards of the population. The housing shortage, together with the slowness of the resumption of the building sector caused by the strategic choices of the *SED*, created a difficult situation which was reflected in the overcrowding and the co-habitation of apartments, which exerted a decisive influence on consumer attitudes, and acted as a brake on the demand for consumer goods. The housing problem hindered the effective economic—and even cultural—modernization of the country. As a result, an ambitious plan was launched for the construction of new and modern apartments, housing estates and settlements which then became one of the symbols of German 'real socialism'.[52]

Thus, *SPK* entrusted the *IfMF* with studying consumer behavior and the influence that the new houses had upon the structure of needs and consumer habits. It acknowledged that the transformation of living habits was linked to the improvement of living conditions and the impact that this had upon the purchases and the choices of socialist consumers.[53]

The surveys were based upon questionnaires submitted to samples of the families that had recently moved into new homes. These families belonged to all the various social strata of the GDR, but were mainly from amongst factory workers, clerks, and members of the intelligentsia,[54] and reflected both social priorities and the fact that the 'new habitations complexes were concentrated around the big cities and the centers of industrial production'.[55] Town planning modules projected the socialist consumer in an urban and industrial context, inhabited not by 'the whole population' but by a socially homogeneous whole, within which all the members shared similar consumption modalities, which had a real and a symbolic dimension.[56] 'Many consumers' wanted 'a good place to live in, to feel at home in (*zuhause*)', wrote the researchers, which meant buying new kitchens, furniture for the living room and the bedroom and so on.

In particular—those that now lived in new homes of one room, or one and half rooms—needed furniture that was space-saving and which could be used to convert rooms to various uses. An example of this was the development of the supply of assembly-unit furniture with which to separate the domestic spaces as though by walls, a method that still fulfilled the need of 'large and flexible spaces that the tenant organized according to the number of rooms and to the dimension of the habitation',[57] in order to develop a new way of living which was characterized by a 'rational control of one's own housing sphere'. Consumer goods and interior decoration were supposed to correspond to the best contemporary material and aesthetic standards. The socialist way of life, in its own way, was 'an unconventional (*unkonventionellen*) housing style',[58] and was adopted mainly by the urban social strata, which comprised the same people who, a few years earlier, had begun to develop a taste for purchasing technical and material goods, which set the standard for the remodeling of the structure of the social needs for the whole society.

Substantially, the studies agreed in indicating that the 'widespread desire for a beautiful, modern and comfortable house' had been fulfilled with the building of modern habitations, although this created new behavior patterns and needs for the consumer, which lent urgency to develop new choices and strategies of production and consumption. The *IfMF* proposed that the authorities pay specific attention to changing needs and that they influence these needs by the elaboration of techniques of persuasion such as advertising, which 'in the socialist context [...] is not a means to influence the consumer, but [...] to inform the potential buyer, in the best possible way, about the function of the product'.[59]

Advertising was therefore necessary to precisely inform the consumer about the goods at his or her disposal, and these were to be 'of important meaning for the organization of future supply'.[60] Thus, the voice of the consumer began to be considered as fundamental for the optimal functioning of the plan. In other words, the results of the research indicated the recognition of people as consumers who manifested complex and modern needs, the fulfillment of which was related to the synchrony between planning and production.

What emerged by 1970, after years of study, from the investigation of the socialist consumers' opinions and behavior, was a 'non-correspondence between goods supply and needs structure'.[61] The consumers were 'understandably angry (*verärgert*) at the lack of choice that did not put the sizes, colors, qualities and variety of desired goods at their disposal', as a result of which many consumers 'could find these goods only after having searched intensely in many shops', which demonstrated a substantial dichotomy between 'the supply of existing goods and the structure of the needs expressed by the population'.[62]

Thus, a substantial disparity existed among consumers, and the economic system was also highlighted by the difference between consumer behavior and the priorities established for particular productive fields.

The complexity of modernization in a socialist industrial society began to bring to light the first cracks in the economic planning system. These were revealed and analyzed by the *Institut für Marktforschung*, although no permanent solutions were found, just as the voice of the consumers remained unheard. Nevertheless, its footprints can be followed through the language used in the surveys and research aimed at establishing the degree of collective and private satisfaction among the 'real socialist' systems that were demolished by the very people which they overbearingly thought they had served.

The figure of the consumer, as first poorly sketched and subsequently refined, remained marginal to the elaboration of production plans, which fostered general discontent, and defined an arena in which the clash between the social life and economic planning occurred. The same consumer, the ideal socio-economic figure, 'longing' for goods and developing needs, probably identified himself in the popular claim during the last months of 1989, *Wir sind das Volk*, We are the People.[63] And it was a much more modern nation than it was officially regarded.

5

Socialist Recreation? Amateur Film and Photography in the People's Republics of Poland and East Germany

David Crowley

In Krzysztof Kieślowski's first feature film, *'Amator'* (*'Camera Buff'*, 1979), the central character Filip Mosz, a factory worker in a small Polish town, picks up his first 8mm camera to record the birth of his daughter. He soon becomes hooked on film. With the hesitant support of the director of the state factory in which he works, he establishes a film club. Bolstered by his successes in film competitions and encouraged by the attention of the cultural élite in the capital, Mosz begins to make bold documentaries which allude to the cronyism and corruption that operates in the factory-town. Released at the time of the birth of the *Solidarność* Trade Union and before other critical commentaries on events of the day, such as Andrzej Wajda's documentary *'Robotnicy 80'*, *'Amator'* reflects on the effects of Real Existing Socialism on Polish society. However, Kieślowski refused to offer a simple political-moral fable. When the film was released, the director was criticized by the anti-communist opposition for his interest in doubt:[1] the culture of dissent in late communist Poland demanded greater moral and political certainty on the part of artists. When the chief character, Mosz is forced to confront the effects of his films, he comes to recognize the complex moral economy in which even party functionaries like the factory director operate. His film has not simply recorded the world: it has changed it.

In selecting this theme for his first feature film, Kieślowski picked the most ordinary subject in the most ordinary of settings. Amateur photography and film-making had become a well-established feature of life in the People's Republic of Poland and elsewhere in the Eastern bloc in the 1950s. Workers were encouraged to establish amateur photography and film clubs in their factories and offices, as well as in the widespread network of houses of culture. The benefits of membership were many:

expensive equipment, such as enlargers for printing photographs, were owned in common, whilst the club offered the promise of obtaining film and other consumables in short supply. Technical knowledge was offered to members as well as opportunities to participate in local and national exhibitions. In his 1978 book offering guidance to those wishing to establish an amateur photography club in Poland, Ryszard Keyser listed 87 such groups, many located in the kinds of small town that provided the backdrop for '*Amator*'.[2] Located in cultural centers and factories, Polish clubs were supported by publications like the monthly *Fotoamator* (a supplement to the leading title, *Fotografia*), national competitions and exhibitions organized by the *Federacji Amatorskich Klubów Filmowych* (Federation of Amateur Film Clubs) and the *Federacji Amatorskich Stowarzyszeń Fotograficznych* (Federation of Amateur Photography Societies). The latter was a self-consciously proletarian organization which had been established in 1948 in competition with the art-minded *Polski Związek Artystów Fotografów* (Polish Union of Art Photographers). These new organizations enjoyed places at the table of government agencies such as the *Centralna Poradnia Amatorskiego Ruchu Artystycznego* (Central Council of the Amateur Artistic Movement) which were organized to promote amateur initiatives. Amateur photography and film were also plugged into an international network which connected Poland, the GDR and Czechoslovakia in ways that seemed to uphold the mythical fraternity of socialist nations. Warsaw in August 1955 was, for instance, host to a heavily promoted and widely reported international meeting of amateur photographers from West and East Europe as well as the Far East.[3] Like a cog in a vast machine, the individual worker photographer was encouraged to feel international and socialist fraternity with his or her fellow enthusiasts abroad.

The regulated setting of the house of culture or the factory club distinguished 'worker photography' as its strongest champions preferred to call organized amateur photography, from the self-indulgent practice of the hobby. In this spirit, German journalist and *apparatchik* Gerhard Henninger wrote:

> Under our new social conditions, photography, for the first time, completely serves to communicate and propagate the great humanist ideas of peace, of friendship among the peoples, and of human happiness. The direct consequence for the practice of our amateur groups is to enhance the amateur's responsibility for the meaning and effect of his images. The less the amateur takes photographs just for himself, the more he takes photographs to communicate his thoughts, feelings and opinions, his experiences and perceptions, the more he lets others participate in them and

> generates similar thoughts and sensations. The stronger and faster that his creations grow out of the private and individual sphere, the stronger and faster his artistic effort and lay-artistic practice will become socially effective.[4]

Amateur photographers were encouraged to produce images which not only met with the socialist realist aesthetic precepts which had been imposed on all forms of art in Eastern Europe in the late 1940s, they were asked to train their lens on 'progressive' themes (Figure 1).[5]

Figure 1: *Fotografia*, September 1955, with a cover photograph by Edmund Zdanowski.

In Poland, mass circulation magazines such as *Świat* (*World*), a photo-journal based on the format of the American title *Life*, held competitions inviting readers to send in their own photographs and to vote for others not just in terms of aesthetic quality but also ideological merit.[6] In East Germany, commentators objected to the aestheticism of 'serious' amateur photography ('the laundry line motifs, the cobblestone motifs, *etc.*') and stipulated socially and politically engaged themes: in 1960 Henninger demanded that the worker photographer pay attention to 'his own practice within production, his life in the brigade, within the family, his holidays, his recreation, his sports.'[7] (Figure 2)

Figure 2: Photograph of musicians by Walter Schröder from the Binz Photoclub in Rügen from *Fotografie*, October 1958.

Locked into the officially-sanctioned infrastructure of amateur culture practiced within the houses of culture and subject to a clear aesthetic creed, it should be clear how amateur photography and film can be understood as a sovietized field. But what were the ideological and historical roots of this phenomenon, and were they to be found in Soviet Russia? Moreover, did sovietization necessarily mean control? And what of the photographs taken and films made by these amateur groups and individuals: do they too represent sovietization? Might their images—like those made by Filip Mosz, Kieślowski's everyman hero—upset the world which licensed their production? This essay sets out to answer these questions by focusing largely on the case of Poland, where amateur films and photographs produced during the socialist era have been collected and exhibited in recent years.[8]

The Problem and Promise of Leisure

The answers to these questions are not to be found in approaching amateur photographs and films as art or propaganda, but as products of official strategies to manage 'free time'. Leisure constituted a problem both for Party ideologues and for official sociology. In its sanctified form, leisure was closely related to the promise of a communist future, a world just over the horizon, free of drudgery and alienation. In an oft-cited passage in *Das Kapital*, Marx described this as the 'realm of freedom':

> The realm of freedom actually begins only where labour which is determined by necessity and mundane considerations ceases ... Freedom in this field can only consist in socialised man, the associated producers, rationally regulating their interchange with Nature, bringing it under common control, instead of being ruled by it as by the blind forces of Nature; and achieving this with the least expenditure of energy and under conditions most favourable to, and worthy of, their human nature.[9]

If leisure, as 'the realm of freedom', was the promise of the future, it was also a problem in the present. Holidays and days of rest were guaranteed by law: in Poland, they were promised in the 1952 Constitution and extended in the form of the two-day weekend in the early 1970s; whilst East Germans enjoyed a statutory five-day week from September 1967.[10] But free time risked encouraging sloth or, worse, it appeared to endorse a calendar of religious observance. Moreover, the image of extravagant leisure was a central feature in the ideological armory of the state, particularly during the Stalin years. The worth and standing of the citizen was closely related to his or her productivity: conversely, the idle enjoyed their leisure at the expense of the majority, as numerous caricatural images of Western '*rentier*' capitalists and anti-social loafers testified. In the binary fashion characteristic of the period, private, wasteful leisure was invariably pitched against public, virtuous labor. Asceticism was, for instance, a marked feature of both the rhetoric and, in some instance, the lifestyles of prominent communists throughout the bloc until the late 1960s.[11]

Production was valorized for ideological reasons as well as for pragmatic ones, not least because industrialization was claimed as the engine of the socialist transformation of consciousness. Work in the factory or the collective farm not only made a better future, it made better minds. In contrast to the capitalist West where leisure and labor were polarized—one seen as a reward for the other—the challenge facing Party ideologues was to make leisure more like production: collective, transformative and progressive. If production, freed of the damaging effects of alienation, was capable of becoming creative, then leisure could be properly productive. This was, for instance, signaled by the widespread promotion of new leafy 'parks of culture and rest' decorated with open-air theatres, leafy avenues and classical statuary in various Eastern European cities including Wrocław and Bratislava in the 1950s. These new sites of leisure followed a Soviet model established in Gorky Park in Moscow in 1928. The worker was to be reinvigorated by the experience of visiting the park, ready for the great challenges in the workplace and ultimately of building socialism. In this way, the park was to be an extension of 'the red corner', the zone allocated to intellectual improvement in the work-place where the worker could access sanctioned culture and political thought. Even at home, the worker was to concentrate on building socialism. Of the new homes being built in Warsaw in the early 1950s, for instance, one commentator wrote:

> The new, bright and comfortable flats are not only a place of rest for the working man. They are also a place where one can work on self-improvement, a place where one may work out many of the ideas about efficiency that present themselves in the course of professional work.[12]

This conception of productive leisure had its roots in the nineteenth century notion of 'Rational Recreation'. As numerous historians have demonstrated, working class leisure underwent a radical transformation in the major urban centers of Western Europe during the course of the century.[13] Rowdy, ludic and sometimes brutal forms of recreation were replaced by 'rational' pastimes. Disciplined, morally-improving and segregated forms of recreation such as visiting public museums and playing organized sport were promoted by the state, whilst, at the same time, traditional pleasures were heavily regulated through the mechanism of the law. Not only were such measures—often laced with a heavy dose of middle class, Christian morality—viewed as means for the self-improvement of the individual, they were also claimed to bring benefits to the whole of society. Healthy bodies, improved by sport, were more efficient; and regularized holidays ensured that the 'tempo' of industry could be maintained and regulated. The conclusion of this new enlightenment was, of course, sinister: disciplined, sober and fit bodies would be best able to serve the nation on the battlefield.

Recast in a sovietized context, 'rational recreation' was accompanied by strong claims on the untapped potential of the working classes for self-development. This is what distinguished socialist leisure from the alienated forms of 'amusement' which prevailed under capitalism. Famously, Theodor Adorno and Max Horkheimer in *The Culture Industry: Enlightenment as Mass Deception* (1947) have characterized capitalist leisure as the eviscerated double of capitalist industry:

> Amusement under late capitalism is the prolongation of work. It is sought after as an escape from the mechanised work process, and to recruit strength in order to be able to cope with it again. But, at the same time, mechanisation has such power over a man's leisure and happiness, and so profoundly determines the manufacture of amusement goods, that his experiences are inevitably after-images of the work process itself. The ostensible content is merely a faded foreground; what sinks in is the automatic succession of standardised operations. What happens at work, in the factory, or in the office can only be escaped from by approximation to it in one's leisure time. All amusement suffers from this incurable malady.[14]

Adorno and Horkheimer's Frankfurt School colleague, Walter Benjamin, provided a contrasting image of the unalienated Soviet worker in his 1934 lecture '*Der Autor als Produzent*'. Benjamin mythologized common readers who picked up the pen and the camera to contribute material to the post-Revolutionary press:

> 'we see that the vast melting-down process ... not only destroys the conventional separation between genres, between writer and poet, scholar and popularizer, but that it questions even the separation between author and reader.'[15]

In becoming producers of culture, the new Soviet man and woman would, he argued, become conscious of the forces of progress in the world. Here was a properly Marxist response to the alienating effects of industrialized culture and a challenge to the prevailing conception of the 'creative personality' which, in Benjamin's words, had long been 'a myth and a fake'.

The programme of 'cultural enlightenment' which was promoted in the Soviet Union was already far more didactic and centralized than Benjamin knew or was prepared to admit. As Anne White has charted, the policy of cultural enlightenment can be traced at least to 1930 when the Council of People's Commissars launched a building programme of educational clubs.[16] Stalin's programme of collectivization was to be accompanied by an infrastructure of new worker's clubs and houses of culture, staffed with professional cultural workers who sought to shape the political consciousness of the working classes through education and the arts. In her words, 'the purpose [of the programme] was to use adult education and collective amateur arts to mobilize the population to industrialize and fight the war'.[17] The spread of houses of culture, rural reading rooms and factory educational clubs throughout Eastern Europe which followed the Second World War was the imperial face of this programme. Houses of culture and workplace clubs promoted not only culture (understood in the highly conventional terms associated with the official aesthetic doctrine of Socialist Realism), but also sought to inculcate positive attitudes to the Soviet Union in the new satellites. Czesław Miłosz, in *The Captive Mind* (1953), wrote about the new programme of cultural enlightenment in Poland in the darkest terms:

> We should … call attention to a new institution, the "club" whose significance is comparable to that of the chapel in the middle ages. It exists in every factory, every school, every office. On its walls hang portraits of party leaders draped with red bunting. Every few days, meetings following pre-arranged agendas take place, meetings that are as potent as religious rites. … People who attend a "club" submit to a collective rhythm, and so come to feel that it is absurd to think different from the collective … as these individuals pronounce the ritual phrases and sing the ritual songs, they create a collective aura to which they in turn surrender. Despite its apparent appeal to reason, the "club's" activity comes under the heading of collective magic.[18]

Visitors to the houses of culture were not simply audiences for indoctrination. They were encouraged to become producers of culture too. A high ideological premium was placed throughout the bloc on amateur cultural activity of various kinds. At the beginning of the new system, much state-support was given to promoting vernacular culture, particularly in the fields of the crafts, dance and theatre. The ideological roots of this support can, it seems, be traced to a fetish made of particular and historically specific constructions of 'authentic' working class culture. Established artistic culture—the 'output' of the gallery and the salon—was often viewed with suspicion, tainted by dint of its élitist associations. By contrast, any form of culture which could be linked to working class or peasant roots was ideologically valuable to the Stalinist regimes. Cultural forms which appeared to emerge from the collective genius of 'the people' and were made without the profit impulse, were celebrated as being instinctively 'correct'. In 1949, ideologue and Minister of Culture, Włodzimierz Sokorski, characterized the forms and themes of amateur and folk culture as a reflex of progress.[19] Ten years later, the East German authorities took a more self-consciously proletarian stance. In April 1959, Walter Ulbricht launched the *Bitterfeld Weg* (Bitterfeld Path), a movement to produce a new generation of worker writers and artists. Under this lead, professional writers were encouraged to go into factories to learn about the industrial production at first hand. These encounters would, it was claimed, take the intelligentsia back to first principles and thus overcome the separation of art and life.[20]

Following Stalin's death, the propaganda function of the houses of culture and worker's clubs was the subject of sharp criticism, particularly in Poland and Hungary. Yet amateurism continued and was even, as White has argued, re-invigorated by the Thaw.[21] Whilst the chief symbols of amateurism in the bloc during the Stalin years had been 'traditional' peasant dance and song, new and unmistakably modern forms of expression – such as photography and film – came to enjoy its protective *marque*. Associations promoting stamp-collecting, gardening and dress-making and other hobbies enjoyed positions in the cultural infrastructure and, as such, were able to draw on the resources of the state. Moreover, the rise in hobbies—many characterized by fetishistic relations with things—paralleled the growing consumerism that was encouraged by the post-Stalinist authorities.[22] Whilst some commentators took a hard line on what they saw as the ideological impoverishment of socialist culture by the rise of hobbies, others continued to press the case for amateurism. This was an echo of a larger debate about alienation unleashed by the Thaw.[23] Reform-minded intellectuals within the *Polska Zjednoczona Partia Robotnicza* (Polish United Workers' Party) such as Leszek Kołakowski proposed a 'Marxist Humanism' to reconcile their commitment to Soviet socialism with new intellectual currents like phenomenology and existentialism.[24] In this context, individual pleasure and creativity were reclaimed and adopted in sharp critiques of Stalinism by the left-wing intelligentsia. Much of the criticism vented during these years was often from a broadly Marxist perspective—albeit one which drew much from the 'young' Marx—stressing humanistic, democratic values. Even when the intellectual freedoms of the Thaw were withdrawn by the state in the late 1950s, the 'battle against alienation' (*'walka z alienacja'*) remained a legitimate intelligentsia preoccupation. Official sociology, for instance, sometimes took a critical line on the malign effects of industrial culture in Poland. In this context, amateur photography continued to have its 'socialist' uses. In the late 1960s, Polish sociologist Wiesław Stradomski argued:

> Along with advancements in specialisation, one of the characteristics of the industrial organisation of production is that the humanistic essence of labour declines, as it is split into minute operations performed by a skilled workforce, who may never see the final product of their common efforts. Their respective jobs require of them neither knowledge nor creativity. The level of responsibility drops down to a minimum ... And here lie the roots and the reasons for the development of amateur film-making, an activity, which at the very core lays a completely creative as well as reproductive act, without the intention of a direct financial gain.[25]

Here, it was not only amateurism's eschewal of profit which lent it its socialist credentials, it was also given a key role in staving off the alienating effects of modernity, even under the superior conditions of socialism.

Promoting Amateur Photography in Poland and East Germany

It is important to note that, within the general patterns of socialist recreation unfolding across the bloc in the 1950s and 1960s, there were national differences. The characteristics that describe the Polish case are not necessarily shared elsewhere. The distinct interests shaping worker photography in East Germany and Poland provides a clearest illustration of this fact. In East Germany, the chief specialist magazine serving amateur photographers was *Fotografie* (Figure 3).

It was first issued in 1947 by Wilhelm Knapp Verlag, a publisher with a long and venerable tradition of publishing specialist photographic literature. Despite its location in Halle, this title had a relatively pan-German character throughout the 1950s as did many of the amateur photography competitions before 1961.[26] *Fotografie*'s status as the leading East German

Figure 3: Cover of *Fotografie*, January 1958, with a photograph entitled 'Blast Furnace Worker' by Erich Angenendt.

title was underlined by the fact that *Fotografik*, a rival title which eschewed 'rigid, limiting rules' in the name of creativity, survived less than a year, closing in May 1958. It was a still-born product of the East German authorities' failure to grasp the reforms launched by Khrushchev.[27] In fact, *Fotografie* underwent an ideological 'renewal' in the late 1950s, becoming a vocal supporter of the *Bitterfeld Weg*. In serving the interests of both amateur and professional photographers, *Fotografie* illustrated a loudly-endorsed social ideal of the movement, that of eradicating the difference between amateur and artist.[28] In 1960, Gerhard Henninger wrote 'the smaller the principle difference between the practice (of the amateur) and that of the advanced photo-artist, the more we begin to bridge the seemingly unsurpassable gap between both, despite their different levels'.[29] 'Already today,' he continued, 'the worker and co-operative farmer who take photographs stand next to the writing, painting, singing and music-making worker.'

Despite the fact that amateur photography was claimed by its writers as a living demonstration of the achievements of socialist culture, the magazine viewed its function in disciplinary terms. Articles regularly promoted the official doctrine of Socialist Realism and amateur photographic clubs were admonished for limiting their discussions to technical matters and for failing to address 'ideological, aesthetic and political questions'. When Western photographs appeared on its pages, they were often used to represent decadence: in 1962, for instance, the magazine published a nude study by celebrated British photographer Bill Brandt. This image of a distorted figure, arranged as 'material' on a beach, was used to illustrate an article entitled 'Western Photography at the Dead End of Late Bourgeois Philosophy'.[30] By sharp contrast, the kind of critical views of the fragmented bourgeois world afforded by photo-montage were a legitimate form of '*volkskunst*' with a politically-correct history supplied by the communist artist John Heartfield, who had returned to East Germany from exile in 1950.[31] West German photographic magazines were particularly targeted for attack, particularly after the erection of the Berlin Wall or what Ulbricht called his 'anti-fascist protection wall' in August 1961. In December 1962, for instance, Otto Croy, the editor of the Munich-based *FOTO-Magazin*, was the subject of a long and aggressive character assassination.[32] *Fotographie*'s writer set out to represent Croy as a supporter of the Third Reich and a war-mongerer, connecting his apparent enthusiasm for images of war technology during the Second World War with his contemporary interests.

Like all publications, the magazine was subject to censorship: all images that appeared on its pages were approved by the *Zentrale Kommission Fotografie* (Central Commission for Photography) which had been established in May 1958.[33] After the erection of the Berlin Wall, security became a pronounced issue. *Fotografie*'s readers were presented with a long list of prohibited subjects with the following justification: 'enemies of our social development use photography to spy and gain information ... Prohibitions and restrictions are necessary to impede ... the enemies of our republic'.[34] Whilst some of the prohibited spheres of photographic activity were clearly determined by Cold War political considerations (aerial and industrial photography for instance) others sought to guarantee the rights of the photographer. A 1962 article on 'unlawful photography' stated with remarkable directness that 'Under no circumstances should a prohibition of photography be used to protect the commercial interests of a private ... photographer'.[35] *Fotografie*'s ideological 'highpoint' was only achieved in the mid-1960s - at the time of the Eleventh Plenum of the Central Committee of the Socialist Unity Party in December 1965. This meeting of the leading members of the Party had been planned as a fanfare for the 'second stage' of the New Economic System. However, the event took on a hysterical tone when the Party leadership used the platform to launch a savage attack on several artists and their work. With culture now clearly marked out as a battleground by the Party, the magazine's writers made strident demands for tendentious photographic practice and aggressive criticism of 'bourgeois' tendencies in photography.

To bolster its political *bona fides*, *Fotografie* presented amateur photography as a revival of the radicalism of the Weimar era when communist activists had organized groups of worker-photographers. They had taken their cameras into the streets, housing districts and factories to record their struggles with brown-shirted fascists and rapacious landlords. Their images had been reproduced in a specialist magazine, *Der Arbeiter Fotograf*.[36] Writing of this generation in 1960, Wolfgang Hütt wrote: 'Those few who are still alive do not make a big fuss about their work and their struggles. This is actually regrettable, for how much could they teach us!'[37] He wrote this sentence following a call issued by the *Sozialistische Partei Deutschlands* to 'make use of the wealth of revolutionary tradition from the workers movement [of the 1920s] in developing an interesting socialist cultural life'.[38] Worker photography's connections with anti-fascist struggles in the 1920s were, it seems, more important than its Soviet 'heritage'. Whilst amateur photography had been encouraged in the Soviet Union during the 1930s with hand-held FED cameras (copies of the *Leica* named after Felix Dzerzhinsky) available through loan schemes,[39] Benjamin's optimism for the wholesale reorganization of the relations of media consumption and production in Soviet Russia, described above, had been excessive. The Soviet camera industry had largely supplied the export market in the 1930s.

Very few cameras found their way into ordinary hands. In fact, according to Elena Barkhatova, the first photography club in the Soviet Union was not established until 1953 under the auspices of the Vyborg Palace of Culture in Leningrad.[40] This was followed by the slow growth of the phenomenon throughout the Soviet Union during the Thaw years. By contrast, amateur photography was relatively well established in the Eastern bloc in the late 1940s as both the East German and Polish cases demonstrate. The fact that it was institutionalized more rapidly and extensively in the satellite states than in the Soviet heartland should not necessarily be viewed as a symptom of local fanaticism, but a reflection of the fact that the transition to state socialism in the late 1940s was a shift from one order of modernity to another. The fact that the camera – the paradigmatic instrument of modernity for Benjamin – existed in Eastern Europe in large numbers was, in part, a legacy of capitalism. The practice and material infrastructure of popular photography had been embedded there in the 1920s with, for instance, American commercial interests such as Kodak and German manufacturers competing for the market for small cameras.[41] The establishment of a network of amateur photography clubs in the late 1940s should be seen, in part, as an attempt to manage the cultural and material legacy of the inter-war years. Sovietization, in this case, was not a simple importation of Soviet practices. In fact, a reverse trajectory can be charted in the traffic in objects and in ideas: entire camera factories were, for instance, transported from Jena and Dresden as war reparations in the 1940s; and twenty years later, an exhibition of photographs from the satellite states of Central Europe at the heart of empire stimulated Soviet interest in social documentary and photo-journalism, practices which avoided the inexorable optimism of Socialist Realism.[42]

In contrast to *Fotografie*, the leading Polish title of the period, *Fotografia*, eschewed the function of regulator performed by the German title. After the Thaw of the mid 1950s, the magazine's editor abandoned the high ideological tone of the Stalin years. Categories like 'Socialist Realism' or 'bourgeois photography' disappeared from its pages in favor of once controversial subjects such as abstract photography and the 'new vision' of the Soviet *avant-garde* of the 1920s, as well as extensive coverage of technical matters (Figure 4).

This lowering of the ideological temperature should not be seen as depolitization. In fact, the magazine can be associated with the interests of a loosely organized group of well-connected Warsaw intellectuals, many of whom were party members. *Fotografia* was staffed by writers and an editor who were associated with the *Klub Krzywego Koła* (*Crooked Circle Club*) which was formed in Warsaw in 1955. This debating club was the intellectual motor of the Thaw; a machine which produced and circulated ideas

FOTOAMATOR

DODATEK DO MIESIĘCZNIKA „FOTOGRAFIA" Nr 10 (148)

NR 10 PAŹDZIERNIK 1965 r.

Kilka lat temu „Fotografia" zamieściła na okładce podobne zdjęcie, diagram naprężeń. Wywołało ono wiele nieporozumień, ktoś mówił, że jest ono „zbyt dekoracyjne, manieryczne, secesyjne". Takie podejście do zdjęć naukowych jest absolutnie nieuzasadnione, zarówno wówczas, gdy ktoś ocenia je jako „ładne", jak i wówczas, gdy się je krytykuje jako „brzydkie".

Zdjęcia takie są poza wszelkimi kryteriami estetycznymi, są śladem zjawisk fizycznych, tylko z zewnątrz niejako kierowanych przez człowieka, a więc człowiek nie ponosi za nie odpowiedzialności na zasadzie odpowiedzialności twórcy dzieła sztuki. Jeśli interesują one ludzi związanych ze sztuką, dzieje się to właśnie dlatego, że powstają tak całkowicie różną drogą, że są wynikiem faktów „obiektywnych", że działają na wyobraźnię raczej przez odniesienie do nieznanego świata niż na „oko" malarza w znaczeniu rozkoszy estetycznych. A wrażliwość wyobraźni na cuda i tajemnice laboratoriów nie jest wcale monopolem ludzi wyrobionych plastycznie; dziś każdy człowiek o pewnym instynkcie poetyckim reaguje żywo na sukcesy techniki w ogóle, a na fotografie niezdobytych planet, niewidzialnych promieni i niezmiernie drobnych cząsteczek — w szczególności.

Zdjęcie Zbigniewa Korbela, stanowiące dokument naprężeń w świetle spolaryzowanym, zostało udostępnione szerszej publiczności przy okazji wystawy „Piękno techniki", zorganizowanej przez redakcję „Przeglądu Technicznego" w Warszawie. Dziedzina fotografii, dokonywanej w laboratoriach naukowych, z pewnością może przynieść laikom wiele cennych doznań i zasługuje na szerszą popularyzację.

ors

ELASTOPLASTYKA

Zbigniew Korbel

Figure 4: *Fotoamator,* 'a supplement to the monthly *Fotografia*', October 1965, with a cover photogram by Zbigniew Korbel.

during the turbulent years of the mid-1950s. Located in the *Dom Kultury* in the Old Town, it shared space and energy with a jazz club and a gallery showing modern art, both of which were fields of culture that had been under prohibition during the Stalin years. The editor of *Fotografia*, painter Zbigniew Dłubak, was the director of the *Krzywe Koło* Gallery, whilst one of the magazine's chief writers, Juliusz Garztecki, had initiated the *Klub* by hosting its first discussions in his home.[43]

The *Klub Krzywego Koła* was closed down in February 1962 in the period known as the '*mała stabilizacja*' ('minor stabilization') when the Polish state sought to rein in the intellectual freedoms claimed during the Thaw.[44] As journalists, educators, curators, film-makers and artists, the associates of the *Klub Krzywego Koła* continued to enjoy access to the public media after the club itself had closed. Magazines like *Fotografia* can be seen as a continuation of *Klub Krzywego Koła* pre-occupations. In this light, three consistent themes addressed on its pages in the 1960s can be understood as mirroring the interests of the editor, Dłubak, and his intellectual *milieu* rather than those of the Party under Gomułka. Firstly, like many such titles around the world in the period, *Fotografia* promoted the role of the photographer as photo-journalist, recording and commenting on injustice. For instance, '*dziennikarz*' (journalist) Marek Holzman's gritty images were regularly reproduced with glowing comments about his investigative approach to society.[45] Secondly, the magazine's fascination with the *avant-garde* of the 1920s - particularly in its Soviet and Weimar varieties – was essentially autobiographical: it reflected a desire to 'reclaim' *avant-gardism* – in the sense of both aesthetic innovation and social function - as the territory of the artist and not the state.[46] (Or, as Dłubak put it at the height of the Thaw, 'the battle against .... the *status quo* is the obligation of every artist'[47]). Thirdly, the magazine's interest in amateur photography – whether in the form of the sanctioned practice emanating from factory clubs or the snapshot – represented a fascination with the potential of the lens and the untrained eye to record the world in unpredictable ways. The official imprimatur of 'amateur' legitimated what might otherwise be understood as an illicit interest in strangeness. In 1963, for instance, 'the unusual amateur', Janusz Krippendorf was singled out for special attention.[48] Anonymous behind his Werra IV camera, Krippendorf trained his lens on the scatological graffiti of the city or on life in the countryside, capturing forms of everyday surrealism. His candid images recorded the broken pots and pans in the hands of children or the odd tenderness of peasant farmers cutting each other's hair. Focusing on the detritus and mundane rituals of everyday life, Krippendorf's photographs disturbed photography's mission of uplifting realism (Figure 5).

Independent and apparently unschooled, it was precisely the unaligned aspect of his practice that appealed to this magazine's editors and the Warsaw galleries which showed his work. In writing about the strange effects and fantasy of these photographs, *Fotografia*'s writers echoed the interest of Weimar intellectuals such as Benjamin in the '*spur*' (the trace) as something hidden in the middle of the unremarkable contours of everyday life.

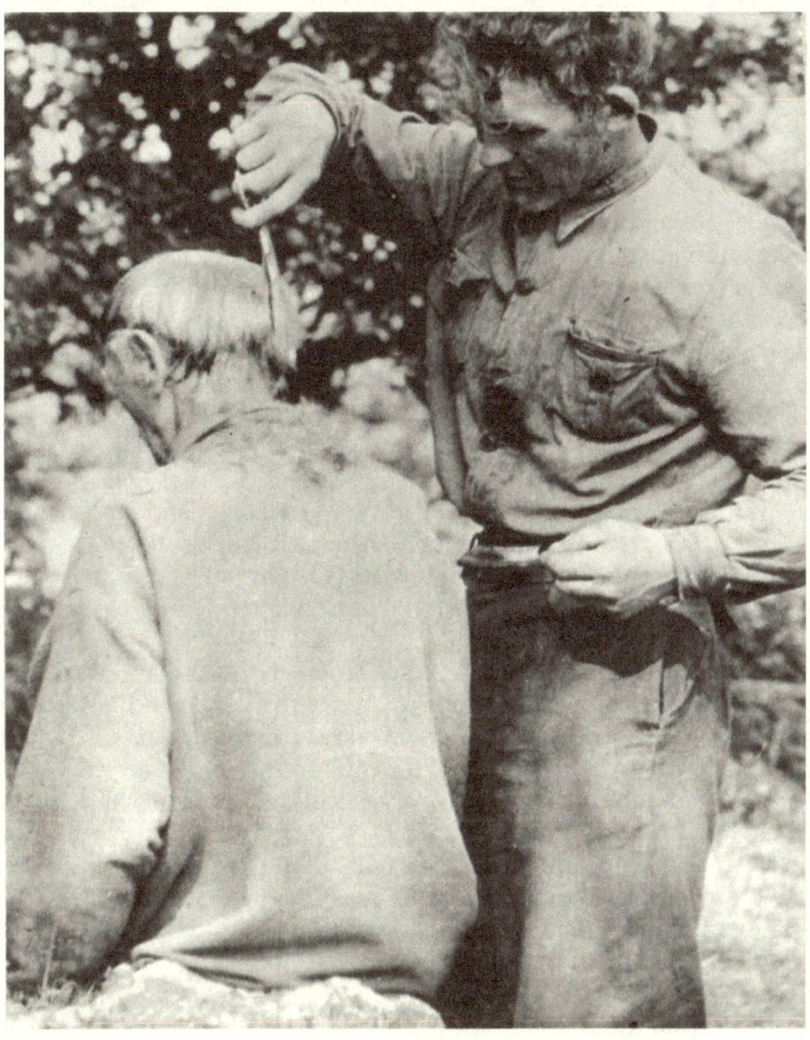

Figure 5: Untitled photograph by Janusz Krippendorf published in *Fotografia*, November 1963.

The fact that the East German and Polish magazines—which occupied the same position in the official cultural hierarchy—could come to hold such different views of amateur photography reveals much about the relationships of the intelligentsia and the state in each country. The Polish art world was gradually released from its ideological obligations over the course of the 1960s, whereas, in the GDR, this pattern reversed.[49] Sovietization—viewed in this light—was hardly as uniform or as choreographed as some commentators have suggested. One should not, however, confuse amateur photography and film-making as represented on the pages of magazines with their practice.

The View through the Lens

The worker photographer and the amateur film-maker may have been licensed by the state and may have used the resources made available, albeit with notorious irregularity, by the command economy. But this does not make the images that they produced 'official'. There is, for instance, relatively little evidence that the disciplinary discourses of Socialist Realism promoted in the popular press in the early 1950s were followed by any of the enthusiastic amateur photographers and film-makers. In fact, what evidence that does exist—in the form of the photographs themselves—suggests a far more ordinary set of uses for the camera. Lenses were trained on friends and families as well as on monuments and landscapes. Reflecting on the practice of amateur photography in the Soviet Union during the Khrushchev and Brezhnev years, Ekaterina Degot has argued that the state inadvertently encouraged the production of private images:

> … taking photographs on city streets without the requisite journalist's identification was a risky business that could result in arrest … The authorities were concerned about unauthorised reproduction (especially in the foreign press). ... As a result, amateur photography in the USSR, especially in post-war times, was actively channeled to "parks of leisure and culture" and the home – areas of intimate life in which there was no (or little) need formultiple reproductions. Thus, the Soviet authorities unknowingly stimulated erotic photography … Photography in the private sphere was ordinarily unartistic.[50]

However, Degot refuses to see all such 'private' images as a reflex of authority or an effect of alienation:

> Life under Soviet post-war socialism was so centred on cheap self-expression – gardening, knitting, poetry writing, and photography – that, even among personal, anonymous photographs of the Soviet era, one comes across impressive artefacts focused on exalted symbols of the private: sex, eroticism, friendship, intimacy.[51]

From this perspective, *some* amateur photographs can be seen not only as an escape or a withdrawal from the ideological imperatives on 'correct' behavior, 'correct' imagery, 'correct' attitudes, they might also be understood as what James C. Scott has described as 'hidden transcripts', *i.e.*, the concealed or disguised expression of anger, frustration or self-assertion by subordinate groups in the face of power. There is, in Scott's words, an important wish-fulfillment component in the 'hidden transcript'.[52] Frustrated by their inability to contest authority openly, the ruled produce hidden transcripts which represent 'an acting out in fantasy'. An instance of this can perhaps be found in a small format black and white snapshot taken by a member of a Warsaw Photographic Club in 1952 (Figure 6).

Figure 6: Amateur snapshot of marchers in Warsaw on 22nd July 1952 (private collection)

It records three young people marching, in a fashion, as members of a sports club through the centre of the city. The caption, hand-written in ink on the back of the photo, indicates that they were recorded, whilst taking part in a public demonstration to open a new section of the Polish capital, Constitution Square on 22nd July, a great state festivity on a symbolic day in the socialist calendar. The stiff jaw depicted on their banner is that of Bolesław Bierut, a member of the Central Committee of the *Polska Zjednoczona Partia Robotnicza* and the President of the People's Republic. The manner of these marchers is conspicuous. The seemingly happy and informal way in which they make their way through the city and their casual style, seems at odds with the banner's sombre jaw. The young man's dark sunglasses stand out. Known as '*mekarturki*' after General Douglas MacArthur, these inky lenses were a familiar symbol in the caricatural iconography of the Cold War. This young man's crest of hair is fashionably heaped above his forehead in a shape that was colloquially known as a '*mandolin*'. His style was constituted by signifiers of sartorial dissidence, interpreted in party discourse as badges of allegiance to the popular culture of the West. Gesture, pose and dress combine in this photograph as a record of fantasy within an event which might otherwise only be understood in the narrow terms of ideological inscription.[53]

This particular photograph could be the platform for a discussion of performativity in the subversive sense outlined by Judith Butler.[54] But what is more important here is the fact that it demonstrates the highly unstable and ambiguous system of signification in the snapshot. In the snapshot, we have a massive archive of dreams, poses, social relations – material through which ordinary citizens projected themselves into the world. In these countless frozen moments, ordinary people, usually *spoken for* (by the state or, later, by the opposition) *speak*. This material is evidently seared with emotion and meaning, yet the problem is how to access it. After all, who or what was this photographer attempting to capture and memorialize in this photograph? Perhaps a psycho-analytical key might open up the photographic archive; one suggested by Benjamin, albeit—this time—in his more surrealist mood. Photography is, he famously noted, an 'optical unconscious' which offers to the waking mind a reality that would otherwise remain hidden: 'the camera introduces us to unconscious optics as does psychoanalysis to unconscious impulses.'[55] However, this line of argument leads to a conception of photography which stresses the involuntary register of the image. The private production and consumption of private images is a kind of *cul-de-sac* for the historian. It is only when private images are projected into the public realm—*i.e.*, when they are projected, exhibited or analyzed on the pages of magazines like *Fotografia*—that they become susceptible to interpretation.

It is precisely the relationship of amateur film-making and photography to publicity which makes them significant. Their products were not what Scott called 'hidden transcripts', *i.e.*, the expression of 'a sharply dissonant political culture' *outside* 'the intimidating gaze of power'.[56] The support and resources that these clubs enjoyed meant that they operated within the sight-lines of authority. Yet, as Jerzy Jernas from the AWA film club in Poznań put it:

> We were not forced to do anything, we only occasionally had to make a "congratulatory scroll" to celebrate the factory's anniversary, something similar to a commercial nowadays. This was taken for granted and in no way interfered with the making of our own films. We didn't identify with those commissioned jobs, but, at the same time, we were aware that film can serve as propaganda. We wanted to talk about our own lives and our own worlds, which didn't resemble what was shown by the official city or factory newsreels.[57]

Amateur image-makers benefited from the relative indifference of the state, at least in the relatively liberal conditions of Poland in the 1960s and 1970s. Largely overlooked and valued largely to illustrate the rhetorical claims of the hegemony of the working classes, these image-makers enjoyed greater freedom of expression than their better-known and more illustrious professional counterparts. A film commissioned to record the achievements of a particular factory could become a wily commentary on working conditions or bureaucracy, and a record of official rituals could map injustice. Describing the first film made by the Radok film club in Rawicz, founded in 1964, Stefan Skrzypek recalls:

> I insisted on calling it a newsreel (*kronika filmowa*). We were filming during Maydays and the 22nd of July celebrations. We would usually film a report that we were asked for but there was always a lot of 8mm footage left over. One day, we started looking through it, and began editing it together … It was a documentary about a Mayday parade but shown, so to speak, through the back door. There were shots that could never have been included in the official version. The film was simply made in conspiracy, while many years later it was presented on television...[58]

Seizing the means to 'talk about their own lives' with their own bodies, homes, workplaces and possessions, and operating in the liminal space between public culture and private life, some amateur film-makers produced exceptional images. '*Impreza*' (Party), a 1972 film directed by Franciszek Dzida from the *Klaps* club attached to the sugar factory where he worked in Chybie, represents the slow drunken drift of a private party into a dreamy sexual encounter. Similarly, '*Nieporozumienie*' (Misunderstanding) of 1978, a film made by Piotr Majdrowicz in Poznań, explored unrequited homosexual desire, a theme which barely surfaced anywhere in Polish culture at the time. Neither film can be seen as an instinctive expression of fantasy, but rather as a commentary on it within the peculiar conditions of the People's Republic of Poland, a land policed by the Party and the Roman Catholic Church. In Dzida's words, 'I would like to emphasise that this place, this club, thanks to celluloid film, was a place where another world ruled … it was a magical place.'[59]

In turning ordinary homes and streets into sets, workers into actors, dreams into celluloid, some amateur film-makers in Poland appear to have escaped the gravitational pull of convention and ideology. Benjamin had once imagined that workers with cameras would be able to overcome the alienation of capitalist modernity: in the People's Republic of Poland, it seems, workers turned to the camera to escape the alienating effects of socialist modernity and morality. Leisure taken in this way might not necessarily be seen as a privatized cosmos of involution or withdrawal. Moreover, its traces – viewed as articulations of fantasy – might well be read by the historian as the expression of dreams, desires and attitudes which are not recorded elsewhere. Far from being minor materials, these transcripts of leisure may well reveal much about the ordinary experience of, and attitudes to, Soviet-style socialism.

6

Male Heroes and Female Comrades: The Image of the Russians in Soviet Films in Post-War Berlin

Sibylle Mohrmann

The situation in Berlin and East Germany at the end of the Second World War differed greatly from the situation in other Soviet-occupied territories as most Berliners accepted the presence of the Red Army as an undisputed consequence of the war and as a punishment for the Nazi regime: after all, the Soviet Army represented one of the four Allied Powers. In this context, the Soviets and the US agreed that the Germans should be 're-educated' to prevent any resurgence of Nazism, even if the victors shared very different understandings of 'humanism' and 'democracy'.[1] Moreover, Soviets and German anti-fascists decided that culture – especially literature, the press, radio broadcasting, theatre and film – should play an important part in implementing the re-education process. In 1945-46, serious attempts were made in Berlin, governed collectively by the four Allies, to negate Nazi propaganda clichés and establish a new positive image of the Russians (at the time, few people distinguished the Russians from the other nationalities of the Soviet Union). This process was connected to the general issue of German guilt and atonement.

Initially, the concepts of re-education implemented by the Soviets and the US did not differ substantially. All the Allies associated re-education with Herder's humanist understanding of culture. The German nation should recall and, once more, value both its national cultural heritage and that of the world as a whole, as suggested by the German writer and communist politician Johannes R. Becher during his exile in Moscow.[2] Culture was the magic word as regards the re-education of Germany. Consequently, Germany's devastated capital witnessed an upsurge in cultural activity. This also meant that Germans learned to look at Russian men and women in a new way. However, it was not easy to create a new image of the Russians. Reports of Russian soldiers looting and raping confirmed, rather than invalidated, Nazi clichés, even if many Berliners were also impressed by the educated Russian cultural functionaries, who were actively supporting the revival of Berlin's social and cultural life.[3]

This chapter analyzes Soviet re-education efforts in post-war Berlin (1945-46), based upon Soviet films and the reviews of them that were published in the Berlin press at the time. While Nazi propaganda had disseminated images of 'barbaric' Russians, the Soviet films tried to erase this negative image and, in its place, propagated images of 'heroic' Russian men. However, a similar reversal of negative Nazi propaganda images in relation to Russian women was more problematical: since the Nazis negatively depicted Russian women as emancipated comrades who neglected their 'natural' roles as housewives and mothers, a simple reversal of that Nazi image would have been in conflict with the Soviet understanding of the emancipated and socially engaged woman. This chapter demonstrates how this problem led to the propagation of mixed messages, which combined depictions of socially and politically active workingwomen with more traditional images. This is of particular interest since these mixed images subsequently became the role model for many women in East Germany.

The images of Russian men and women have always been a controversial issue in Germany. It was not merely a matter of whether Russians were seen as enemies or allies (as during the Napoleonic Wars). Interest in developments in Russia, both approving and critical, greatly increased after the October Revolution. As the agents of a new historical, political and cultural social order, Russians became the focus of attention for those who saw in them a promising sign of new hope. This was also the case in relation to the (socialist) women's movement, since the Bolsheviks also challenged both traditional role models, which confined women to the house, as well as claims that husband and wife should belong to each other.[4] Consequently, Germans who did not want to question the traditional division of power and labor between the social classes and the sexes saw Soviet Russia as a major threat. This fear of Bolshevism had been stoked by Nazi propaganda, which utilized images derived from the late 16th and 17th centuries that depicted Russian men as barbarians.[5] The Nazis also scorned the image of active Soviet women and contrasted it with their belief in a natural role of women as housewives and mothers.[6]

As a result, the images of Russian men and women oscillated between two poles: Russian men varied between barbarians and heroes, and Russian woman between traditional and emancipated roles. To explore this phenomenon, we will analyze articles from daily Berlin newspapers in the years 1945-46, which have, until now, received only insufficient attention from researchers.[7]

The importance of films in Soviet propaganda was underlined by Richard Taylor, who asserted that cinema was the 'most important of all the arts' for Lenin, the 'greatest means of mass agitation' for Stalin, and 'the best instrument of propaganda' for Trotsky.[8] As the German communist Willi Münzenberg said in the 1930s, 'film is the most advanced means of propaganda', and he insisted that Soviet films should be shown in Germany.[9] As Peter Kenez pointed out, Soviet leaders had an extremely well-functioning propaganda machine and did not hesitate to provide it with ample resources, even in difficult wartime circumstances. It was therefore possible to produce several war films[10] and feature films.

In Germany, Russian films have always been received very differently. Oksana Bulgakova depicted the reception of Russian films in Germany as a war of stereotypes. She claimed that attempts were repeatedly made in this 'war' to process everything that was new by adapting old stereotypes to make them conform to new images or dominant stylistic trends.[11]

Figure 7. Election poster of the NSDAP, viz Nazi Party , "The Red War – Mother or Comrade", about 1930, Bundesarchiv Plak 002-038-011. "The Red War. Mother or Comrade? God or Devil? Blood or Gold? Race or Half-Bred? Folk Song or Jazz? National Socialism or Bolshevism?"

The most famous Soviet film was probably *Battleship Potemkin* by Sergei Eisenstein, which became world-famous following its screening in Berlin in 1926. Clearly, the post-war Soviet military administration tried to continue along this path, by bringing Soviet films to the cinemas of Berlin immediately after Germany's capitulation in May 1945. These were, first and foremost, documentaries, historical and contemporary Soviet films. It goes without saying that the Soviet cultural officials in Berlin were greatly interested in Soviet films which, in their opinion, communicated a positive image of Russians. The Soviet distribution company *Sovexportfilm* assumed control over the showing of Soviet films in Berlin; in this company, Soviet administrators worked with 'untainted' figures from the German film industry. A cultural council, which included German theater directors, critics and other artists, decided which Soviet films should be shown in Berlin; the German members of the council attempted to explain how Soviet viewing-habits differed from German ones.[12]

So, what images of Russians were conveyed by these films and how were they perceived by the Berlin newspapers? Can we identify common patterns for both the image of the Russian man and the Russian woman? To answer these questions, we examine the following films, which are examples of the most important genres screened in Berlin's cinemas at the time: documentaries – *Stalingrad* and *Berlin*; historical films – *Ivan the Terrible* (part 1) and *Peter the First*; and feature films – *Circus* and the *Rich Bride*.

In each case, one has to bear in mind that writing a very negative statement about these films was virtually impossible: the Allies would probably have interpreted a critical review as anti-Sovietism. Instead, some reviewers of the films highlighted the acting of the 'happy' and 'lively' Russians in 'extremely beautiful' landscapes. However, this over-emphasis of positive Russian features may, actually, have also been understood as criticism, by leaving the aspects of the film that the reviewer disapproved of unspoken.

Documentaries: Soviet Soldiers as Ordinary Men

To promote a positive image of Russians, no Soviet films that displayed hatred of Germans were screened in post-war Berlin, even though the war had been a life or death fight for the USSR. Instead, the authorities selected pre-war Soviet films, which showed what life was like in the new society of Soviet cities and rural districts. The war was addressed primarily via historical films or contemporary documentaries such as *Berlin* and *Stalingrad*. Soviet and German footage alike was used for both documentaries.[13]

	Documentaries	Historical Films	Contemporary Films
Released in 1945	***Stalingrad*** ***Berlin***	***Ivan the Terrible***	
Released in 1946		***Peter the First***	***Circus*** ***The Rich Bride***

Table 1. Selected Soviet films that were released in Berlin 1945-1946

Berlin

The documentary *Berlin* (written and directed by Yuli Raizman) was ready for screening as early as 17th of June 1945. Soviet cinematographers from the 1st Belarusian and 1st Ukrainian Fronts, where more than half of the combatants had been wounded and one fifth had died in combat,[14] had filmed the run-up to the assault on Berlin and the subsequent capture of the city. This Soviet footage was assigned such high priority that military leaders gave the film-makers every possible support.[15] The film shows, in quick sequences, Soviet artillery bombardments, aircraft and tanks, and, behind them, Soviet soldiers running, shooting and dying. Ruined buildings burn and collapse, houses are stormed. As a contrast, these scenes are intercut with footage of military parades from German cinema newsreels, full of exhortations to maintain the fighting spirit, and with footage of civilians trying to reach safety. The red flag over Berlin's *Reichstag* and the signing of capitulation in the Berlin district of Karlshorst not only signaled the end of the war, but also the end of the Third Reich.

Berlin was in the city's cinemas by July 1945 and was instantly acknowledged as depicting Germany's immediate past:

> 'It is our wives, children and mothers who, driven by fear, bolt for safety as rubble falls around them … It is our Berlin in which the soldiers of the Red Army storm forward.'[16]

The suffering of the civilians documented by the film amid the ruins of Berlin and the undeniable presence of Soviet troops again demonstrated Germany's defeat in real, graphic terms. Soviet soldiers were seen as military victors, men in whose faces the strains of the bitter fighting were readily visible. The chief commander was no exception, as Marshall Zhukov, the victor of Berlin, was depicted as a worn-out man while he was marching through the Brandenburg Gate.[17] Russians and their military leaders were perceived as ordinary men and not as glorified heroes. Russian women were not mentioned in the reviews, in stark contrast to 'our' German women, children and mothers, who embody the suffering of the civilian population in a manner corresponding to the traditional female role.

Stalingrad

The documentary *Stalingrad* was made in 1942-43 under the direction of Leonid Varmolov. Wartime camera teams on the Stalingrad and Don fronts shot the film; their footage was combined with captured German film material. This documentary has the same structure as many others:[18] it starts with pictures of the peaceful town of Stalingrad with its inhabitants, their work (for instance, in the famous tractor factory) and their leisurely walks through museums and pleasant parks. Then, war breaks out. German troops bombard the city; encircle it, and the struggle for Stalingrad begins. Tanks are now built in the tractor factory. The viewer sees civilians, women in particular, who start to dig trenches and then have to flee the burning city with the possessions that they have managed to save. A stone monument of dancing children stands in front of a burning house; a tired horse stands immobile in front of ruins. Soviet soldiers run, attack, fight, save the injured. Men can be seen dying. In a break from fighting, a soldier repairs clocks and watches; another one plays the harmonica. As in *Berlin*, Russians are depicted as ordinary men who love their homeland and fight for it. The heady victory celebrations of the Red Army are interspersed with striking scenes depicting individuals who long for peace, for example a Soviet soldier who ties his hat over the mouth of a cannon as a sign that the battle is over. The inhabitants of Stalingrad return to their devastated city. German footage is then shown, depicting German soldiers during and after the fighting in Stalingrad. Intercuts contrast brisk *Wehrmacht* parades with columns of German prisoners of war stumbling through snowbound Russia, German military orders are contrasted with the crosses on German soldiers' graves, with the corpses of German soldiers and with destroyed German military equipment.

Stalingrad was shown in Berlin in November 1945 and was held in high regard by German viewers. There were several reasons for this. The Battle of Stalingrad represented the moment when the German *Wehrmacht* lost its aura of invincibility, and marked the turning point of the war. However, the capitulation of the army led by Friedrich Paulus had never been officially acknowledged in the Third Reich, and instead, the regime had announced that all its soldiers had died as heroes. After the end of the war, many relatives hoped to discover if their men had somehow managed to survive, so the topic of Stalingrad remained important for Germany. This factor was also compounded by the fact that Germans were, by 1945, familiar with scenes of wartime suffering and of people fleeing the ruins.

In her review of *Stalingrad,* Rosemarie Knop recalled the sufferings of Soviet civilians and mentioned both the scenes with the horse and the breaks from fighting in which Russian men used to play folk tunes and write letters – in other words, you see Russian men engaged in civilian activities during the lulls in the inferno of the war around them. This significantly influenced the reviewer's appraisal of *Stalingrad* as a 'realistic, unvarnished report', and she described the impact that it had on the German cinema-goers.

> The viewers leave the cinemas shaken. They all know it, and they will never forget it - Stalingrad.[19]

The reviewer for *Der Kurier* also commented upon this image of Soviet soldiers, observing that *Stalingrad* depicted 'an image of Russian soldiers which is completely different from the distorting representations shown in a Goebbels newsreel'.[20] Already the headline 'The heroic song of Stalingrad' in *Das Volk* was an early sign of a changing perception of the Soviet defenders of Stalingrad. The bravery and heroic resistance of both the inhabitants and the soldiers of Stalingrad that finally halted Germany's advance was instrumental in creating a new image of the Russians. After watching the film, there were no more discussions about the collapse of Germany. Soviet cinematographers had filmed their material in such a way that it looked as real as a documentary, and it made clear how physically and emotionally draining the fighting had been. It was revealed that the number of Germans taken as prisoners of war was 91,000.[21] Thus, the review contained an important item of information for its readers. Together with 'bravery', 'heroic' now represented not only the highest praise for the military prowess of the Soviet soldiers, but it was also an explanation for their victory (until the end of the war, both words had only ever been used to describe how Germans fought). Now, the dominant image was one of Russians as brave, helpful soldiers during fighting, and as normal men during the breaks in the fighting, men whose love of peace was represented by small, symbolic gestures.

Berlin's cultural commentators saw both documentaries as depictions of real warfare and, by and large, they perceived Russian men as active, fighting soldiers. The reviewers' images corresponded to the current feeling of the time: Soviet soldiers were not primarily glorified as heroes, but were, instead, (in accordance with traditional roles) more frequently seen as ordinary men who had had to fight to defend their homeland and to bring the war to an end.

Relatively few Soviet women were visible in either film. There were no representations of the Soviet women who had fought as soldiers in the Red Army. Apart from the scenes of life before the war and the trench-digging, *Stalingrad* generally depicted Soviet women in traditional roles, as suffering mothers and victims of war. This meant that the reviewers in Berlin equated the German (*Berlin*) and Soviet (*Stalingrad*) mothers and children, and were, in this way able to identify themselves with the civilians who had suffered during the war. This kind of identification was derived largely from the fact that Soviet documentaries showed suffering and devastation, whereas, in contrast, German propaganda films had shown victorious armies pressing forward.[22]

Historical Films: Heroes and Barbarians

As mentioned above, the Western image of Russian men frequently oscillated between the two poles of *heroes* and *barbarians;* heroes because the '*homo sovieticus*'[23] was seen as a heroic creator of a new society, but conversely, as barbarians, because the Russians had been frequently represented as such in the West ever since the 16th century. This reflects an image that was particularly associated with the figure of the Tsar Ivan the Terrible.[24] Given the 'barbarian' connotations of Ivan the Terrible—which stood in sharp contrast to the image of the radiant Soviet hero—it is particularly interesting to see how this figure was seen by the Berlin press, and how it was perceived in comparison with that of Peter I, or Peter the Great.

As David Gillespie has pointed out, the main task of Soviet historical films was to harness the perceived glories of the past in order to legitimize the present through the lives of great men. Both *Ivan the Terrible* and *Peter I* represented Russian rulers who had 'to be cruel to be kind' and who claimed, like Stalin, to embody the will and the spirit of the Russian nation.[25] By apparently accepting the official phraseology as dogma, Eisenstein knew how to infuse it with irony as he sought to show the tragedy of absolute power in *Ivan the Terrible*.[26]

Ivan the Terrible

The first part of *Ivan the Terrible* deals mainly with the following events from Ivan's life: his coronation as ruler and tsar of the Russian empire, his wedding to Anastasia, the conquest of the city of Kazan, Anastasia's death, and his flight to the town of Alexandrova Sloboda. It closes with the procession of citizens asking the tsar to return to Moscow. Eisenstein, commissioned by Stalin to make *Ivan the Terrible* in 1941, had originally envisaged a three-part film. The first two parts of the controversial film were filmed almost simultaneously. Part I was completed in 1945 and received the Stalin Prize that year, while Part II was suppressed in 1946, and only a fragment of Part III was made. Part I of *Ivan the Terrible* was shown in August 1945, the first dubbed Soviet film to be screened in Berlin. Eisenstein's expressive imagery, his fast editing, impressive close-ups and crowd-scenes were admired. However, the reviewers did not consider Ivan to be a barbarian, which, it has to be admitted, is a view that fits the plot of Part I. This reflected Stalin's intention of conveying an image of Ivan as a ruler who was bound to his people and who was forced to act cruelly against internal and external enemies. *Neue Zeit* went even as far as to propose substituting Ivan's epithet 'the Terrible' with 'friend of the people'.[27]

The reviewers acknowledged and enthusiastically praised the first part of *Ivan the Terrible* as Eisenstein's cinematic masterpiece, but they did not engage in any psychological interpretation. This meant that the female characters were hardly mentioned, despite the fact that the dualism of Ivan's wife, Anastasia (good mother), and his aunt and opponent, Efrosinia (bad mother), played a significant role in the plot of Part I. That Eisenstein's genius had created a double-edged, psychological masterpiece in the dangerous climate of the cult of Stalin[28] was something the reviewers could not, of course, mention due to censorship. Instead, they interpreted the historical figure of Ivan as a Russian leader-hero, one who had to assert himself in difficult circumstances. In conformity with the interpretation that was dominant in the Soviet Union, Ivan was, indeed, partially re-interpreted as a 'friend of the people'.

Peter I

Directed by Vladimir Petrov in 1937-38 and based upon Alexei Tolstoy's play of the same name, the first section of *Peter I* describes the developments during Peter's reign and his personal happiness with Catherine, a commoner. The second part of the film focuses on the boyars' conspiracy, which leads to the execution of Alexei, Peter's son. As David Gillespie points out, Peter is represented as a leader closely connected with the people, one who embodies the people's will and who sees himself as the protector of the Russian people to such a degree that he orders his own son's execution.[29] The film received the Stalin Prize in 1941.

Both parts of the film were shown in December 1946. As early as 1946, Berlin's *Telegraf* commented on the film in a slightly ironic tone, while the reviews of other Berlin newspapers kept a low profile. On this occasion, however, the *Telegraf* wrote, for instance, about the smoke of the gunpowder, which prevented the viewers from seeing a clear picture, and about the huge number of ragged or uniformed extras that were made to laugh ecstatically and explode with anger by the stage manager. The Russian acting tradition was usually praised, but here the depiction of *Peter I*, was ridiculed:

> The tendency is nonetheless clear: overcoming dearth and death to achieve victory and prosperity... And all thanks to the political thinking of a single person, one who looked neither right nor left, who was as reckless as he was sure of victory and who succeeded – according to history – in overcoming all obstacles.[30]

In the film, the baroque Peter is not only shown as a leader-hero, but also as a robust workingman. He laughs, drinks, brawls, saves lives, all of which is, however, due to his impetuosity, not cultured and is, for this reason, a little dangerous.

> Infinite vitality in a huge, bull-naked body, a childish giant with a bright and wide smile, a dangerous tamer who surpasses all restrictions set on him.[31]

Despite the much-praised first part of the film, the *Neue Zeit* also made some mild criticisms of the second part, which was dominated by large-scale events such as the Battle of Poltava. The newspaper criticized the misery of the serfs in Russia's mines and the fact that the Cossacks had only been sketchily treated. However, the *Neue Zeit* also gave much more attention to the conspiracy, which led to execution of Alexei, the son of Peter I.[32]

Peter, but also his confidant, the statesman General Menshikov, Catherine, who was later to become his wife and tsarina, the boyars and farmers' sons are all presented as vivid beings full of energy. In his review in *Der Tagesspiegel*, Friedrich Luft speaks of a 'pompous historical painting' that loves the 'plump, the sturdy' and in which 'the bluntly naked bodies of burly farmers' sons' are in action.[33] By way of contrast, Alfred Maderno of *Der Morgen* wrote about Russia as a new cultural force in the east, one, which had been actively formed by Peter, the populist aristocrat who thought and acted in a human way.[34] Maderno saw Peter I as a good tsar, a view which was shared by the *Neues Deutschland*, which characterized

Tsar Peter as a careful statesman, a friend and comrade of his subjects, as well as a clever politician. With regard to the acting, the film was described as having a compelling earthiness, and therefore being free of all heroic pathos. As a documentary based on strictly historical facts, it was claimed that *Peter I* could be viewed as one of the best historical films.[35] The film obtained gushing praise which certainly corresponded to the image conveyed by the Stalinist propaganda.

By contrast, *Der Kurier* describes the celluloid Russians as stupid, primitive barbarians in terms that could have come straight from Nazi propaganda. They are called a herd of dull, vegetating humans who are sometimes whipped into action, sometimes driven from their homes, howling and sniveling as they pointlessly run helter-skelter, to and fro; the camera had discovered huge numbers of craggy, animal-like faces along with masses of monks with wild heads of hair, who were good for nothing.[36] The second part of the film was seen as having a 'compressed form of nationalism' as its theme, which is why the film was stated to have lost the admiration of the German audience; one was meant to see the tsar's actions only as good and progressive, while the politics of the other European states, including the conspiracy of the tsarevich Alexei, were motivated only by vain despotism and the desire for power. *Der Kurier* continued by describing the violent battle scenes full of smoke and armies pressing ahead, sea battles with wild broadsides: in these, the victorious Russians displayed great valor, but their opponents were capable only of malicious deviousness.[37]

Reviewers in Berlin ascribed qualities such as 'energetic', 'active' and 'allied with the people' to the character of Peter, as well as 'unpredictable', 'lusty' and 'lively' – in other words, he was part leader-hero and part uncivilized barbarian. As for the figures from his on-screen Russian nation, some were brave patriots, but most nonetheless remained barbarians, albeit ones whose action could be anything from 'active' or 'uncivilized', to 'members of an uncouth mob'.

Peter I also conveyed a rather mixed image of Russian woman. However, only traditionally female characteristics caught the attention of the Berlin reviewers. While the boyars' wives in *Peter I* represent old Russia, the boyars' daughters represent the new Russia, in that they obey Peter's clothing reforms. The most impressive female character in this history film is Peter's future wife, Catherine. Just like a traditional mother, she cooks, cleans and rocks her child's cradle. But she also actively takes part in government affairs as a woman. This aspect, however, received little attention from reviewers, and instead, Catherine was described with synonyms which related to carefree sexuality and robustness: *Der Kurier*, for example, described her as a healthy girl from an ordinary background, who had belonged in succession to a soldier, Peter's confidant Menshikov, and finally to the tsar himself.[38] She is the only woman singled out by *Der Morgen,* but even then only on account of her cheerful nature amid all the men: with her healthy and unpretentious sense of humor, she dispels tension when things become too serious with a simple smile for the men or for the masses, before whom Catherine is the only woman to appear.[39]

Historical facts are, in part, ignored and historical figures transformed, or their Russian nationalist pathos is given special emphasis. Tsar Ivan was represented as a strict, rather than a cruel, ruler, despite historical evidence to the contrary, while the reviews of *Peter I* convey a much more mixed image. Of the women, only Catherine is mentioned; her sexual attractiveness seemed unusual because it did not correspond to the traditional gender roles in Germany, those of wife and mother.

Contemporary Films: Worker-heroes, Mothers and Comrades

In contrast to Nazi propaganda, which discredited all Russian women as 'comrades' who neglected their traditional duties as mothers, the USSR championed a new female role model, which was part of a new understanding of marriage and family. Women were no longer supposed to be economically dependent upon their men, and they were meant to dedicate themselves to the political and social re-organization of the Soviet Union via their own active participation. Maxim Gorky's novel *The Mother* came out in 1905 and was included in the repertory of most important Soviet literature in 1932, as an example of socialist realism. Its contents can be regarded as a typical example of a process of development by which the tolerant and suffering mother is transformed into an active comrade. In the mother's development, the process of maturing politically is represented as a path of suffering that also includes elements of Christian martyrdom.[40] This pattern was maintained in Vsevolod Pudovkin's silent movie *The Mother,* made in 1925 and based on Gorky's book; it was shown in Berlin in 1927. However, the new role of the Soviet woman implied combining motherhood and working, social awareness and political involvement, *i.e.,* being mother and comrade at the same time. This is an image that also featured in the two films discussed below.

Another particular feature of contemporary Soviet films was the representation of worker-heroes. The creation of this new type of hero played a major motivational role in Soviet iconography, namely, the spreading of heroism into all spheres of life. As a result, the whole of society turns into a battlefield where wars are fought and victories won.[41]

Circus

Since these worker-heroes appeared in all genres of contemporary Soviet films, it is not surprising that they were also present in musicals such as the film *Circus,* which was produced in 1936 and shown in Berlin cinemas in 1946. Here, it is the Soviet artist and main hero Ivan Martynov who manages to outdo the circus performance of a German-American, *i.e.,* capitalist, couple. While the German artist sends his American partner, Marion Dixon, to the moon (a trapeze high up in the circus tent's ceiling) from a cannon, the Soviet acrobat manages to do a double performance by sending himself and the American through the air in a stratospheric flight from an even bigger cannon. She once again lands on her trapeze-moon, while he flies in circles through the circus tent with his wings that he built himself. This not only symbolized the victory of the Soviet worker-hero over gravity, but also a kind of Soviet-American love, their common enthusiasm for new technology, the cult of aviation as well as the possible future conquest of space.

As Richard Taylor points out, part of the structure of *Circus* deals with the new Soviet Constitution of 1936, which served as a guarantee of greater rights for minorities in Stalin's earthly paradise. According to Taylor, the entire rhetoric of the film has to be seen within the context of speeches in praise of the cult of Stalin, which was at its peak at the time.[42] For German viewers, however, this was not as important as the humane ideal of all people being equal, upon which the film is based and which belonged to the program of re-education to counteract German notions of national superiority. Instead, the Berlin papers, such as the *Deutsche Volkszeitung,* emphasized concepts of racial equality as the Soviet ideal.[43] *Das Volk* reminded its readers of the appalling phrases from Nazi terminology, such as racial shame and racial inferiority, and claimed that these terms were alien in the Soviet Union.[44] In *Circus,* the view of the Soviet Union as a society without race-based differences was clearly more important to reviewers than analyzing and evaluating Martynov, the shining example of the diligent Russian worker-hero.

The American Marion assumes the role of the working mother, and she does not seem to have any problems reconciling her motherhood with her work as a circus performer because a dark-skinned nanny looks after her dark-skinned child. In this respect, she is, in fact, a modern woman and mother. The problem of her illegitimate child's dark skin, however, is expounded when her jealous German impresario, Franz von Kneischitz, tries to use it to blackmail her. Clearly, he is destined to fail because there was not supposed to be any racial segregation in the Soviet Union. Without further complications, the American woman, Marion, changes into a

Soviet one, Masha, *i.e.*, a *mother* and a *comrade*. Later, she performs with her beloved Soviet artist in an even more successful show, stays in the Soviet Union with her child and, at the end, marches together with her Ivan among the big cheering crowds of the May Day parade to the sounds of Isaak Dunayevsky's *Song of the Motherland*, which itself refers to the mother understood as the archetype of the home country.[45]

The workingwoman portrayed by Marion, equal in both the professional and the social sphere, was not emphasized in the reviews in Berlin newspapers. Nor was the transformation of an American into a Soviet citizen with equal rights. Instead, the entertainment value of the film was ascribed to the fact that the Soviet director Aleksandrov had worked in America and thus had introduced American influences into the imagery of the film and the technology used to make it.[46] Marion corresponds to the image of a modern, working woman and mother. Through her love for a Soviet worker-hero, the American working mother turns into a Soviet comrade who is professionally and socio-politically active like him. Their love and their work together lead to the fact that, at the end of the film, she corresponds to the ideal image of a modern Soviet woman that is a working mother *and* comrade.

The Rich Bride

For John Haynes, the film *The Rich Bride* is the origin of the '*kolkhoz* musical'.[47] These were also films that glorified the Soviet work ethic and focused on the working hero as the new Soviet man or woman in collective farms. In *The Rich Bride*, made by director Ivan Pyryev in 1937, the protagonists on the collective farm are the young Ukrainian countrywoman Marina and the young tractor driver Pavlo. Both are exemplary workers. They are in love, but the jealous (petty bourgeois) bookkeeper Alexei alters their results to interfere with their love. Each believes their beloved has to be equally hard working and ambitious, so a conflict arises as neither allegedly manages to fulfill their work quota. Only after both have fulfilled their aim and the cheating accountant has been exposed can the couple get married.

The Rich Bride was shown in Berlin cinemas in 1946. It received mixed reviews. The reviewers expressed their belief that the film lacked conflict by saying the plot was, in itself, simple.[48] They praised the beautiful Ukrainian landscape, the people, their work ethic and so forth, and they included carefully formulated comments about the broad, indeed, for German audiences too broad, humor.[49] Along with their folkloric, exotic view of the Soviet Union, for example, that of the Ukrainian landscape, the talented actors, the music, *etc.*, the reviewers emphasized Soviet values as socio-political differences to post-war Germany. However, *Das Volk* praised the film as an outstanding collective achievement, which was largely due to the perfect co-ordination of direction, camerawork, acting and music. All of this was held to have resulted in a musical comedy in which the 'splendid humor of Russian humanity' could unfold.[50] Very little mention was made of the characters, however. They were described as healthy, jolly young people with tanned faces, who needed no make-up. Naturalness was used as exemplifying simple, normal people. Der *Tagesspiegel*, in contrast, was less interested in Soviet exoticism, and instead commented on the plot with some irony:

> Marina is the capable field worker on a Ukrainian collective farm, Pavlo the busy tractor driver. There would be nothing in the way of their union were it not for the jealous bookkeeper. He does a terrible thing: on the big board mounted at the side of the road in the village, the board which announces everyone's productivity week by week, he tampers with the high results of Marina's enthusiastic work. And his grudge against Pavlo leads him to create a misleading report about him, too. Now, the two lovers both think that their beloved is not committing themselves 100% to their work. And there can, of course, be no mention of attraction under such circumstances. Until the profiteer is caught red- (or green-) handed at work on his typewriter and the exemplary performance of the two innocent people is recalculated and re-acknowledged.[51]

This review is remarkable for a number of reasons. First, there is the undisguised amusement of a German critic writing in an American-licensed newspaper about the apparent conflicts of life on a collective farm as depicted in a Soviet film. Secondly, the review probably corresponded to the view of many German viewers who found worker-heroes depicted in such a manner only of minor interest. Thirdly, these viewers did not want to, or could not, recognize that, despite the low degree of conflict in the plot, a new type of hero made its appearance in this kind of Soviet film: the ultimate worker, the Stakhanovite whose heroism did not consist of feats of military prowess, but, instead, consisted of their work-related performance for the community. In this view, Russians work hard, but also love to drink vodka, sing beautiful sentimental songs and dance. The behavior of the political and military leader-heroes matches these characteristics. The new Soviet human-being had primarily been conveyed through the optimistic Soviet films of the 1930s: the positive working hero is happy when he can work for, and in, the collective, dance the most passionate dances, sing the most emotional songs and invent the most impressive machines. He is exemplary, courageous and selfless.

The Rich Bride is not a film about women mastering new technology, but about their work ethic in a competitive situation. Marina is not a tractor driver, but a field worker, and wears - like all other rural women - traditional Ukrainian dress. The cheerful women are faster at binding the sheaves than the cheerful tractor driver is at mowing. Whoever works fast and efficiently serves both the people and society by supplying food, and can also earn well. Everybody can do something at his or her own place for the country's welfare. Wealth no longer has to be inherited or obtained through a dowry. The new Soviet woman is rich because she can earn well through her own work.

The *Neue Zeit,* in particular, emphasized the competitiveness represented by harvesting on the collective farm, as well as the realization that the term 'riches' was obviously associated with different things in Germany and in the Soviet Union: the paper saw riches in Germany as meaning material prosperity, while, in the Soviet Union, it was the capacity to receive an impressive wage along with respect and recognition by dint of one's own work in the community.[52]

Marina – together with all the other women shown in this film – corresponds to the prototype of a hard working, but cheerful comrade as envisaged by Stakhanovism. They work, are socially and politically active, and are emancipated. Their plump forewoman corresponds to the image of both a mother and comrade, because, on the one hand, she encourages her women to compete, and, on the other, she assumes the role of the affectionate, but strict, mother who also cares about the personal fate of her women (real children do not really appear in this film).

In the contemporary films presented here, the young, hard-working peasant woman on the collective farm, Marina, corresponds to the ideal of a young cheerful comrade. She earns her money with her own hands and is an active participant in the harvesting competition, while her superior, the forewoman, symbolizes the new image of the Soviet woman as mother and comrade embodied in one. Similarly, the forewoman combines her duty as expected by society with a (surrogate) mother role in her work brigade.

In early Soviet films, women were not portrayed as sexual objects but as emancipated active women, who are financially independent, but bear a double burden: work and home.[53] In both the films described here, the combination of work and children is not a problem for a Soviet woman. Instead, her personal and political confidence and her pleasure in her work are emphasized. This woman apparently masters her new double role as comrade and mother without any problems. The image of the radical comrade put forward by both the Bolshevik feminist Alexandra Kollontai (in a positive way) and in Nazi propaganda (in a disapproving way) was not the image of the woman conveyed by the Soviet films and observed by the reviewers in post-war Berlin. Instead, the images of the caring mother and the working comrade were combined.

Conclusion

The images of Russian men and women as conveyed in the Soviet films that were selected to be shown in Berlin at the end of the Second World War emphasized particular characteristics and virtues. Nevertheless, the German reviewers of these films perceived and replicated amazingly different images of Russian men and women. The German reviews of the Soviet documentaries *Berlin* and *Stalingrad* perceived Soviet soldiers above all as ordinary men. In turn, in Soviet historical films, Russian tsars act as ruler-heroes and warrior-heroes. The reviews of *Ivan the Terrible (Part I)* and *Peter I* in the newspapers of Berlin even reversed the traditional images of Ivan and Peter in Western Europe. Regardless of his epithet 'the Terrible', Ivan was perceived as a strict, but just, ruler, bound to his people – just like Stalin. In contrast, Peter was celebrated as a ruler-hero, but was simultaneously seen as an unpredictable barbarian. The Berlin reviews of *Peter I* oscillated between the perception of the Russian people as depicted on the screen either as earthy peasants or as ignorant barbarians. Consequently, the Berlin reviews discussed here conveyed a rather mixed image of Russians: in historical films, as heroes and barbarians; in documentaries, as ordinary men and only partially as heroes. In contrast, the contemporary Soviet films portrayed Russians as cheerful, uncomplicated, good-natured, hard working and undemanding people.

These films and the corresponding reviews tried to convey a new image of the Russians. This was an attempt to substitute the old negative image of the Russian barbarian, spread by Nazi propaganda, with a new positive image of the Soviet hero. In this way, the former Nazi image of the Russian barbarian was not only to be changed into a Soviet-friendly image of heroes from different walks of life, but also augmented by the new type of worker-hero. Though the working hero remained a role model in the socialist realism of the GDR, the creation of a new image of Russians succeeded only in part. The Soviet films that were shown in 1945-46 had been made in the Soviet Union for propaganda purposes in order to enhance patriotism. This, however, often did not go down well with the Berlin audience. Incidentally, the comparatively uncritical reviews of Soviet films also led to the fact that those who later became citizens of the GDR commented sarcastically on the complexities of their daily lives by saying 'you won't find that in a Russian film'. Soviet films clearly did not always achieve the desired effect with regard to the image of Russian men. But can the same be said of the image of Russian women?

While there were hardly any women in the documentary *Berlin*, some were shown in *Stalingrad* as active participants in defense preparations and as mothers who sought to find refuge from the fighting. The Berlin newspapers reviewed the latter film sympathetically. In history films, women featured mainly as mothers, but they were scarcely noticed by the German reviewers. In contrast to this, Soviet films were set in the contemporary world and the corresponding reviews frequently portrayed women as comrades *and* mothers. The Berlin newspapers perceived them as lovable, active, hard working and cheerful: in short, as modern superwomen. After the war, the term 'female comrade' was to be relieved of its negative connotations which resulted from Nazi propaganda. To do this, the image of the workingwomen was combined with the traditional image of the caring mother. This combination of the caring mother and independent comrade continued to exist later on in the GDR, and it influenced the perception of many women living in East Germany. They started to be economically, socially and politically active without giving up their families and children. This suggests that the propagation of a new image of the (Russian) woman was more effective than the propagation of a new image of the Russian men.

Part IV

Sovietized Rituals

7

Continuity and Innovation: Itineraries of the May Day Ritual in Czechoslovakia

Roman Krakovsky

In the Soviet Union from 1917 onwards, mass demonstration became central features of political life. What had initially been developed as displays of working class unity and solidarity came, in time, to be highly orchestrated events whose main function was to demonstrate popular support for the regime. In the absence of meaningful elections, these mass displays functioned as a kind of popular plebiscite, which claimed to demonstrate popular consent and support for the ruling party and its leaders. To this end, great efforts were expended on organizing these events, and in reconfiguring the urban architecture to accommodate these mass displays. The ability of the regime and its agents to produce large turnouts for such events became a test of their ability to mobilize the masses.[1] Here, we examine the way in which the Czechoslovak Communist Party used the May Day celebrations for such ends from 1948 until 1989, through the study of the routes of the parades. This provides an illustration of the extent to which the Czechoslovak Communist Party employed the same devices as were developed in the USSR, and how far the May Day celebrations were sovietized. What emerges from this study are the significant changes in the routing of the May Day parades, which reflected domestic political exigencies, and demonstrated how the model which was partly taken from the Soviet Union had to be molded to meet local needs.

When the Czechoslovak Communist Party came to power in February 1948, May Day gradually became one of three major holidays in the socialist calendar. This was codified by law in 1951.[2] These dates signaled the three 'holy traditions' of the regime that had evolved in the USSR, and were gradually exported to Central and Eastern Europe after 1945.[3] These embodied the revolutionary tradition, the tradition of the building of socialism and the patriotic tradition. They were celebrated every year on the three most important dates of the socialist calendar: the anniversary of the October Revolution, May Day and the Day of Liberation. On these occasions, three emblematic heroes were celebrated: the revolutionary, the Stakhanovite and the soldier-liberator. By sharing their personal experience with the audience, or simply by their presence at the rituals, these heroes restored the legendary past and constituted an important part of the regime's strategy to strengthen its claim to legitimacy amongst the populace.

Before 1945, May Day was a traditional political holiday that was commemorated by communists, social democrats and even the Nazi Party. The communist regime intended to turn this day into a national holiday: 'Labor Day'. At the same time, May Day was supposed to represent the present, an idealized socialist future, and the regime's fundamental values. In order to achieve this objective, the organizers redesigned the structure and the itinerary of the parades. Here, we concentrate on the routes of the May Day parade, and explore the relationship between the traditional and the new, Soviet-type celebrations.[4] We will consider the routes in three cities: Prague (capital of the country), Bratislava (capital of Slovakia) and Žilina (regional capital). This will allow us to follow the evolution on a national, republican and regional level, and to come to conclusions regarding the whole country. However, in order to maintain clarity, much of the analysis will focus on Prague.

The Czechoslovak Communist Party's freedom to manage urban space was constrained by the dictates of Soviet policy as regards Stalinization and de-Stalinization. Following the decisions of the Twenty-second Congress of the Soviet Communist Party to institute a further phase of de-Stalinization, including the removal of the dictator's body from the mausoleum, the countries of the Eastern bloc were required to followed suit. The Central Committee of the Czechoslovak Communist Party decided on 15 November 1961 to remove the name of Stalin from certain streets and squares. The giant statue of Stalin erected in Prague on the Letná overlooking the Vltava in 1955 was demolished in 1962.[5]

The Invention of New Routes in the 1950s

In all three cities, the traditional routes of the May Day parade were modified between 1948 and 1955. Paradoxically, the new routes that were chosen were not related to locations which had connections to the labor movement. The organizers did not try to return to the earliest traditions of the May Day celebrations of the late nineteenth century, when the participants gathered outside the cities, in industrial estates or in the countryside, because demonstrations were forbidden. Nor did they seek to resurrect inter-war traditions. In Prague, during the inter-war period, the Communist Party held May Day demonstrations on Republic Square (*Náměstí Republiky*), whereas the social democrats celebrated on Gunner's Island (*Střelecký ostrov*). In 1948, the new communist regime ignored the historical precedents and chose Wenceslas Square (*Václavské náměstí*) as the principle venue for its parades.

The same development can be observed in Bratislava. One part of the traditional route was abandoned. From 1948 until the mid-1970s, the May Day parade was held on Stalin Square, which, in 1961, was renamed the Square of the Slovak National Uprising, where the stage for the dignitaries was set up. The parade followed the traditional route of labor demonstrations. It started at Gottwald Square – sometimes, if the size of the parade required, it started from a different place – and led towards Stalin Square. Nevertheless, the old town centre with Fish Square (*Rybné námestie*), which had been the traditional destination during the inter-war period, was abandoned. In Žilina, in 1955, the parade proceeded from Gottwald Square towards Stalin Square (renamed Lenin Square in 1961) where the stage for the officials and guests was set up.

To sum up, in Prague, the Communist Party completely abandoned the traditional route of labor demonstrations that had been followed during the inter-war period. In Bratislava and Žilina, only one section of the traditional route was maintained. What was the explanation for this new strategy? The reasons for abandoning the traditional May Day routes were both of a symbolic and practical nature.

After coming to power, the aim of the communist leadership was to replace the 28th of October, the anniversary of the creation of Czechoslovakia and a national holiday, with May Day. The idea was to add a national meaning to the traditional political meeting, by linking the date to the history of the whole community. Thus, it reflected the transformation of the Communist Party into the permanent party of government, and its attempt to appropriate the most fundamental symbols of national identity. The re-configuration of space and the investing of certain urban sites with symbolic meaning played an important part in this strategy, which was reflected in the decisions to place the parade in locations with strong national or local connotations.

However, in order to achieve this, the organizers of the May Day parade did not exorcise all reminders of the past. In all three cities, the parades never crossed into historically 'virgin space'. Furthermore, the routes did not pass by places that were linked to the origins of the working-class movement.

In Prague, Wenceslas Square is associated with significant events in the nation's history. At one end of the square, the National Museum, built by Josef Schulz in 1885-1890 (modeled on the museum of Vienna and the Louvre), contains a Pantheon with statues of prominent figures in Czech history. In 1912-1913, an equestrian statue of Saint Wenceslas, the patron saint of the nation, was erected in front of the building on the initiative of Czech nationalists. The figures of Saint Procope, Saint Adalbert, Saint Ludmila and Saint Agnes emphasize the national symbolism of the place. Whenever an important event in the history of the nation occurred – elections, the death of a statesman, declarations of war or beginnings of occupation – the people gathered at the square. Political parties, including the communists, held important meetings there. For these reasons, Wenceslas Square had always been an ideal location for national festivals.

Similarly, the parades in Žilina and in Bratislava passed by places that were associated more with local history than with the history of the labor movement. The aim was to attract more participants. By relying on such places, the organizers attempted to gather large sections of the population at local '*lieux de mémoire*' (places of memory) which were unconnected with the history of the labor movement.

The changing of the routes in the first half of the 1950s can also be explained by reasons relating to urban-planning and the choreographing of these mass parades in order to achieve the maximum impact. The layout of squares was exploited in order to maximize the effects of the new festival. The organizers favored closed spaces and tended to draw the attention of the population to the spot where the principal event of the festivities would occur. This had the effect of providing a focal point for the parade, which marked the climax of the event, where the party dignitaries were assembled on a podium to view the passing crowds. This had the result of producing a concentrated dramatic, acoustic and visual effect. The selection of the location as well as its arrangement favored the viewers on the official stand. However, the spectacle could also be observed by ordinary spectators from the pavement.

In Žilina, the most impressive view was from the official stage that was erected at the citadel, on a slight slope overlooking the parade. From there, the viewer could see the whole crowd and enjoy a complete view of the parade. In 1956, the May Day Committee noted:

> From the official stage, the viewer has a beautiful view of the Street of the Slovak National Uprising and the parade advancing towards him, with four lines of flags and streamers floating in the wind.

No gaps in the procession were visible and its 'continuous character can only be praised'.[6] The May Day Committee recommended retaining this route in the future and using the Street of the Slovak National Uprising for the deployment of the parade instead of for the gathering of participants.[7]

In Prague, Wenceslas Square slopes slightly. It descends from the National Museum towards the place called Můstek, on the opposite side of the square. From Můstek, the whole square is visible and the slope enables the parade to be viewed in its entirety. It appears almost natural that the stage at the May Day celebrations was set up at this place, opposite the National Museum. The intention of the organizers – that the parade could be read as an open book – was manifest in this arrangement. The stage, erected at Můstek, also stressed the opposition between the old élites, immortalized in the Pantheon of the National Museum, and the new élite, who stood on the May Day stand, a kind of contemporary Pantheon.

In Bratislava, Fish Square was considered unsuitable to accommodate the large crowd that was envisaged for the May Day celebrations. The streets leading to the square are irregular and narrow, and thus prevented the parade from spreading out. Moreover, the trees which lined the square reduced the visual impact of the spectacle. Historical continuity was sacrificed in the interest of the new objectives of the day – convenience and visibility.

In the same way, in Žilina, the old route did not permit a fluid and comprehensible procession. Gottwald Square was too small to accommodate the crowd. In 1955, the May Day Committee discussed the problem and decided on a new route. Two projects were considered at the time. One proposed the setting up of the official stand in front of the cinema, the *Dawn* (*Úsvit*). The parade would depart from Gottwald Square and follow the *Veľká Okružná* Boulevard, which was wide, but surrounded the entire town center. The other proposal suggested directing the procession from Gottwald Square towards the railway station, turning off along the Street of the Slovak National Uprising and leading the procession to Lenin Square, beneath the citadel. From there, the crowd would go up towards the historic Dukla Square where it would disperse. The second proposal was eventually adopted. The circumstances were in favor of this. Lenin Square, extending under the citadel, was an ideal place to set up the platform. Since it was spacious enough, it could easily accommodate both the participants and the spectators. The Street of the Slovak National Uprising, which was long and straight, and led to Lenin Square, enabled the procession to spread out before arriving at the official stage. After passing the stand, the crowd could settle on the steps of the citadel and observe the parade from there. In 1956, the official stage was moved permanently from Gottwald Square to Lenin Square.[8]

The Necessary Adaptations

Since the May Day parade made its way through a space charged with historical symbols, it was necessary to change the holiday in order to establish its own space marking. A judicious use of space contributed to a great extent to the smooth organization of the celebration. The preliminary work made it possible to avoid conflicts and mishaps. In order to appropriate historic space, the organizers carried out some complex modifications to the architectural space.

The first concern was to remove all obstacles on the route, which could block the advance. The movement was to be continuous, fluid and without any interruptions. Since the parade was meant to re-enact an idealistic representation of society, the movement of the crowd was not to be hindered by obstacles. On a normal day, 'the workers must step over the crevices of old human mistakes, the gutters of bureaucracy, the stones of dishonesty'. But on May Day, the road must be perfect. The marching people were not to be disturbed by any defects: they were to walk 'on a perfect pavement and a shining route, passing through broad avenues and spacious squares'. On this route, cleansed of all imperfection, 'the future is certain'.[9] In the 1950s and the 1960s, Wenceslas Square was gradually restructured in order to facilitate the movement of the procession: the flowers and the barriers in the middle of the square were removed. These objects and even olfactory defects that could disturb the festivities were removed. The public toilets were closed with the approach of May Day. If buildings were being repaired at the time, the scaffolding was taken down before the festivity and was re-erected the following day.[10] The removal of obstacles prevented delays in the program and precluded any misinterpretation: a gap in the parade could be perceived by the spectators as a subversive act or as an indicator of a lack of popular support. In cases of malfunctioning, the censors intervened and official photos were modified to create the right impression.[11] In order to control the route of the crowd, the members of the Popular Militia (*Lidové milice*)—the paramilitary force of the Communist Party—spread out across the square before the participants arrived and—with their bodies—marked out the lanes along which the participants would advance. In the same way, the Militia created a barrier in front of the gallery in order to protect the officials from the participants and to direct the crowd towards the exits.

Without characterizing the communist regime as a 'political religion', the distinction between the 'sacred' sites, whose function was exclusively ritual, and 'sacralized' sites, which only had a temporary ritual quality, can still be applied to the analysis of the routes.[12] Wenceslas Square was not a site devoted exclusively to the May Day ritual. Other 'sacred' sites of the regime fulfilled their ritual function permanently in an exclusive way (military cemeteries of the Second World War, memorials, the cities of Lidice and Ležáky destroyed by the Nazis). Wenceslas Square, on the other hand, acquired this function only for a specific time period. In order to sacralize the square, it was decorated with strong symbolic markers for longer periods.

With the help of such space marking, the organizers sought to evoke emotional responses and to transmit a political message. Attention was focused on the aspects that emphasized verticality. The streets all along the route were covered with Czechoslovak and Soviet flags, banners and streamers. These emblems forced the spectator to look to the sky and created a dynamic and merry environment. The decorations, which were fixed to the ground, interacted with a multiplicity of flags, streamers, banners and organization logos flying over the parade.[13] Some emblems delivered a much more formal message. The portraits of statesmen as well as leaders of the party and Central Committee members decorated the buildings along the route and transformed them into a spontaneous gallery which gave the impression that the statesmen were observing the crowd. The front of the National Museum was a place of honor: until the middle of the 1950s, it was reserved for monumental portraits of Gottwald and Stalin.[14] After the denunciation of the 'cult of the personality' in 1956, the portraits were replaced by the May Day motto that was chosen each year by the organizers, and was more neutral and impersonal. Some of these mottos became emblematic, like 'Proletarians of the world, unite!' or 'With the Soviet Union for eternity'.

As the crowd approached the lower part of the square and the official stage, space marking gradually became more emphatic. From the crossroad of Vodičkova and Jindřišská streets, the frequency of the emblems intensified. The portraits and the flags covering the urban backdrop became denser. Certain buildings were entirely covered with streamers or paintings representing the central ideas of May Day: peace, the Five-Year Plan, international solidarity.[15] The decoration of the buildings of this part of the square was given special attention. The organizers sent special orders to the owners of these buildings.[16] Decoration was to be—at least roughly—connected to the activities of the organizations located there. In 1956, the House of the Hungarian book (*Dům maďarské knihy*, N° 772) was decorated with the streamer: 'Fraternal greeting to all the nations fighting for the consolidation of peace, democracy and socialism!' The headquarters of the Czechoslovakian Youth Union (ČSM, N° 785) carried the banner 'Long live our youth and its avant-garde – the Czechoslovak Youth Union'. The Tatran Hotel (N° 782), where Western guests stayed during the festivities, was decorated with the banner, 'We greet the members of the socialist parties of the capitalist countries'. The increase of attention meant that the parade entered the center of sacralized space, the symbolic center of power. A special authorization was required to gain access to this area. From the Vodičkova—Jindřišská crossroad until Můstek, small galleries bordered the square on both sides. Access was reserved for official guests, the best workers, who had been granted awards by the government the day before May Day, the media and the representatives of political parties and other public organizations. The symbolic forms led the crowd to the very center of the festivities, towards the official stand.

The Change of the Routes in the 1970s

In the 1970s, the procession routes were again changed, reflecting a changing use of urban space that also corresponded to a deeper change in relations between the regime and society. The goal of the regime since 1948 had been to replace the traditional national holiday of 28 October with the celebration of May Day. This 'instrumentation' also occurred through the recovery of national '*lieux de mémoire*', such as Wenceslas Square in Prague, or Stalin Square in Bratislava and Žilina. The 1970s, therefore, marked a rupture in the continuity of the official tradition.

Such a rupture was dictated by the need to deal with the critical attitude of the population towards the regime of normalization that was gradually installed in Czechoslovakia after August 1968. The regime was conscious of its unpopularity and tried to avoid any events that could potentially turn into a manifestation of opposition. In 1969, the celebration of May Day was cancelled in Prague because of the fear that it could get out of control. The holiday was re-instated in 1970, and was also strengthened by two anniversaries in the same year: the 100th anniversary of the birth of Lenin (22nd of April) and the 25th anniversary of the Liberation (9th of May). However, protests against the regime of normalization continued, and included the defacing of the decorations on the streets and on buildings. In spite of their efforts, the authorities were not able to ensure total control over the centre of Prague. From 1974, the procession was moved outside the city centre, to the Letná esplanade. This choice corresponded to the new political situation which the regime had to face.

The Letná esplanade, which could host large gatherings, was, in the inter-war period, the site of the Sokol mass sporting events (*sokolské slety*).[17] The communist regime developed this empty and flat space so that it would accommodate large military parades, notably that of the anniversary of the October Revolution, on 7 November. With the erection of a large platform and the construction of access roads and exits it gained a permanent structure. The esplanade became a 'sacred' space and was no longer 'sacralized'. But the esplanade's southern end remained haunted by the remains of the gigantic statue of Stalin that had been destroyed in 1962.

The Letná esplanade seemed to respect the primary concern of the organizers of the demonstrations of the 1970s: to control space. Here, the structure of space prevented the crowd from getting out of control. Access to the area was provided by broad avenues which the police could control without difficulties. The space in front of the platform was flat and empty.

The transferral of the Prague procession to Letná could be explained mainly by the dictates of crowd policing. In the middle of the 1970s, the routes of the May Day procession were radically modified. A similar tendency took place in all the cities under discussion here and can also be observed in other countries of the Eastern bloc.[18]

The procession in Bratislava was moved from the city center to the periphery. From 1975 onwards, it was held on Malinovski Street and after 1979 on Vajnorská Street, which was the principal axis of the new residential district *New City* (*Nové mesto*), built in the 1950s and 1960s. Whilst some authors explained this change as a move to free up the town center, which was completely paralyzed by traffic on May Day,[19] the change also underlined a new relationship between the regime and its history, as well as a search for legitimacy by establishing new references.

The example of the Žilina procession also supports this hypothesis. The processions in Žilina were also transferred from the old town center in the mid-1970s.[20] The official stand was moved to the new Lenin Square, which was the *chef-d'oeuvre* of socialist town planning in the 1950s and 1960s, and became the center of the new residential district of *Hliny*. The square was located at the end of the Street of the Defenders of Peace, a broad commercial avenue, which became the local symbol of the new socialist consumer society which began to emerge in the 1960s. The Street of the Defenders of Peace enlarged the old town center and the inhabitants of Žilina integrated this space into their Sunday walk, thereby creating a 'course' *(korzo)* which started in Gagarin Street in Hliny, crossed Dukla Square and ended on the Street of the Slovak National Uprising. Lenin Square, with a statue of the Soviet revolutionary, became the new town centre and affirmed its aspiration as a place of modernity and new leisure activities. The largest and most modern hotel in the city (*Slovakia*) and the House of the Trade Unions *(Dom odborov)* including a theatre, a cinema and the most important stage for shows in the city, were all located on the square. Nearby, there was a large building site where the future headquarters of the Communist Party was completed in the mid-1980s. The socialist ritual of May Day took place at this new space, which was truly virgin, and where no compromise with history was necessary.

The change of the routes of the demonstrations in the mid-1970s had several explanations. Firstly, the regime of normalization was searching for a new identity. The Prague Spring of 1968 had demonstrated the dangers of 'national Communism'. By creating a socialist identity based on pre-1948 national traditions, the regime had become exposed to the danger of creating socialism in one country, which the representatives of normalization considered to be revisionist. Pre-war national history, even if it was re-interpreted, was generally considered dangerous, and the regime sought to focus on its own past, the history of the labor movement, the Communist Party and the construction of socialism. Henceforth, the regime would use such references to reinforce its identity, which would then be propagated amongst the population.

In March 1973, for the 25th anniversary of February 1948, a major conference in Prague considered the monuments of the Communist Party and the labor movement in the capital.[21] For the first time in the history of the regime, historians and art specialists focused on monuments dedicated to the history of the labor movement. However, in the majority of cases, this came too late: most of the workers' inheritance had been dismantled by the regime itself. Several speakers criticized the regime's indifference to its own history and its long-term neglect of its own monuments. Marie Benešová declared that the '*lieux de mémoire*' of the labor movement had been neglected and treated as though they 'are not of any historical and artistic relevance' and that there were few opportunities to stimulate the interest of young people in this subject. She evoked the examples of the dilapidated worker's districts of the capital, such as Žižkov, Vysočany, Libeň or Smíchov. Other speakers underlined the difficulty of organizing celebrations next to monuments that had been erected to commemorate events which took place clandestinely and left no noticeable trace. Such were the meetings of communist militants that were held in inns and cellars, or the great strikes in the industrial zones in the 1930s. Two architects, Jaroslav Heyduk and František Peťas, noted that, due to the indifference of the regime, many of these monuments had simply disappeared during the years of the building of socialism, to make way for motorways or new residential districts.

Others were transformed into warehouses or general-purpose buildings, thus fundamentally changing the appearance of the monument.[22] A few years later, in 1976, the *Rules for the future development of heritage protection* denoted the priorities for the conservation and erection of monuments in Slovakia in the following order: 1. Monuments of the Labor movement and the Communist Party; 2. Monuments connected with the Slovak National Uprising; 3. Monuments connected with the Second World War and the liberation of Czechoslovakia by the Soviet army; 4. The period of the building of socialism; 5. The History of Slovakia.[23]

The regime's attempt to strengthen its claim to legitimacy was facilitated by the generation change that happened in the first half of the 1970s. The younger generation entering professional life after 1968 was born at the time of the people's democracy and grew up with the new socialist reference points. The ambition to create new references was thus easier to achieve.

The transfer of the Prague demonstrations to Letná, in 1974, imposed and confirmed a new relationship between the organizers and the participants of the event. The rectangular and flat space that was chosen for the procession imposed a circumscribed character, almost a military one, on the event. The delegations representing the various districts of Prague, came together on the plateau, and stood in blocks each aligned behind one another. At the beginning of the procession, the group furthest away from the platform advanced, turned right and passed in front of the stage, greeting the officials to the sound of music. After passing the stage, the group turned to the right, and returned to its starting point. When the parade finished, all the districts were in exactly the same position as at the beginning of the demonstration.[24] The organizers expected the same number of participants (180,000 people) every year and the authorities 'ensured' that the requirements were fulfilled. This was not a mere detail. The perimeter of the place was not extendable. With the exception of those on the official stage, there were no spectators at Letná and the individual who might have liked to join the procession, could not. The procession lost its capacity 'to recruit' new participants and thereby its ability to create surprise. Those who were there had to be there. Thus, participation in the national demonstrations did not vary much in the 1970-1980s. It remained generally around 190,000 people, and a 'better year' was noted. In 1983, the organizers were pleased with the participation of 280,000 people, 'one of the largest successes during the last few years'.[25] However, this figure was far below the numbers recorded in the 1950s and 1960s, when around 400,000 people participated.

However, the selection of new routes failed to recreate social cohesion between the party-state and the population. In its circumscribed form, the parade became 'de-personalized' and exclusively political, and appeared as though it was intended primarily for the official élites. A change of vocabulary confirmed this evolution. From the end of the 1970s, the National Front abandoned the emotionally charged term 'celebration' (*oslava*), and started using the term 'manifestation' (*manifestace*), instead. The event was gradually drained of any emotional content, and was replaced by a sense of boredom.

The Bratislava manifestations returned to the Square of the Slovak National Uprising (the pre-war Stalin Square) in 1985, and the manifestations in Prague returned to Wenceslas Square in 1988. Nevertheless, such a 'return to the tradition' of May Day as it had been constituted in the 1950s and the 1960s should not be considered as a self-criticism of the regime. Instead, it was the last attempt to save the ritual, which had been gradually abandoned by those for whom it had been created.

The study of the routes of the demonstrations elucidates the continuous evolution of the ritual. During the communist regime's almost 40 years of existence in Czechoslovakia, the routes of the May Day processions were radically modified twice; first, between 1948 and 1955, during the foundation period of the people's democracy, and for the second time in the mid-1970s. In the 1950s, continuity with pre-1948 workers' traditions was abandoned in the interest of convenience and visibility, and in accordance with the new objective of the processions: the mobilization of the population. Through the procession route, the festival adapted the history of the community, since it gathered the participants around historical references, either national (Wenceslas Square and the National Museum in Prague) or local (Stalin Square in Žilina and Bratislava). This strategy discarded the original political memory of the holiday.

The political mobilizing effect of the procession was achieved through on-site installations of varying complexity. The intensity accentuated as the demonstrators approached the stage, the symbolic centre of the political ritual. The initial aim of these installations was to trigger emotional response by accentuating verticality (flags, posters, decoration of the buildings), and to transmit a closely supervised political message (especially with the help of portraits and streamers).

The 1970s represented both a rupture and a new impulse. In search of a new identity, the regime tried to re-invent the traditions of May Day, by establishing symbolic spaces for the new socialist society. The re-organization of the routes in the 1970s was justified partly by security reasons (in particular in Prague), but it also aimed to attach the participants to the regime, by making use of the urban zones that were built in the 1950-1960s, during the period of the building of socialism. By celebrating the successes of socialism on May Day, the Communist Party sought to widen its appeal, and to re-assert its claim as the legitimate authority, which had been weakened by the intervention of the armies of the Warsaw Pact in 1968. The partial failure of this attempt led the organizers of the ritual to return in the middle of the 1980's, to the tradition of May Day as it had been codified in the 1950s and the 1960s.

8

Spatial Aspects of the Communist Leader Cult: The Case of Mátyás Rákosi in Hungary

Balázs Apor

The construction of communism had an undeniably spatial aspect in the Soviet bloc after the Second World War.[1] The process of building up a whole new world became a largely spatial project that involved the reconfiguration of space, both physically and symbolically, as well as horizontally and vertically. The exploration and conquest of vast landscapes were coupled with the implementation of monumental architectural schemes. Besides the physical reshaping of the landscape, the socialist undertaking also meant the symbolic transformation of traditional spatial structures. Monuments and memorials of revolutionary heroes replaced tsarist monuments in the Soviet Union and pre-1945 memorials in Central and Eastern Europe. The redrawing of the country's symbolic map also involved uncountable renaming rituals. A great many street and place names, factories, *kolkhozes* (collective farms) and geographical locations were named after historical events or figures selected from the communist historical pantheon of heroes, such as the martyrs of the working-class movement or the leaders of the party.

The ideological obsession with spatial re-organization, tightly chained to the idea of social transformation, permeated the concept of space with an element of sacredness. As has been argued in scholarly literature, 'sovietized space' was arranged in concentric circles based upon 'spheres of relative sacredness', all of which pointed towards the center of centers, Moscow.[2] With the emergence of the Stalin-cult in the mid-1930s, the sacred center gradually became personified by one man, the secretary of the Communist Party, surrounded by his closest companions, or brothers-in-arms, who also bathed in the great leader's halo. The centrality of the leader was mainly constructed through the attribution of all progressive measures to his name. He was depicted as the main inspiration and driving force of socialist construction. In eulogies, the leader was frequently described in terms of spatial metaphors, and he was generally staged in paintings and public cult rituals as an 'artist-creator', or the 'unmoved mover' who made the whole world turn with a single stroke of his pen, while, in the continuous swirl, he stood still in the center like an indestructible rock or an all-powerful giant.[3]

The association of socialist construction with Stalin was also manifested in the spatial spreading of the leader's name. The numerous renamings after the Soviet party secretary were supposed to function as symbolic signposts to indicate the distance already taken on the road to socialism. Naming collective farms, industrial plants or the Constitution of 1936 after the head of the CPSU, made tangible the slogan: 'We are building socialism with Stalin's name'. Apart from the numerous representations of the leader as the epitome of socialist construction, the sacred center of Soviet space, and as a distant and abstract mystical entity who possessed superhuman powers, he was also portrayed as a close, easily approachable and accessible person, a 'man of the people', someone capable of paying attention to the everyday problems of the 'little men', and who was there for them even while directing the grandiose construction of socialism. The image of the ever-caring, omnipotent and omnipresent leader was enhanced to a large extent by the wide-scale proliferation of leader images (paintings, posters, photos and statues) and the placement of portraits of him at all possible locations in private and public spaces alike. In general, the relative success of the Stalin-cult was essentially indebted to the spatial organization of cult artifacts and cult practices, and to the subtle manipulation with the distance between the leader and the led. The technique of a constantly shifting emphasis between the remoteness and the closeness of the leader, in fact, became a fundamental method of constructing the cult of the Soviet leader.[4]

The transformation of symbolic spatial structures in Central and Eastern Europe was launched by the advancing Soviet Army, well before local Communist parties were in possession of political power. The sacrifices of the Red Army conferred a certain sacral aura upon the territories for which the Soviet soldiers had fought. In order to provide a visual testimony of its struggles, the Red Army promoted the erection of war memorials in the countries of the would-be bloc, including Hungary. The location, size and design of these monuments were mainly decided upon in the army headquarters, which intended to occupy the strategically most important symbolic spaces of the countries that had been 'liberated'. It was the competence of local authorities to carry out the Soviet plan. The place of the Liberation Monument in Budapest, for example, was personally decided by Marshal Kliment Voroshilov, and the construction of the monument was supervised by his artist client, A. Gerasimov.[5]

The take-over of communist parties in Central and Eastern Europe in 1948-49 and the launching of rapid sovietization in the region, entailed the importation of the Stalin-cult from the Soviet Union and the adaptation of the leader worship to local party secretaries. The cults of mini-Stalins, such as Bolesław Bierut, G. Gheorghiu-Dej, Klement Gottwald, Walter Ulbricht, Georgi Dimitrov, Mátyás Rákosi and so on, which were mainly constructed through emulating the cult of Stalin, became all-pervasive in the respective countries in the late 1940s and early 1950s. Nevertheless, the transplantation of the cult to Eastern Europe was not a uniform process, because the systematic veneration of party leaders had to be adapted to local political contexts and national traditions in order to overcome the resistance that was frequently encountered from among the respective societies. While, in most of the countries, the implementation of the Soviet-type leader cult was impeded by many obstacles (in Poland and the GDR in particular), in other places, the development of the cult was smoother. The cults of Tito in Yugoslavia and Enver Hoxha in Albania, for example, combined the myth of a war leader with the myth of the party secretary, and managed to acquire genuine popular support without the need to rely on the Soviet techniques of mass persuasion. Here, a Soviet-type leader cult emerged even before the launching of the sovietization project.

Besides copying the essential techniques of representing the *vozhd'* from the Soviet Union, the veneration of local party secretaries, conducted mainly by the party's *agitprop* departments, also mimicked the fundamental patterns of the Soviet leader cult's spatial organization. Party leaders in Central and Eastern Europe normally stood in the centre of mass demonstrations and festivities, towering above the masses on their podium or stage. Their portraits and statues were ubiquitous, dominating the spectacle of the national public sphere and even reshaping the outlook of private spaces to some extent. As in the Soviet Union, countless institutions, streets, collective farms or industrial units were named after the party leader, which provided lucid markers for the citizens who tried to orientate themselves in the Soviet cosmos. Even though local party secretaries were usually presented as being omnipresent and were often portrayed as the main directors of socialist transformation in their own country, the peripheral nature of their cults remained apparent throughout the entire period. The status of Moscow, or the Stalinist Rome, as the sacred center, was unquestioned, as was the spiritual dominance of the man, Stalin, who personified the building of socialism until 1953. The construction of monumental statues of Stalin in the countries of the bloc – the most remarkable were the ones in Prague and Budapest – functioned as permanent visible reminders of the hierarchical relationship of the leader cults within the Soviet empire.

The period that followed the communist take-over in Hungary (1948) also witnessed the physical and symbolic occupation of the environment, the radical reshaping of urban, as well as rural, landscape, and the 'utopianization' of the representation of space in political discourse, which could all be grouped under the heading: 'the sovietization of space'.[6] The process involved the rapid spreading of the Hungarian party leader's name and his images throughout the country, and triggered a sudden increase in the number of representations that depicted Mátyás Rákosi as the symbolic center of the transformed spatial structure. This specific aspect of spatial sovietization, which could be termed as 'the leader-ization of space', resulted in the construction of a circular spatial structure pointing towards the leader, and in the construction of the image of the omnipresent party secretary.

The introduction of the leader cult in Eastern Europe, however, did not simply mean the reconfiguration of space according to the Soviet pattern. The spreading of the cult gradually led to the ritualization of state-societal relations, and to the sovietization of political rituals, political iconography, communication codes, national traditions, and even the calendar. Traditional holidays were replaced by Soviet holidays, the most significant being the anniversaries of Stalin and Lenin, May Day, the anniversary of the October Revolution, *etc.*, which were celebrated simultaneously across the communist world. The leader cult, therefore, can be regarded as the indicator, as well as the essence, of the sovietization project. The degree to which the cult was promoted was also indicative of the commitment of Soviet-type societies to implement Soviet patterns. Due to the complexity of cult propaganda, the spatial aspects of the leader's veneration should be viewed and interpreted with reference to the sovietization of rituals, celebrations, national traditions, and political iconography.

Rákosi, the 'Sacred Centre'

In the same way that Stalin was portrayed as the great designer and conductor of the building of communism in the Soviet Union, Rákosi was also frequently described as the heart and soul of socialist transformation in Hungary. His name was regularly linked to progress and construction in the communist propaganda that contributed to the shaping of the image of the omnipotent leader. Rákosi had already been called the 'cautious leader in the battle for the democratic rebuilding of the country'[7] in 1945, which only marked the beginning of the tide of associations that were about to flood the public sphere after 1948. The party secretary was labeled 'the father of the forint' after the introduction of the new currency in 1946, the 'creator of the constitution' in 1949, but his figure was also attached to the repatriation of Hungarian prisoners of war from the Soviet Union, the unraveling of the 'Rajk-conspiracy', and the drafting of the First Five-Year Plan, launched in 1950. Although the idea that Rákosi was the major source of the social, economic and cultural transformation of the country was unmistakably implied by communist propaganda, clear cut depictions of Rákosi as the 'artist creator', or the 'unmoved mover' who possessed divine characteristics were less frequent and less forceful than in the case of Stalin in the Soviet Union. Nonetheless, there were several literary attempts that tried to bestow god-like qualities upon the party leader's persona. One of the most well-known examples is the poem by László Benjámin which portrayed Rákosi as an all-powerful poet (an artist) who created the world (a work of art) out of nothingness.[8] A similar effort at deification can be recognized in the poems of yet another young poet, Tamás Aczél. Here, Rákosi again appeared as a god-like figure, who granted the essential pre-requisites of existence – such as air for breathing and water to drink – to the Hungarian people.[9]

In addition to the rare descriptions of Rákosi as creator, the literary representations of the Hungarian party secretary were only occasionally assisted by the use of spatial metaphors. Although comparisons with Stalin and high mountain peaks, indestructible rocks, or even the sun became almost indispensable constituents of the eulogies written to the Soviet leader, Rákosi was rarely portrayed in such a way.[10] The Hungarian leader was occasionally presented as a 'larger than life' figure (a giant, for example), but the divine features of the leader were not accentuated often, and were restricted to literary representations.[11] The basic image of Rákosi constantly transmitted by communist propaganda was that of the wise teacher – the god-like characteristics of the secretary of the Hungarian Worker's Party (MDP) were less pronounced elements of his cult.[12]

Despite the fact, that Rákosi was not represented as an 'artist creator' as categorically as Stalin was, the position of the Hungarian leader as the spiritual centre, and the motor of socialist transformation in the country was often re-enacted by the participants of leader cult rituals, especially at festivities which culminated in mass demonstrations. Several scholars who have discussed Soviet rituals have pointed to the fact that, during such occasions, the leader was usually positioned at the centre of all activities, standing on a podium, watching the crowd marching in front of him.[13] The spatial organization of mass festivals – *i.e.*, the leader standing on a stage high above the people in a stationary position watching the permanent movement of the crowd – reproduced the image of the leader as the 'unmoved mover', the great director of the building of socialism. Furthermore, the placement of the party secretary during demonstrations was a clear indication of the relationship of the leader and the people, and an explicit portrayal of hierarchical relations within the party leadership.

In the era of High Stalinism in Hungary (1949-1953), the most imposing mass demonstrations which Rákosi attended took place on the 4th of April (the Day of Liberation), and on the 1st May.[14] The official celebrations in both cases were held on Heroes' Square (*Hősök tere*), at the meeting

Figure 8: Mátyási Rákosi in a field of wheat

point of the magnificent Andrássy-avenue (renamed after Stalin in 1949), and the almost equally wide *György Dózsa út*. Heroes' Square, besides providing a perfect location for mass processions, was also a symbolically-laden place. The grandiose Millenary Monument, with statues of Hungarian kings and the seven legendary captains who led the Hungarian tribes into the Carpathian basin, infused the square with the aura of history and national traditions, and turned it into a site with symbolism of a value which proved difficult to supersede. It is no wonder that the square became the major spot of communist celebrations, a place where social relations were ritually re-enacted within the framework of mass demonstrations. The status of Heroes' Square as the centre of festivals was only challenged by the erection of the statue of Stalin on *Dózsa út*, a few hundred meters away, in December 1951. Stalin Square, however, never really became a sort of sacred center in Budapest. Although it became the location of communist mass demonstrations in 1953, the death of the Soviet leader, and the subsequent waves of de-Stalinization left the square bereft of its symbolic aura. (The statue of Stalin was torn down in October 1956.)

The celebrations which took place in Heroes' Square, or in Stalin Square (from 1953), followed a well-established ceremonial routine, which remained more or less unchanged throughout the period. The distinct ranks of demonstrators, arranged according to various social categories (occupation, age, gender), were already positioned on Stalin Avenue and on *Dózsa-út* by the time Rákosi and members of the Politburo usually arrived. The party leaders were greeted by the amassed crowd often by the rhythmical slogan, '*Éljen Rákosi! Éljen a Párt*!' ('Long live Rákosi! Long live the Party!'), then, the procession began.[15] (The 4th of April celebrations always started with a military parade, opened by the Minister of Defense, Mihály Farkas.) Rákosi and members of the party élite were located on a monumental stage erected in the middle of Heroes' Square, generally in front of the statues of the seven captains. From 1953, the Party leadership was seated on the platform on the Stalin statue. Hierarchical relationships in the Party, and the status of members of the political elite were clearly demarcated by the placement of individual party functionaries and members of the government. In the middle stood the leader, Rákosi, surrounded by his closest companions (Ernő Gerő, Mihály Farkas, József Révai), members of the Politburo, and a few ministers. On occasion, distinguished Soviet guests, such as Voroshilov on the 5th anniversary of the 'Liberation', were placed next to the Hungarian party secretary.[16] Delegations from abroad, lesser party functionaries, generals of the army, leaders of trade unions and mass organizations were normally seated on smaller podiums, erected close to the main stage. From their richly decorated podium, dominated by the giant portraits of Lenin, Stalin and

Rákosi, the Chief Secretary of the Hungarian Worker's Party (Magyar Dolgozók Pártja – MDP) and his closest companions watched the endless rows of marching people carrying the pictures of the 'holy trinity', and continuously expressing loyalty and devotion towards the Soviet and Hungarian party leaders. Because of the number of leader portraits that people carried during the demonstrations, Rákosi, and the other party leaders, were continually looking at their own faces. The image of the thousands of demonstrators marching with the face of Rákosi in front of them was meant to symbolize the inseparable unity of the leader and the led. The never-ending procession of the Rákosi-portraits added further emphasis – in a ritual form – to the idea of the leader being the personification of both the Hungarian people and progress.

The placement of the leaders at the focal point of the celebrations, towards which all the participants marched, was a clear indication of the central status of Rákosi and his *entourage* on the country's symbolic map. Reports about the holidays in the communist press, however, tried to add additional emphasis to the idea of the leader's centrality and his image as an 'unmoved mover', mainly through contrasting the static posture of Rákosi during festive events with the permanent motion and dynamism of the masses. 'Everything is on the move', the official newspaper, *Szabad Nép*, informed its readers in a front page reportage about the 4th of April celebrations in 1950, and continued by portraying the festive crowd as a 'colorful waving meadow'.[17] Metaphors taken from nature, frequently used by communist journalists emphasized the vibrant character of the processions. The *Szabad Nép*'s article about the 1st of May celebrations in 1949, for example, called the first, early morning gathering of demonstrators a 'brook', which slowly turned into a 'stream', continued to grow into 'four mighty rivers' and finally became a 'sea', which was 'waving through the country from Zala through to Somogy'.[18] Subsequent 1st of May demonstrations were also described as 'flooding rivers', 'rolling tides of men',[19] or 'endless tides'[20] by the same newspaper. However, due to the uncontrollable, unpredictable and spontaneous character of water, metaphors contrasting the masses to elements of nature gradually disappeared, giving way to images implying discipline, order and consciousness.[21] Descriptions of incidents in which the strict line of procession was broken because someone wanted to look at Rákosi longer than he was supposed to, or paragraphs illustrating the 'tide of love', which almost dislocated the stage of the leaders[22] became unacceptable after a while, and were gradually replaced by metaphors comparing festive demonstrations to military parades. The various guidelines for participants published at the time were also supposed to educate them as how to behave, and how to march as a disciplined mass that displayed political consciousness. Such guidelines requested the participants not to break the line, not to giggle, and to act as if they were the atoms, or constituents of the utopian socialist community.[23] Although these celebrations, or at least their verbal representations, became gradually tamed, newspaper accounts about mass holidays continued to report on the vitality, vigor and enthusiasm that allegedly characterized these events.

The highlight of the demonstrations for those participating in the processions, according to communist propaganda at least, was the time when the individual, after walking for several hours (some demonstrations lasted for more than 5 hours), passed by the central podium, and could catch a glimpse of the party leader. Communist newspapers reported on numerous incidents (fictitious or real) in which the sight of the leader triggered emotional outbursts and the slackening of discipline among the marching crowd.[24] Some people started to dance in front of the MDP secretary others started to play music happily. Women usually raised their children in the air, in order to show them to Rákosi, their collective father, and pioneers normally sang songs or cried out 'homemade' slogans invoking the name of the leader. As the rows of demonstrators were permanently on the move, expressions of devotion to the leader were continuous, further intensifying the whirl around the party secretary, who, in the midst of all the motion, remained static, and his movements only involved waving to, and smiling at, the people who went past.

Figure 9: Mátyás Rákosi among pioneers

Due to the fact that the image of Rákosi as a god-like figure, directing the great construction works of socialism, was not backed up by visual propaganda materials, nor emphatically present in press reports, and was only rarely depicted by literature, representations of the Hungarian party secretary in divine categories remained in an embryonic stage. Although verbal, as well as visual, illustrations of the party leader's centrality were few in number, on the occasions of mass political holidays and festive processions, Rákosi was clearly staged as the 'sacred center'.

The Spatial Allocation of Rákosi's Images

The gradual conquest of symbolic space by the Communist Party was signified by the multiplication of leader images in the public sphere. Although the take-over of the visual realm following the Communist Party's coming to power, attempts to populate public spaces with the portraits of the Hungarian party leader had already been evident before 1948. Besides supervising the production of the leader's visual representations, the *agitprop* department of the Hungarian Communist Party (Magyar Kommunista Párt – MKP), along with the Orgburo, also monitored the usage of such images, including their spatial allocation. Guidelines and instructions regarding the distribution and placement of Rákosi portraits were usually issued at the time of general elections (1945 and 1947), or before mass-festivities, such as the 1st of May celebrations. However, despite the predominance of central planning, some space was still left for individual initiatives in the decoration of public spaces in the coalition years. The *agitprop* department once had reported enthusiastically that non-party member tradesmen and craftsmen in Veszprém decorated the windows of their shops with the portraits of the MKP leader during the 1st of May demonstration in 1947.[25] Children in Szerencs were also reported to have hung the portraits of Rákosi on the walls of their schools after the local festivities, and some even placed the picture of the MKP leader on their walls at home.[26]

The occupation of Hungarian symbolic space by the Communist Party was signaled by the decree of the Ministry of Religion and Public Education in 1947, which ordered the removal of undesirable images (irredentist pictures, such as the map of Greater Hungary, portraits of pre-1945 politicians, images related to the era of Habsburg rule) from public institutions and schools. At the same time, another decision forbade the decoration of public premises without the permission of the ministry.[27] Besides purging public spaces of the visual remnants of the past, the allocation of the images of the new power, and the arrangement of related images were prescribed by central directives. It generally remained the responsibility of the *agitprop* department to work out in-depth proposals concerning the positioning of portraits of the leader during festivals or political events. Such schemes usually paid attention to the international, as well as the domestic, cult hierarchy and suggested the allocation of portraits accordingly. It was often emphasized that the pictures of Rákosi should dominate over the portraits of regional party bosses, in order to prevent the exaltation of local party officials, and the emergence of the cult of 'mini-Rákosis'.[28] Although the propaganda bureau remained in charge of designing the appearance of mass demonstrations, including the placement of images at various locations, the Secretariat of the MDP, and various governmental bodies also intervened on occasion.

One of the first examples of central planning with regard to the allocation of pictures occurred during the election campaign of 1949, when the Propaganda Department (Országos Propaganda Osztály – OPO), in addition to securing the uniformity of leader portraits, defined the way in which and the location of where the various types of images were to be placed. Immediately before launching the wide-scale agitation, the OPO compiled various packages of propaganda material for local party organizations, which included officially approved portraits of communist leaders as well as figures from the communist historical canon. The packages were designed primarily for decoration purposes, and contained portraits of Lenin, Stalin and Rákosi in three different sizes, and were accompanied by the OPO's detailed instructions concerning their use.[29] Most of the pictures were designed to be carried at celebrations, or used for decorating buildings. One group of pictures was meant to be used to decorate indoor places, primarily, the offices of public institutions, such as ministries or party headquarters.

As soon as the position of the Communist Party was cemented in the Hungarian power structure, the Propaganda Department, which was reorganized under the name Agitation and Propaganda Department (APO), put forward another initiative to centralize the production and dissemination of leader portraits used for the purposes of decoration. In a proposal issued in 1950, the department argued for the primary importance of the portraits of leaders, and considered them to be 'the most effective tools of agitation and propaganda towards the politically backward masses in particular'.[30] The proposal emphasized the necessity of standardizing the pictures of leaders carried at mass demonstrations, or used as decorations in offices, 'in order to avoid political mistakes and manifestations of bad taste, and to eliminate occasional manifestations of the personality cult'.[31] As in the case of the 1949 election campaign, the APO advocated the publication of a centrally-designed set of portraits for the further popularization of leaders. The document planned the production of portraits of the most prominent members of the communist pantheon (Marx, Engels, Lenin, Stalin and Rákosi), as well as respected historical figures (Dózsa, Sándor Petőfi, Mihály Táncsics and Lajos Kossuth).[32] There were several proposed formats for the images, involving posters, paintings, colored drawings and photographs, and the portraits were meant to be used for indoor decoration, primarily in party and governmental offices, in the premises of police departments, as well as in military buildings.

Figure 10: Rákosi amongst Hungarian prisoners of war during the Second World War (Painting of the Szemerei collective)

A preferred placement was advised even for the pictures that were published for commercial use, and were meant to be used in private settings. In February 1950, anticipating an enthusiastic reception of purchasable Rákosi images the APO, came up with the idea of producing portraits of Lenin, Stalin and Rákosi in diverse formats, for sale. One set of pictures were recommended for hanging indoors, another one was to be framed and placed on writing desks, while the third set was supposed to decorate the façades of houses, or the entrance of apartments.[33]

The instructions of the party's propaganda section, and governmental organs, or the published guidelines written by professional decorators usually prescribed the exact way in which the portraits of Lenin, Stalin and Rákosi should be installed at various meetings or celebrations.[34] Although the images of the three leaders would occasionally appear at the same level in the coalition years, the sovietization of symbolic space also entailed the introduction of cult hierarchies expressed through visual means. The arrangement of the portraits of the major figures of the communist universe became similar to an iconostasis, with the images arranged according to a triptych-pattern. Lenin's portrait was normally placed on the left-hand side of the viewer, taking the first place in the row of images. The picture of Stalin, however, was also located on the same horizontal line that indicated the spiritual equality of the two politicians. The portrait of Rákosi was generally hung in the centre, with the picture of Lenin on its left and Stalin on its right, but the image of the Hungarian leader was placed vertically lower than the other two. It seems that the visual syntax of leader portraits (*i.e.*, the way they were arranged in relation to each other) in communist celebrations, or demonstrations, fostered the visual reproduction of the international leader cult hierarchy, and determined the local party leaders' position in it.[35] Although the centrality of Rákosi's picture could have been regarded by contemporaries as an indication of the Hungarian leader's central prominence within the communist pantheon, the obvious vertical inferiority of his portraits overtly indicated the boundaries of the party leader's sub-cult.

The actual number of the portraits and busts of Rákosi produced and disseminated in the period of 1945-56 is difficult to estimate. As pictures of the leader were ubiquitous, even the most modest approximation would go beyond millions of print-outs. The absurdity of the number of portraits in circulation could be paralleled with the absurdity of the locations in which a great proportion of these images were placed. They were hung in offices and in school classrooms, where they replaced the images of Miklós Horthy. Thousands of portraits were carried at festivities and mass demonstrations, and were also used as decoration for public holidays, where they dominated the sight of such events. Workplaces – factories especially – were supposed to install their own 'Red Corner', which functioned as local shrines of the communist movement, similarly to the 'Lenin Corners' in the Soviet Union.[36] Besides displaying the portraits of the factory's privileged shock-workers, 'Red Corners' were packed with portraits of, and quotations from, Rákosi, Lenin and Stalin.[37] According to contemporary memories and reminiscences, photos or small busts of Rákosi were present in hospitals,[38] at sporting events, but could also end up 'on the top of a pyramid of fat' at a butcher's, or even among female underwear in clothes shops.[39] The portraits of Stalin, Lenin and Rákosi even featured at fashion-shows, overlooking the parade from above the stage.[40] The memoirs of Ákos Major, an ex-judge of the People's Tribunals, recalled the incident of a Budapest butcher, who, in order to popularize his own shop and increase his profits, sculpted the bust of Rákosi and installed the product in his shop-window. The example became infectious and the bust of the leader started to appear in the windows of neighboring shops. As the weather turned to spring, however, the sculpture started to melt, revealing the true nature of the material the butcher had worked with: pork fat. In order to prevent public ridiculing, and, more importantly, the intervention of the authorities, the butcher quickly removed the image of the great leader, and sold the rest of the fat.[41] Miklós Szabó remembered a similar incident, when a butcher placed a bust of Rákosi in his shop window, on the occasion of the leader's sixtieth birthday.[42]

In addition to recurrently accompanying mass celebrations and communist festivities, the representations of the leader were tightly linked to everyday collective rituals. Party membership meetings, commemorations and agitation briefings normally took place in places sanctified by the image of the leader: in a 'Red Corner', next to a bust of Rákosi, in front of wall-newspapers or 'glory boards', and so on. After the unveiling of the statue of Stalin in 1951, Tamás Aczél argued that such effigies could be communicated with in the leader's physical absence. People were meant to turn to the visual representations of leaders in their misery, as well as in their happiness, when they were in need of advice, or after the fulfillment of individual plans.[43] The images of Rákosi could also become the objects of individual cult rituals, in private apartments. As is well known, pictures of the leader often replaced the icons of saints in many houses in the Soviet Union, and often inherited the mystical function of Orthodox Christian images.[44] Although examples of adoration of Rákosi's portraits are extremely rare, a certain spiritual aura was conferred upon the pictures of the MDP secretary by communist propaganda. Newspapers, such as *Szabad Nép*, frequently reported pioneer children swearing an oath, or workers offering pledges to the portrait of the leader, in the physical absence of the subject of veneration. The one-act play by Márta Gergely from 1952, entitled *Az ígéret* (The Promise), provided an ideal-typical representation of the presence of the leader in the private sphere through his images.[45] The drama, which was clearly influenced by A. Laktionov's painting, *Moving Into a New Flat* (1951), describes the moment when a family moves into their new apartment.[46] Although the rooms are already furnished, the walls are still empty. The spiritual climax of the play is the moment when the little girl hangs the picture of Rákosi on the wall, expecting that, through his portrait, the leader would also move into the flat. 'Comrade Rákosi lives with us, too, doesn't he?' asks the girl to her mother. Since no father-figure appears on the scene, the Rákosi-portrait, which represents the mystical body of the leader, assumes the role of the absent father, through being ever-present in the life of the family.

Signposts of Progress: Renamings

An emblematic manifestation of the cult of the Hungarian party leader was the multiplication of renaming rituals. Street or place names, and markers of socialist progress such as factories, collective farms, and cultural and educational institutions were named after the party secretary – and some of his close lieutenants – with the aim of establishing symbolic signposts for the citizen who wished to orientate himself in the realm of sovietized space. Despite the increasing number of renamings, the redrawing of the country's symbolic geography remained a sensitive issue throughout the period. Although it is difficult to recognize the careful planning of, or a consistent policy towards, renamings, it is clear that the party organs that were responsible for authorizing name changes generally tried to avoid the devaluation of the symbolic currency of the sacred names through occasionally declining proposals which they regarded as inappropriate by the decision-makers. Thus, it is not surprising that the baptisms of a highly symbolic nature (prominent educational institutions, or factory complexes) were mainly proposed by one of the central party organs (the Orgburo, the *agitprop* department or the Secretariat). On the other hand, submissions put forward by local party organizations or non-party institutions were sometimes rejected by the highest authorities. Irrespective of the original source of suggestions – from above or from below – proposals requesting permission to apply Rákosi's name to a particular institution were normally presented in communist propaganda as 'initiatives from below'.

Soon after the end of Second World War, a minor wind of name-changes swept through the country's symbolic scenery, which eradicated the remnants of fascist influence and conservative authoritarianism in Hungary. Squares and streets named after Hitler and Mussolini were hastily removed, while the names of historical figures, mainly from the leftist deposit of heroes (Táncsics, Petőfi, Dózsa and Kossuth), emerged in their place. Nevertheless, as a result of some prodding from Rajk, the Minister of Internal Affairs in 1948, by the end of the year, place-names bearing the names of Marx, Lenin, Stalin, Voroshilov, Malinovskii and Molotov already featured significantly on the symbolic map of the country.[47] One of the first institutions to be named after the Hungarian party leader, Rákosi – except for the Hungarian 'Rákosi-brigade' that fought in the Spanish Civil War – was an orphanage founded in 1945, but the coalition years witnessed several other renamings after the Secretary of the Communist Party, as well as other leaders of the MKP. A newly built residential district in the city of Debrecen, for instance, was given the name '*Rákosi-prolitelep*' (proletarian neighborhood), one of the first ships renovated after the war was christened '*Mátyás Rákosi*', but even sport events became associated with Rákosi's name at the time. In January 1947, the Orgburo for example, approved the organization of a Rákosi chess competition,[48] but *Szabad Nép* also reported on a certain 'Rákosi Cup' in August 1947: an annual football tournament organized by the College of Gymnastics in Budapest.[49] Even if the party center had often lent its consent to the proliferation of Rákosi's name before 1948, renamings only started to multiply in the years of the communist take-over.[50] One of the first examples of such renamings was the request by the Szeged Party Committee in December 1948 which asked for the Orgburo's permission to rename the newly rebuilt bridge of the town, over the Tisza-river, after Rákosi.[51]

Although the renaming of institutions – especially those under MKP control – after prominent party leaders was a common practice in the coalition years, the process became standardized only after the communist take-over. Alongside the various proposals that were all meant to secure control in the field of cult production, the *agitprop* section of the MDP worked out the general scheme of renaming rituals in late 1949. The proposal, which was submitted to the Secretariat for authorization, laid down the major principles of future renaming rituals, and also suggested the specific name categories to be used for industrial plants. (The first category was comprised of the names of Soviet and Hungarian party leaders.) According to the document, the main function of such rituals was to strengthen the population's loyalty and allegiance towards the regime, and to enhance the political consciousness of the masses by setting exemplary figures for them.[52] The *agitprop*'s proposal authorized the Orgburo and the National Economic Council (*Népgazdasági Tanács*) to evaluate the individual appeals, and also prescribed the procedure of requesting and granting the privilege of acquiring the leader's name. According to the suggestion, renamings were to be organized in such a way that they would seem to be initiatives from below. In the event that the requested name was that of a living leader, the workers were supposed to address him by letter, giving details of the previous successes of the factory and of the pledges they would offer after they became worthy of carrying the leader's revered name. Renaming rituals were always preceded by an intense agitation campaign in the respective factories, during which the workers were expected to assess the significance of the renaming, and to recognize the new obligations that the name change brought with it. Since the major pre-condition of granting permission to the usage of a certain name was outstanding production, the toilers were expected to perceive the renaming as a gift, or as a reward for their good performance. The regime also anticipated that the workers of factories that received such a privilege would express their gratitude in return, through increasing their work efforts.

Although the *agitprop*'s proposal was actually removed from the agenda of the Secretariat at its meeting on the 26 of October 1949, the planned changes were executed later according to the initial plan. The procedural routine established by the propaganda department for renaming rituals was closely followed by the individual factory committees that aspired to acquire the leader's name. Workers, under the influence of their local party officials, wrote letters to the leader requesting name changes, and, at the same time, offered their pledges to the party in the event that permission was granted. Whenever the right to append the sacred name to an institution was guaranteed, the employees would not hesitate to express their gratitude for the honor, by intensifying their workload. As the letter-writing bureau of *Szabad Nép* reported, the news that the factory on Csepel Island would be named after the secretary of the MDP re-invigorated the on-going labor competition.

> This decree triggered true enthusiasm, and happiness among the workers which they expressed through pledges offered en masse.[53]

The renaming of Hungary's largest factory-complex at the time, the former Manfréd Weiss Works on Csepel Island, after the Chief Secretary of the MDP (*Rákosi Mátyás Művek*) in 1950, signaled the beginning of the most symbolically-laden name changes. The utilization of the party leader's name was particularly widespread in the sphere of production. The number of Rákosi-brigades in factories and collective farms gradually increased, and they all participated in the country-wide Rákosi shift, before the leader's 60th birthday. Besides industrialization, the sacred name of the party leader was also linked to culture and education. Apart from the Mátyás Rákosi House of Culture in Budapest on Attila József square, the central school of the Trade Union Council was bestowed the name of the leader in August 1949,[54] like the special college for officers at the armored divisions of the army, which took the name of Rákosi in 1951 (*Rákosi Mátyás Páncélos Tiszti Iskola*).[55] Following a similar pattern, a secondary school was named after the party secretary in Tatabánya, and a Rákosi-room was established in Sopron, in the primary school where the leader had once studied.[56] The most significant renamings, however, were implemented for the occasion of Rákosi's 60th birthday in 1952. The University of Miskolc, which specialized in training mining and mechanical engineers, was christened *Rákosi Mátyás Nehézipari Műszaki Egyetem* (Mátyás Rákosi Technical

University for Heavy Industry). At the same time, the party established a Rákosi study contest (*Rákosi Mátyás Tanulmányi Verseny*) for secondary school students, a Rákosi grant for outstanding university students, and a Rákosi award for exceptional academic achievement.[57] By 1953, at least 30 collective farms bore the name of Rákosi all over the country, and several cities had a Rákosi street (Kalocsa, Kiskunfélegyháza and Szarvas, for example).[58]

The renaming process had a remarkable international aspect. The practice of renaming institutions and place names from other bloc countries – the most obvious example being Stalin – was a common practice in the countries of the 'peace camp' in the 1950s. Hungary was no exception: it had factories named after Gheorghiu-Dej, Wilhelm Pieck and Klement Gottwald. Renamings in this context were meant to provide additional symbolic backing to the cults of local party secretaries, but, most importantly, such rituals were part of the effort to promote the idea of friendship and unity in the states of the Soviet bloc.[59] The frequency of appearance of a party leader's name on the symbolic maps of foreign countries was also indicative to his international significance among the hierarchy of mini-Stalins, and it also designated his position in the constantly changing international pantheon of leaders.[60] Following the pattern of mutual renamings in the Soviet bloc, the name of Rákosi was also exported abroad, which fostered – to some extent – the transfer of his cult beyond the country's boundaries. The Hungarian newspaper, *Szabad Ifjúság* (Free Youth), for instance, reported on the christening of a machine tractor station in the GDR (in Mecklenburg), as well as the renaming of a collective farm in Bulgaria (in Uzondzovo) after Rákosi in 1952.[61] At the same time, a factory in Bucharest in Romania was given the name of the Rákosi Works, but war-stricken Korea also expressed her gratitude for Hungarian – mainly medical – aid, and renamed a hospital after the leader of the MDP.[62] In one case, a Soviet new-born – a girl – was baptized Matiasa, in honor of the Hungarian leader.[63] Renaming requests from abroad were submitted to the Hungarian government even after the Rákosi cult had reached its peak in 1952. The *Andreas Schule* in Berlin, for example, sought the consent of the Hungarian government to rename their school after Rákosi in March 1955.[64]

The process of renaming institutions was meant to convey symbolic allegiance and absolute loyalty to the leader. Through bearing the leader's name, the workers of the chosen factory or *kolkhoz* expressed their commitment and full association with the goals of the leader, without the possibility of deviance or doubt. These industrial units or collective farms, honored by the name of Rákosi, were also expected to perform better than the rest. In fact, they were anticipated to show an example in production that could be emulated by their less (or more?) fortunate partner institutions. The drive to match the expectations of the party was compensated by the rise of the renamed institution to a semi-privileged status. The industrial or educational units that were named after Rákosi received widespread publicity in the press, and more attention from the party, which often involved easier access to rare goods and scarce commodities. Indeed, one of the incentives behind requesting permission to rename a place or an institution after Rákosi or other communist leaders at local level was often the hope of gaining economic advantages through the exploitation of the symbolic currency of the leader's name.[65]

Despite the distinguished status of various institutions bearing the leader's name, such organizations did not always display outstanding performance. The attachment of Rákosi's name to an orphanage in Budapest, for example, could not save the institution from the notorious financial lapses of the management. Shortcomings were also reported with regard to the functioning of other educational institutions bearing the name of the MDP secretary. The Maxim Gorky School was once criticized for not dealing with the early manifestations of sexuality among children in an appropriate way. As the report claimed, such problems were observed among the children who had come from the Rákosi Kindergarten in Budapest.[66] The Hungarian party leader was also heard to have complained about the bad reputation of the Rákosi kindergartens in the country in 1954. Rákosi blamed Árpád Szakasits for suggesting such renamings, and claimed that the only motivation of the ex-leader of the Social Democrats behind proposing the idea was to disparage him.[67]

The sensitive nature of the reconfiguration of symbolic space in Hungary was signified by the occasional rejections of appeals that tried to obtain the right to rename a particular institution or street name after the leaders of the Communist Party. Besides declining propositions to rename institutions after second or third rank party leaders, there were a few instances when the party authorities rejected renaming requests which involved the names of Lenin, Stalin or Rákosi. A suggestion in 1945, for example, to rename a mine (St. Stephen's mine) after the MKP leader, was rejected by the Orgburo without much hesitation, which indicates the general sensitivity with which name changes in the coalition period were treated by the organs of the Communist Party.[68] Similar rejections were nonetheless recorded even after the conquest of symbolic space in 1948-49. For the 60th birthday of the Hungarian party leader, the party committee of Székesfehérvár proposed the idea of renaming the new theatre of the town and Dózsa Square after Rákosi, and a plan for changing the names of the main streets in the villages of the county was also submitted to the party center. Although Rákosi hesitated at the beginning, Révai rebuffed both ideas.

> It is not desirable: 1. What kind of an idea is that, to suggest the renaming of György Dózsa square, or the renaming of a theatre after Comrade Rákosi? 2. We don't do such things in Budapest, therefore it is not possible to rename streets in the countryside after him, either. It is impossible to check if worthy streets or squares have been selected.[69]

The initiative of the Nagykanizsa Party Committee to rename the main street of the town after the secretary of the MDP was also vetoed, this time by the Orgburo, in November 1948.[70]

Notwithstanding the numerous occasions in which renaming proposals were rejected, the number of place names, educational institutions, collective farms and factories bearing Rákosi's name rapidly increased. Although no towns were named after the Hungarian party leader, unlike *Gottwaldow* in Czechoslovakia, *Gheoghiu-Dej* in Romania, or *Dimitrovgrad* in Bulgaria,[71] the baptisms of the indicators of the socialist transformation after the party secretary, accompanied by the permanent association of progressive measures with the leader in communist propaganda, were all meant to reinforce the image of Rákosi as the sole physical embodiment of socialist transition in Hungary.

Conclusions

The 'leader-ization of space' was a fundamental constituent of the sovietization of symbolic space in post-war Hungary. The politics of renaming and the allocation of leader images were all meant to bolster the image of the leader as the epitome of progress and socialist transformation. Through the staging of the leader as the focal point of symbolic space, Rákosi was represented as the great director of the building of socialism in Hungary. Nonetheless, despite the fact that the spatial extension of the cult was centrally co-ordinated, the flooding of public spaces with the leader's name and his pictures – Rákosi was not distinguished for his good looks – triggered the de-valuation of the symbolic value of the party secretary's name, as well as his visual representations. Furthermore, the monotony and grayness of leader images and the drill-like character of mass processions inevitably led to the inflation of the cult of Rákosi in Hungary. It, thus, seems tempting to claim that the spatial arrangement of the cult (*i.e.*, being all-pervasive) proved to be somewhat counter-productive, and instead of sparking devotion and admiration for the leader, it caused disapproval, irritation, and hostility in Hungarian society. It is not surprising that the dismantling of the Rákosi cult was initially marked by the renaming of institutions that bore the leader's name, and by the gradual withdrawal of the portraits of the party secretary from the public sphere, culminating in the iconoclastic acts of the 1956 Uprising.

Nevertheless, the failure of the regime to attain social support through the Rákosi cult cannot be solely attributed to the monotonous spatial structure of cult objects and ritual practices. In Hungary – and in many countries of the Soviet bloc – the problem of transplanting the Soviet-type of veneration of the leader could not be resolved during the relatively short period of 'High Stalinism'. In the Soviet Union, the Stalin-cult flourished for a quarter of a century, whereas in the bloc – with the exception of Yugoslavia and Albania – Stalinist leader cults only prospered between 1948 and 1956, and were even toned down to a significant degree after 1953. Moreover, the triumph in the Second World War largely contributed to the solidification of the Stalin–myth. However, the first secretaries of Eastern European communist parties – again, with the exception of Tito and Hoxha – had no such symbolic capital at their disposal. Besides the shortness of the Stalin era in Hungary, cultural resistance and the problem of reconciling national traditions with the fundamentally Soviet veneration of leaders also contributed to the failure to create a demigod out of Rákosi.

9

Mass Gymnastic Performances under Communism: The Case of Czechoslovak Spartakiads*

Petr Roubal

By their nature, social rituals have the capacity both to display and to disguise certain power relations. This is even more so when the ritual centers on the symbolism of the human body—the most versatile symbol of them all—as is the case with mass gymnastic displays. The mass gymnastic displays popularized in the GDR and in Czechoslovakia after 1945 had specific roots in the nineteenth century nationalist movements in Central Europe. Such displays had also been popular in the Soviet Union in 1920s and 1930s.[1] But the displays in the GDR and Czechoslovakia were not directly imported from the Soviet Union. On the contrary, it could be said that the cultural transfer went the other way round. Nevertheless, the 'Soviet experience' served to transform these rituals, particularly in the case of *Turnfeste* in the GDR, where, through sovietization, the core underlying message of these displays was modified. In this sense, mass gymnastic displays are yet another example of the successful application of the more general 'national-in-form, socialist-in-content' strategy.

The core message of the mass gymnastic displays, with the synchronized movement of thousands of bodies in a stadium, always centered on the representation of 'the people'. But whereas the mass gymnastic displays of the gymnastic movements, *Sokols* or *Turners,* tried to portray their members as the embodiment of the ideal (future) *volk*, the communist organizers of these displays faced a far more intricate task.[2] Their task was to represent 'the people' as both a sovereign and a docile subject at the same time, thereby offering a visual answer to the most complex conundrum of communist ideology, namely, the relationship between the masses and the leader(ship). Whereas the displays of *Sokols* or *Turners* in the inter-war period were, in most cases, directed against the state and its vision of a national community, the communist states—and

Czechoslovakia in particular—perceived, in the long established culture of gymnastic exercises, the most convenient visual strategy to present itself as something more than just a state.

Although the Czechoslovak *Spartakiads* at the Strahov Stadium in Prague—by far the biggest sporting arena in the world, covering an area larger than eight football pitches—were the most spectacular mass gymnastic displays ever held, the ritual of synchronized mass movements played an important role in all communist countries, either as an independent event, such as *Turn- und Sportfests* in the GDR or as part of a ritual cycle. The latter was the case in the Soviet Union or Hungary, where May Day parades at Red Square or at Felvonulási Square were accompanied by mass gymnastics displays in front of the tribune of the Politburo. Similarly, in Romania, the 23rd of August, the national holiday celebrating the country's liberation from fascism, was the occasion for organizing such displays. Yugoslavia incorporated mass gymnastic display into Tito's cult by fusing the Day of Youth with his birthday.

Historically, mass gymnastics were characterized by that same equation of body with machine, which constituted the basis for the modern military drill[3] or working process.[4] Although the underlying logic behind the technique of the performances was the same as that behind the working process or military drill, the final goal was, however, different. It did not aim at greater efficacy, but at greater effect. The highly rational approach to body movements led to a purely irrational, aesthetic experience. Thus, mass gymnastic performances were less part of the implicit politics of domination than part of explicit politics of representation. The display of gymnasts was intended to represent the community in a situation where other means of representation were not available. This explains the geographical distribution of mass gymnastic displays, which concentrated in ethnically German, Czech and several other Slavic areas. To paraphrase Walter Benjamin, where parliaments were deserted, the stadiums had to be full, offering a symbolic representation both of popular consent and of legitimate authority.[5]

The political history of modern gymnastic performances goes back to F.L. Jahn—commonly known as *Turnvater Jahn*, the father of gymnastics—the radical liberal and democrat, who saw gymnastics as a way of overcoming the weakness and disintegration of Germany. The initial impulse for organizing the German gymnasts, *Turners*, was the desire to avenge the humiliating defeat inflicted upon them by Napoleon. The long-term role of the *Turners* was, however, to create an exemplary community that would show the rest of Germany what an ideal society could be. The gymnasts, Jahn demanded, must be 'chaste, pure, capable, fearless, truthful and ready to bear arms'.[6]

The aspiration of the *Turners* to model the whole of society was taken over by the Czech gymnastic association, the *Sokols* (falcons), founded in 1862, and was succinctly expressed in the slogan 'Every Czech a Sokol'. Public displays of the *Sokol* gymnastic association – *Slets* – were deeply influenced by the regular festivities of German *Turners*, *Turnfeste*. Their common purpose was to visualize the emergence of a new, single national identity as opposed to the numerous separate classes and regional identities of the pasts. Mass gymnastic displays thus document the gradual shift of European nationalism from the older 'linguacentric' emphasis of intellectuals of the first two-thirds of the 19th century to a more 'iconocentric' form, accessible to the broader public.[7] The synchronized movement of the male gymnasts was the main symbolic means of expressing the idea of the unified and uniformed national community. Moreover, the mandatory uniforms of the gymnasts, instead of being designed to facilitate the exercise, aimed at creating an equal and democratic mass.[8] It is precisely the abstract character of gymnastics, free of any regional or class characteristic, which made it so suitable for the bridging of class and regional barriers, and thus for modeling the ideal community.

Jahn's ideal gymnast possessed a strong male body modeled upon the example of Teutonic warriors. But how could a man be a Teutonic warrior in the era of rational, civilized modernity? Gymnastics, as Jens Ljunggren shows, offered an answer to this problem of modern masculinity by combining the military virtues of forefathers with the self-restraint and control of the modern citizen.[9] The primitive masculine strength of the Middle Ages was to be re-awakened in modern society as obedience and discipline.

Even though it mirrored, to a large extent, the development of the *Turners*, the Czech nationalist *Sokol* movement could hardly be described as proto-fascist. It shared, with the *Turners*, a radical claim towards society, stressed democratic values, addressed one another as 'brother' or 'sister', and portrayed the movement as a force above political parties and social classes. Not unlike Jahn, Miroslav Tyrš, a Prague professor of aesthetics of German descent, became the charismatic leader of the movement, and it was his writings – strongly influenced by A. Schopenhauer and C. Darwin – that determined the future orientation of the movement. However, as the key political aim of the *Sokol* movement was not to unify and purify the nation, but was instead to overcome the modest size of the nation symbolically through the display of national grandeur, there were significant differences between the *Sokols* and the *Turners*. To increase the strength of the nation, the *Sokols* also formed a kind of gymnastic geopolitics. Through the help of the Czech *Sokols*, strong gymnastic movements were established among the Southern Slavs, in Bulgaria, Russia and in the Austrian part of Poland. In contrast with the *Turners*, who, after the unification of Germany, gradually lost their political influence and were finally disbanded by the Nazis,[10] the *Sokols* remained an important political force throughout the 1930s and 1940s. Their two last *Slets* in 1938 and 1948 marked turning points not only in the history of the *Sokols*, but also in the whole country. The 1938 *Slet*, according to the eyewitness Karel Čapek, was no longer a mass display of bodies, but 'a dream created out of a crowd of souls' which culminated in the performance of the 'Oath to the Republic', a solemn declaration, made by 30,000 men, to defend the country against Nazi Germany, against which more than 3,000 *Sokol* members lost their lives. The 1948 *Slet* was the last massive protest against the recently established communist rule, which resulted in mass persecution and the banning of the movement.

National regeneration was only one of the two most important topics that mass gymnastic displays were used to 'embody'. Social justice was the other. Social Democrats, and later on, Communists, considered nationalist gymnastics to be a trick of the bourgeoisie against the workers, whose purpose was to conceal both the anarchy and the class struggle within capitalist society behind the harmony of the body movements of the gymnasts. However, instead of rejecting such practice, they created their own gymnastic associations at the end of the 19th century and organized their own mass gymnastic displays. These displays offered a practical realization of the political and aesthetic dream of the *avant-garde* theatre, in which the masses were both directed and free to act. In mass gymnastics, the gymnasts became the artists and still remained true to the original design. There was also another reason why the left embraced gymnastics. In the Soviet Union, the *Proletkultists* despised competitive sport and fair play as 'remnants of the decadent past and emanations of degenerate bourgeois culture'. They called for a fresh start, through the 'revolutionary innovation of proletarian physical culture, which would take the form of labor gymnastics and mass displays, pageants and excursions'.[11] It was in this context that the name *Spartakiad* emerged. The Communist physical training specialist Chalupecký, argued:

> All medieval and modern history of workers' movement does not offer any person whose name would connect three ideas: proletariat – social revolution – physical education. Only antiquity offers such a name: Spartacus, gladiator, it means trained wrestler, the slave and soul of the first organized proletarian revolution.[12]

Equipped with hammers and sickles, the communist gymnasts performed their first *Spartakiad* in Prague in 1921 expressing, through their co-ordinated movements, 'the determination of our revolutionary workers to fight under the leadership of the party to overthrow capitalist supremacy'.

Even though spectacular mass gymnastic displays in communist Czechoslovakia and elsewhere inherited the name '*Spartakiad*' from the radical left gymnastic movement, their role was much nearer to those of nationalist displays: the *Sokols* and the *Turners*. Both nationalist *Turnfests* or *Slets* and the communist *Spartakiads* were an attempt to visualize a radically new political theory based upon an interpretation of the concept of 'the people' which was radically different from that of parliamentary democracy. However, whereas nationalist gymnastic displays aimed at presenting the movement as the exemplary center of the national community, and were often targeted against the existing state, the communist displays had a far more complex róle to play. The bodies of the communist gymnasts had to perform two radically different roles, they had to embody 'the people' in such a way as to be the sovereign, in other words, to provide the *raison d'être* for the Party, and, at the same time, be the docile subject of the care of that self-same Party.

In '*The King's Two Bodies*', Ernst Kantorowicz studies the key concept of medieval political theory - the duality of the king's body.[13] The medieval king had two qualities, for he had two Bodies: the Body Natural was subject to mortal sins and mortality itself, the other one was the Body Politic, which was moral and immortal. The Body Politic of the king was the representation, the 'embodiment' of the medieval polity. It 'incorporated' and 'headed' all 'members' of the society. An elaborate system of transition, including the display of the effigy and the feeding of the dead corpse of the king, was developed to bridge the gap between the Body Natural and the Body Politic at the time of the king's death. Gluckman described a similar 'native' political theory among the *Shilluk* of East Africa, who, through an elaborate rite of '*translatio*', express the inalterability of the Body Politic which culminates in a mock battle, in which the 'kingship captures the king'.[14]

In communist political theory, as 'embodied' in the mass gymnastic performances, the body of communist gymnasts served the same purpose as the body of the king in medieval and East-African political philosophy. It was literally the embodiment of political collectivity. And it also had two bodies. The first gymnast's body was the Foucauldian Body Docile. The body of the gymnast was constituted by discourse based upon social geometry, which operated with a set of analytical body techniques. These techniques transformed the individual gymnast into an analytical unit and constituted him as a docile subject, who sacrificed his or her individuality for the sake of the collective. Whereas the Body Docile was physical and apolitical in the traditional sense of macro-politics, the second body of the communist gymnast – the Body Collective was immaterial and political. The synchronized movements of the gymnasts—established by the procedures creating the Body Docile—testify to the existence of one symbolic collective body of the communist polity in 'a direct manifestation of the people for socialism, an expression of their faith in the policy of the Communist Party which successfully led Czechoslovakia out of the crisis and turbulence of 1968-1969'.[15] For some two hours of the performance, the body of the gymnast was the sovereign; its symbolic power was unchallenged by the other symbolic powers. It represented the totality, the life and the meaning of the socialist society. *L'état c'est gymnast.*

The Body Docile consisted of the physical body of the gymnasts, physical in both senses of the word. His or her body was subjected to the gaze of a physician and a physicist as well. The physician's gaze analyzed the gymnast's body as a single organism, studying the possibilities and the 'usefulness' of the movements, noting sex and age differences, and suggested improvements in the body techniques. The physicist's gaze looked at the mass of gymnasts as a dead matter, it distributed the bodies at the stadium according to geometrical grids or measured the speed at which the bodies were able to pass through the gates of the stadium. They both constituted the Body Docile as a building block of the performances.

The Body Docile of the gymnast was constructed by the discourse and techniques of ritual specialists. The ritual specialists were mainly former organizers of the *Sokol* performances and were not directly connected with communist political power. They consisted of a strictly hierarchical organization of several hundred full-time employees who worked on well-defined specific tasks in the organization of the display.[16] Though they shared a discourse strongly resembling Foucauldian disciplinary practices, they did not see their task as transformative, but as emancipatory. Discipline was not understood, as Vladimír Macura showed in his semiotic analysis, by the communist organizers as an outward principle, something to which the natural character of individual behavior must be sacrificed, but as an inner principle of human beings and society, which is deformed by everyday life[17] and ought to be 'purified' and cleansed of 'unaesthetic involuntary habits'.[18] According to one of the key organizers, there was no artificiality in the gymnastic performances; on the contrary, they presented an ideal, which was to be fulfilled in everyday life. 'It is, after all, a matter for all people to know how to march properly, keep in step, and form the ranks.'[19]

In a similar way to other disciplinary practices, the bodies of gymnasts were subjected to elaborate techniques of social geometry. However, the dynamic interplay between the social and architectonic geometry that occurs between the gymnastic performances and the stadium contributed to a specificity of mass gymnastics as a disciplinary practice. The design of the stadium was shaped by the hegemony of gaze,[20] which, in effectiveness, surpassed even the visibility of the subject in J. Bentham's panopticon. The concrete structure of the stadium surpassed the one-dimensional panopticon in its all-dimensional character, which did not, in any sense, reduce its control over the acts of every individual. The architectural geometry of the stadium allowed for social geometry by a simple but powerful measure. Instead of prison walls isolating one inmate from the other, the stadium field was divided by an invisible geometrical grid, which determined the position of each and every gymnast. A gymnast standing on his mark at the stadium was no longer part of the masses, but became an analytical unit, an intersection of axis x and y which could be directed, controlled and analyzed from any point of the stadium, as the ultimate purpose of the display was not the efficiency of external control but the effect of individual inner discipline. The extensive use of this grid to design the movements of large masses of gymnasts was probably the most important innovation of gymnastic performance under communism. Previously, the even distribution of bodies in the stadium was ensured by the relative distance between the gymnasts' bodies that was based upon bodily proportions. The gymnasts used to stand at arms-length or two-steps distance from each other, there were no abstract geometry imposed on them and they truly exercised 'together'.[21] What communist gymnastics invented was an analytical mass, a peculiar variant of the lonely crowd, in which each member of the mass stands in solitude under the gaze of the spectators and power. The solitude of the gymnast was not complete. He or she performed as part of a 'Basic Unit' consisting of square number of gymnasts – 16, 25 or more – who exercised together throughout the whole training process, and were the building blocks of the final performance. By multiplying the numbers of such units and directing them in the sporting arena large spectacles were created. In this way, a class, a military unit, or sports club could easily be trained independently. They later joined other units in their category and performed larger or smaller parts of the final figure.[22]

The discourse of discipline, or—one may say—of the plasticity, of 'the people' that governed the gymnastic display was further strengthened by the organization of the spectacle in the wider sense. A whole administrative network was mobilized in order to transport the gymnast to Prague, dress him/her, accommodate him/her and manage all his or her bodily needs. The specialists of the bureaucratic ritual determined how many square meters each gymnast needed,[23] how many calories he or she was supposed to consume (specified according to sex and age),[24] with how many other gymnasts he or she was going to share a bathroom.[25] As the event took place in Bohemia, the bureaucrats had to manage an additional technical task: the consumption of beer, which can be characterized in no other way than excessive.[26]

In his anthropological study, *Models and Mirrors,* Handelman distinguished three types of public events: events-that-model, events that represent, and events-that-present.[27] Whereas the first—such as presidential inauguration—makes change happen inherently, which directly affects social realities—the second, for example, carnivals—does its work in comparison with, and in contrast to, social realities. The third type of public event—events-that-present—has the task of presenting society to itself. Not accidentally, the examples of such events which Handelman named, the Nuremberg Rallies and Soviet parades, both included or were constituted by a gymnastic display. As was observed by Abner Cohen, the less obviously political in form the symbols employed in ritual are, the more effective they are politically.[28] As the human body is an 'ideological variable' which is a rich reservoir of meanings without having direct political affiliation,[29] the mass display of bodies was an ideal symbolic system to portray the communist *communitas*. Similarly, as a young, strong and beautiful body of a sportsman is capable of offering an optimistic answer to the basic question of philosophical anthropology of what is a human being,[30] the mass gymnastic display through the multiplication of its symbolic potential offers an affirmative answer to the basic question of political theory, of what is the polity?

'Today, the masses will speak at the Strahov stadium', claimed president Antonín Zápotocký at the opening of the 1955 Spartakiad.[31] The performances made up of different age and social groups was intended to represent 'the masses' in their variety, but still as 'the masses' united and fully concentrated upon a common goal.[32] 'Stadion—eto my', 'stadium— that's we/us', claimed a Soviet daily, demonstrating that the crucial element of the displays was to communicate 'the simple and mighty "We/us" whose power we have now fully realized'. The 'mighty We/us' was embodied by the synchronized movements of the gymnasts symbolizing a single will, purpose, shape, common breath and step, in a word one body. This Body Collective, composed of thousands of gymnastic Bodies Docile, was seen to act 'as a single man.[33]

> These are the days when the people, as a single poet with thousands of heads, compose verses of love in Prague in honor of humanity and their socialist homeland.[34]

Not only the synchronized movements but also the sheer magnitude of the display was used to represent the communist collectivity through metonymy: 'Strahov stadium is a cinnamon field/...The entire country dance here/ As if all the people gathered for a feast/ Men and women go. A forest of hands is raised./ A vibrant forest of hands bound by an oath'.[35]

This stress on the self-representation is what constitutes the specificity of the communist gymnastics and clearly distinguishes it from the Nazi display, which would not be able to balance the self-celebration of society with the cult of the leader. Susan Sonntag mentioned in her analysis of the work of Leni Riefenstahl a photograph from the Nuremberg Rallies showing Riefenstahl, Albert Speer, and Adolf Hitler studying 'some plans'[36] to prove that Riefenstahl, the famous film director, was involved not only in the documenting but also in designing the ritual.[37] What, in our context, is more striking is the presence of Hitler, who here is captured not only studying 'some plans', but also with the help of strips of paper, each representing several thousands of SA members actually designing the performance. Such a photograph would have been unimaginable in the context of communist displays. Here the designer was an anonymous collective bureaucratic institution, which remained hidden, the masses were 'spontaneous', and the leadership motionless. In the need to show 'the people' as the sovereign, the communist gymnastics resembles the Negara State, described by Clifford Geertz, where the state serves the pomp, not the pomp, the state.[38] The leadership was not totally absent, but it was included in the totality of the representation. The president or the Politburo may be presented as the head of the collective body of the gymnasts, but never as standing above, that is to say, outside of the collective body. Its role was passive and was determined by the same ritual specialists who designed the whole performance. The Body Collective was also defined negatively. In contrast with the proclaimed 'friendship among the brotherly nations' and especially with the 'Great Friend', there was no display of foreign gymnast during the performances. Originally in the 1950s the displays by 'friendly' visiting gymnastic delegations were part of the program, as was also the practice in the pre-war and inter-war *Sokol Slets* where, in particular, the Yugoslav gymnastic performances were prominent.[39] From the 1970s, however, nothing was allowed to interfere with the Body Collective of the Czechoslovak gymnasts; foreigners with their symbols were restricted to the stands of the stadium. Even the Soviet flag, accompanied by the Soviet anthem – a necessary part of the displays in the 1950s – was removed from the ceremonial and was substituted by a 'symbolic red' one, thus avoiding playing of the Soviet anthem. The structure of the stadium was purified of all the decorations and the sculptures built there during the 1950s and 1960s, so 'nothing interferes with the powerful impact of the display of the human body'.[40]

In contrast with Kantorowicz' *The King's Two Bodies*, both bodies of the gymnast were immortal. As collective constructs, they were not threatened by the finality of the physical human existence and offered stability of political representation that the physical body of the king could not offer. Immortality of the communist gymnast was of a peculiar sort; it was the immortality of a dead body. The price which the discourse of communist gymnastics had to pay for the immortality of these bodily constructs was that the very individual body of the gymnast was eliminated.

In the late 1980s, the masses in Central and Eastern Europe ceased to be 'precisely docile and legible'. With the emergence of a new type of crowd in central squares, disorganized and discontented, the mass gymnastic display lost its symbolical power. The body symbolism of choreographed displays of the sovereign, yet disciplined, 'people' was displaced by the body symbolism of the spontaneous crowd, who, by much simpler means, took over the role of representing society. Mass protest demonstrations, with corporeal choreography of their own, had, in essence, the same agenda: to represent 'the people'. They present a variation of the same topic of the 'mighty we/us'. In fact, in Czech dissident movements, the demonstrations caused a serious dispute between those building up 'alternative *polis*' and those, who were in favor of demonstrations as a means of challenging the regime on its own grounds. The latter group proved to be the stronger, the core slogan of the Prague demonstrations was 'už jsme tady', that is simply: 'here, we are'. No doubt the mass protest demonstrations were more convincing than the mass gymnastic performances. Even the leadership eventually believed that a tiny (a hundredth, at best) section of the population occupying bodily central squares eventually represented 'the people'. While the central squares were full, the central stadiums started on the road to oblivion and decay. They proved to be too rigid a structure for political demonstrations and too big to host any profit-oriented events, the only exception being the central stadium in Warsaw, which was transformed into a huge and rather shady bazaar.

10

Agitation, Organization, Mobilization. The League for Polish-Soviet Friendship in Stalinist Poland

Jan C. Behrends

In the summer of 1944, the Red Army crossed the Curzon Line into territory which the USSR considered Polish.[1] On 22 July, the Polish Committee of National Liberation (PKWN) issued the Lublin manifesto, the first statement of communist rule in post-war Poland.[2] The manifesto proclaimed the need for Slavic unity against the German enemy, and called for a 'historic turnaround' in relations between Poland and her eastern neighbors. Centuries of conflict and struggle were to make way for a future of co-operation, brotherhood, and friendship. Behind the rhetoric of the Lublin manifesto lay the fundamental problem of Polish communism, namely, the historically strained relationship between Poland and Russia, her imperial neighbor. In order to overcome distrust and hatred, Polish-Soviet friendship was invented. In Stalinist Poland, propaganda which stressed friendship with the Soviet Union gained a prominent place in representations of power.[3]

Overcoming History: Polish-Russian Relations as Background for Sovietization

In inter-war Poland, the Polish Communist Party had been at the margins of political life. The party was widely regarded as an agent of Soviet Russia; it was declared illegal and, as a result, had little political influence. In 1938, Stalin dissolved the Polish Communist Party, and many of its members fell victim to the Great Terror.[4] Polish communism thus ceased to exist. When Hitler and Stalin partitioned Poland in the autumn of 1939, her eastern territories became subject to instant sovietization, which was especially harsh towards ethnic Poles.[5] Thousands of Poles were deported to Siberia, and the 1940 massacre of Polish officers in Katyń by the People's Commissariat for Internal Affairs (NKVD) became a symbol for the anti-Polish policies of Stalin's regime.[6] In 1941, after the German attack, Poland and the USSR inevitably became allies, albeit uneasy ones. Thus, Stalin and G. Dimitrov decided to give Polish communism a second chance. By a Soviet initiative, the Polish Workers Party (PPR) was founded in 1942. Stalin instructed Polish communists to talk less about ideology and the Soviet Union, and more about the Polish nation, in order to gain the trust of the Polish people.[7] But the events of 1939 and the subsequent sovietization of eastern Poland — not to mention the betrayal of the Warsaw rising by the advancing Soviet Red Army in 1944 — eclipsed attempts to establish a Polish-Russian *entente*. Grievances between the two countries, and between Polish and Russian communists, ran deep. Opposition to Russia, which was seen as a backward giant and source of oppression, was deeply embedded in the Polish national identity. Catholic Poles despised Bolshevik atheism and the anti-Semitic stereotype of 'Jewish communism' (*żydokomuna*) was widespread.[8]

In August 1943, the Polish communist-in-exile Alfred Lampe reflected on the difficulties facing his party. Lampe asked himself, 'What kind of Poland would not be anti-Soviet?' Looking back into the inter-war period, Lampe's answer was pessimistic:

> With the exception of the communists, all traditional Polish political movements are anti-Soviet: the Piłsudski-party, the National Democrats, and the Socialists. ... An orientation towards the Soviet Union, as it exists in Czechoslovakia, never existed and cannot exist in any political party. The historical development of Poland took a different path and political traditions differ widely between these countries.[9]

Lampe referred to a history of confrontation which dated back to the times of the partitions of Poland in the late 18th century.[10] If communist rule was to gain legitimacy and public trust, far more than just the events of the Second World War stood in its way. After 123 years of partitions, Poland had regained its statehood as a result of the parallel collapse of the Russian and German empires. Poland consolidated her eastern border in the war that had followed the 1920 invasion by Lenin's Bolshevik Russia.[11] The existence of the modern Polish state had thus been achieved through a series of struggles against Russia. In 1944, Polish communists had to convince a hostile public that history would not repeat itself. In order to overcome historically-grounded public distrust, Polish communists applied Soviet methods of persuasion — namely, agitation, organization, and mobilization.

Preaching Pan-Slavism: The Foundation of the TPPR

In 1944, the political power of the PPR was borrowed from its Soviet patrons. Stalin and Beria closely monitored the situation in Poland, and the NKVD co-ordinated military actions against anti-communist resistance.[12] In order to stabilize their own rule, Polish communists faced great challenges. The PPR had to transform itself into a mass-party, and it had to build up a loyal state bureaucracy. As a Communist Party, it also had to construct the two main pillars of authoritarian rule – the security apparatus and the propaganda-state. It was the task of the propaganda-state, to legitimize communist rule and to help overcome the deep-rooted distrust of the USSR, which dominated the collective Polish memory and political culture.

In the autumn of 1944, while the Soviet advance against Nazi Germany was stalled on the Vistula, Lublin Poland became the laboratory of the propaganda-state *in statu nascendi*. There were already early indications of sovietization. On 27 August, hardly a month after the arrival of Soviet troops, and at a time when Polish insurgents were battling against the *Wehrmacht* amidst the ruins of Warsaw, the new regime unveiled a monument on Lublin's central square, *Plac Litewski*.[13] This monument symbolized the brotherhood of Slavic peoples and, in particular, the friendship between Poland and the USSR. It was further supposed to express the gratitude of the citizens of Lublin to the Soviet army. This monument was the first public symbol, which marked the birth of the new regime, and erected after the liberation of Lublin. Its hasty unveiling underlined the obvious urgency that the new rulers felt was required to reshape Polish public space. The new government, however, did not restrict its propaganda to the erecting of monuments: throughout the weeks that followed the unveiling of the statue of friendship, the PPR's propaganda apparatus initiated a wave of events which manifested support for Polish-Soviet friendship.[14] On the anniversary of the October Revolution, communist propaganda in Lublin reached a peak. In the presence of Nikolai Bulganin, a high ranking official from Moscow, the Soviet holiday was celebrated in Lublin's theater. A telegram was sent to Stalin congratulating the Soviet Union on its 'achievements'; it praised the 'brotherhood in arms' of Soviet and Polish forces, and spoke of the 'friendship of the Slavic peoples'.[15]

On 22 November 1944, the *Towarzystwo Przyjaźni Polsko-Radzieckiej* (TPPR), the League of Polish-Soviet Friendship, was established in Lublin. Although it was later claimed that Polish citizens had initiated the founding of this organization, archival evidence points towards the Soviets as the masterminds behind the TPPR.[16] From the moment of its establishment, the Friendship League was materially and ideologically supervised and supported by the Soviet agency for propaganda abroad, the USSR Society for Cultural Relationships with Abroad (VOKS), in Moscow. The Polish news agency, *Polpress*, reported that, at the first meeting of the TPPR, Professor Józef Wasowski was elected league president. In its first statute, the TPPR claimed to facilitate 'harmonious co-operation' between Poland and the USSR,[17] and it called upon scientists, writers, artists, and army officers to join. The TPPR was clearly an instrument of the propaganda-state, which was used to seek out 'fellow travelers' in the process of sovietization. Its first goal was to foster support among the intelligentsia.

When the Red Army finally liberated Warsaw in January 1945, the TPPR moved to the Polish capital. Although the city had almost been leveled in the wake of the Warsaw uprising, the TPPR was given a prominent location on the *Aleja Marszałka Stalina*, (formerly *Aleje Ujazdowskie*), one of the main arteries of Warsaw. The Polish Government further supported the TPPR with a starting capital of 300,000 Złoty. In addition to these benefits, the Red Army and the Soviet Embassy also helped the Friendship League. At this early stage, the TPPR was actually part of a stage-managed civil society, a front organization whose moves were orchestrated by the emerging party-state. In the public sphere, however, the TPPR was portrayed as an independent organization; officially, it was registered as a voluntary club of Polish citizens who acted upon their own convictions. Its public appearance as an independent actor was supposed to give the message of friendship with the Soviet Union additional legitimacy. In this initial phase of its establishment, the supposed distance between the TPPR and the ruling PPR was strongly emphasized. In January 1946, however, the TPPR began moving closer to Polish politics. Henryk Świątkowski, a member of the Socialist Party (PPS) and Minister of Justice, was named as its new president. By this time, the actual propaganda work of the TPPR was being carried out by professional functionaries who remained in the background, well out of the public eye;[18] officially, the TPPR was just another public association.

TPPR propaganda reproduced the nationalist rhetoric that was characteristic of post-war Polish communism.[19] Its close alliance with the Soviet Union was legitimized along *völkisch* lines.[20] A document from 1945 stated that the TPPR was founded to celebrate the victory of 'brotherly Slavic nations', which, under the leadership of the Soviet Union, had thrown off the yoke of German oppression. Through the 'brotherhood-in-arms' of Soviet and Polish soldiers and the 'spilled blood of the peoples of the Great Soviet Union and Poland' an independent Polish state had been resurrected. In this historic moment, the TPPR wanted to fight for the 'greatest possible realization of the idea of democracy' in both countries and to ensure the 'peaceful co-existence of all democratic nations, especially the closer unity of the Slavic peoples'.[21] The rhetoric of the TPPR was nationalist, laden with *völkisch* metaphors, but lacked open reference to socialist ideology. The very term 'communism' was avoided. The radical nationalism which dominated Polish propaganda in 1945 was a mixture of Stalin's revived pan-Slavism and Roman Dmowski's nationalist rhetoric.[22] Re-inventing Polish nationalism meant adopting ideas from the 19th century while, at the same time, sovietizing its discourses and restructuring its narratives along Stalinist lines.

For the Polish public, pan-Slavism was not an easy ideology to embrace.[23] In the 19th century, pan-Slavism was perceived as an idea which legitimized Russian dominance in Poland, and, as such, it enjoyed little popularity among Polish intellectuals. A century later, in TPPR publications, pan-Slavism was still the order of the day. Authors such as Wiktor Kornatowski and Henryk Batowski argued for the historic necessity of a Slavic alliance. They constructed an analogy between the defeat of the Teutonic Knights in the battle of Tannenberg, in 1410, and the outcome of the Second World War. In their view, Tannenberg and Stalino — the first battle fought by Polish communist forces alongside the Red Army — proved that Poland and Russia could be strong if they stood together against the 'Teutonic' threat.[24] The TPPR Secretary, Jan Karol Wende, and the TPPR President, Henryk Świątkowski, argued along similar lines.[25] Beyond the TPPR, the Polish party-state initiated Slavic Committees in major Polish cities. In 1946, the government passed yet another resolution designed to disseminate further the idea of Poland's ethnic brotherhood with Russia. They, however, stressed the fact that the new Slavic movement was not connected to the 19th century notion of pan-Slavism and the Russian empire:

> The Polish nation has understood that the contemporary Slavic movement is a new one, a natural expression of our national instincts, the instincts of survival and self-defense.[26]

The aim of pan-Slavic propaganda was to create a sense of ethnic proximity, a feeling of close 'blood-ties' between the two nations. However, post-war pan-Slavism could not conceal from people the realities of post-war Poland.

Despite all of these propaganda efforts, during the course of 1945, communist rule was plagued by crises. Many Poles regarded the PPR as mere agents of Moscow — in a popular saying, the acronym 'PPR' was translated as *Płatne Pachołki Rosji* or 'paid servants of Russia'. The Red Army's mistreatment of Polish civilians, the terror of the NKVD, and the large reparations exacted by the USSR in the western territories along the

Oder and Neisse rivers caused widespread anger and resentment.[27] In eastern Poland, there was pervasive talk of a 'new occupation', accompanied by the persistent fear that Poland was about to be annexed by the USSR.[28] Local authorities in Cracow reported on the increasingly negative attitudes of the Polish population toward 'the Russians'.[29] In April 1945, the PPR's *éminence grise*, Jakub Berman, admitted during a meeting of the Central Committee, convened to discuss its failures, that, 'Our propaganda is weak'.[30]

The Road to Mobilization: Building a Mass-Organization

The PPR's main crisis was a crisis of legitimacy. In a plenary session held in May 1945, the General Secretary, Władysław Gomułka, admitted that the party was facing a public relations *débâcle*.[31] He was quick to blame the public attitude towards 'the Russians' for the diminishing popularity of his government. Gomułka pointed to the historic burden which communist rule had to carry:

> Many see in Russia just a continuation of the old Russia and the heritage of that old Russia— namely, war and centuries of oppression. This undermines the consciousness of our nation. To overcome these attitudes will take a long time.

Gomułka blamed Marshall Piłsudski's inter-war regime for further strengthening anti-Russian sentiment. But he also mentioned the problems caused by Soviet policy. The new borders had led to a 'deepening of mistrust'. The General Secretary acknowledged the fact that ordinary Poles had come to the conclusion that 'Russia has robbed Poland of a considerable amount of territory. This impression has … far-reaching significance'. The violence of the Red Army and the NKVD against Polish civilians, however, were addressed only in euphemistic terms. He spoke of 'mistakes' that had influenced public opinion, and claimed that the majority of the [Polish] working class was still behind the party. Nevertheless, he conceded that 'agitation by reactionaries over the sovietization of Poland has shaken the Polish soul. … The enthusiastic, positive attitudes toward the Red Army have evaporated'.[32]

Other party leaders joined Gomułka in his critical assessment. Aleksander Zawadzki reported strong anti-Soviet undercurrents reigning in Silesia, and Edward Ochab complained about the lack of discipline in the Red Army. Ochab demanded that future propaganda should strongly stress Polish sovereignty. Zenon Kliszko, head of the department of party cadres stated that there were widespread rumors in the country of mass arrests by the NKVD and deportations to Siberia; and Helena Kozłowska of the propaganda department conceded that pro-Soviet propaganda had been too 'stereotypical'.[33] In a world where one could speak only in positive terms about the USSR — where problems had become taboo — gaining public trust was difficult to accomplish.

On 1 January 1946, the daily *Wolność* declared 1946 to be the 'year of friendship' which would bring in an 'important harvest' in Polish-Soviet relations.[34] The year began with an unprecedented step. The General Secretary of the PPR wrote a letter of complaint in which he criticized the conduct of the Red Army:

> The attitude of the Red Army towards the Polish population is often hostile ... its behavior includes violence, theft, pillaging and murder of the Polish population [all of which make] co-operation in the regained territories difficult.

In the 'name of Polish-Soviet friendship', Gomułka demanded that concrete measures be taken by the Red Army, which included an end to the billeting of Soviet soldiers in private homes and a strict policy against the Soviets fraternizing with the remaining German minority. Additionally, Gomułka demanded an end to the excessive consumption of alcohol, and insisted on harsh punishment for rape or the theft of Polish property.[35] By speaking out in these terms, Gomułka had broken an established taboo: Stalin strongly disapproved of any such criticism of Soviet troops.[36]

On 3 May 1946, anti-Soviet sentiment in Poland was confirmed. On this traditional Polish holiday, celebrating the 1791 constitution of the *Rzeczpospolita*, religious processions in Cracow and other Polish towns turned into anti-Soviet rallies.[37] The communist regime was challenged in the public sphere. The opposition voiced its protest against official friendship with the USSR. Polish citizens protested against communist propaganda and declared their opposition to the revised eastern borders of their country. Demonstrators across the country questioned the legitimacy of the Soviet annexation of eastern Poland. In the end, the police force and the security apparatus had to be called in to disperse the demonstrations. In the aftermath of 3 May, Jakub Berman declared it the 'ironclad right' of the Party, not to leave the public arena to 'the reactionaries'.[38] One month later, as a counter-measure, the Polish party-state staged a grand show of Polish-Soviet friendship. The government strengthened its grip on the public sphere, and, in subsequent years, the celebration of many traditional Polish holidays became illegal. Soviet holidays began to structure the calendar of Polish festivities.

In 1946, at the beginning of June, the first all-Polish congress of the TPPR assembled in Warsaw. The entire event became a massive show of support for Polish-Soviet friendship. Two thousand five hundred delegates arrived from all corners of the country – many in traditional costumes. The auditorium where the assembly met was decorated with Polish and Soviet banners; this display was intended to confirm that the whole nation stood behind the friendship with Soviet Russia.[39] The TPPR President, Henryk Świątkowski, greeted members of the Polish government, the Soviet embassy, the Red Army, and the Polish army among the congress delegates. During the event, Polish and Soviet representatives praised the friendship between their nations. Again, the Second World War and pan-Slavism were the dominant topics of the speeches. In contrast to the TPPR propaganda of 1945, the Germans were no longer the only enemy. The 1946 congress declared former British Prime Minister Winston Churchill to be an 'enemy of peace', because he had warned the world about the prospects of Soviet domination in Europe. The orchestrated response at the TPPR congress to Churchill's speech in Fulton, Missouri, underscored the fact that the Soviet camp was ready to take its place on the Cold War front in the ensuing war-of-words propaganda battle. The high point of the congress was the unanimous passing of a resolution which called for further dissemination of the 'truth' about the Soviet Union. In a telegram to Stalin, TPPR congress delegates promised to tear down the 'wall of lies' erected between 1918 and 1939, which still separated the Polish and the Soviet peoples.[40] With the TPPR congress, the first major manifestation of friendship with the Soviet Union had taken place, although only handpicked delegates had actually participated in this show of sovietization. From this point on, however, the drive of the propaganda-state was toward mass mobilization. This called for the transformation of the TPPR into a mass organization.

Towards Cultural Revolution: Friendship Campaigns and the Making of Polish Stalinism

In order to penetrate the population deeply, the TPPR began to establish circles (*koło*) of its members.[41] Its propaganda increasingly portrayed the Soviet Union as the ideal form of modernity, a modern society without contradictions, and an example which Poland should follow.[42] In May 1947, the PPR's Central Committee discussed the transformation of the TPPR.[43] The decision to turn it into a mass organization to support the state's propaganda drive coincided with a radicalization of Soviet policy toward Central Europe, marked by the formation of the Cominform. The

Soviet ideology tsar, Andrei Zhdanov, declared that 'two camps' existed in the post-war world. One could only be for or against the Soviet Union. *Tertium non datur*. The Polish population was taught that being against friendship with the Soviet Union meant questioning the *raison d'être* of post-war Poland. A Polish patriot *had* to be a friend of the USSR. Criticism of the Soviet Union was effectively criminalized.

In October 1947, the PPR leadership urged its members to support the friendship propaganda in every conceivable way. The Party claimed that most Poles already supported close ties with the USSR, and that only 'the most backward circles' were still sabotaging the great cause. The British Broadcasting Company (BBC) and the Voice of America (VOA), the main organs of Anglo-American propaganda, were becoming increasingly popular; these broadcasters were thus identified as real menaces. TPPR membership had grown to 250,000 members organized in more than 1,000 circles. Notwithstanding this, the party-state admitted that, while the friendship propaganda effectively impacted upon the Polish intelligentsia and the working class, women, youth, and many rural inhabitants were still beyond its reach.[44] The party-state's goal was to mount an all-out display of friendship in celebration of the 30th anniversary of the Bolshevik October Revolution. It was the first Soviet holiday which was to be celebrated with a campaign designed to mobilize the whole Polish nation.

Celebrations of the 'Great October' were to increase Polish awareness of the cultural and economic 'achievements' of the USSR and its utmost importance for 'independence, sovereignty over regained territories, and the industrial development of Poland'. Furthermore, the 'leading role' of the USSR in the 'struggle for peace' was to be emphasized.[45] During the friendship campaigns, officials, writers, and artists from the USSR visited Poland. They toured the country and gave lectures on Soviet 'achievements'. On Soviet holidays, the Polish people were asked to lay flowers on the graves of Soviet soldiers.[46] The month of friendship was the first attempt to carry the official discourse about the Soviet Union — the USSR *qua* 'first socialist country' — to every corner of Poland. In 1947, on the anniversary of the October Revolution, the TPPR President, Świątkowski, presented a new version of Polish history. According to his address on this occasion, it was the Bolshevik Revolution that brought Poland's independence and freedom after 'centuries of oppression'.[47] Świątkowski linked Polish nationalist rhetoric, which had dominated communist propaganda, with the Polish-Soviet friendship discourse. This attempt to fuse nationalism and sovietization became characteristic of High Stalinist Poland. When the sovietization of Polish public life reached its apex in the early 1950s, it was claimed that this was in the Polish national interest. The *völkisch* ideology of pan-Slavism, however, was replaced by the discourse of emulating the 'achievements of the USSR'. The inherent contradictions of nationalism and sovietization could not be discussed, and this was certainly one of the weaknesses of communist propaganda. Thus, the discourse of Polish nationalism was forced to merge with the ideals of Soviet modernity.[48]

The expansion of the TPPR into a Soviet-style mass organization signaled a change in the pace of sovietization. In the autumn of 1947, the TPPR already had 500,000 members, and the Soviet Union cult had become a part of everyday Polish life.[49] This development – the growing significance of strong emotional ties to the Soviet Union – affected Polish politics. In the spring of 1948, when General Secretary Władysław Gomułka defended his tactical distance from the USSR, his days as party leader were numbered. It was simply inconceivable that someone who expressed even the slightest doubt as to whether Poland ought to be transformed according to the Soviet model could lead the party. Gomułka opposed the collectivization of agriculture and thus came into open conflict with a rival group, headed by Bolesław Bierut, in the party leadership. In August 1948, Gomułka was attacked by his comrades for expressing 'distrust in the policies of the Soviet Union'.[50] Two weeks later, during a Central Committee session, Gomułka was overthrown. Again, he was charged with 'distrust of the USSR'. Another national communist, Mieczysław Moczar, managed to save his own career by telling his comrades what they wanted to hear:

> The Soviet Union is not just an ally. This is a piece of propaganda for our people. For us, comrades, the Soviet Union is our fatherland [*nasza Ojczyzna*], and I cannot say where her borders may be: today they are west of Berlin, tomorrow they may be in Gibraltar.[51]

By the summer of 1948, the Polish Communist Party had become part of the tightly woven discursive net of Stalinism. Now, it had to bring cultural revolution to the country.

Only a few weeks after Gomułka had been sacked, another TPPR congress was celebrated in Wrocław in newly acquired western Silesia.[52] This assembly marked the beginning of the next friendship campaign. Nationalist propaganda about the 'Polishness' of the western territories was merged with the rhetoric of sovietization. In yet another way, however, the Wrocław congress marked a watershed: it saw the introduction of the Soviet leader cult. After 1945, Stalin's *persona* had only played a limited role within Poland.[53] The Soviet leader was lauded for organizing the victory during the war and liberating Poland from German occupation. In 1948, however, a new Stalin appeared on the Polish stage. The Soviet dictator was now praised as 'Poland's best friend' and credited with always having supported the Polish cause. During the 1948 TPPR congress, the establishment of the leader cult manifested itself in the introduction of Soviet ritual. Time and again, statements made at the congress were interrupted by exclamations in praise of Stalin, and speeches ended with canonical hails to the leader.

In the autumn of 1949, Poland was shaken by yet another example of the imposed friendship. On 6 November 1949, Soviet Marshall Konstanty Rokossowski, an officer of Polish origin, was appointed Polish Minister of Defense. At the height of the Cold War, the Soviet leadership chose to install Rokossokwski as their watchdog in Warsaw. The event bore enormous significance because, traditionally, the army was one of the most respected and revered symbols of the Polish nation.

Within days of Rokossowski's taking office, the propaganda apparatus had produced three short biographies of the new incumbent.[54] The picture painted in these hagiographic texts was one of a model soldier and war hero. Additionally, Rokossowski's career was to exemplify the reborn Polish nation. His life story related how he, as a Pole, had not taken part in the Second Polish Republic, but had decided, instead, to fight for the Soviet cause immediately following the October Revolution. In the USSR, Rokossowski was educated to become the ideal communist officer.[55] Now, the propaganda claimed that the lost son had returned to his fatherland in order to lead it to a better future:

> With pride, happiness and trust, the Polish nation entrusts its Armed Forces into the hands of Konstanty Rokossowski, a great Pole, warm-hearted patriot and revolutionary, and a faithful son of Warsaw's working class.[56]

Polish and Soviet reports reveal, however, that popular reaction was quite mixed.[57] The conversion of the Soviet Marshall to Polish Defense minister sparked the fear that Poland could soon become the '17th Republic' of the USSR. Nevertheless, Rokossowski became an icon of the invented friendship. At the Third TPPR Congress in November 1949, the delegates adopted a rhythmic 'Sta-lin — Bie-rut' and 'Sta-lin — Bier-ut — Ro-ko-ssow-ski' as their enthusiastic chants.[58] The leader cult had been introduced in the form of a Polish-Soviet *troika*.

The Rokossowski campaign was hardly over when the lavish celebrations for Stalin's 70th birthday began in December 1949.[59] In the course of these celebrations, the TPPR was to become the 'organization for the whole nation'. Knowledge and adoration of the Soviet Union had to be brought to 'all working people'.[60] The self-proclaimed goal of the

TPPR was to establish member circles in every community and village of Poland.[61] Stalin's official biography was the focal point of the birthday campaign; the stations of Stalin's life were supposed to become household knowledge.[62] The party-state now openly pursued the objective of complete mobilization in the name of sovietization. At the same time, the friendship discourse was becoming progressively more emotionalized: 'friendship' with the Soviet Union was punctuated by declarations of 'love' for Stalin. *Przyjaźń*, the TPPR's official periodical, proclaimed:

> This is a friendship which is in our blood, under our skin, in our hearts and souls...[63]

The Stalinized Polish nation was discursively tied to the USSR and its leader. It was the TPPR's task to create a dynamic through which the 'enthusiasm' of friendship campaigns would spread throughout the society. The ultimate vision was to create a nation of non-party-Bolsheviks. According to the representations by the Polish mass media, this goal had been achieved.

The TPPR in Polish Stalinism, 1949-1955

Like the PPR, the TPPR was affected by the post-war purge which swept through the party-states of communist Europe.[64] Increasingly, those who had a less than perfect past came under pressure. Emigrants from Moscow replaced Polish communists in important positions. Changes in the TPPR's leadership confirmed that this organization was not immune to these pressures of the party-state. In November 1949, the TPPR's General Secretary, Stanisław Wroński, lost his position because he was accused of having had close ties with the anti-communist underground during the war. Mieczysław Tureniec, who took over from Wroński, only held the post until November 1950, when he, too, was sacked for allegedly insulting the Soviet ambassador.[65] The presidency of the TPPR was also affected. In July 1950, Edward Ochab, the head of *Agitprop*, took over the TPPR presidential office from Henryk Świątkowski, who was charged with contributing to anti-Soviet publications prior to 1939. In Stalinist Poland, the record of the TPPR president as a devoted and life-long 'friend of the Soviet Union' had to be spotless. Thus, Ochab, a veteran communist was an obvious choice. On 4 July 1950, the Politburo confirmed Ochab's appointment, thus putting the mass organization under the direct control of one of the regime's most powerful men.[66]

During the years of Polish Stalinism, the TPPR's tasks stagnated. Whereas official membership rose into the millions, it became unclear just what being a TPPR member actually meant. The organization was supposed to grow, to gather ever more recruits, and it was supposed to organize the annual campaigns around Soviet holidays, especially the 'month of friendship'. No other campaigns during Polish Stalinism reached equivalent proportions. The internal instructions proclaimed that the aim was to use this period 'to teach the masses of Polish society about the peaceful policies of the USSR and its struggle for the freedom of the peoples, against imperialist aggression'.[67] Dozens of Soviet guests toured the country, and a Polish delegation was chosen to travel to Moscow for the October celebrations — one of the highest honors the party-state could bestow on model citizens such as 'shock workers' or activists. While there was little unsupervised contact between Polish and Soviet citizens, a tight net of symbolic communication was woven. Factories, ministries, or collective farms sent telegrams to Soviet sister institutions, in which they committed themselves to work better and praised the friendship between their two peoples. The TPPR circles or town meetings sent telegrams to Stalin and to other Soviet leaders. The modern mass-media reproduced and disseminated the cult around the USSR in newsreels, magazines and papers, on posters and banners. Between 1948 and 1955, these rituals of friendship changed little.

An important aspect of the annual friendship campaign involved the sovietization of public space. The TPPR held its members responsible for decorating their workplaces on Soviet holidays and during the month of friendship. Small exhibitions about Soviet 'achievements' were staged and large banners were displayed. Portraits of Soviet leaders, above all, the iconic representations of Stalin, loomed large. During the month of friendship, the 'achievements' of self-sovietization were also extolled. Lectures were given on the construction of the giant Nowa Huta steel works, and excursions to Warsaw were organized, where the on-going construction of the 'Palace of Culture' — a Stalinesque skyscraper officially portrayed as a 'gift' of the Soviet people — could be observed.[68] These projects were supposed to prove that Poland was no longer backward, and that it had successfully taken the Soviet path to modernity. However, while the mass-media and propaganda hailed the achievements, reality at the construction sites of socialism was often grim. Contrary to the official picture, the Stalinist path to modernity produced its own array of social problems.[69]

The spread of the Russian language was another aim of the campaigns. People were asked to sign up for language classes or to subscribe to Soviet publications such as *Pravda*.[70] Many institutions and enterprises organized the sale of Soviet literature. On shop floors and construction sites, Soviet methods of rationalization and mobilization such as 'shock' or 'Stakhanovite' work were introduced. Hardly a sphere of life was left that was not subject to attempted sovietization. Soviet superiority was claimed in politics, work, culture, and leisure. In Stalinist Poland, becoming a modern person meant sovietizing oneself. In the long run, this propaganda was to leave the Polish population humiliated. Implicitly, the friendship propaganda devalued many things that were Polish. Combined with a lack of sovereignty, feelings of anger and frustration were the most likely results of the sovietization of the public sphere and the imposition of Soviet values. For Poles who traditionally considered themselves as more western, cultured, and advanced than Russians, the TPPR campaigns could be perceived as a continuous insult to national pride. In 1954, the Polish writer Maria Dąbrowska discussed the mood of her fellow citizens in her diaries:

> At this very moment, the Polish nation is a single cup full of bitterness. There are things the nation cannot bear and will not bear, unless, its neck were to be broken, which, of course, for Russia would require no great effort.[71]

For the TPPR and its functionaries, there was little choice. The inherent contradictions of the propaganda — *e.g.*, between its nationalist rhetoric and the policies of sovietization — could not be discussed. Central elements such as the Stalin-cult or the discourse on 'Soviet achievements' could not be questioned. Additionally, there was mounting pressure from Moscow to transform Poland in accordance with the Soviet model. In a way, Stalinist propaganda in Poland suffered from the ideological consequences of communism. The more the regime sovietized itself, the less it considered how these policies could be 'sold' in the political marketplace. In exile and during the first years of their rule – under Gomułka – there had been some discussion in the PPR about the consequences of the strained relationship with the USSR. After the fall of Gomułka, however, and with the onset of utopian sovietization, such discussions were no longer tolerated. Hence, the party and its propaganda apparatus were further isolated from the population. The leaders themselves had long ago accepted the absolute superiority of everything Soviet and now they expected their subjects to follow suit.

The Prolonged Decline of the Great Friendship: 1956-1989

The rituals associated with Poland's great friendship with the Soviet Union survived Stalin for almost three years. The end of Polish Stalinism began in Moscow. When Nikita Khrushchev condemned his predecessor in his 'Secret Speech' at the 20th Party Congress in February 1956, he spoke to a Soviet audience.[72] The gravest consequences of de-Stalinization, however, were to be seen in Poland and Hungary. In order to gain new legitimacy, the Polish regime decided to jump on the rolling train of de-Stalinization.[73] In March, the party organized meetings in which the secret speech was discussed. Following the Soviet model, Stalin's 'cult of personality' was condemned. Subsequent discussions, however, proved impossible to contain: the Party had opened Pandora's Box, and the façade of friendship crumbled.

Within weeks, the Polish leadership encountered the Tocqueville effect: the most dangerous moment for an authoritarian government is when it starts to reform itself. In the spring of 1956, even Party members were not willing to limit their criticism to the excesses of Stalin's rule. The Polish intelligentsia, which had partly participated in the sovietization of the country, started to press for more radical liberalization. The entire issue of Polish-Soviet relations—past and present—became the subject of heated debate. What the Party had intended as a campaign to discredit Stalin and his rule, threatened to loosen its grip on Polish society. Taboos which had dominated public discourse in Poland for the last decade tumbled one by one. Utopian discourses about the USSR faded, and discussion on long-suppressed subjects such as the Hitler-Stalin-Pact of 1939, the eastern border, the deportations to Siberia, and the Katyń massacre re-surfaced. By the summer of 1956, the TPPR was paralyzed. One of its functionaries proclaimed: 'The 20th Congress has ended our flight through the spheres of mythology and brought us back down to earth.'[74] It was certainly a hard landing.

In June of 1956, the industrial workers of Poznań went on strike. What began as a labor conflict turned within hours into a full-scale uprising against communist rule.[75] It took several days and the introduction of the armed forces to defeat the insurgents. A close look at the events in Poznań reveals the anti-Soviet dimension of the uprising. During the insurgency, Polish workers destroyed what they saw as the symbols of Soviet domination: red flags were replaced by Polish banners. They chanted 'down with the Bolsheviks' and 'down with communism'. During this summer, explicit anti-Soviet sentiment dominated the mood of the country. This led to the paradoxical situation in which a stern, staunch communist with anti-Soviet credentials eventually saved the regime. In October 1956, the party re-installed Władysław Gomułka as General Secretary. This was an overwhelmingly popular choice because Gomułka was perceived as always having resisted sovietization. His anti-Soviet charisma saved the Polish regime from drowning in the deluge of anti-Bolshevism, and saved

Poland from Soviet invasion. After 1956, there could be little doubt about the limited impact of the friendship campaigns on popular attitudes towards the USSR. For the regime, ten years of the most extensive propaganda had not improved things: it had made them more difficult.

Nevertheless, even under Gomułka, 'Polish-Soviet friendship' was not abandoned. For decades to come 'friendship' remained the only term officially used to describe Poland's relationship with the USSR. Although the TPPR had failed in its task to re-educate the populace and had almost completely disintegrated in the course of 1956, the Polish regime did not dissolve it. Instead, the friendship league survived all Polish upheavals until it was finally privatized, like everything else, in the early 1990s.

Polish-Soviet Friendship: Glances from afar

The invention of Polish-Soviet friendship is an illustration of the ambition and the ultimate failure of cultural sovietization. The sovietization of existing institutions such as the state, workplaces, or the universities represented only one dimension of the complex process of forced transfer and transformation. Additionally, institutions, discourses, and practices from the Soviet Union were imported. In the case of Polish-Soviet friendship, we can observe the construction of the propaganda-state. The friendship league, the TPPR, initially had the limited task of attracting members from the Polish élite. Throughout the years of Polish Stalinism, between 1948 and 1955, the TPPR's goal was to mobilize the masses for the cause of sovietization. In the decades that preceded the collapse of communism, it became an icon of the invented friendship and a reminder of the Stalinist years, of the times when Polish-Soviet friendship was portrayed as the ultimate path to communist modernity.

The building of the propaganda state can be divided into two distinct phases. Between 1944 and 1947, the Soviet leadership and the Polish communists adopted a policy of pragmatic sovietization. They targeted only limited groups, such as the intelligentsia and the working class. What they tried to achieve in these early years was an understanding of the necessity for Polish-Soviet friendship. The communists used the discourses of nationalism and pan-Slavism to get this point across. From the autumn of 1947 onwards, the pace of sovietization accelerated. Poland was now to be modeled after a discursively constructed, ideal Soviet Union — a utopian place which existed only in Bolshevik propaganda. In this phase of utopian sovietization, cultural revolution became the goal. The political culture of Poland was to be transformed along the lines of the Soviet model. At the heart of the propaganda was the assumption that the Soviets were superior in all spheres of life: during Stalinism, modernizing Poland meant sovietizing the country. Despite contradictory messages, Polish nationalism and Soviet discourses fused and created the contradictory culture of Polish Stalinism. The task of the TPPR was to mobilize the entire nation for the cause of sovietization. This proved to be too arduous a task. By the beginning of the 1950s, both the campaign and the mobilization had become ritualized and stagnant, but nothing actually changed until 1956 when the whole system imploded. The TPPR's value was its symbolic significance. Although it was dysfunctional as a mass organization, it represented the close ties of communist Poland to the USSR. The idea that Poland needed to be modernized persisted after 1956. The new model to follow, however, was much closer to western ideals. While the Communist Party would not loosen its grip on power, it tried to create a socialist consumer society. Terror and cultural revolution made way for repression and consumption.

What did the TPPR's propaganda for Polish-Soviet friendship achieve? The TPPR was successful when it acted as the mouthpiece for the regime. Between 1944 and 1949, the TPPR's propaganda can be read as a barometer of sovietization. Throughout communist rule in Poland, the TPPR reflected the official status of Polish-Soviet relations. Through TPPR publications, the public learned how a loyal citizen ought to speak about, or relate to, the USSR. By joining the TPPR, citizens could make a symbolic declaration of loyalty to the communist state without actually joining the Communist Party. Carrying a TPPR card could thus be a way of obtaining a secure job or of concealing a compromising past. This was true in the 1950s, and it remained so until the 1970s.

The actual effect of the friendship propaganda, however, may be described as limited. Neither in the short run, during the years of Polish Stalinism, nor in the long run did it have the expected impact. The failure to change public attitudes, collective memory, or national consciousness had several causes. First of all, the communists underestimated the force of collective memory. Despite all efforts, the problematical history of Polish-Russian relations did not disappear. Secondly, the best propaganda could not distract Poles from the harsh realities of their existence. Despite all of the talk about brotherhood, friendship and independence, the Red Army behaved like an occupation force and was thus perceived as such. Finally, Stalinist propaganda did not sufficiently adjust to Polish conditions. It tried to cater to Polish nationalism but did so in a clumsy way. The notion of pan-Slavism served as an uncomfortable reminder of the Russian empire; later substitutes for this concept, in attempts to create or strengthen the supposed bonds, such as the introduction of the cult of Stalin, did little to improve the USSR's standing in Poland. Like pan-Slavism, these later forms of propaganda represented the unity of the Soviet empire to Poles; they were not useful as tools for successful re-education.

Despite the immense powers of the communist propaganda-state, its impact on Polish attitudes towards Russia was marginal. Distrust towards Poland's eastern neighbor, deeply rooted historical myth and lasting experience superseded the attempts to force change upon the Polish people. In the *longue durée,* Stalinist campaigning, so it appears, was unable to redirect the undercurrents of modern Polish nationalism which dated back to the long 19th century. Polish Russophobia was an adversary that could only be overcome in the mode of representation, modern mass-media and mass mobilization permitted grandiose displays of friendship. As a mass organization, the TPPR played a crucial role in the stage management of this show. At the level of attitudes, mentality, and memory, however, the impact of the propaganda matched neither the efforts nor the expectations of the party-state. Today, Polish-Soviet friendship is a post-communist *lieu de mémoire*. Popular attitudes towards Russia and diplomatic relations between Poland and its eastern neighbor remain strained, and Polish society has wholeheartedly embraced a western path in the modernization of the economy.

Part V

Sovietization and Religion

11

Mechanisms of State Control over Religious Denominations in Romania in the Late 1940s and Early 1950s

Anca Maria Şincan

The relationship of the communist states in Eastern, South Eastern and Central Europe to the various religious denominations was, in most cases, shaped by the Soviet pattern. In Romania, the relationship between the state and institutionalized religion functioned on a similar mechanism to the one employed in the Soviet Union. However, employing this mechanism had distinct results, as in the Soviet case. Recent studies that focus on this relationship have come up with several hypotheses to explain the means by which religious denominations succeeded – with few exceptions, such as the Greek Catholic Church – in safeguarding the functioning of religious life, and in maintaining the *status quo* with regard to the number of believers and places of worship during the communist period.

One interpretation put forward by Romanian historians explains the survival of religious denominations in relation to the weakness of the Communist Party, the lack of a charismatic communist élite that could promote the banning of religious institutions, and even the lack of a functional atheist dogma that could replace the religious worldview. The traditionalism and conservatism of the population, which remained predominantly rural, and centered its universe upon the Church, prevented the new regime from enforcing its authority on the religious denominations.[1] Another explanation, advanced by Olivier Gillet, refers to the Orthodox Church tradition of caesaro-papism. The compromise that allowed the survival of the Orthodox Church was inherent to this tradition and was extended by the state to encompass all religious denominations. The policy of compromise with the religious denominations included infiltration of their ranks and their use as *port-parole* for the communist state.[2] This interpretation is highly contested since it is based upon a cultural model and leaves economic and social explanations aside.[3]

The historiography of the subject focused on the imitation of the Soviet model of state-church relations in the communist states of Eastern, South Eastern and Central Europe. The relationship with the religious denominations under the Soviet regime in the 1940s was fundamentally different from that which existed in the inter-war period. Researchers who favored an explanation *imitatio dei* noticed the adoption of the Soviet model of compromise and the instrumental use of the Church for solving national problems, and the use of the Church as *port-parole* of the state's policies, which was functional in the 1940s. It was this model of 'compromise' that was adopted by the 'people's democracies' – with certain variations.[4]

The process of defining the relationship between the Soviet state and the Church underwent several phases over more than 20 years, from the October Revolution of 1917 to the Second World War. In this period, the fundamentalist views that 'opposed [...] any form of co-operation between church and state' were inter-twined with the more pragmatic ideas that were in favor of the 'utilization of the churches' influence at home and abroad'.[5] Researchers who designed a chronology of behavioral patterns of the Russian Orthodox Church in its relationship to the Soviet regime described the various stages of development. The initial period was characterized by overt hostility, whereas the second period was marked by the withdrawal of the Church from political activities. The final period was characterized by the 'commitment to unconditional loyalty to the state and positive support of its policies' from 1941 onwards, shaped by the exigencies of the war against Nazi Germany.

In the Romanian case, the model of compromise functioned throughout the communist period. The *status-quo* was achieved in a short period of time, between 1946 and 1952/53. This was not a one-way compromise, however. Historiography usually divides the religious denominations into collaborationist and oppositionist groups, depending on the individual stance regarding the agreement. Nevertheless, this was also a compromise on the part of the communist state, which permitted the functioning of institutions that contested the communist (atheist) doctrine, and, in certain cases, also managed to influence the public sphere by advocating their own model and discourse. A paradoxical hybrid relationship was created, in which the state allowed the functioning of religious denominations and their access to the public sphere in order to use them for its own purposes. Thus, religion, which was supposed to have been confined to the private sphere, remained present in the public sphere in its institutionalized form.[6] This paradox is noticeable in the relationship at the level of state control over religious denominations. Government documents express concern that the religious 'liberties' which the state granted would be extended by the denominations, that opposition to the regime would be harbored within the religious institutions, and that the authority of the state might be undermined.[7]

In adopting the Soviet model of church-state relations, the Romanian communist regime encountered difficulties, because of the lack of the kind of pre-conditions that had existed in the Soviet Union. While, in the Soviet Union, the complete subordination of the denominations to the state preceded their co-optation, in the Romanian case, the imposition of a model of collaboration with the regime occurred at the time when the state attempted to exert its control over the religious denominations. Thus, the state, which was not adequately prepared to take control of society, was compelled to make compromises. The mechanisms of control that were developed, and the conditions of this compromise, meant that they occasionally backfired.

The relationship between the state and the religious denominations in Romania initially entailed three types of solution to the problem of religion and the religious denominations. The same behavioral patterns and types of solutions appeared in the Soviet Union in the process of forming the relationship between the state and the Church. Although, in theory, religion, as part of the superstructure, was supposed to wither away with the advent of socialism, in practice, the Soviet regime never had the 'patience' to test this Marxist hypothesis, and adopted extreme measures to advance the development of atheist society. The duality of the policies against religious denominations, in the phase of legal regulation,[8] as well as in the phase of the forceful imposition of hierarchical allegiances, was characteristic to the Romanian case.

One document dealing with the problem of monastic life in the Orthodox and Roman Catholic churches exemplifies the pragmatism of the state and enhances our understanding of the situation. This document, drafted between late 1947 and early 1948, reveals the activity of the state and summarized its possibilities in confronting the spread of religion in its institutional form. According to the specialist who drew up this policy guideline, the state had three options in dealing with religion: noninterventionism, the complete banning of religious activities and religious denominations, and interventionism. The first option meant the toleration of the Church's activity 'hoping that in time and with the country's transition to socialism which would bring about a raising of the cultural level of the masses, its [the Church's] power will weaken'.[9] The specialist never considered this option seriously. He compared this option to 'the peaceful integration of the bourgeoisie into socialism', and claimed that the state would encounter 'surprises' if it left the denominations uncontrolled before socialism had succeed in disposing of them naturally. Nevertheless, the presences of such an option in a policy document formulated by a state representative reveals the complexity of the situation in which the new regime found itself. The government always considered the Soviet example, but remained realist at the same time, and realized that the transition to 'socialism' would not come naturally and the state would have to intervene.

The second option was also discarded. It was described in the document as the ideal solution, although the word 'ideal' was eventually cut from the draft.[10] The implementation of the proposal, however, would be a strategic mistake and one that the new regime could not afford to make. The banning of the religious denominations would have meant opening Pandora's Box, and extending the scope of the 'fight' from the denominations themselves to the mass of the population.[11] The document envisaged the Church as a distinct entity, separated from the mass of believers. The double meaning of 'Church' should be noted here. It was described as a hierarchical and centralized institution, and, at the same time, as a diffuse organization which could reach the most remote corners of the country.

> Since religious organizations live and are powerful because of the adherence of the masses, any radical measures directed against them would raise the dissatisfaction of the masses, dissatisfaction that would be used to trouble the waters, for enemy actions of a political type.[12]

This measure would have had more negative effects for the state than the granting of permission for the denominations to function.

What was left was the last solution: the limitation of the power of religion by intervening in religious activity at three different levels: organizational, economic and ideological. This solution meant infiltrating the religious denominations, *i.e.*, suffocating them with rules and regulations. The denominations should be subordinated to the state from an economic point of view, and any opposition should be brutally suppressed. This could be accomplished at a central level, leaving 'the masses' aside. Through legislative measures, the state gradually limited the number of priests and pastors.[13] Nevertheless, the state would provide the salaries for a limited number of personnel, forcing the denominations, which were no longer self-sufficient, to go to extreme lengths to preserve the number of clerics. Two-thirds of the priest in the Orthodox Church received a salary from the state in 1948. Instead of reducing the number of priests, the church negotiated with the regime to keep the priests and fund them from the parish budget. This system was preserved throughout the communist period.[14] All these measures were protected by regulations that the denominations were obliged to respect. Intervention in the administration of the religious denominations could become coercive whenever the state felt threatened by their activity – as was the case with the Greek Catholics, the monastic life of the Roman Catholic and Orthodox churches, or the proselytizing activities of neo-Protestant denominations.[15] In most cases, however, this relationship was based upon constant compromises from both sides.

The transition period until the consolidation of the communist dictatorship was marked by an ambiguous attitude towards the religious denominations, especially towards the Orthodox Church and the neo-Protestant denominations.[16] The communist leadership encouraged the frequent appearance of communist officials in public together with church hierarchs and clerics.[17] The regime collaborated with the clergy in order to justify the arrest of 'reactionary priests'. Nevertheless, the hierarchs, known to the party as supporters of the former regime, were retained in their positions. Their presence in the church administration created the illusion of normality and continuity. Archbishop Nicolae Bălan, Metropolitan of Transylvania, for example, was one of the voices of 'opposition' in the Orthodox Church. He nevertheless kept his post. Moreover, he was also entrusted with the administration of the 'Greek Catholic unification', which could be regarded as a reward for toning down his criticism of the regime.

In the construction of a new relationship with the religious denominations, the fact that the administrators of the state were selected from specialists of the former regime meant the first setback in the attempt to enforce complete control over religious denominations. The religious denominations benefited – with few exceptions (the neo-Protestant churches) – from the lack of trained communist functionaries. The state also took advantage of the situation, since it received first-hand information from insiders from the denominations, concerning power struggles, the mechanism of administration and hierarchical deficiencies. The state utilized the functionaries that it inherited from the Ministry for Religious Denominations. After they had been replaced by communist cadres, the state infiltrated the new functionaries into the denominations, where – with a few exceptions – they continued to work for the state. Valerian Zaharia, for example, who had worked in the department as a consultant until 1952, was later appointed as Bishop of Oradea, after the former bishop was forced to resign. Zaharia was the 'party mole' in the Holy Synod of the Romanian Orthodox Church. The theologian Liviu Stan, who worked for the Department of Religious Denominations, also retained his position in the Theology Institute. Patriarch Iustin Moisescu worked for the Department as an inspector. This was not specific to the Orthodox Church alone. Greek Catholics, Roman Catholics and Protestants also worked for the Department and were later rewarded with important positions in their respective churches.

The Ministry for Religious Denominations, later the Department for Religious Denomination of the Ministry for Internal Affairs, supervised the activity of the religious denominations. It functioned according to the same precepts as the Council for Religious Affairs in the Soviet Union. Its duties included mediating between the state and the religious denominations, and monitoring the denominations' activity. Supervision, the collection of data and monitoring, was also assisted by the Secret Services. The administrative center in the ministry centralized financial activities, imposed rules and regulations, monitored their application, and, in general, supervised the state's policy towards religion and the religious institutions. The policy of the department was shaped by second-rank specialists who were connected with the religious institutions (theology professors and clergy). They reported at the request of the Council of Ministers or at the Ministry's initiative, and they responded to problems raised at regional and local level, the second and third layer of the structure of the Ministry (the Empowered for Religious Denominations – [*Împuternicit de culte*]). Their implementation depended on the urgency of the matter.[18] At local and regional levels, the ministry had functionaries who were dependent on the center and whose latitude was also restricted by local authorities.

For the departments that oversaw the activity of the churches the recruitment of personnel was a serious matter because of the sensitive affairs that they had to administer. It seems that specialists who could be blackmailed because of their past were preferred by the Ministry for Religious Denominations.[19] However, their status as specialists gave them no decision-making power.[20]

In 1952, there were substantial changes in the party hierarchy, when the 'national' faction defeated the 'Muscovites'. This triggered a change in the administration, and a change in policy towards the religious denominations. The archives of the ministry demonstrate that the functionaries, at least at local and regional level, were replaced by trained communist cadres, as of 1952.[21] In many cases, the new cadres transformed the state administration of religious denominations into personal authority. The shift from 'administering authority' to 'owning authority' derived from various factors. On the one hand, the central system failed to supervise and control the large spectrum of problems caused by the denominations. The most telling example was the shift from a centralized system of control imposed upon the Roman Catholic Church towards the local control of local churches.

> The Ministry for Religious Denominations was wrong when it forbade the local Empowered to deal with the Catholic problem, leaving it exclusively to the central administration of the Ministry for Religious Denominations (...) Since the Ministry for Religious Denominations gave the Empowered the task of keeping close contact with the priests and persuading them to join the local committee for peace, we have noted the weakening of their reticence and even a change in their attitude in some cases. (...) Also, because of involving the local Empowered, the Ministry for Religious Denominations now has the possibility of knowing the serious problems better, such as what means are used by the enemies of the state, what is their system of support in various parishes and so on.[22]

During this shift, the regional functionaries of the Ministry for Religious Denominations (the Empowered) received more leverage in dealing with the religious denominations. They were granted more authority, and could question central directives if they failed to suit local conditions.

There were certain shortcomings in the relationship between the state and the religious denominations before 1952. In this period, the denominations established a system of negotiation with governmental representatives. Once directives had been issued, the denominations tried to bypass them, and attempted to create a mechanism of negotiation with the regime, in order to enlarge their liberties and weaken the control of the state. In this context, one can observe the decentralization of the system and an increase in the authority of the representatives of the state. For example, at local level, state functionaries lost their connections with the church: they were usually uneducated men with allegiance to the state. They were asked to respect regional directives and no negotiations were to be undertaken with local priests or believers.

A regional and local Empowered (*Împuternicitul*) of the Ministry for Religious Denomination, especially in areas where numerous religious denominations were active (as in parts of Transylvania and Moldova, for example), had an extremely demanding work schedule. The connections that this person established between the Ministry for Religious Denominations (state) and the religious denominations were based upon his constant involvement in the life of the particular denomination. In order to be able to verify, supervise, control and impose the measures and rules established by the central government, in order to be able to inform the Ministry about the level of suspicious activities or the support for the new regime, and in order to be able to give advice on solving the problems that arose or to solve the conflicts, the Empowered had to be familiar with the organization, structure, administration and hierarchy of the respective religious denomination. He had to infiltrate the local or regional leadership of the denomination with persons, whom he trusted, or he had to use those who were already in position, he had to exploit any potential tensions among the priests, between priests and the hierarchy, between the believers and the priests, and the tensions between denominations. Close attention had to be paid to the ways with which to reward loyalty and punish disloyalty. To fulfill these duties the Empowered was obliged (from the early 1950s) to participate in the activities of the religious denominations: inter-confessional conferences, conferences in support of the struggle for peace, conferences of deans, conferences of priests, administrative gatherings, religious services, and meeting of the hierarchs. The Empowered had to be familiar with problems ranging from the number of priests, whose salary was paid by the state, to the number and title of books that were held in parish libraries.

The Empowered provided the connection between the representatives of the religious denominations and the local authorities. The religious denominations were sometimes used by the state as a medium of communication with the local authorities, and the representatives of the religious denominations could not but be aware of this. The important role which the parish priest could play in various social and cultural activities organized by the state (collectivization, support for the new constitution, the fight for peace, the integration of believers into the regime) were not the only issues that needed explanations. The role that the Empowered played at local level had to be explained as well. Since they responded directly to the center, they remained outside the control of the local administration, which left the relationship between these two institutions fairly problematical.[23] More problematical was the close connection of the Empowered with the Romanian Secret Police (*Securitate*), because, in most of the cases, they worked as informers for the Secret Police.

These were the privileges and obligations of the Empowered before 1952. After that, together with a change in the type of personnel administering the relationship between the state and the religious denominations, their rights were extended. They were authorized to offer advice. They were no longer data collectors, but could also intervene together with the local authorities on occasion. The Empowered had to respect the rules and requirements of the Ministry for Religious Denominations, but, in most cases, they had the right to intervene. The Ministry for Religious Denominations elaborated its policies on the basis of the information and the suggestions that it received from the Empowered. There were problems that were left entirely to their authority, and the center even intervened in favor of extending the competence of the Empowered. The Empowered knew who collaborated, and where they had to exert pressure to enforce collaboration. They also intervened in the entourage of the hierarchs in order to find out their intentions, and used intimidation or rewards to achieve their goals.

In most cases, the intervention of the Empowered in the life of the church was visible and this led to friction between them and the clergy. For example, they were present at the elections of parish councils 'to make the lists, according to the instructions received from the center, (...) and in collaboration with the local authorities, but as many reports suggest, in doing so they allowed some hierarchs to disregard the elections seeing them as a problem of the Ministry for Religious Denominations, as in the Buzău or Cluj eparchies'.[24] The replacement of the leadership of the religious denominations with supporters of the new regime was achieved by exerting influence and pressure at a middle level, and this was accomplished on the basis of reports sent by the local and regional Empowered. The Ministry for Religious Denominations had to approve the nomination of the candidates and the election of any person in the hierarchical chain of the denominations, such as the deans.

This period was supposed to mark the end of the transition in the process of imposing state control over the religious denominations. The increase of the authority of functionaries, the success in infiltrating the hierarchy of the religious denominations – at least at a lower level – with persons loyal to the regime, the legislative stability with regard to denominations and the routinization and adoption of the rules and regulations by the denominations were all meant to strengthen their subjugation to the state. Nevertheless, this period, until 1953, provided the religious denominations with sufficient time to discover opportunities to bargain, and to establish a place of their own in the state administration. Thus, the denominations developed a system of checks and balances in their relationship with the state.

The religious denominations developed various methods of protecting themselves from the interference of the state. Firstly, it was an imperative that they knew about the activity of the Empowered.[25] Although most often the Ministry of Religious Denominations sent its requests to the hierarchy, there were a number of cases when the local Empowered decided to talk with the second in command in the leadership of the denomination, people who were linked to the ministry, especially in cases concerning reactionary hierarchs who were reticent in implementing governmental decisions. Doubling the hierarchy and inserting a second level with loyal functionaries was a common practice in the period. In the documents of the Ministry for Religious Denominations, one can observe two types of reactions. One is that of the collaborator, who complained about injustice and the hardships that he had to endure inside the organization (jokes, threats or being impeded of access to the activities of the hierarchical body or from exercising his duties).[26] The other one was the reaction of the Empowered, who reported such obstructions. These records show that the church body had its own way of protecting itself and had its own means of isolating the collaborators within its hierarchy. It thus remains unsure what the Empowered were interested in, what their arguments were, whom they interacted with and what actions were taken. In many cases, such information proved useful for the authorities. One Empowered admitted that their plans had failed because of the involvement of the hierarchy. Priests were moved from their parishes to avoid contact with the Empowered. Priests, who, as a punishment, had their state-salaries stopped, were paid instead from the budget of the Bishopric or with money collected from other parishes until the Empowered discovered the situation and alerted the center.

The documents very rarely offer the possibility of following the correspondences of the Empowered and the clergy and especially with the hierarchy. Examples of when the hierarchy of religious denominations openly expressed discontent with the Empowered to the Ministry for Religious Denominations are scarce. One can assume, however, that there was a code of conduct that was respected in the majority of the cases. Nonetheless, at the lower rungs of the hierarchical ladder, the Empowered had more authority over the clergy. There were records of brutal intervention on the part of the Empowered.

The state adopted a more aggressive stance towards the neo-Protestant denominations,[27] a more deferential attitude towards the Orthodox Church and the traditional Protestants, and one of reciprocal control towards the Roman Catholics. There are various explanations for this variation. The lack of a centralized leadership and a fully recognized hierarchical center of the neo-Protestant churches left them less protected against the authoritarian behavior of the local Empowered than the Orthodox Church, which, in many cases, had direct links to the Ministry through the hierarch, who could thus denounce such behavior. The activity of neo-Protestant denomination was focused on proselytizing. Their number was insignificant in the late 1940s, which was one of the reasons why they were authorized to sustain their activities under the new communist regime. However, they became one of the most serious problems that the system had to confront while dealing with religious denominations. They were escaping state control because the lack of a center made it difficult for the local and regional Empowered to monitor their activity.[28] The control and supervision of these denominations was advanced by the collaboration of religious denominations that lost believers due to the proselytizing activities of the neo-Protestant churches. Such an attitude was characteristic of the Orthodox and old Protestant clergy, who were often targeted by the missionary activities of neo-Protestant pastors. Nevertheless, before 1952, more than half of the Empowered[29] in the country were working with the neo-Protestant or Roman Catholic denominations.

The Roman Catholic Church received special treatment. It was subject to close supervision and control by governmental representatives. The supervision was stricter due to the special position of the denomination. All clerics and believers were considered to be potential collaborators with the regime, or seen as reactionaries. The methods were, therefore, subtler. The authority of the Empowered was also evident in this case, however, since the authorities responded to the activities of the clergy based upon their reports. The response could mean imprisonment, the stopping of a state salary or, on the other hand, the lifting of house arrest, or the payment of special endowments.

The strict supervision of the Roman Catholic Church was implemented due to the failure of the unification of the Greek Catholics with the Romanian Orthodox church. It was closely connected with the attempts of the Roman Catholic clergy to win over the Greek Catholic believers who refused to 'return' to the 'mother church', namely, the Romanian Orthodox church. The Empowered were required to closely monitor areas where the population had belonged to the former Greek Catholic church. The believers were followed in order to observe which church they regularly attended, whether they participated in religious services or whether they had contacts with former Greek Catholic or Roman Catholic priests. They had to produce statistics about the age, social status, job and attitude towards the new regime. They described reality differently from the way official discourse and the Romanian Orthodox church usually portrayed it. This information encouraged the Ministry for Religious Denominations to design policies, to use an entire apparatus of state employees to implement them, and to offer leverage to the Romanian Orthodox church in its struggle to integrate the Greek Catholics.

Wider latitude was offered to traditional Protestant churches in order to counter-balance the influence of the Roman Catholic Church in Hungarian communities in Transylvania. In the same way, the Romanian Orthodox church was provided with more space to counter the proselytizing activity of neo-Protestant denominations. Two quasi-failures of the state – *i.e.*, the failure of the unification of the Greek Catholic church with the Romanian Orthodox church,[30] and the authorization of the four neo-Protestant denominations – made the state more open to compromises with traditional churches and more cautious in using force as a solution to the various problems that surfaced in the uneasy relationship of the communist state with the institutionalized religions.

On the one hand, the mechanism involved the adoption of the rules and regulations by the religious denominations and the development of a system of checks and balances; a way of negotiating their way out of various restrictions imposed by the state administration. On the other, there was a weak state, in a constant legitimacy crisis, which tried to turn the actors against each other and sought to control them at the same time. Although the use of force was restricted by the unpredictable impact of such measures on the population, the state's authority was almost total. The religious denominations developed a mechanism of collaborating with the state in order to secure their own institutional survival. The state's compromising attitude could be explained by various shortcomings, such as the lack of strong communist élite, and the lack of communist cadres who were prepared to control the religious denominations. This, in turn, made it impossible to displace institutionalized religion. The shortcomings in this mechanism were linked to the specific political context and were manifested either in the use of force by the state (as in 1958 with the regulation of monastic life in the Orthodox Church) or in the liberalization of the relationship. As a result, various denominations could maintain their position in the public sphere, and their support for the state triggered a more relaxed environment for church life. The co-existence of the communist state and institutionalized religion, and the special compromises that contributed to the emergence of functional relationship, make the Romanian case unique.

12

Cuius Regio Eius Religio. The Relationship of Communist Authorities with the Catholic Church in Slovenia and Yugoslavia after 1945

Mateja Režek

The policies towards religion adopted by the people's democracies after 1945 reflected, in large measure, the practices adopted in the Soviet Union, although these policies were shaped in accordance with local circumstances, and the relative strength of the local communist parties and religious communities. Religion and the communist ideology were incompatible, and, consequently, the elimination of the church from public life was one of the basic goals of all communist regimes. In Yugoslavia and the other East European countries, the constitutions and special laws that followed the Soviet model separated the church from both the state and schools, while, at the same time, guaranteeing freedom of conscience and religion – which was, however, often interpreted arbitrarily. There were restrictions throughout on both the religious press and education, church property was nationalized, religious holidays were abolished and clergymen prosecuted – often by means of political trials. These measures were accompanied by aggressive atheistic propaganda, which relied heavily on both the education system and the press for its dissemination. Militant atheism was an integral part of communist ideology, whose main weapon of implementation was administrative measures.

In establishing the relations between the state and the church, the people's democracies followed the Soviet example; however, as it presented an approach to the Orthodox Church, they were forced to modify the Soviet model in their relationship with the Catholic Church due to an external factor – the Vatican. Some of the East European communist regimes, including Yugoslavia, initially made efforts to separate the local Catholic

Church from the Vatican, based on undefined ideas of a national church, but all attempts to form such national churches failed, with the exception of Albania. Subsequently, the communist authorities began to establish priests' associations, which opened their doors to 'progressive' members of the clergy. Through these associations, the authorities tried both to control and to divide the clergy with the intention of separating the internally disintegrated domestic church from the Vatican.

In Yugoslavia, the strength of the Communist Party and its deep roots within the wartime partisan movement conferred upon the new regime a degree of political militancy as well as impatience with the claims of the diverse religious communities, especially with those of the Catholic Church. The Yugoslav policy was also shaped by domestic and external priorities, the tasks of state and nation building, which sought to minimize external impact, including that of the Vatican, on domestic development. Following the rift between Yugoslavia and the Soviet Union in 1948, the policy of the Yugoslav government towards the Catholic Church was, if anything, even more radical. The escalation of this policy, *i.e.*, the attempt to make a final reckoning with the Catholic Church at the beginning of the 1950s, coincided with the Soviet-Yugoslav break merely by chance, as the Yugoslav authorities had planned this campaign earlier. The Yugoslav policy towards religion reflected the internal dynamics of the regime's ideological priorities, and was a part of the Yugoslav government's attempt to find its own particular form of socialism – a sort of authentic 'sovietization', in which Yugoslav communists were increasingly critical of both Stalinism and the Soviet model of socialism. However, this was not the case in the sphere of state-church relations. The attitude of the state towards the Catholic church was, at the same time, the only important political area that was completely avoided during the general wave of political 'liberalization' that swept through Yugoslavia following the dispute with the Soviet Union. Thus, one may say that the relations between the state and the church, as established by the Yugoslav authorities, were still based on the Soviet attitude even after 1948, and were, in effect, nothing but a modification of the Soviet role-model, adapted to local circumstances.

In 1945, the Catholic Church in Yugoslavia found itself in completely new circumstances. In political opposition, an opposition with which the communist authorities intended to settle accounts. In the perspective of the new government and its ideology, religion was an unscientific illusion that reflected the alienation of man. The church was considered to be a class enemy that could potentially threaten the revolutionary authorities. Relations between the state and the Catholic Church had also been damaged by the behavior of the church authorities during the war, because of their refusal to side with the resistance against the German and Italian occupiers. Moreover, a part of the clergy had collaborated with the occupying forces against the partisan resistance movement. In July 1945, the clergy of the Ljubljana diocese issued a declaration of loyalty[1] in which they deplored all wartime violence and condemned the collaboration. The government, however, ignored the statement. The intransigence of the Catholic Church led by Pope Pius XII regarding socialism and communism only enraged the revolutionary authorities further. In addition, the Yugoslav leadership believed that the Vatican acted according to Italian interests, and that the local clergy, loyal first and foremost to the Vatican, were not sufficiently patriotic. Finally, it was concerned with the prospect that the various religions in the multinational state might sow hatred among the Yugoslav nations.

The Catholic Church, in turn, with its strong rearguard of Yugoslav Catholics, was the sole well-organized opposition to the new communist power. It also drew strength from its close relationship with the Vatican. Consequently, the Yugoslav government tried to weaken these ties by asserting its power over the local church leadership. On 2 June 1945, when Josip Broz Tito, the President of Yugoslavia, met the highest Croatian church dignitaries, he remarked that the new authorities were well aware of the influence of religion and were, therefore, prepared to come to an agreement with the local Catholic church, but the church would have to be less reliant on the Vatican, *i.e.*, to be more inclined toward Yugoslav national interests. He said that, as a Croat – he supposedly said 'as a Croat and a Catholic',[2] although the word Catholic was omitted in all printed versions – he was displeased with the wartime behavior of the Catholic clergy. He again emphasized the government's awareness of the importance of religious influence and their readiness to come to an agreement with the church, but also stated that:

> ...Our church should be more national so that it can better adapt itself to our nation. ... I must openly say that I do not take the right to condemn Rome, your supreme authority. ... But I must say that I look critically on such things, because I see this authority as being increasingly inclined toward Italy rather than our own nation. I would want the Catholic Church in Croatia ... to be more independent. I want this fundamental question to be resolved, since all other questions are secondary to it and can be resolved easily.[3]

At that time, Tito's words were understood as an effort to create a national church, something that the leadership of the Catholic Church strongly opposed. Important decisions could only be taken by the Holy

See, and the church authorities insisted that any decision about the relationship between the church and the Yugoslav state should be reached by concordat. The church leadership, especially in Croatia, had no desire to negotiate directly with the government, and similarly the Yugoslav authorities rejected the Vatican as a potential negotiating partner for resolving internal political matters. Moreover, anti-communist forces in the Catholic Church were not prepared to accept orders from communist authorities, and the communist authorities, in turn, would tolerate no opposition. Thus, relations between the Yugoslav state and the Catholic Church remained tense at least until the mid-1950s.

The central figure in the Catholic Church in Yugoslavia during this period was the Archbishop of Zagreb, Aloysius Stepinac. As the President of the Yugoslav Bishops' Conference, he was the principal author of the pastoral letter addressed to the state authorities and the believers on 20 September 1945. The Yugoslav bishops accused the government of pursuing anti-church policies and condemned their materialist philosophy, along with other ideologies and social systems that were not based upon Christianity. They demanded the return of all the church assets that had been seized, freedom for the Catholic press, Catholic religious education and upbringing, as well as Catholic charitable works and all other activities of the church. They also drew attention to the violence against the clergy, pointing out that, according to their records, 243 priests, 19 seminarians, 3 friars and 4 nuns had been killed in Yugoslavia since 1941; 169 priests had been jailed and 89 were missing.[4] The bishops issued the pastoral letter during the pre-election period and signed it on the same day that the united opposition announced its boycott of the election. As a result, the government authorities treated it as a direct attack or, as President Tito put it in an interview in the French communist daily *L'Humanité*, as 'a kind of official declaration of war'.[5] Boris Kidrič, the President of the Slovenian government, was also indignant about the contents of the pastoral letter. In an interview to *Slovenski poročevalec*, he rejected the charges of persecution against the Catholic Church and described the pastoral letter as 'much ado about nothing'.[6]

The communist government tried to break the political and economic power of the church and confine its activities to religious services. The economic foundations of the church were weakened by agrarian reform and nationalization, and its ideological and political power by restrictions placed upon the religious press and education, including the closure of church schools. The first post-war Yugoslav constitution enacted the separation of church and state, and the separation of schools from the church. The Catholic Church was only allowed to retain schools for the training of the clergy. The religious instruction of children and young people in elementary and high schools was allowed only within certain limits. Formal and informal education was as important to the state as it was to the church, and this only exacerbated the conflict between church and state authorities.

The party leaders were constantly taken up with the question of how to draw the masses, especially the young, away from the church and religion, and their response was usually through recourse to various administrative measures. Catechism classes were restricted in schools and prohibited in churches. Children could only attend such classes with the written permission of their parents. In Slovenia, priests needed written permission from government authorities in order to teach catechism classes. Despite administrative barriers, according to the records of the Slovenian school authorities from 1949, 67% of the pupils attended catechism classes at elementary schools that offered religious instruction more or less regularly, which means 47% of all Slovenian pupils.[7] This led the communist leadership to think of other ways of limiting the attendance of religious services and catechism classes. With this goal in mind, the Politburo of the Central Committee of the Communist Party of Slovenia decided in June 1950 that it would be necessary 'to radicalize the question of religious education and not to perceive it only as part of the campaign' and 'to provide youth with entertainment, especially at times when there are church services and to provide field trips as an alternative to pilgrimages'.[8]

The administrative interventions into the educational activities of the church, something which was undertaken as a fundamental mission, continued to increase the tension between church and state authorities. At the end of 1950, the Slovenian Bishops Anton Vovk and Maksimilijan Držečnik sent letters to the president of the Slovenian government in which they noted the impediments to religious education in schools and churches, and called upon the government to desist as this amounted to a gross violation of the constitution and of the international conventions which guarantee the freedom of conscience and religion.[9]

The idea of forbidding the teaching of the catechism in schools gained momentum at the end of 1951, and such activities were prohibited in Slovenian schools in the spring of 1952.[10] In January 1952, Boris Kraigher, the Minister of the Interior for Slovenia, defended the decision by stating that attendance of catechism classes in Slovenian schools had been increasing. He claimed that the teaching of the catechism in Slovenian schools was allowed for easier control and supervision, although 'this practice has not entirely solved the problem'. Thus, it was decided that the time had come for catechism classes in schools to be abolished, which 'of course, does not mean and must not mean that we will reduce our supervision of catechism classes and the manner in which they are taught'.[11] But that does not mean laxer control over the teaching of the catechism, but that it instead meant 'the achievement of a more principled attitude in our struggle to eliminate the church both as a political and as a kind of cultural factor' and gradually 'to rid ourselves of the legacy that gives Slovenia an explicitly religious and Catholic character'.[12] At the same time, the party considered introducing classes in social and moral education. These were added to the curriculum of elementary and high schools as well as to grammar schools and teacher training colleges in the autumn of 1952.

In the spring of 1952, *Slovenski poročevalec,* the leading Slovenian daily, began to publish articles about the abolition of catechism classes in schools. In March 1952, the author of an article about a conference of Slovenian schoolteachers reported:

> There can be no true teacher of socialist youth who teaches one thing and does another. Therefore, there is no place for teachers who teach according to the official curriculum, while at the same time indulging in the mysticism and obscurantism that is taught by the church.[13]

A month later, *Slovenski poročevalec* published a report about four teachers who had been dismissed because of their attendance at religious services. The author of the report unhesitatingly approved the action:

> Yes, that is precisely why they were dismissed, because they were cooked and baked in the church!
>
> The author continued:
>
> Let's not beat about the bush! Our constitution guarantees each citizen religious freedom and nobody is persecuted because they go to church. But that does mean that we are obliged to look to religious people even in socialist schools, to let them teach one thing while propagating another with their own personal example, and thus contradicting themselves and sowing doubts and uncertainty in our youth. No, we are most certainly not obliged to endure such hypocrisy in our socialist schools and we have already endured it for too long, because school is not a bakery or a cobbler's workshop where it wouldn't make much difference if the craftsmen and their assistants adhered to this or that world view.[14]

In April 1952, Ivan Regent, a member of the Slovenian Politburo, also contributed an article to *Slovenski poročevalec* about what a socialist school should be like. He wrote that 'our schools must be laic, which is to say strictly scientific. ... There is no place for religion where science resides'.[15] When the journalists seemed to be going too far in expressing their anti-church and anti-religious fervor, Boris Ziherl, the head of Slovenian *agit-prop*, advised the newspaper to be more cautious in its rhetoric, since:

> ...we did not dismiss any teacher because he or she was religious, but because anti-socialist actions stems from being religious. It is because they considered our schools to exist in opposition to their own principles and were therefore in a struggle against socialist education and socialist development in general. That is why we attacked them, not because of their religion, but because their religiousness was united with anti-socialist actions and so we legitimately acted against those actions.[16]

Janez Janžekovič, an influential theologian and priest, also responded to the articles in *Slovenski poročevalec* by writing to the gazette of the Slovenian priests' association called *Nova pot*. He concluded that the question of the freedom of religion and conscience in Yugoslavia had been worked out in principle, but that the path to the actual implementation of this principle was a long one. He wrote that many Marxists were convinced that dialectic materialism and socialism were so intertwined that one could not be a good socialist without being also a good materialist, and that, from this, one might also conclude that religious people could not be good citizens of the socialist homeland. He also noted the contradictions in the articles in *Slovenski poročevalec*: namely, that politicians and journalists denied foreign accusations of religious persecution in Yugoslavia, while, at the same time, the articles about the dismissals confirmed it. 'A country that takes bread from someone because he or she attends a church persecutes religion, even if it is "not only" because of that.' Otherwise, Janžekovič agreed with Regent's statement that 'there is no place for religion where science resides'. He added, however, that 'nor is there any place for dialectical materialism or any other worldview' and that:

> in any worldview, there is some kind of extrapolation that makes man take a leap, and that, therefore, approaches faith. A laic school must teach science, true science, all science and its meanings – yes! But it must not teach a worldview – no!

In Janžekovič's opinion, to introduce a specific worldview into schools meant 'reviving the disreputable, defeated and condemned principle from historical development: *cuius regio et eius religio*', and, for this reason, he strongly opposed it.[17]

The Yugoslav government was preparing itself for a long-lasting ideological war with the Catholic Church. On the one hand, it allowed religious activities so as not to turn away the faithful masses; on the other, it restricted catechism classes and the training of priests, and endeavored to strengthen the atheistic upbringing of school children. When Tito received a delegation of teachers and high school professors at the end of April 1952, he made the following comment:

> We do not persecute religion and indeed we leave this matter to each individual person. But we cannot allow children, who have yet to be educated, to be educated according to the desires of those who have chosen a very different path than the one we would like to take. The state has the right and the duty to educate its children. In this regard, we will never bend to any outside pressure.[18]

Despite the political thaw that began after Yugoslavia split from the Soviet Union, the gap between the government and the Catholic Church deepened during the first years of the 1950s. In Slovenia, increased pressure from government authorities was applied, especially with the abolition of catechism classes in schools, in the exclusion of the Theological Seminary from the public school system, and in the banning of the publications of the Ljubljana and Maribor dioceses. Catholic printing houses were nationalized immediately after the war and the religious press, in general, was restricted: the Catholic press particularly suffered from frequent 'paper shortages' or the printers 'spontaneously' refused printing of Catholic newspaper. The most important religious holidays – Christmas, Easter and All Saints Day – also underwent great changes. From 1948 onwards, Easter Monday was no longer a work-free day and All Saints Day was renamed the Day of the Dead. Balancing the religious implications of Christmas, which, starting in 1953, was also no longer a work-free day, the government encouraged celebrations on New Year's Day and smoothed the arrival of the secular Grandfather Cold. The Slovenian state authorities also called Catholic intellectuals to account. At the end of January 1951, the Minister of Interior, Boris Kraigher, concluded that 'more or less, all organized reactionary positions against us are represented by the various Catholic-oriented groups among our writers and artists, and, to a great degree, also among our scientists' and that 'they hold very important positions in scientific academies, universities and a variety of institutes, especially those related to the humanities'.[19] Here, he also had the Christian socialists in mind, including those who were communist allies and those who had long before distanced themselves from the Liberation Front. Edvard Kocbek, the last Christian socialist to occupy a high position in the government, had to step down from all political functions in 1952 and withdraw from public life.

Government authorities also acted harshly against priests. The most spectacular and internationally noticed trial was that of the Archbishop of Zagreb, Aloysius Stepinac, in the autumn of 1946. The court trials of priests served two purposes: to condemn the opposition, and to show the government's anti-church position publicly and thereby to warn the Vatican. In Slovenia, judicial proceedings against the clergy culminated in 1952 when a group of priests were accused of anti-government actions or collaboration with the country's former occupiers. According to the 1955 records of the Slovenian Commission for Religious Questions, in the first ten years after the war, 319 priests were tried in Slovenia, and the majority of them were sentenced either to prison or to monetary fines, while 4 of them were sentenced to death. During the same period, administrative bodies penalized 1,033 priests.[20] In 1952 alone, 735 priests were charged for minor offences and tried before the courts, and 490 of the accused were punished.[21] Most of them were accused of 'spreading false information', of conducting catechism classes without authorization from the proper state organs, of having organized various unregistered processions, and the performance of baptisms and funerals prior to their being officially registered. The increase in the number of verdicts against priests was in complete contradiction to the general trends in Yugoslav penal policies, since, at the beginning of the 1950s, convictions for political crimes fell sharply as a result of a more liberal penal legislation.[22]

The daily press frequently reported on the trials against priests, and articles about the malice of the Catholic Church aroused a certain hostility among the public against priests. Harsh rhetorical assaults directed at the Catholic Church triggered numerous riots against priests, among which the attack against the Bishop of Ljubljana, Anton Vovk, stands out. In January 1952, a large group of people attacked the bishop at the train station in Novo mesto. One of the attackers poured gasoline on him and set him alight. The bishop survived the attack, although he was badly burned, but his attacker was only given a nominal punishment.

The government publicly censured these excesses, warning of their negative political consequences. At the plenum of the Central Committee of the Communist Party of Slovenia on 26 January 1952, Boris Kraigher warned that the attacks on priests could have undesirable consequences: namely, that they 'make it possible for the priests to affirm their role as persecuted martyrs, and, on this basis, create new foundations for their struggle against us'.[23] Edvard Kardelj, the leading Slovenian and Yugoslav communist ideologist, used the opportunity to remark that 'the enemy's power today rises, above all, from the church and the peasants' backward religiosity' which must be decisively marginalized, though not with 'administrative measures, and also not by burning bishops and similar excesses', but, instead, with strong ideas that would allow Party members to realize that 'socialist democracy is for the working class and for its socialist allies, but is not for our enemies'.[24] The top echelons of the Slovenian party did, at least, pretend to have been concerned about the attacks against both priests and sacred buildings that continued in the subsequent years. In October 1953, Vida Tomšič, an influential Slovenian politician, again emphasized that it was necessary 'to strike back strongly against such physical reprisals', since as 'Comrade Kardelj has said on many occasions, we can kill the priest but unless we kill him politically, we accomplish nothing. What must be accomplished is that he becomes a political corpse'.[25]

The government was much more tolerant towards the priests who were organized into priests' associations. Through such associations, the authorities tried to exert control over the clergy, above all, by turning them away from the leadership of the Catholic Church and the Vatican. Political leaders were convinced that, through direct negotiations, they could more easily achieve a *modus vivendi* with local priests. The priests' associations served a further political objective; according to Boris Kraigher, 'they were actually only a matter of internal disintegration of the church and its hierarchy'.[26] Membership in priests' associations conferred certain advantages, in particular rights to social security and health insurance, the right to teach catechism at schools, financial support for the renovation of churches, and, sometimes, even the release of certain priests from jail.

The first priests' association began to operate in Istria in 1948 and attempts were made to establish a similar association of Slovenian priests, too. In October 1948, the initiating committee of the Slovenian priests' association met and soon afterwards it published the first issue of its news bulletin *Bilten*. This was published by the members of the clergy who had rejected both Vatican policies and those of local church authorities, who condemned the collaboration of the priesthood with the occupation forces, and demanded the dismissal of Gregorij Rožman, the Bishop of Ljubljana, who had fled to Austria in 1945. He had been convicted *in absentia* in 1946 and had been condemned to eighteen years of forced labor. In April 1949, the Vatican responded to the articles in *Bilten* by prohibiting its publication. Soon afterwards, the initiating committee of the Slovenian priests' association dissolved itself and recommended the establishment of a new priests' association. This was established on 20 September 1949 under the name of the Cyril-Metodius Association of Catholic Priests in Slovenia

(CMD) and it also began to publish its own gazette called *Nova pot*.[27] From 1949 to 1952, 526 priests and monks joined the CMD, which represented roughly half of the Slovenian priesthood. The following year, however, membership had already begun to fall.[28] The highest church dignitary to join CMD was Mihael Toroš, the Bishop of Gorica, although he soon distanced himself from the association because of the negative opinion of both the Vatican and the Yugoslav Bishops' Conference. In December 1953, he officially resigned from the association.[29]

An association of Catholic priests was also established in Bosnia and Herzegovina, while attempts to establish such an association in Croatia encountered stiff opposition from the church leadership. An association of Croatian priests was established only in 1953, and it had just 188 members, less than a tenth of all the priests and monks in Croatia.[30] The Vatican saw the priests' associations as the specter of a new national church, which is why it so adamantly opposed them. On 26 April 1950, the Yugoslav bishops proclaimed that membership in such associations was undesirable or, in other words, *non expedit*. In August 1950, the Vatican excommunicated Anton Bajt, the President of the CMD, and Jože Lampret, the founder of the association, and issued written reprimands against several other priests, while Silvio Oddi, the papal nuncio, orally reprimanded the Bishop of Gorica, Mihael Toroš.[31] These rigorous measures triggered a period of alarm among the priests. At the end of January 1951, Anton Vovk, the Bishop of Ljubljana, wrote to Oddi, informing him that the CMD would dissolve on its own accord because, after all, 'who would dare to be the President of the association? Members say publicly that they can no longer belong to the association since its current president has been excommunicated'.[32]

The Yugoslav government saw this as Vatican interference in its internal affairs and demanded the reversal of the excommunications and the *non expedit* measures, but this proved in vain.[33] The government believed the greatest obstacle to the normalization of its relationship with the local Catholic Church lay with the Vatican, since the Pope had demanded total freedom with regard to religious upbringing, education and the Catholic press, as well as the release of Archbishop Stepinac and other imprisoned priests. In May 1951, Boris Kraigher announced that the Yugoslav authorities were prepared to release Stepinac, but only on condition that he leave the country. The Vatican rejected these terms.

> As long as the situation remains as it is, responded Kraigher, it is illusory to speak of the rebirth of Christianity, or that religion could be freely practiced alongside dialectical materialism, as long as the Vatican exists. First, we must liquidate the organization

> of the church such as it is today, and only then can we begin an open discussion of these matters. In other words, the question of freedom of religion is the question of liberating the church from the Vatican.[34]

Western public opinion also expressed dissatisfaction over Stepinac's fate. In the summer of 1951, the United States placed conditions on its military assistance to Yugoslavia, namely, the release of Stepinac. As a result, the archbishop was released from Lepoglava and confined to Krašić, the village of his birth. But despite this, the tension between Yugoslavia and the Vatican did not abate, as the Pope insisted that Stepinac be allowed to perform his duties as Archbishop of Zagreb. To exacerbate matters, the Yugoslav political leadership had become convinced that the Vatican was supporting Italian demands regarding the inclusion of the entire Free Territory of Trieste into Italy. Dissatisfaction was also expressed about the behavior of the papal nuncio Silvio Oddi, who opposed any efforts to normalize relations between the Yugoslav state and the Catholic Church and was spreading rumors abroad about the persecution of the church in Yugoslavia.

At the end of January 1952, Edvard Kardelj, the foreign minister, met with the papal nuncio Oddi, who protested against the attack on the Bishop of Ljubljana, Anton Vovk. Kardelj rejected Oddi's interpretation of the event, saying that the church alone was responsible for its persecution since it had failed to adapt to the revolution and still demanded a privileged position. In his contention, the event in Novo mesto served as a warning to the church, that it should cease taking action against government authorities because the people would not abide by it. 'What's more, we could say that the development of such matters begs the question of relations between the Vatican and Yugoslavia. If the Vatican is not prepared to support the development of normal loyalty of the clergy to the state, then what is the point of having a relationship with the Vatican at all,' wondered Kardelj, and added that 'our relations with the Vatican under such conditions only aggravate the normalization of relations between church and state' since 'Yugoslav public opinion has got the impression that the policies of the Vatican towards Yugoslavia are often not guided by the interests of the Catholic church, but rather serve the political goals of a foreign power.'[35] He also said that the government demanded nothing more of the priests than loyalty, and added that the Catholic Church was taking advantage of the tolerance of the Yugoslav government and the delicate international situation that Yugoslavia was in in order to obtain more rights than it enjoyed anywhere else in the world. On 11 May 1952 at the meeting in Zrenjanin, Tito spoke in a similar vein about relations with

Italy and the Vatican. He emphasized that every citizen was first obliged to serve the interests of his own country and people; this comment was directed at the church authorities and priests who 'see only Rome'.[36] At that time, the Yugoslav press was inundated with articles about the ill will of the Vatican. *Slovenski poročevalec* was at the forefront of the campaign, reporting day after day about the intervention of the Vatican in the Trieste crisis and in Yugoslavia's internal affairs, printing caricatures with political content and articles about the belligerent behavior of priests.

Relations between the state and the Catholic Church were stretched to the limit following the resolutions made at the Yugoslav Bishops' Conference in September 1952 in Zagreb. Before the conference, Josip Ujčić, Archbishop of Belgrade and president of the Yugoslav Bishops' Conference, requested from the Vatican, in the utmost secrecy, a statement regarding the priests' associations. The response expressed the hope that the Yugoslav bishops would know how to resist the threats posed by priests' associations.[37] With this decree of *non licet,* the bishops prohibited the priests' associations. However, the prohibition did not apply to the Slovenian priests' association, as the Slovenian bishops chose cautiously not to announce it.

The Yugoslav bishops also addressed a letter to Marshall Tito in which they asserted that there was no complete freedom of religion in Yugoslavia and that a *modus vivendi* could not be reached as long as the state encroached upon the rights of the church. They strongly opposed the establishment of the priests' associations, saying that the state was using them to undermine church discipline. They added that they would only recognize the priests' associations if their regulations were in agreement with canon law and if church authorities had full control over their activities. In conclusion, they confirmed that they respected the existing government authorities and that the Catholic Church demanded no special privileges, simply more respect for God and natural law. They demanded total freedom for religious education, the Catholic press and other religious organizations, as well as access to the financial means that would be adequate for the smooth running of church operations.[38] The Slovenian Bishops Vovk and Držečnik took notes of the Zagreb conference, but the notes, which included the Vatican's opinion about the priests' associations, were confiscated by the secret police during a search.[39] Now that the government authorities possessed evidence that the bishops stood shoulder to shoulder with the Vatican, the breaking off of diplomatic relations was only a question of time.

The government authorities were enraged by the Vatican's prohibition of the priests' associations. On 1 November 1952, Aleš Bebler, deputy foreign minister, sent papal nuncio Oddi a note protesting against the Vatican's intervention in Yugoslav internal affairs. Instead of the long-expected papal response to this letter, the Vatican elevated Archbishop Aloysius Stepinac to the position of cardinal and announced the promotion on 29 November, Yugoslavia's national holiday. In mid-December 1952, Bebler sent another memorandum to Oddi in which the Yugoslav government demanded the closure of the Belgrade nunciature and accused the Vatican of interfering in Yugoslavia's internal affairs, of elevating Stepinac to the position of cardinal, instead of responding to the previous letter of protest, of refusing to co-operate with the Yugoslav government in the normalization of mutual relations, and of trying to give Yugoslavia a bad name in the sight of international public opinion.[40] At that time, the foreign minister received a papal response to the first letter, which had been sent on 1 November 1952, but the letter was returned unopened to the papal representative and diplomatic relations were broken off.[41] In the response dated 15 December 1952, the Pope noted that the Vatican had the inalienable right to protect Catholics everywhere in the world, and, for this reason, he rejected the accusation regarding intervention in Yugoslavia's internal affairs. In addition, he listed several examples of persecution of the Catholic Church in Yugoslavia.[42]

Edvard Kardelj explained the reasons for the breaking off of diplomatic relations to the Yugoslav federal assembly. He said that the Yugoslav government had strived to normalize relations with the Catholic Church, but had not succeeded—as it had with other religious communities—because of the Vatican's intervention. In his opinion, the Vatican itself had triggered the breaking off of diplomatic relations by naming Archbishop Stepinac a cardinal and by its provocative policies towards Yugoslavia. Kardelj emphasized that the Yugoslav government did not persecute religion, claiming that 'religion is a social phenomenon that cannot be uprooted with persecution and decrees even if it were desirable to do so'. He continued by naming the Vatican as one of the main promoters of Italian irredentism, and pointed out that the positions of the Vatican and the Italian state on the question of Trieste were identical. He also mentioned the government's on-going policy towards the Catholic Church, and highlighted the constitutional principle of the separation of church and state. He added that the government did not expect the Catholic Church to become an agitator for socialism, nor did he demand the separation of the church from the Vatican, but stated that socialism in Yugoslavia was a fact to which the leadership of the Catholic Church would have to adapt.[43]

With the appointment of Stepinac, the Archbishop of Zagreb, to the position of cardinal, the conflict with the Vatican reached boiling point, and though this did not provide the reason for the breaking off of diplomatic relations, it did provide the much-expected pretext. The priests' associations that the Vatican had so decisively rejected had also played an important role. Despite the political thaw at the beginning of the 1950s, the Yugoslav leaders repeatedly emphasized that there could be no democracy for the opponents of socialism. It was the Catholic Church that was the harshest opponent of socialism, and that was why the authorities had acted so strongly against it. The conflict had also been exacerbated by the diplomatic and propaganda activities of the Vatican. The Yugoslav leadership believed that the Vatican had tried to push for a resolution of the question of Trieste which was unfavorable for Yugoslavia and that it had launched a propaganda offensive in the West that had aimed at stirring up anti-Yugoslav sentiment.

Although the Vatican perceived the priests' associations as the beginning of a possible schism, the conditions, in fact, were not ripe for such a radical break, since not even the leaders of the associations agreed with the concept of a national church. In the 1968 memorandum, the members of the Slovenian priests' association decisively rejected the claim of the Vatican and church officials that the CMD represented the beginnings of a national church. On the contrary, they stressed that they had continually strived for the church endorsement of the CMD. They also denied the accusation that Mihael Toroš was being considered for appointment as the bishop of the Slovenian national church. The memorandum concluded that 'the desire to establish a national church may have existed outside the clergy, but no one in the association itself had ever mentioned it'.[44] The idea of a national church, however, persisted among the Yugoslav leadership. Tito made no secret of his wish to separate the Yugoslav Catholic church from the Vatican. He expressed this desire during a conversation with the Croatian bishops in June 1945 when he presented the idea of a more independent national church, and again in November 1949 when he posed the following question to the members of the CMD:

> If we have liberated ourselves from Moscow, why have not you [liberated yourselves] from Rome?[45]

The idea of an independent national church also circulated among Slovenian communists, and, in June 1943, the Christian socialist Edvard Kocbek recorded his opinion in his notes. He mentioned that certain comrades had suggested the establishment of a Slovenian Catholic church and characterized it as 'an utterly foolish notion'.[46]

After the breaking off of diplomatic relations with the Vatican, government authorities tried to normalize relations with the Catholic Church in Yugoslavia. On the invitation of President Tito, Catholic bishops met him in Belgrade on 8 January 1953, although they insisted that they could not come to an agreement with the government without the permission of the Vatican.[47] They only agreed to the proposal for the establishment of a proportional commission that would study the disputed issues. Later, the bishops also responded to an invitation to participate in a provisional federal commission for the normalization of relations with religious communities that sought to become acquainted with the bishops' opinions concerning the proposed law on the legal status of the religious communities. The law guaranteed the independence of religious life from the state on condition that religious communities confined their activities to religious matters. Organizations and individuals would be prohibited from taking advantage of religious sentiments for political ends. In terms of the most sensitive questions – education and training – it was anticipated that classes in public schools would be taught by laymen and would be guided by the principles of science and free thought. Lessons in the catechism would only take place at churches, and religious communities would be allowed to establish their own schools for the education of the clergy. Finally, the proposed law explicitly allowed the functioning of priests' associations, but did not mention the religious press.[48]

On 19 February 1953, Josip Ujčić, the President of the Yugoslav Bishops' Conference, sent his comments about the draft to the federal commission for the normalization of relations with religious communities. Although he once again emphasized that he had no authority to negotiate with the government, he mainly dwelt upon the fourth article on the teaching of the catechism. He wrote that the proposed law violated the right of religious freedom since it limited religious education, and prohibited the expression of religious beliefs. In contrast, the law in no way prohibited the expression of anti-religious beliefs or the dissemination of atheism, and thus grossly violated the equal rights of citizens. Ujčić was convinced that the government's fear of religion was not justified:

> Each religion teaches morals, and especially the Christian religion (to which the majority of our people belong) teaches cleanliness, diligence, justice, rendering unto Caesar the things that are Caesar's and rendering unto God the things that are God's: that is, it is necessary to respect authority because every authority comes from God, not out of fear of punishment but out of conscience! How could such elevated instruction harm school children? And does the world know any more elevated morality than Christian morality?

He declared that the church had the right to establish religious schools at elementary, high school and college levels. As far as the priests' associations were concerned, Ujčić would adhere to the decision of the Yugoslav Bishops' Conference, which had prohibited such associations. He added that the law must explicitly guarantee the freedom of the religious press because 'if people are allowed to attack religion, then the religious press must at least be allowed to defend it to the same extent'.[49]

At this point, Ujčić received a letter from Domenico Tardini, the deputy state secretary of the Vatican. He reminded the Bishop of Belgrade that any agreement with the government fell outside his competence. He emphasized that the Vatican was not opposed to the normalization of relations with the government, but that the bishops could take no decision without the Vatican's consent because 'what is not in accordance with the standards about which we spoke is to the greatest degree harmful to the good of the church and its souls'.[50] These instructions were sent through ordinary mail so that the state authorities were aware of the content, which is a fact that Aleksandar Ranković, Vice President of the Yugoslav government, admitted in his speech on the occasion of the acceptance of the law regarding religious communities.

The Slovenian government established a special commission led by Boris Kraigher to negotiate with the representatives of Slovenian religious communities. On 17 April 1953, the Slovenian Bishops, Anton Vovk, Maksimilijan Držečnik and Mihael Toroš, met the commission, although, even before the talks began, both sides had stressed that they had no intention of reaching an agreement. On behalf of the Slovenian clergy, Mihael Toroš, the Bishop of Gorica, read a memorandum in which loyalty was pledged to the legal state authorities, while, at the same time, total religious freedom was demanded as well as the rectification of all the injustices that the church had endured since 1945. Kraigher threatened to cancel the talks if the memorandum was not withdrawn. In response, the demand for total religious freedom and the rectification of all injustices were replaced with a new passage that merely stated the willingness to negotiate with the government about the actual problems of church-state relations. Maksimilijan Držečnik, the Bishop of Maribor, stated that the original memorandum had been written in order to 'forestall all possible recriminations from the Vatican'.[51]

One week later, the Yugoslav bishops led by Josip Ujčić met a provisional commission of the federal government for the normalization of relations with religious communities, which was also led by Boris Kraigher. The bishops once again stressed that they were not authorized to negotiate with the government and that they did not want to accept responsibility for any law that might not be in harmony with the interests of the Catholic Church and canon law. Because of this, the talks ended on 24 April 1953 and the federal commission for the normalization of relations with religious communities ceased to function.[52] In mid-May 1953, representatives of the Slovenian clergy met the Slovenian commission for the normalization of relations with religious communities. Mihael Toroš read the original memorandum of the Slovenian clergy, which included the explicit demand for total religious freedom and the correction of previous injustices. He concluded that the bishops could not come to any agreement with the government and considered the continuation of the discussions to be unnecessary:

> because the government can grant the church as much freedom as it wants without any talks, and if that is complete freedom then we will applaud, the whole world will applaud, and reactionary forces will be disarmed.

The President of the commission, Boris Kraigher, agreed with stopping the dialogue, commenting that 'if we are speaking about injustices, then, of course, these talks make no sense'.[53]

In May 1953, the federal assembly passed the law on the legal status of religious communities.[54] In his presentation of the law, Aleksandar Ranković stressed that the Catholic Church, unlike the Orthodox and Muslim communities, had been unwilling to reach an agreement with the government. He put the blame for this intransigence on the Vatican, which had shown little concern for the true interests of the Catholic Church and its followers in Yugoslavia.[55] The law on the legal status of religious communities formally guaranteed the freedom of religion and conscience as well as equality among the various religious communities. Religion was defined as a private matter of the individual. In addition, the law prohibited the abuse of religion for political ends, as well as any hindrances placed upon the expression of religious beliefs. The separation of church and school was emphasized once more in Article 4. Religious education would be permitted only in churches and other places specifically designated for such use. The religious communities would only be allowed to establish schools for the education of the clergy. The permission of parents or guardians was required before children could attend religious classes. Schools established for the training of the clergy could be attended only by students who had completed mandatory elementary school. The baptism of minors could be performed with the permission of one parent and after they had been officially registered. Church marriages could be performed only after the civil ceremony had been carried out in front of the appropriate state authority. The law permitted religious communities to publish and distribute printed material as well as the establishment of priests' associations. It also stated that no one could be persecuted because of adherence to a particular religion, but likewise that no one could enjoy any special privileges, for instance, exemption from military service. State authorities could provide material assistance to religious organizations, and the clergy would be allowed to accept voluntary contributions from the believers or payment for the performance of religious rituals. These rituals were only allowed to take place in churches and other spaces specifically designated for such use. Exceptions for family celebrations, weddings and funerals could only be made with the permission of the local authorities.

After the enactment of the law on the legal status of religious communities, the dialogue between the government authorities and the Catholic Church became even darker. The number of attacks on priests and religious buildings increased in all of the republics, and the Western press frequently reported these incidents.[56] Political leaders, who had hitherto encouraged such attacks in their public announcements and in their instructions to members of the Communist Party, soon realized that violence would only lead them into a *cul-de-sac*. The results of a census report, which revealed that only slightly more than twelve per cent of the citizens claimed to be atheists, may have also contributed to an easing of the policies towards the church. In September 1953, President Tito once again emphasized the significance of political efforts to work with the young and claimed that violence and administrative measures against priests were inappropriate, since:

> the strongest means that you have are restraint and your own disbelief in what they [the priests] are telling you; with this, you will create the conditions in which they will no longer have fertile soil for their hostile actions. This will make it much harder for them than if priests are actually physically attacked.[57]

At the Third Congress of the League of Communists of Slovenia in May 1954, Edvard Kardelj emphasized that the communists must ensure the equality of the various religious communities and their inclusion into socialist society, since:

> it seems to me that this is the only way that we can de-politicize the church, de-clericalize religious belief and truly transform religion into a private matter for each individual, a matter that has no connection to the socialist orientation or the activities of the state.[58]

In contrast to this statement, religion began to be actively persecuted among Party members. Many of them secretly attended church services, were married at church, baptized their children and sent them to catechism classes. Surveillance of such members increased after the Sixth Congress of the League of Communists of Yugoslavia in 1952, which had included in its by-laws that Party membership was irreconcilable with religious observance. In 1953, as many as 1,105 members of the Slovenian party were expelled because of their attending religious services.[59]

After 1953, the Catholic Church in Yugoslavia became isolated for a long time. Most church dignitaries declined any contact with government organs and thus expressed their passive resistance to the regime and its institutions. In this period, relations between the Yugoslav government and the Catholic Church remained cool, although the original reasons for their mutual distrust began to fade away with time. In 1954, the question of Trieste was finally resolved and Pope Pius XII named Franjo Šeper as the Archbishop coadjutor of Zagreb. This was a quiet admission of the fact that Stepinac could no longer perform the functions of the archbishop. Pressure from government authorities relaxed to some extent, although the church continued to face strict surveillance, trials against priests, administrative annoyances and frequent unexpected taxes.

With John XXIII's assumption of papal duties in 1958 and his replacement by Pope Paul VI in 1963, and especially after the second Vatican Council (1962-1965), the Catholic Church began to adapt to new global circumstances and the dialogue between the church and the Yugoslav state was resumed. After several years of negotiation, a protocol between Yugoslavia and the Vatican was signed on 25 June 1966. It included the principled positions of both sides with regard to relations between the church and the state.[60] The Yugoslav government recognized the jurisdiction of the Vatican over the Catholic Church in all spiritual and church matters. The Holy See confirmed the position that church activities would be restricted to matters of the faith and would not intervene in politics. In September 1966, Yugoslavia and the Vatican resumed ambassadorial relations and full restitution of diplomatic relations remained only one step away, although four more years were needed to take this final step. From this time onwards, the dialogue between the state and the Catholic Church remained continuous and relations did not fall below the level of a relatively peaceful co-existence.

Despite the initial determined resistance of the leadership of the Catholic Church, the Yugoslav authorities were, nonetheless, relatively successful in their efforts to exclude the church and religion from the public sphere. The Catholic Church in Yugoslavia soon no longer figured as a significant social force capable of guiding or noticeably affecting the development of society. In the 1960s, the policy of the regime, which no longer felt seriously threatened from this quarter, became more tolerant. The subsequent agreement between the communist authorities and the Catholic Church was also helped by the realization of the church authorities that they had no alternative but to adapt to the political situation, which, at the time, showed all signs of there being no hope for any fundamental change.

Part VI

The Sovietization of History

13

The Sovietization of Hungarian Historiography. Failures and Modifications in the early 1950s

Árpád von Klimó

The sovietization of historiography should be understood as a process of attempting to transfer (1) Soviet models of ideological contents, (2) Soviet models of narrative structures, and (3) Soviet institutional models, into a different academic context. These three different aspects are concerned with the cognitive, aesthetic, and practical questions that are raised by the idea of transferring Soviet models, or models believed to be Soviet, into the field of the professional history of other countries, in this case: Hungary. These aspects cover only a small part of the much more complex and broader process of the sovietization of historical beliefs and the professional practices of historians and others who dealt with ideas and images about the past. It should be borne in mind that, in general, professional historians were not the most important actors in the field of historical culture. Historical culture, or *Geschichtskultur*, can be defined as the sum of ideas, symbols, representations, practices and beliefs that relate to the past as imagined by the society.[1]

Sovietization should not be understood as a process that took place in the historical profession of Soviet occupied or dominated countries, but as a metaphor that represented the process of institutional changes and ruptures of historiography in a broader context. The beginnings of the sovietization of Hungarian history can therefore be dated back at least to 1937 when, during the 7th Congress of the Comintern, Dimitrov demanded the re-conquest of national histories by the communist parties, particularly of those countries which were part of the fascist sphere of influence, including Germany, Italy, and Hungary.[2]

Sovietization should also be distinguished from the 'Stalinization' of historiography, which took place during the 1930s.[3] It meant the introduction of strictly authoritarian, centralizing practices and ideas, as well as certain aesthetic forms, including the monumentalization and personalization of historical narratives, a preference for dualist structures representing progressive 'heroes' versus reactionary 'enemies', the dynamization of narratives, and a tendency towards 'national' forms, instead of 'Marxist' or 'sociological' ones.[4] In the case of Hungary, the Stalinization of the historical field took place between 1948 and 1953. In these years, however, the impact of this process was more or less superficial. The *Kratkii Kurs* (Short Course) was translated and implemented, textbooks were written, speeches were delivered and programmatic articles were published, which were oriented towards a Stalinist and Soviet model. Historiography, however, was only touched superficially.[5] Only a few, albeit highly representative, books or articles which treated historical subjects in a Stalinist way were produced, and most published works remained unaffected by this phenomenon.

The term 'Marxism' could also be a source of several misunderstandings concerning this period. 'Marxist' historiography is not the same as 'Soviet' or 'Stalinist' historiography, because in Italy, France, the USA and Japan, there were many Marxist historians who would have been shot or imprisoned in the Soviet or Stalinist context. Thus, 'Marxist' historians were a very colorful and manifold species. Even in Eastern Europe, Marxist historiography displayed a wide range of different, often opposing, approaches.

Thus, 'Marxism-Leninism' is best understood as a metaphor to describe the fiction of a unified and coherent historical profession in the countries of the Soviet hemisphere, including Hungary.[6] This was the official label for a specific historiography, as imagined by Party officials, although it was never fully realized.

The 'Conference of Hungarian Historians' in June 1953

One particular event illustrates both the culmination and the failure of the first attempt to sovietize Hungarian historiography. This event was the so-called 'First Conference of Hungarian Historians', which took place on 7 June 1953 at the Institute of History of the Hungarian Academy of Sciences in Budapest.[7] Fifteen months before, a similar conference had been organized in Warsaw (December - January 1951/52), where Polish and Soviet historians had met. Delegations from the Soviet Union, Poland, Czechoslovakia, Romania and the GDR participated in the Budapest conference.

The conference started with the opening remarks made by Erik Molnár, a member of the Politburo of the Hungarian Worker's Party (MDP) and Director of the Institute. Molnár greeted the guests in an order that reflected hierarchical relations. The seven representatives who spoke after him reflected the same hierarchy. The first to speak was Yuri Andropov, Soviet ambassador to Hungary from 1954. After him, Anna M. Pankratova, who was the leader of the Soviet historians' delegation, which consisted of three members, entered the scene. The third speaker was the Polish historian Henryk Jabłoński, who, together with Leon Grosfeld, represented the two leaders of the Polish group. After him, his Czech colleague, who headed a group of two Czech and one Slovak delegates, followed. His place on the stage was then taken by the Romanian and the Bulgarian speakers, who were followed by the very last speaker, the GDR-historian Leo Stern, who was rector of the University of Halle at that time. Stern, who was of Austrian origin, recalled his stay in Budapest in 1945, when he was stationed there as an officer of the Red Army. He thus disclosed his identity as a Muscovite. He remembered the devastated state of Budapest at the time, and appraised the impressive reconstruction work of 'democratic' Hungary. After his praise of the Hungarian regime, the German delegate made the position of 'progressive' German historians clear by stressing the need to fight against:

> cosmopolitism, existentialism, schematic idealism, personalism, mysticism, symbolism, positivism, pragmatism, national nihilism in every form, in which Anglo-American imperialism in West Germany is spreading it among the larger part of the German people. [...] We have to learn in particular from the Soviet Union, [...] We also have to learn from the peoples' democracies, how we could raise the moral and political energies of the German people by the great examples of its past, so that we can move the German people towards the building of a united, democratic, independent and peace-loving Germany.[8]

The scene provides us with the opportunity to analyze some important features of the relationship between Stalinism and historiography. First, we can observe how the political leadership of the Soviet Union was staged: the first and most important guest to speak was the representative of the Soviet state, followed by a historian and a member of the Soviet Academy of Science, and so on. The particular importance of the Soviet delegation was also marked by the fact that the Soviet colleagues not only participated as the most honored guests at the conference, but that they also participated at a workshop after the conference, where they gave advice to both their Hungarian colleagues and others. Soviet historians were thus regarded as the 'teachers' of other historians. This was a Stalinist metaphor, which represented not only the hierarchical relations between the historians within the Soviet world, but also the idea of the transfer of values, knowledge and practices from the center of this world – Moscow – to the periphery.

Rituals of subordination, such as the control of language by party officials and propaganda specialists, as well as the selection of personnel by the newly founded institutions, with the Historical Institute of the Academy of Science in Budapest at its head, were important for the internalization of the new values. Thus, Erik Molnár, as head of this institute, was the most appropriate person to speak in the name of the new Marxist-Leninist Hungarian historiography. But what the institutional centralization of professional historiography really meant, and what practical and cognitive consequences the institutional changes had, needs to be researched further.

With regard to ideology and historical narratives, the attempt to introduce Soviet models as the unquestionable and only possible ways of understanding, explaining and aesthetically shaping the past became obvious. From the speech presented by Leo Stern from East Germany, it became clear that the Soviet model meant the exclusion of several 'enemy models' from sovietized historiography. It should be stressed that this list, which included 'cosmopolitism, existentialism, *etc.*', embraced the main philosophic and historiographic trends of the time, not only in terms of ideological systems and concepts, but also in terms of aesthetic forms. The sovietization of historiography was not only about ideas and ideology, but also about form. We should not speak only about Marxism-Leninism, but also about Socialist Realism with regard to Stalinist historiography. How this program was implemented and what results it had is still an open question that needs more research.

Actors: Who Introduced Soviet Methods and Language?

The introduction or the attempt to introduce Soviet historiography after 1945 was not a product of one, homogenous social group. According to their educational backgrounds and/or Party positions, five different groups contributed to historical production during the centenary of 1948 – the central propaganda campaign which focused on the remembering of the Revolution of 1848 and which attempted to legitimize the erection of the dictatorship of the Communist Party historically. These were: 1) party theorists; 2) party theorists who held academic positions at the same time;

3) young communist historians, who were not high ranking functionaries; 4) non-communist historians who were 'tolerated'; and 5) non-communist historians who were defamed for their 'falsification' of history. This classification allows us to differentiate between propaganda and scholarship, and to measure the extent of overlaps between the two.

1. Party Theorists

József Révai was the leading party theorist, who articulated the official interpretation of the events of 1848/49. In the strictly hierarchical bibliographies of the history textbooks of the early 1950s, his contributions were ranked first, immediately after the 'classics of Marxism-Leninism'. The 'Short Summary of the History of the Hungarian people', first published in 1951, was the first textbook of Hungarian history that was in accordance with the Party line.[9] It presented Hungarian history from 'prehistoric society' to the 'triumph of the people's democracy after 1945' on slightly more than 700 pages, divided into sixteen chapters. On pages 708-715, there is the recommended literature, beginning with the essential *Rákosi Mátyás és a magyar történettudomány* (Mátyás Rákosi and Hungarian Historical Scholarship) published in *Századok* in 1952. The second recommended title for Hungarian history in general was one of Révai's work *Marxizmus, népiesség, magyarság* (Marxism, Popularism, Hungarianness), followed by the brochure written by Erzsébet Andics, entitled *Munkásosztály és nemzet* (The Working-Class and the Nation). In the fourth position, there was the program of the MDP from 1948. After Chapter IX ('Bourgeois Revolution and the fight for National Freedom'), the same hierarchical ordering of books can be observed. The titles first recommended were the 'classics', beginning with Marx-Engels-Lenin-Stalin, *Proletárnemzetköziség és hazafiság* (Proletarian Internationalism and Patriotism), the Stalinist interpretation of scientific socialism, published in 1952. In the group of classic texts on 1848-49, Révai was to be found alongside Marx and Engels. This illustrated his position as the top theorist on historical problems.

Révai's theses on the Hungarian Revolution of 1848 had one main goal: to discredit Ervin Szabó's pre-1918 Marxist interpretation of the Revolution as a revolt of noblemen. If the revolution had not been 'bourgeois', Hungary would not yet be ripe for a socialist revolution.[10] For people who did not believe in the laws of historical materialism, such an effort might seem to be far removed from reality. But the country's future was, thanks to the Soviet military machine, in the hands of the high priest of this belief system.

2. Party Theorists who Held Academic Positions at the Time

In the bibliography of the handbook from 1951, the classics were followed by the official narrative of 1848, *Revolution and Struggle for Freedom 1848-49*, (Szikra, 1948), written by Party theorists who were also in academic positions (Group 2), such as Aladár Mód, Dezső Nemes and Erzsébet Andics. They were assisted by younger communist historians, who were not functionaries, such as Péter Hanák (see Group 3 below), and non-communist sympathizers, such as Győző Ember (see Group 4 below).

Mód and Andics were important party functionaries who worked as historians at the same time. Mód wrote the first summary of Hungarian history which was a specific mixture of Marxism and populism. The *400 Year-Struggle for Hungarian Independence* (published in 1945), became the most important general overview of modern Hungarian history, although it was ranked at a lower level than Révai's theoretical texts. Mód once wrote in the theoretical journal of the Party, *Társadalmi Szemle*, that the struggle of the working-class developed into the 'struggle of the whole *people*, of the whole *nation*'.[11] Mód and Révai both used the term *people* in a Marxist, as well as in an ethnic, sense: it was also characteristic to the policy of the people's front during Stalinism.

Another representative of Stalinist historiography was Erzsébet Andics, who belonged to the Muscovite group in the Party. During the war, she had been the director of the Anti-Fascist school at Krasnodarsk. Since her return home in 1945, she had become responsible for the transferring of Soviet history-writing to Hungary.[12] Her books and articles in the Stalin-years were mixtures of Stalinist propaganda and traditional diplomatic history. In the *Revolution* volume published in 1948, Andics discussed her favorite subject, the 'treason' of the 'church reaction' in 1848-49.[13] She 'unmasked' the class-biased stance of the higher clergy and of the Habsburg-loyal aristocracy during the Revolution, which determined their 'reactionary' behavior. She denounced the Catholic primate János Hám as a 'national traitor'. Only a few months later, the Primate of the Catholic Church, Cardinal József Mindszenty, who had held the position since 1945, was put on trial as a 'traitor to the nation'. Like a hundred years earlier, Hungarian public opinion was made to believe that the cardinals seated in Esztergom were 'enemies of the people'. It was in these years that Erzsébet Andics reached the peak of her career. In 1949, she was elected president of the Society of Historians in Hungary. She was also a member of the commission for the radical transformation of the Academy of Sciences, publisher-in-chief of *Századok*, and chair-holder of modern and contemporary history in Budapest, the only position she kept after 1956.

3. *Young Communist Historians*

In the bibliographical hierarchy, monographs and articles of younger historians with communist orientation, such as Sándor Fekete and Gyula Mérei, were ranked in fourth position after the contributions of the 'classics' and the leading theorist, Révai (first), the official volume of 1948 (second), and some source editions (third). Stalinism provided an opportunity for young historians, Marxists and non-Marxists alike, to assume influential positions quickly.

In *Revolution and Struggle for Freedom*, Péter Hanák wrote an article about the 'suppressed peoples of the Habsburg monarchy'. He applied a comparative approach that made him conclude that: 'The failure of the Italian struggle for freedom was also due to the insolvability of the land question' (p. 454). Using a wide range of German, Italian and Romanian literature and sources, Hanák constructed a narrative based on an orthodox Marxist perspective: the forces of progress fight against the forces of reaction, and their actions are determined by class affiliation. The 'lesson of 1848', according to Hanák, was that 'the progressive peoples can only defend their freedom and independence in a close union of friends and against the reactionary forces' (p. 467). This approach was suitable to the propaganda of communist parties in Eastern Europe in 1948, when the bloc was established. Nevertheless, in contrast to Erzsébet Andics, Péter Hanák's work was less 'Stalinist'. He was not 'unmasking' enemies and traitors, but searching for the possibilities of the 'progressive peoples' to fight together against the Habsburgs. The article contained valuable historical scholarship, and was far from being worthless despite the doubtful conclusions.

4. Non-communist Historians who were Tolerated

Interestingly, disciples of 'bourgeois' historian Gyula Szekfű, arguably the most important Hungarian historian of the first half of the 20th Century, also contributed to the official volume on 1848, like Győző Ember.[14] Ember's article on the revolutionary peasant movements in 1848 had a central argument: the peasants had remained loyal to Lajos Kossuth by postponing their claims for social justice, whereas the leaders of the revolution had missed the opportunity to introduce radical agrarian reforms. His critique of the literature was balanced and fair. He emphasized that 'Marxist historians [Ervin Szabó, Imre Nagy, Sándor Haraszti, *etc.*] stressed the significance of the peasant movements of '48, non-Marxist [historians] did not find it very important'.[15] Ember concluded that the literature on 1848/49 mainly studied the Revolution from a legal, national or military historical perspective, but left contradictions, and economic and social problems aside. Surely, this was not a Stalinist historical work. It indicated that the take-over of the Communist Party did not simply trigger the production of narrow-minded propaganda material, but also left some space for comparative or social history, as long as they did not violate the official master narrative. This was also a tactical compromise in order to include some 'bourgeois' historians into the ranks of new Hungarian historians.

5. Non-communist Historians who were Defamed for their 'Falsification' of History

Stalinism, like other dictatorial systems, was marked by arbitrariness. No matter how impressive their academic merits, the destiny of 'bourgeois' historians was sealed, especially if they held positions that were important for the party. The treatment of Ferenc Eckhardt, one of the leading legal and social historians, illustrates this tendency. From 1929 on, Eckhardt held the chair of legal history at Budapest University. He almost lost his post in 1931 because of his criticism of the 'idea of Saint Stephen', a cornerstone of the 'Christian-national' ideology of the Horthy regime. As a consequence, Eckhardt enjoyed the reputation of being an independent scholar after 1945. This made him the perfect candidate to be the successor of Bálint Hóman in the presidency of the Historical Society (*Magyar Történelmi Társulat*), who had been accused of 'war crimes' and had died in prison. Eckhardt was eventually elected president in 1946. He recognized the necessity of opening towards Marxist theory in historical science, and had long been arguing for a broader inclusion of social and economic factors in the history of the Hungarian state. His contribution to the centenary was the volume entitled *1848 – A szabadság éve*, (The year of freedom). The newspaper of the Communist Party, *Szabad Nép*, severely criticized the book. The author of the review claimed, that 'the *people* don't play a role in the book', and '*Petőfi's name* is only mentioned twice in the volume'. The journalist also complained that 'he [Eckhardt] cherishes his open sympathy towards any form of compromise', 'rehabilitates Windischgrätz, the "old man"', and 'justifies even János Hám and his bishops'.[16] The conclusion was clear: 'This piece of writing is unworthy for the book-week of the centenary.'[17]

The critique exemplified what a Stalinist historical narrative on 1848 had to contain: (1) the 'personality cult' of Petőfi – Kossuth – Táncsics, the Holy Trinity of the official narrative; (2) the damnation of the 'enemies' of the past, who resembled contemporary 'enemies' such as Cardinal Mindszenty; (3) the glorification of revolutionary radicalism, instead of 'bourgeois' compromises.

In his inauguration speech as President of the Historical Society, Eckhardt emphasized the importance of the independence of historians from the state. He regretted that, in the period after 1918, society had been too dependent upon the state. The Stalinists regarded such ideas as 'petty bourgeois'. In April 1949, Erzsébet Andics replaced Eckhardt as president of the Historical Society.

Institutional Changes in Hungarian Historiography in 1948 and 1949

With Eckhardt, Vice President Domokos Kosáry also had to resign. During the discussion, the very flexible Győző Ember mentioned the 'inner causes that made the resignations necessary, first of all, the fact that our Society cannot keep step with the progress of our country which needs the development of progressive scholarship which serves the interests of the *people*'.[18]

Two historians, András Alföldi and József Deér, who had emigrated to Western Europe, were excluded from the Society. The new secretary (Ember) of the Society reported to Révai, on 19 August 1949, that the Eastern Europe Institute, headed by Kosáry and Kálmán Benda was 'disorganized'.[19] Four days later, Ernő Gerő's wife, Erzsébet Fazekas, recommended the secret informer of the state security as secretary of the Institute, with the striking logic 'because he knows the Institute well'.[20]

Next to the new President Andics, Révai was elected 'honorary president'. The text in *Századok* reported his election in a typical Stalinist way, followed by 'continuing enthusiastic applause'. Andics began her new job with the withdrawal of an issue of *Századok*. Jenő Berlász, editor of the journal after 1943, whom Eckhart had appointed to 'follow a strict professional line' against the attempts to introduce 'foreign [that is, Nazi] political ideas', had already finished the volume of 1948 by the end of the year.[21] After the change of the presidium of the Historical Society on 20 March 1949, the new editorial staff rejected this issue entirely. It could only be published forty years later. Instead of the issue prepared by Berlász and the old editorial board, Andics and her staff edited a new issue of the journal some months later. The Stalinist era of *Századok* began with Andics' inauguration speech, in which she fiercely criticized 'bourgeois' historiography, and called for the imitation of the example of Soviet historical scholarship. In the following years, the Scientific Council of the party completed the *Gleichschaltung* of Hungarian historical scholarship in the Academy and the universities by replacing most of the older 'bourgeois' historians (such as István Hajnal, Deér, *etc.*) by loyal scholars.[22]

Stalinism and Historiography: Older and More Recent Explanations

Stalinism and the Tension between Nationalism and Internationalism

Ferenc Glatz, the Director of the Institute of History at the Hungarian Academy, defined Stalinism as 'a united, monolithic, in an every day expression: uniform system'.[23] Its 'enforced internationalism' prevented, according to Glatz, the individual nations from finding their real place in Central-Eastern European co-operation, and led to the suppression of 'bourgeois nationalism'.[24]

By examining the history texts produced during the Stalinist period more closely, numerous traits of nationalism could be found. Polish, Hungarian and Czech historiography of the period were all, for instance, were all marked by anti-German tendencies, which were also related to the attempt to justify 'population transfers' executed on dubious 'ethnic' grounds. At the same time, these texts were written in a heroic manner, stressing the permanent 'liberation' struggles of the 'peoples'. 'People', in this context, stood for 'nation' constructed by the exclusion of the ruling classes, and distinguished from external and internal enemies. The Stalinist concept of 'people' was, thus, not a sociological category, but an entity to which propaganda addressed its messages.[25] In order to distinguish militant class-nationalism with its *völkisch* elements from the so-called 'bourgeois' nationalism of the pre-1945 era, a sophisticated engagement was needed on the ideological front. It is difficult to assess how many contemporaries were actually able to distinguish between tolerated and forbidden forms of nationalism. Differentiation became more complicated after the publication of Stalin's linguistic theses in the summer of 1950.[26] Stalin argued that language had nothing to do with basis or superstructure, nothing to do with class or society, nothing to do with historical change, but only with the entire people, whose language would not merge with other language registers. It either remained dominant or it perished. This opinion had nothing to do with 'proletarian internationalism', but was a typical product of nationalism. Ferenc Glatz, however, was right to point out the miraculous disappearance of national conflicts between Hungary and its neighbors, and of the danger of pan-Slavism that had been emphatically present in textbooks before 1945.

Stalinist propaganda tried to capitalize on certain aspects of nationalism, but its success remains in doubt. Stalinist art was characterized by the selection of traditional and modern elements in order to create a new Socialist art.[27] Stalinist internationalism in the field of history disappeared in the 1960s, and was replaced by various Marxist-Leninist approaches and the introduction of certain elements of Western social history. Conferences like the ones in Warsaw or in Budapest in the beginning of the 1950s were not repeated after the crisis of Stalinism in the Socialist camp.

Totalitarian and Historicist Approaches

A second type of controversy about soviet historiography relates to the debate between 'totalitarian' and 'historicist' approaches.[28] From a totalitarian perspective, two kinds of historians were imaginable in Eastern

Europe: 'politicized' or 'real' scholars, those who wrote history as a sort of propaganda, and those who tried to defend the 'pure' science of history. This simplified picture resembled the dualistic perspective of Stalinism. 'Revisionist' views that became popular in the era of co-existence modified this dualistic structure to a limited extent. Such revisionism claimed that a process of professionalization was taking place in socialist countries: the number of institutions and the production of historical works increased and became more diversified. Marxist-Leninist history-writing, from this point of view, became more 'scholarly' and less 'political' in the 1970s.

In the last decade of the Soviet system, new approaches tried to describe historiography within the Soviet system by using a 'historicist' method. Such an approach sought to explain the system not only by analyzing the institutional and legal framework of the historical discipline, but also by understanding the internal logic by which it functioned and the discourses to which historians appealed. It seems as if the unwritten rules of socialist academia had been interiorized by its members. This would explain why some of them continued writing according to the old rules even after the fall of the dictatorship.

Gwidon Zalejko defined Soviet historical science as a 'normal' science.

> They [the Soviet historians] really try, to their best knowledge, and within the framework of what is considered real, to acquire the knowledge of the world, to explain it and to change it in the desirable direction. Everything is decided at the moment of the first decision, the moment when science accepts a given set of assumptions originating from the outside and not from itself.[29]

Soviet historiography for him was 'in the specific sense formulated by Kuhn - discipline pursued under abnormal conditions. The ontological assumptions resulting from the Soviet interpretation of Marxism pre-determined, however, the results of the research carried out by historians. But this research itself was conducted in accordance with the methodological rules binding all over the world'.

Soviet-type historiography in Hungary began with the election of Erzsébet Andics. Hungarian historiography, however, was only superficially Stalinized and sovietized in the 1950s. It was only in the late 1950s, that the ideas and forms of Marxism-Leninism penetrated into the field of historical studies. In addition, as early as the conference of 1953 the model of Stalinism was abandoned. Soviet historian Pankratova, a member of the Hungarian Academy of Sciences, criticized Leo Stern for his Stalinist ideas at the workshop following the conference. When Stern pleaded for 'the publishing of another volume of studies about the deeds of such extraordinary personalities who strengthened the friendship of peoples in their age',30 Pankratova sharply replied:

> It is absolutely incorrect to treat the heroes as a particular topic instead of the masses.

The statement made it clear that the Stalinist approach with its cults of heroes and leaders and its demonization of enemies was no longer the only possible way of writing history in the Soviet context. Thus, historians studying sovietized history should always consider the sometimes contradictory internal logic, changes and limits to the 'sovietization' process.

14

Marxist History of Historiography in Poland, Czechoslovakia and East Germany (late 1940s – late 1960s)

Maciej Górny

After the end of the Second World War, the new communist leaders of the Soviet bloc faced the problem of legitimization. Nationalism was clearly the most natural source of political legitimacy, and, indeed, a strong anti-German resentment – a common experience of post-war Europe – was used to the full by pro-Soviet East-Central European regimes. Poland and Czechoslovakia belonged to the group of countries which expelled the German population from their western areas and introduced very severe policies towards the remaining minority, while also tolerating the brutality of the Czech and Polish population towards the remaining Germans. Three communist parties, in Poland, the Czech lands and Slovakia were successfully able to refer to a long history of conflicts with the Germans, simultaneously stressing the meaning of Slavic brotherhood in both past and future battles. At the same time, East German leaders often repeated the catalogue of German crimes, committed mainly on Soviet territory, in order to justify Soviet exploitation. But playing on the German danger and German guilt was not enough to form a new historical consciousness: there was a need for a new interpretation of the entire national history.

One of the most important means of proving the indigenous origins of the communists was the search for the so-called 'progressive traditions' in national history. Clearly, it was historical scholarship that was expected to accomplish this task. At the same time, Marxist-Leninist historiography[1] was expected to re-interpret and judge national history, focusing not only on its glorious, 'progressive' parts, but also on its negative, 'reactionary' heritage. One of the first problems that the Polish, Czech, Slovak and East German historiographies of the 1950s had to deal with was the critical re-assessment of modern national historical science from its birth in the Enlightenment to the last years of the inter-war period. Researchers were supposed to find their way between two extremes: between the total repudiation of previous historiography and the 'positive' search for a progressive historiographical tradition. One of the few Polish Marxists, Wanda Moszczeńska, for example, called this dubious venture the 'dialectical negation' of this heritage.[2] Looking from a different angle, one could say that what Marxists were expected to do was simply to construct a self-identity for the new school by writing the history of the nation through carefully selected predecessors. The following study analyses the Marxist-Leninist history of historiography in the Stalinist period, from *circa* 1948 until 1956 in Poland; from 1948 until the mid-1960s in Czechoslovakia; and from *circa* 1949 until the end of the 1960s in the GDR.

The changes in 1989 gave historians access to archives which included those of the Communist Party. It provided them with the possibility of studying issues such as the balance of power in historical institutions, the ways in which the authorities dominated historians, personal connections, interdependences and conflicts. Regarding the history of historiography in the 1990s, in Germany, in particular, one could observe an immense interest in these areas.[3] This methodology was widely accepted in Poland, in the Czech Republic and in Slovakia. This approach focused primarily on the question of continuity: whether historical science remained resilient, or, on the contrary, Stalinism caused personal and institutional breaks.[4] The first works of post-modernism in research on Marxist historiography also appeared in Germany.[5] The advantages and disadvantages of this method is aptly illustrated by Martin Sabrow's book *Das Diktat des Konsenses. Geschichtswissenschaft in der DDR 1949-1969*.[6] It is based upon meticulous archival research and Sabrow describes not only the various aspects of the party line in historiography, but also the initiatives originating from professional circles. He analyses the mechanisms for the creation of the rules in East-German historical discourse. The author manages to draw a much more complicated picture than the straight model depicting the subordination of science to politics. Sabrow points to instances when historians themselves disciplined their colleagues, creating an efficient system of self-control and thus reducing the need for direct political intervention. But, surprisingly, Sabrow fails to address the crucial topic of de-construction: he ignores the analysis of historical narratives, rhetoric, style or strategies of argumentation. His work is based not upon historical texts proper, but on institutional and personal documents. Thus, the outcome of the examination is not a de-construction of the factual and methodological canon of GDR historiography, but the re-construction of a case of Soviet-type historical science.

Although historiography is not always a central question to students of sovietization, it is frequently referred to as an important means of obtaining legitimacy. In most cases, however, historians, who deal with the question of legitimacy acquired through historical writings, look at their object from the perspective of rulers and their need for history (or fear of history) and avoid discussing historiography as a science or an art with its own particular traditions. Furthermore, in some cases, the period of research interest (*i.e.*, the communist or Nazi dictatorship) is detached from the continuity of national history and is described as an 'abnormal period', in contrast to supposedly 'normal' eras before and after.[7] This method is even more striking if we take into consideration the usual conclusions of these works. Most of these authors agree that the communists eagerly clung to nationalist ideas, or, in other words, that they borrowed a lot from their predecessors. But we may follow this path even further to stress the need for continuity in interpreting the history of historiography without excluding the 45 years that followed the Second World War. John Connelly, among others, has shown that what is really interesting is how tradition merged with 'sovietization', how, in the process of pressure and concessions, a new compromise was built. This is because continuity and discontinuity in historical scholarship should not refer to personal links alone. The question of how Marxist historiographies walked in the footsteps of their bourgeois predecessors is of equal importance. Arguably, Sabrow's title *Das Diktat des Konsenses* could refer not merely to relations between historians and the authorities, but also to the way historians reflected national traditions in Poland, the GDR and Czechoslovakia. Hence, in my research, I combine the sociology of the science of Marxist historiography with a comparative textual analysis of historical publications from 1940s - 1960s.

Historical debates in Poland and East Germany occurred more frequently and were relatively fiercer than in Czech or Slovak Marxist-Leninist scholarship. Czech and Slovak Marxist interpretations of the national past borrowed a lot from the traditional liberal-nationalist ideas that had been prevalent in Czech culture since the first edition of František Palacký's gigantic historical work, and, in the Slovak context, since Ľudovít Štúr had formulated the programme of national awakening. The painful task of reducing the national tradition to its 'progressive' elements had already been fulfilled in the 19th century. Excluding Czech Catholics or Czech and Upper Hungarian gentry from the national tradition prepared the ground for subsequent Marxist interpretation of history.[8] Neither German nor Polish Marxists followed their own liberal-nationalist tradition so consistently. In these two countries, scholars hesitated among the various historical traditions, and this led to more frequent and often extremely sharp ideological disputes among Marxist historians themselves. It is also worth mentioning that interest in the history of historiography in the 1950s seems to have been more evident in Poland than in any other historiographies under scrutiny. The number of Polish Marxist publications devoted to this issue was incommensurably larger than in the GDR or in Czechoslovakia.

Despite these differences, it is possible to develop a scheme that could encompass all these four Marxist historiographies and their research on the history of historiography, one that could help us to understand each of them in comparison to the others. In my research, I have concentrated on the main methodological problems of Marxism that featured in the agenda of the debates on East-Central European historiographies as well as the attitudes of the researchers towards the tradition of national historiography.

'Romantic' versus 'Positivist' Interpretation

The crucial problem of Marxist history of historiography was how to define the criteria of progressiveness. It goes without saying that this problem remained unsolved. On the one hand, it was quite obvious to search for progressive values in romantic historiography. Joachim Lelewel, František Palacký and Ľudovít Štúr (the latter two in their early works) praised the pre-historic freedom and equality, condemned German feudalism and looked to the future with the optimism of the liberal democrats of *Vormärz*.[9] They stressed the 'democratic' element in the history of their respective nations: the Hussite Revolution, the previous Slavic freedom, *etc.* In many ways, future Marxists simply agreed with their conclusions. Official post-war Soviet Pan-Slavism strengthened the romantic myth of the peaceful, calm and gifted Slavs who heroically opposed German feudalism. Moreover, in many respects, the new language of communist Russia and its allies simply used the vocabulary of the 19th century Pan-Slavists. As Hans Kohn had noted already in the 1950s:

> The Yugoslav defection created in the Slav "family of nations" a situation similar to the one which between 1839 and 1945 existed as a result of the enmity of Poles and Russians. Like Poland then, Yugoslavia now became the "Judas" and "traitor" to the Slav cause and a "tool" of "Western scheming against the Slav world which the Russians then as now magnanimously identified with Moscow."[10]

But, on the other hand, it was also obvious that romantic historiography was 'idealistic' and methodologically less developed than later positivist or historicist schools. Thus, in several cases, the Marxists made their choice of 'more progressive' predecessors. In fact, some Polish Marxists regarded the pre-positivist historian Karol Boromeusz Hoffman or the conservative Galician politician and brilliant positivist researcher Michał Bobrzyński as more progressive than Lelewel. This idea, however, was by no means uncontroversial. On the contrary, by doing so they found themselves being criticized for simplifications and 'sociologism' – a serious methodological error. It was precisely this type of methodological conflict that led to the problematization of the 'objective' and 'subjective' criteria of progress. To make the complicated issue simple, we can say that not every change brings progress. For instance, if a liberal thinker prepared the fundaments for the development of capitalism, he still remained a liberal and a capitalist despite the fact that what was to succeed capitalism was socialist revolution. In fact, his activity might be interpreted as an attempt to repair and preserve the existing social order, and thus the implications to social progress might have been more dangerous than open feudal reaction. According to this conception, Joachim Lelewel and other 19th century democrats and liberals could always count on a more favorable response from Marxists than from those historians who were active later in the period of imperialism (and were not Marxists).

To make the picture a little bit more complicated, the same Marxist historians who rigidly opposed the rehabilitation of positivism, historicism and social conservatism used to defend their own 'favorite' bourgeois historians using similar arguments. To give one example, Celina Bobińska (who once condemned all attempts to canonize the positive Marxist picture of pre-positivist Karol Boromeusz Hoffman) stated that clear-cut conservative historiography – above all, Michał Bobrzyński – was, in a way, much less problematical for Marxist researchers since they did not need to unmask it, in contrast to liberal historiography which needed new critical Marxist examination.[11] In the language of Marxist historical criticism, this meant that, according to Bobińska, there had been better and worse positivists; the better ones could be even more progressive than romantic historiography, whereas the worse ones were positioned far below the level of the tolerated historiographical tradition.

Both options – the 'Romantic' and the 'Historicist-Positivist' – had equal chances of being described as genuine Marxist approaches, and, in fact, both were regarded as the Marxist response to previous misinterpretations. A highly interesting appendix to the Polish debate on positivist historiography was provided by the East German interpretation of the Prussian school, which was considered more 'national' and less conservative than Leopold von Ranke. Although Ranke never belonged to the favorite heroes of Marxist historiography, we can observe certain shifts in his evaluation. In one of the first East German reflections on historiography, Ranke was accused of moral indifferentism disguised in misconceived objectivity that allegedly could lead to the justification of any crimes committed in the past. Surprisingly, the author of this judgement, Leo Stern, did not accuse Ranke of being a reactionary political thinker, and also believed that Ranke's striving for an objective picture of the past was meant both seriously and frankly. He merely observed that, through this erratic attempt, Ranke weakened the moral strength of German historiography, thus, rendering it unprepared to face the historical outcomes of 1918 and of 1945.[12]

In 1956, Jürgen Kuczynski recognized completely different aspects of Ranke's impact on German historiography. He wrote that Ranke had simply been a brilliant historian who had raised the professional level of historiography. This judgement of Ranke was subsequently used as one of the main arguments in an official campaign against the German 'revisionist' historian. However, thanks to his good political relations with the German and foreign communist élite, this did not affect his personal life seriously.[13] The last Marxist image of German historicism was constructed throughout the 1960s and was much more simplified than the interpretations of Stern or Kuczynski. 'In brief,' – argued Ernst Engelberg – 'Ranke was useful in order to justify the imperialist aggression outside as well as to fight against the German workers' movement.'[14] This putative Rankean legacy was perceived as resilient and enduring even in the 'NATO' West-German historiography.[15] Ranke's portrayal by Marxists was gradually losing its charm.

The interpretation of the Prussian historical school followed a similar path, albeit in the opposite direction. In the late 1940s, when the Marxist vision of the German past was still under the influence of post-war criticism (with Alexander Abusch as the most prominent representative of the new historical direction), the role of Sybel, Treitschke and Droysen seemed to be quite clear: through their works, they paved the way for the subsequent coming of Hitler.[16] Despite all this, East German Marxists recognized certain positive aspects in the Prussian school, and – interestingly enough – discovered these mainly in its difference from Ranke and his followers. Hans Schleier explained this problem in a similar way to that of Polish authors who tried to include positivism in the catalogue of 'progressive traditions':

> Political historians, representatives of an alliance between the great bourgeoisie and the Junkers, the adherents of national and

> political unification of Germany represented the new, more progressive school of historiography than the conservative, romantic Ranke.[17]

Surprisingly, even such features of the Prussian school as its German nationalism were interpreted as Ranke's heritage and, thus, not as a sign of difference between Ranke and the national-liberals. Schleier noted that:

> there was much more methodological and political similarities between Ranke and the Prussian-German historians than they or the succeeding bourgeois history of historiography were ready to admit.[18]

Naturally, one can, arguably, claim that it was Sybel's, Treitschke's and Droysen's attitude towards the unification of Germany that played the main role in this Marxist interpretation. The Prussian school, which ardently supported the unification, must have been finally classified as being more progressive than Ranke, who was rather skeptical towards every attempt to change the map of Europe. In the German case, even the 'late' liberals were seen to fit the Marxist frame better than the adherents of less 'national' historical schools. Droysen, Sybel and Treitschke were at the center of the German national movement of their age, and, thus, could functionally play the role of romantic historians and politicians in Poland, the Czech lands or Slovakia.

Pan-Slavism versus Social Progressiveness

Within this general problem, a separate unit of investigation can be created, namely, the category of socially and politically conservative researchers who shared a weaker or stronger pan-Slavic conviction. Among them, Zorian Dołęga Chodakowski was particularly interesting (although completely forgotten), to whom Andrzej Poppe devoted a lengthy article in *Kwartalnik Historyczny* in 1955.[19] The author stressed the democratic and pro-Russian commitment of Chodakowski, and incorporated him in the group of the progressive heirs of the Polish Enlightenment and the forerunners of the revolutionary democratic historiography. Poppe pointed to the enormous influence of Joachim Lelewel on Chodakowski, which seems to be even more interesting if we take into consideration that Chodakowski was older than Lelewel and died before the publication of the most important and popular works of the latter Romantic historian. Despite this, Poppe claimed that almost every progressive feature of

Chodakowski's ideology had been borrowed from Lelewel. On the other hand, all the problematical aspects and limits within the works of the Polish slavist were also considered to be an effect of Lelewel's influence. A diligent reader of this article may get the impression that, according to the Marxist researcher, Chodakowski's positive elements belonged to his own courtesy, while Lelewel was responsible for all his ideological shortcomings. This attempt illustrates the historian's attitude towards Russia as a crucial model that was thought to be capable of redemption from ideological or methodological backwardness. Unfortunately, neither Polish history in general, nor the history of historiography could deliver many examples of pro-Russian sympathies.

To demonstrate this was much easier in the case of Czech or Slovak historiography. In many respects, František Palacký could be seen as a Czech counterpart to Lelewel. He was also a national political leader. His vision of national history is perceived even today as a Romantic one. He shared the belief in ancient Slavic democracy, the German nature of feudalism and the glamorous future of his nation. The most striking differences between Palacký and Lelewel were of a political nature. Lelewel belonged to the radical democrats, while Palacký shifted from liberalism to social conservatism with pan-Slavic undertones. The Marxist evaluation of the Czech historian was, interestingly enough, quite positive. Josef Macek considered Palacký's interpretation of Czech history to be progressive. Palacký appreciated the Hussite movement. He did not distinguish between the more progressive radical Hussite movement of Tábor and moderate Hussites, but this minor fact did not change the opinions that he had already arrived at. As a historian and a politician, Palacký represented the most progressive part of the bourgeoisie in its glorious days, especially before the Revolution of 1848.

However, as a liberal, and soon-to-be a conservative, politician, Palacký could not always expect such positive responses from Marxist historians. A Soviet researcher, Ivan Ivanovich Udalcov, accused Palacký of being not only conservative but also a nationalist (chauvinist). Palacký's idea of austro-slavism was, according to Udalcov, reactionary. The Czech national movement as a whole was also reactionary, since it supported the Habsburg monarchy in its struggle against the revolutions in Vienna and in Hungary. This opinion, which came from a Soviet historian and a prominent Soviet diplomat in Prague, could not be openly rejected by Czech historians. There were only two people who challenged Udalcov in order to defend Palacký from Marxist criticism. In 1948 (when the approach of the Marxist-Leninist 'methodological revolution' was still not obvious) Josef Macůrek, the 'bourgeois' historian from Brno, confronted the Soviet researcher during his visit to the congress of Polish historians in Wrocław.[20] Several years later, the first president of the Czechoslovak Academy of Sciences and the main codifier of the Czech Marxist vision of history, Zdeněk Nejedlý firmly (and successfully) resisted Udalcov, who tried to erase Palacký from the Museum of National Literature (*Památník národního písemnictví*).[21] Nevertheless, the only promising way to defend national values was to try to 'reconcile' Udalcov with Palacký. In the university handbook on Czech history, Udalcov was cited as 'the best expert on the Revolution of 1848'.[22] Josef Kočí, the reviewer of Udalcov's book in *Československý Časopis Historický*, shared the same positive assessment, but added that Udalcov failed to pay attention to some positive aspects of the Czech national movement, especially to the role of Palacký as a historian.[23] Bedřich Šindelář formulated the same idea in a different way when he wrote (in 1952 in *Časopis Matice Moravské*): 'We must distinguish between Palacký – the historian, and Palacký – the politician.'[24] The Marxist evaluation of Palacký, despite his political beliefs and despite the harsh criticism of Marx and Engels, which had been directed against the Czech national movement as a whole, was more benevolent than the same Marxist evaluation of Lelewel.

The Slovak Marxist interpretation of one of the leaders of the national rebirth, Ľudovít Štúr, shows striking analogies with the image of Palacký. He was regarded almost as a creator of the Slovak nation. As Vladimír Mináč put it, 'at the beginning there was a Word. And this Word was by Štúr. [...] So, it was Štúr at the beginning'.[25] Štúr was described as a fighter for social and political progress, for Slovak national identity and for Slovak culture as well as for universal values.[26] Although he remained critical towards the idea of Czecho-Slovak national unity, he always expressed his sympathies with the Czechs.[27] He was an internationalist and political moralist on his way to becoming a revolutionary.[28] He was said to have been the best student, economist, linguist, educator, publicist, poet, politician, and – last but not least – the best Slovak historian of his times.[29] Karol Goláň stated that he had possessed some prophetic abilities, for Štúr was supposed to foresee the decline of capitalism in Slovakia.[30] In his latter years, he became a pan-Slavist, who proposed the assimilation of all Slavic nations to the Russian language and culture, but this conservative turn did not change the positive attitude of Marxists towards Štúr.[31]

In fact, if there was anything that could overshadow this picture of a national hero, it was his attitude towards the Hungarian Revolution of 1848-1849. This particular revolution belonged not only to the 'progressive traditions' of the neighboring socialist Hungary, it was also one of the democratic movements that were vehemently supported by Marx and Engels. In 1954, the young Slovak historian and ethnographer, Vladimír Matula, drew attention to this element of ideological inconvenience. According to

Matula, the ordinary Slovak interpretation of the national movement was highly subjective and idealized. According to him, the truth was that Štúr and other Slovak politicians had supported reactionary Austria against the European revolution embodied by the Hungarian leader, Lajos Kossuth. Only some marginal radically democratic Slovak groups that supported the Hungarians were truly progressive (Matula mentioned the names of Janko Kraľ and Jan Francisci in particular). The mainstream of the Slovak national movement was far from any democratic ideology. Matula classified their attitude as enlightened-liberal. After 1848, Matula found no signs of social progressiveness in the Slovak national camp.[32]

Such a re-assessment of Štúr was shocking, and attempts to question Matula's theses were published almost immediately. Although Karol Goláň admitted that the Slovak national movement had collaborated with Vienna, he stressed that it had simply had no other choice, as 'The national chauvinism of the Hungarian movement [...] excluded any other option'.[33] In January 1955, Matula faced his opponents at the conference of the Historical Institute of the Slovak Academy of Sciences in Bratislava (*Historický ústav Slovenskej akadémie vied*). This time Karol Goláň was supported by a strange coalition that consisted of the Stalinist Academy-member, Andrej Mráz and a young, bright and 'apolitical' sociologist and historian, Július Mésároš.[34] The first phase of the debate ended in 1955 when the Slovak Academy of Sciences published the so-called 'theses' for the Marxist university handbook for history students. According to the authors, Štúr was partly wrong because the agenda of the Hungarian Revolution had a clearly progressive impact on all the nationalities. But, on the other hand, he was right in noticing that the Hungarian liberal opposition decided to respect historical-feudal rights while ignoring national ones (and ignoring the postulates of the Slovak national movement accordingly).[35]

In 1956, the Slovak scientific community celebrated the 100th anniversary of Štúr's death. The central historical journal *Historický časopis Slovenskej akadémie vied* printed Štúr's portrait on its front page, and the foreword gave an account of the recent debates about the Slovak national movement in the 19th century. Its author also criticized the two allegedly extreme options - bourgeois nationalism and national nihilism - with equal measure.[36] The following study by Július Mésároš was entitled *'Boj Ľudovíta Štúra proti feudalizmu'* (Ľudovít Štúr's struggle against feudalism). Mésároš pointed out the important social differences between Hungarian revolutionaries and the members of the Slovak national movement. Slovaks belonged to the common people, whereas the origin of Hungarian liberals was from the gentry. Thus, their social radicalism was seriously limited. For Štúr and his fellow-fighters – according to Mésároš – the Hungarian Revolution was simply not progressive enough.

> The bourgeois reforms in the form given by the liberal gentry in March 1848 was only a shadow of the ideas for which Štúr fought. The abolishment of serfdom, the radical change of the feudal means of production and the elimination of the privileges of the gentry was accomplished only partly. It was not enough.[37]

These opinions were supported by Soviet researchers during the Štúr conference in Moscow in 1956.[38] Several weeks before, a gigantic conference in Bratislava had taken place in which the participants had simply ignored any critical remarks concerning the national hero. Vladimír Matula himself delivered an address on Štúr's Slavic idea, stressing its 'healthy features' and not reiterating his previous critical remarks.[39]

In the meantime, Matula's critical re-assessment of Štúr was completely abandoned. The new Hungarian uprising in 1956 was one of the reasons for the posthumous victory of Štúr over Kossuth. In 1959, the Czechoslovak university handbook described Štúr as an unquestionable source of progressive and national values. The Hungarian Revolution was then compared to the current Hungarian 'counter-revolution' and was thus excluded from progressive traditions.[40] Matula, however, tried to defend the remnants of his theory claiming that the old Štúr, while being politically conservative and pan-Slavist, had been close to the radical democrats of 1848, Kral' and Francisci, 'without their revolutionary strategy of course'.[41] Matula's attempt to interpret a 'conservative revolution' as a democratic one did not trigger any further discussion.

The better and more progressive that Štúr and the Slovak national movement became, the more reactionary the Hungarian Revolution of 1848 began to be seen. In the mid-1960s, Vladimír Mináč wrote:

> This revolution we fought against was odd from its very beginnings: *drôle le revolution*. The figures were moving: the casino in Pest instead of the Viennese court; five Hungarian aristocratic families instead of the emperor. It was characteristic for this strange revolution that no other reaction, restoration or counter-revolution was needed to stop it. This revolution had an inborn protest, reaction and restoration – revolution with a victorious seed of reaction.[42]

Vladimír Matula's article has been extensively quoted since 1954, especially during the period of political liberalism in the Slovak Spring of the 1960s. His attempt to re-interpret Štúr and the Slovak national movement was considered a Stalinization of historiography. Moreover, it became the main example of all the anti-national features of the Stalinist period. Ľudovít Holotík (director of the Historical Institute of the Academy) wrote in 1963 that:

> the ideological campaign against nationalism was one-sided, it was restricted to Slovakia and accompanied by the system of distrust and terror. In those conditions, the need to search for Slovak progressive traditions was wrongly understood, they were labeled as nationalist (for example, when it came to the characteristics of Ľudovít Štúr, *etc.*).[43]

The allusion to Matula's text was quite clear. Moreover, the idea of an anti-national Stalinist historiography attempting to 'destroy' Štúr is still present in the Slovak public and in scientific discussion. In 1991, during the Congress of the Slovak Historical Society (*Slovenská historická spoločnost*), Richard Marsina claimed that, in the communist period, only the small nations had been accused of nationalism, while it had to be made clear that, whatever they had done, they had done to defend their existence against the suppression of the 'great' nations.[44] Neither the Štúr controversy nor any other element of the Slovak Marxist interpretation of history justifies these propositions.

Another aspect of the debate on progressiveness was the adoption of the idea of historical progress. No Marxist evaluation of historical forces could fail to address this issue. Romantic historians, although idealist (and, in fact, simply because they were idealists), believed in the linear progress of history, which was also shared by Marx and Engels. The adherents of positivist philosophy, although in many ways different, also shared the belief in linear and constant progressive evolution. This rendered them, in part, at least, adjustable to the Marxist vision of history. In contrast, Ranke with his critique of the Hegelian philosophy of history, with the vision of separate epochs to be judged according to their own rules, was unacceptable. In comparison with Ranke's historicism, the nationalist tendency of the Prussian school was much easier to justify.

'Optimism' versus 'Pessimism'

The differences between the Polish communist reluctance towards Lelewel, perceived as being only partly progressive, and the Czech and Slovak admiration for Palacký and Štúr, is not at all a unique phenomenon. On the contrary, many historians of historiography recognize the immanent difference between more and less 'nationalist' Marxist historiographies. The Czech and Slovak cases illustrate a more 'optimistic' model, the Polish case seems more 'pessimistic' and the East-German – being the most dependant on current political developments – was also the most flexible, shifting from radical post-war 'pessimism' to the nationalist and Prussian 'renaissance' just before the collapse of the state. Let us now focus upon these two extremes of Marxist interpretations: on historical 'pessimism' and 'optimism'.[45]

The 'optimistic' model was highly unified. We find hardly any important historical controversies in the Czech or Slovak context. If such a controversy appeared, it was almost immediately silenced. The interpretation of national history depended on the liberal-nationalist historiographical tradition in so far as it did not confront Marxist dogmas. The Marxist vision of the past shared certain liberal-nationalist convictions in general (it described the history of the nation, not of class struggle or economic development) and in specific details (such as the interpretation of the Hussite movement, Palacký or Štúr, *etc.*). Paradoxically, such a development meant that any other Marxist (but non-orthodox) interpretation was hardly possible.

The 'pessimistic' model of the Polish and – partly – the East German historiography of the Stalinist period were much more open for historical discussions. It differed from the model of 'normal science' because it stressed the need for a single exclusive 'true' interpretation of every single topic. The debates between Polish or German historians who supported the progressiveness of Lelewel, Hoffman, Ranke or the Prussian school led to the canonization of one chosen solution. After the canonization, no other interpretation could be formed, because there could not be two distinct Marxist interpretations of the same phenomenon. Thus, within various models of Marxist interpretation, some non-national (and sometimes even openly anti-national) ideas could appear much more often, as happened in the Czech or the Slovak cases. Paradoxically, their presence was, instead, seen as a sign of a relatively open historical debate within Marxist limits. In reality, the 'pessimistic' version appeared when the Polish or German history interfered with the privileged Soviet vision of the national past. Polish democrats of the 19th century (such as Lelewel) were, unfortunately, doing their best to fight against the Russian tsar. Similarly, the anti-Slavic features of German history were condemned (at least until the late 1960s) by GDR-historiography.

One should also take into consideration the relatively significant German and Polish historiographical traditions as the 'internal' cause that led to the multiplicity of opinions within Marxist historical science that so often stressed its unity and uniformity. It was often too difficult to decide which ones to capitalize upon and which ones to condemn and forget. Whether to praise the democratic Lelewel or to choose the positivist historians as representatives of the new socio-economic formation remained an unresolved dilemma. Paradoxically, it could be said that German and Polish Marxists of the Stalinist period had prolonged and copied the historiographical debates of the 19th century. In the 1950s, albeit in a rather simplified way, the controversies between Romanticism and Positivism or Conservatism and Liberalism had their equivalent in the polemics of German and Polish Marxist historians.

The 'optimistic' and 'pessimistic' model of Marxist historiography can be seen as a conflict between the 'right' and 'left' interpretations described by Lutz Raphael. The 'left' always sought for class struggle and perceived only the lower classes as being progressive. A more moderate 'right' interpretation considers the continuity of the progressive development towards the peak of national history: the independent, people's-democratic state. In this latter model, certain knights, kings and burghers were also included in the progressive traditions.[46] It should be made clear, however, that neither the 'optimistic' nor the 'pessimistic' (or 'right' and 'left') Marxist interpretation of national history can be perceived as being better than the other by any standards. Both of them were simply the variants of the same Soviet type of Marxism. In addition, both types aspired to achieve a monopoly status in all topics under discussion.

The Model

To sum up, Marxist ways of interpreting the history of historiography encountered several important problems in methodological, cultural and political terms. The first group of problems emerged during the process of translating the historiographical tradition into the language of Marxism. Nineteenth century historians were detached from their original cultural and scientific context, and were transposed into different theoretical frames. They had to answer ahistorical questions from the point of view of Soviet Marxism and not from the point of view of their age or of the history of historiography. The best illustrations of this problem were the Polish debates on the criteria of progressiveness or the discrepancies between the Marxist adherents of Ranke and of the Prussian school.

The second group of problems can be described as essentially geopolitical. Marxist historiographies in East-Central Europe often praised the historical phenomena that were pro-Russian in their political implications without paying too much attention to their social or political context. Thus, the conservative pan-Slavists were less problematical than the progressive anti-tsarist democrats. Even Marx and Engels could be wrong in those instances where they criticized or neglected the historical role of

Russia. Clearly, it was Polish historiography that suffered most from this geopolitical factor.

Finally, the third group of problems raises the question of 19th century nationalism. Since Marxist-Leninist historiographies in East-Central Europe never adopted the radical Pokrovski-type of 'Bolshevik' historiography with all its non-national and anti-national features, they remained deeply indebted to the national traditions that had been shaped by such personalities as Palacký, Lelewel, Štúr, and the Prussian, the Krakow or the Warsaw school. It would have been a drastic step for them to have cut the ties that bound Marxist historians to the tradition of national movements. They gradually became more 'nationalist', but, even in the Stalinist period in the 1950s, one could find many instances of continuity between the previous historiographical tradition and the new methodological tendency. Marxism - understood as a scientific revolution - never fulfilled what it had promised: it never managed to go beyond the tenets of its objects of study.

The following three aspects could be grouped among the common elements of Marxist historiographies in Poland, Czechoslovakia and the GDR: Marxist translation of historiographical tradition, the geopolitical situation, and nationalism (or the national tradition). One should note that Marxist historiographies were not only a 'prolongation of politics through the means of historical science' as Jan Herman Brinks has argued in his book on East German historiography.[47] It was, in many respects, a highly problematical and difficult attempt to cope with the tradition of national historiographies. Although Marxism sometimes challenged those traditions, it often integrated them into its vision of the past with or without making any footnotes.

15

The Origins of Symmetry: A Micro-History of the Birth of Communist Historiography in Hungary

Péter Apor

1

The basic popular history book of the 1950s on the origins of the counter-revolutionary regime that had ruled Hungary between 1919 and 1944 retrospectively classified the Horthy regency as a fascist system.

> The Hungarian ruling class developed the first European fascism by applying old and new means of oppression, thereby showing—for the first time—what fascism, which would wildly ravish Europe two decades later and drive millions of people to war, looked like. One can hardly find a characteristic feature of Hitler's and Mussolini's dictatorships which cannot be immediately found in Hungarian fascism. The fear of Bolshevism, the ruthless oppression of the working class and the wild racist incitement were the same in all these regimes. They all demonstrate the same unrestrained rule by the big capitalists and landowners, the same anti-progressive and anti-culture attitudes, the same depreciation of the working man and the same social demagogy.
>
> Thus, in 1919 and 1920, it was not merely the seeds of fascism that appeared in Hungary, but, rather, fascism itself. In Hungarian fascism of the twenties and forties, not only the fundamental idea, but even the participants were the same. In 1919 in Orgovány, and in 1942 at the massacre in Újvidék, the same Horthy stands at the helm; in the middle of the thirties, it was the same Gyula Gömbös, who adjusted Hungarian fascism to the newly emerged

> Nazi movement, who led the extreme right wing MOVE in 1920. László Endre (a major figure in the Hungarian Holocaust), who was a brutal county leader in the Gödöllő district in 1920, and who became state secretary in the Ministry of Interior in 1944, threw hundreds of thousands of innocent people to the German fascist murderers. The same people, the same crimes: from 1920 to 1944, to the reign of terror of the Arrow-Cross hordes, our history has a direct road.[1]

The authors argued that the rule of the Hungarian fascist Arrow-Cross Party in 1944 and 1945 had its roots in the activity of the white terror commandoes that persecuted Communists, Jews and leftist persons after the collapse of the short-lived Hungarian Soviet Republic of 1919. The similarity of the violence convinced communist historians that fascism in Hungary had been born in 1919. Thus, the inter-war Hungarian system was closely associated with the crimes committed by the Nazis and their companions throughout Europe. As a result, it became possible to claim that the counter-revolutionary regime of Admiral Miklós Horthy was genuine fascism. At the same time, it was also claimed that fascism had emerged during the struggle against communism, and was, in reality, nothing else but anti-communism. Consequently, communism was the real opposition to fascism. This peculiar interpretation of history emerged to justify the power of the Party, because the narrative entailed that the only genuine alternative to the Horthy regime was the communist system. Moreover, since counter-revolution was equated with the rule of Evil, communism represented the rule of Good. This teleological interpretation of history that leads to the inevitable victory of the Communist Party was a typical example of Stalinist historical writing. In fact, this belief in historical inevitability had already featured the interpretation of the 1917 October Revolution and the fall of the Provisional Government, which were considered to guided by historical laws. An attempt was made to adapt these principles, which were based upon a Manichean view of the struggle between light and darkness, good and evil, proletarian revolution and bourgeois reaction, to the particular records of contemporary Hungarian history.[2]

The second source of the sovietization of Hungarian historiography were the post-war political trials in which communist and leftist intellectuals – after 1945 – first encountered a substantial amount of historical records and faced the pressing challenge of interpreting the recent past. The newly founded People's Tribunals in 1945 called to account those who were accused of committing war crimes. This conformed to international expectations and was also required by the armistice treaty. In spite of the fact that the trials of the major war criminals ended in 1946, the people's courts had an unusual history thereafter. They were authorized to deal with crimes committed 'against the order of the republic'. The People's Tribunals prosecuted László Rajk, the most well-known victim of Stalinist purges in Hungary. After this trial, the courts ceased to exist. However, they were resurrected after the uprising in 1956, when crimes against the people's democracy were dealt with once again by People's Tribunals.[3] Using the records of a local trial which ended with capital punishment, this essay concentrates on the procedures and practices of connecting abstract historical constructions to actual individual lives in order to render them tangible and provide evidence for their credibility. The chapter also seeks to demonstrate that popular forms of memory-biased and politically-biased history writing both contributed to a peculiar way of individualizing history. Focusing on the method of proof, the essay draws conclusions concerning the form, as well as the structure, of communist historical representations.

2

At the beginning of 1947, Lőrinc Latorczay, whose original family name was Szim, was denounced for assaulting people in 1920, when he had been commander of the Military Department of Investigations in Northern Hungary. He was apprehended and tried by the People's Tribunal in the provincial city of Miskolc in 1947-1948 and was sentenced to death as a war criminal. The People's Tribunal condemned Latorczay for crimes committed in 1919 and 1920, which was an obvious legal error.[4] Although political crimes committed in 1919 and the following years belonged to the competence of the People's Tribunals, these acts were not classified as war crimes.[5]

There were ninety-six witnesses present at the court and most of them accused Szim of murdering and assaulting people. As one of them put it, 'there were serious beatings' in the cells of his headquarters. Another witness, who had been in jail there for two days, saw a lot of people covered in blood. When he was beaten he 'wailed so much that it could be heard even on the street'. A third witness was assaulted so badly that he lay ill for three months. One of the witnesses gave evidence that beatings happened daily. Even more cruel tortures were inflicted. According to one witness, the defendant hit one of his victims in the face 140 times and knocked out all of his teeth. One man testified that he received twenty-six beatings in a month and said that Szim had hit him even with a seal ring. On one occasion, he was bound to a chair, a stick was put into his mouth and Szim's men spat into it; they tore his hair out and hit his head with a stick causing a wound that did not heal for ten years. Another witness stated that he had seen a person whose face had been torn to pieces. One of the testimonies claimed that Szim and his subordinates had beaten a war invalid who was amputated below the knees. One of the ex-prisoners remembered that one of the victim's noses had been bleeding after the 'treatment'. The blood had been collected in a glass and he had been forced to drink it. Several statements claimed that people had been killed whilst under interrogation, and that Szim had personally shot two men. Another recalled a case in which Szim had killed a person, because he had struck back. A third witness had given account of the extra-judicial murder of a railwayman. This testimony described a scene in which the victim had begged for his life, but the lieutenant gave the order to fire.[6]

These testimonies described the defendant as a disgustingly violent person. 'Szim abused a thirteen year old child, women and even the seventy-one year-old man to satisfy his sadistic propensity.' One of the witnesses remembered that the lieutenant injured children: his fifteen-year old brother had been taken away and had returned home severely bruised. Another witness recalled the times when, as a twelve-year old, he had delivered cigarettes and meals to the inmates. Szim disliked this and had, therefore, had him beaten. The officer had pulled his ears until they started bleeding. Another testified that a woman had been beaten with an iron bar. Another one had seen that 'women were treated in the same way as male captives'. One of the testimonies described how Szim showed no mercy even to elderly women. This witness recollected that the officer had kicked his fifty-five year-old mother. Often, prisoners were not fed. Moreover, one witness remembered that, if a relative brought a meal, it would be overturned, and the captive had to lick the food up from the ground. The same witness also said that, due to the mental injuries which his wife had received during her visits to the police station, his baby had 'sucked milk poisoned by his wife's nerves' and the child had died in its fifth year.[7] Szim preferred interrogating his victims at night. One of the victims remembered the rumor that Szim and his men investigated by day and interrogated at night. Another witness recounted that he had been taken to Szim for a beating at night. A third one remembered that screaming could be heard every night. Executions were generally carried out at night, 'One night somebody cried, then, I heard a shot and the crying stopped. I was taken to Szim for interrogation twice late at night'.[8] The popular memory formulated by the witnesses during the trial took on the genre of a thriller. One may construct the blurb of a pulp fiction by using the text of the testimonies. This was 'the horror-story of the Szim-nursing home'. 'In the cell of his institution called the house of terror' sat Szim, 'the monster of the Csabai kapu (the street where the building stood) and those caught in his grasp' were tortured cruelly. 'Here it is impossible to sleep due to the constant wailing, corpses are transported weekly' from the prison.[9]

The tropes by which Latorczay was characterized by the witnesses are very old ones. The defendant was described as a person who treated children cruelly. The early Christians as well as the Jews later were accused of slaughtering children. In the Middle-Ages, heretics and witches were also accused of the same sins. The murdering of children is generally considered by every society to be a crime that breaks very basic norms. Therefore, a group which denies or is believed to deny the fundamental rules of its society is usually accused of killing children. Latorczay's night activity has very similar ancient meanings. Those who act in the night, under the veil of darkness are usually suspicious characters. The practices of the Knights Templars at nightfall was emphasized in their trials, witches flew and also held their meetings at night. The night recalls an alien, unknown world full of dangers. The night is the world of monsters.[10]

The narrative of the defendant presented by the witnesses was a narrative of a monster, of a cold-blooded resolute killer. He 'subjected large numbers of people to long-lasting torture revealing unrestrained cruelty, with which he aimed to kill his victims. Only persons of very strong constitutions and mental strength could withstand such treatment'.[11] Such bloodlust may trigger an extreme sense of danger. 'When Lőrinc Latorczay-Szim, once an officer of Horthy's clique, was escorted from the Military Political Department to the juridical lock-up, the detective who accompanied him noticed a shocking scene. A dog was sitting in front of the gate of the County Hall. When it saw Szim, it started to whimper showing its teeth, and then it ran away in fear. Even the dumb animal suspected the bloodhound in him.'[12] The figure of Latorczay-Szim, as formed by the witnesses, obviously meant a significant danger to normal people.

The general popular understanding was connected with politically more meaningful concepts in some of the confessions. A musician remembered that he had played a song recalling Béla Kun at the beginning of 1920 and that, as a result, he had been taken in and beaten with a stick. A witness recollected that, when he stood before Szim in November 1920, the lieutenant had shouted at him, 'So, you are that renowned communist' and had beaten him up. Others were allegedly taken away, either because of abusing the Horthy-army or singing the *Marseillaise*. One of the confessions claimed that the victim had been beaten because he had delivered a speech by the grave of a Red Army soldier. Another man was convinced that he had been victimized because he had participated in suppressing the counter-revolutionary uprising of the Ludovika Academy during the Soviet Republic. A third one remembered that Szim's men had raided his premises searching for a red flag, a typewriter and leaflets. During the house-search, he was beaten and was also kicked with a spur. The defendant was characterized as a fanatical anti-Communist. According to one statement, he remarked after killing a person, 'this is your common fate, dirty communists!' Szim was also said to have shouted: 'I will kill all of you like flies in autumn, bloody communists!'[13]

As a cruel anti-communist, Latorczay-Szim was associated with the white terrorists in the report of the investigation. 'The white terror commando committed a series of brutal tortures and executions. All the responsibility is Szim's, he was the leader; in his lock-up, left-wing people were tortured.'[14] The description of Latorczay-Szim as a white terrorist helped to explain his deeds. On the other hand, his figure personalized the crimes of this group. Numerous witnesses believed that they could explain Szim's cruelty. As one of them put it, Szim had been the cruelest figure of white terror in Miskolc. White terrorists played a significant role in the establishment of the counter-revolutionary system. They were usually recruited from the officers of the Hungarian army in the First World War, and, after the fall of the Hungarian Soviet Republic, they persecuted communists and Jews. Such groups are generally described as 'officer commandos'. One of the witnesses remembered that the defendant 'had also been the commander of the widely-known Szim-commando'. Nevertheless, Latorczay-Szim's unit was not a military detachment like the officer-commandos. His men were regular military troops, who conducted political investigations between 1919 and 1921. Nevertheless, the witnesses remembered that he had been a bloodthirsty sadist who had gained a reputation in Borsod county equal to that of Iván Héjjas (the most notorious figure of the white terror executions) in the Trans-Tisza region. Therefore, it was logical for the witnesses that Szim had also been a white terrorist of that time.[15]

Other witnesses attributed more direct political meaning to the defendant's figure. As one of them put it, 'Szim was a lieutenant with a crane-feather who acted on Horthy's highest order with unlimited power'. The crane-feather was the symbol of Horthy's 'national army' which distinguished the soldiers from the Red Army troops who wore the red star. Another witness claimed, 'I definitely remember that the defendant was mounted on a white horse at the corner of the engine-house'.[16] The color of the horse was not a neutral element in this description. It recalled the well-known scene of Miklós Horthy's marching into Budapest on a white horse. The witnesses thus posited the defendant as a typical member of the Horthy-regime. Such political meaning was amplified by the politically conscious People's Tribunal and the left-wing press. In their perception,

> Lőrinc Szim was Horthy's bloody handed henchman in Miskolc.[17]

> He was a wicked murderer of the counter-revolution who became a colonel due to his brutality in the Horthy-regime.[18]

> He appeared in Miskolc with a special commission after the takeover of the white terror. He was granted an absolutely free hands to crack down on the leftists, he had unlimited power to achieve his goal. The place of his operation was the so called Szim-sanatorium where he interrogated the leftist people who came into his hands in the cruelest manner together with his subordinates.[19]

> His aim was to silence every freedom-loving Hungarian by causing fear and dread, and to lead the murderous counter-revolution to power.[20]

Thus, Latorczay-Szim was depicted as a brutal criminal, who, in addition, had made the Horthy-regime tangibly comprehensible. 'Lőrinc Latorczai Szim was the type of the regime-knight, of this darkest type of human beings which had been produced by the previous decades.'[21] 'The defendant who let the children of the people languish, this was the counter-revolution and the Hungarian terror.'[22] In the courtroom, Latorczay-Szim became the embodiment of the alleged brutality of the Horthy-regime in its entirety.

According to the Act on the People's Tribunals the 'illegal execution and torturing of people' – which could not be persecuted in the previous regime – had to be investigated and punished as 'crimes against the people and humanity'. In describing Szim, the judge made reference to this act, and did not utilize the term 'war crime'. Nevertheless, the reasoning of the verdict consistently stated that the defendant's deeds met all the criteria of war crimes. According to the Act of the People's Tribunals, a war criminal was a person who promoted the expansion of the war to Hungary in 1939, or the involvement of Hungary in the war. The question was, thus, how political crimes committed in 1919 had contributed to Hungary's war catastrophe. The sentence argued:

> After the fall of the Hungarian Soviet Republic which happened on 1 August 1919, the counter-revolution that spread over its ruins wrote the most baneful and disgraceful pages in Hungarian history.
> This is the first page in a chapter that was concluded by Ferenc Szálasi's insensate reign of terror at the end of 1944 and the spring of 1945 as the Russian Red Army of liberation was forging ahead. The war against the Hungarian people was started by Miklós

> Horthy in his sanguinary frenzy in the year 1919 on behalf of his class and clique with his slayer henchmen, and was pursued by him through various means during the next 25 years, when he insanely passed the murderous weapon into Ferenc Szálasi's hands in shameful conditions on 15 October 1945, who cut the last strokes with it on the Hungarian people until the liberation.
> This war, the struggle of the counter-revolution against the Hungarian people was constant during a period of a quarter of a century, it was waged by the same forces, was motivated by the same goals, the difference was only in the means shaped by the circumstances of the age.[23]

The history here ended with a real 'apocalypse': the catastrophe and destruction of the Second World War. The collapse, however, was attributed to one single cause by the judge: the fall of the First Hungarian Soviet Republic. According to the sentence, the road from 1919 towards 1944 was straight and unambiguous: history left no alternative but war after the defeat of the proletarian regime.

> There passed 25 years between 1919 and 1944. The oppression, the struggle of the reaction against the Hungarian people started in 1919. In the year of 1945, the glorious soldiers of the Red Army liberated the country from oppression and subjugation. Essentially, throughout the 25 years, the reaction continued its struggle against the Hungarian people with the same means in 1919 and in 1944... Here is a politically uniform process which started in 1919 and ended at the time of the liberation.[24]

Apocalyptic or prophetic histories see in the past only pre-histories and pre-figurations, and attempt to represent inevitability and dismiss all alternative possibilities. They are usually based upon the rhetorical device of mirroring back the knowledge of the present into the past, which seeks the signs of events in the past to prove that the eventual outcome was the only possible historical outcome.[25] The historical interpretation of the People's Tribunal implied that the war catastrophe had been the inevitable consequence of the defeat of the revolutionary forces; namely, the Soviet Republic. As the Horthy regime had been born to crush the genuine movement of the people, it had to maintain a constant struggle against the people. The judge argued that the war itself had been nothing other than another means of fighting against the Hungarian people. From this point of view, the only satisfactory explanation of Hungary's participation in the war was that it was a means of perpetuating the survival of the Horthy regime. The counter-revolution in 1919 had been the beginning of this political system; thus, it was also the start of the war.

In the interpretation of the People's Tribunal's, the collapse of the First Hungarian Soviet Republic was the cause of the war-catastrophe, since it was in 1919 that the fascist regime of 1944 had been born in Hungary.

> Not without grounds, Horthy boasted that the first manifestation of fascism appeared in Hungary in 1919, while Hitler and Mussolini admitted the fact resignedly. This fascist era continued during the next twenty-five years.[26]

The events of 1919 convinced the court that the 'Horthyist-fascist dictatorship' had come to power with the single purpose of eliminating communism; therefore, it concluded that communism was the only true enemy of fascism. The essence of the fascist systems was to fight communism. Consequently, the inevitable fall of the fascist powers meant the inevitable triumph of communism, because, besides these two historical forces, there were no other alternatives. In turn, this straightforward historical interpretation was a powerful means of justifying communist rule. The judge argued that the defeat in the war had become unavoidable from the very moment that the first communist regime in 1919 was overthrown. Furthermore, as the war resulted in the destruction of the counter-revolutionary system, its fall had been encoded at the time of its genesis. With this reasoning, the sentence sought to demonstrate the thesis of the inevitable downfall of all non-communist social and political structures. The judge believed that, by such a historical argument, the thesis of the inevitable victory of communist systems could be justified.

The purpose of the trials of war criminals in Hungary was, from the beginning, the creation of historical narratives. The foundations of this peculiar representation of the recent past were laid down by the communist or leftist political attempts to discredit the constructed history of the Horthy-regime in order to bolster the legitimacy of the new political system.[27] The preface to the decree on the People's Tribunals in 1945, written by István Ries, then social democrat Minister of Justice, already claimed that the beginnings of the road leading to the war catastrophe had to be sought in the events of 1919:

> The destruction of Hungary did not start with Hungary's drifting into the war and less with Sztójay's or Szálasi's Arrow-Cross rule. The counter-revolution succeeding the revolution of 1919 laid the grounds for the Hungarian catastrophe... It could almost be

> foreseen that they would set the country on fire. They systematically prepared the Hungarian people for suicide.[28]

In this regard, the Hungarian trials and their similar Central and Eastern European counterparts differed from the Western European pattern from the beginning. In the West, the post-war trials of those accused of war crimes were principally aimed at amending the victims' memories of wartime sufferings, without any explicit claim to the construction of overarching historical interpretations.[29]

The formal similarity of legal and historical practices, lends credence to the judge's claim to ascertain the truth about the historical past. History and jurisprudence share common epistemological roots: in fact, both historiography and legal proceedings originated in the demand to establish the reality of the past. Generally speaking, a juridical verdict needs the notion of the past in order to make statements about the present. This means that, in order to claim titles, rights or judgments in a legally appropriate way, one has to know the preceding events of the case in question. In order to claim these rights or the basis for legal actions, one has to prove that something actually took place. Thus, it is necessary to demonstrate the actual *reality* of a happening. Legal reasoning in Western law ordinarily takes the following form: the established facts indicate a plot that is always related to the past, whereby the proven events are organized in a chronological order. The argumentation is always retroactive: an action that is known by the judge is conceived of as having been done because of certain reasons which, however, are only assumed to be probable. This is also the way modern historiography operates.[30]

Szim personified and realized the narrative described above. The sentence declared: 'The defendant was one of the outstanding leaders of this exterminating war led by executioners.'[31] One of the articles of a newspaper claimed, that 'the Hungarian people were offended by the activity of the defendant!'[32] Another paper wrote that 'The honor of the Hungarian people requires Lőrinc Szim to suffer for the crimes committed against the people!'[33] 'The People's Tribunal in Miskolc sentenced the bloody handed executioner of the workers and peasants in Upper-Hungary to death',[34] as one article informed the population. Later, it gave an account of the trial in the following way:

> The terrifying crimes of the counter-revolution have been revealed during the trial. The true face of the counter-revolution born in crime and blood, and which perpetrated the killing of peasants and workers was shown in its own nakedness.[35]

The public trial itself was abundant in horrific details. The court attempted to show tangible or visible evidence wherever it was possible. When one of the witnesses stated that, 'The defendant kicked even the flesh from my chest,' then 'according to the People's Prosecutor's proposal the witness takes off his coat and, pulling up his shirt, shows his chest. The Chairman and the People's Judges inspect the witness' breast and state that a mark from a bruise can be seen on that.' Later, the 'witness takes his upper set of teeth (a dental plate), shows it and declares: all of my teeth were knocked out'.[36] These details had no direct relationship with the course of the historical narrative. They played no role in advancing the story. According to the judge, the existence of counter-revolution would have resulted in the downfall of the regime during the Second World War, even without the committing of ruthless crimes. Such particulars fulfilled no narrative function. Having no symbolic function, such details could only state and indicate that the story *really happened*.[37] The press also emphasized the horrifying details. Press articles bore titles such as the following: 'Horrors of the Szim trial',[38] 'Witnesses confess of brutal torture in Szim's trial',[39] 'Gruesome testimony of terrors in the Szim-sanatorium',[40] 'Szim knocked out all teeth of a craftsman with his own hands',[41] 'First blow given by Lőrinc Szim to victims taken to the house of terrors in Csabai kapu, old handicapped invalid beaten until he was covered with blood'.[42] The articles gave accounts of similar events. 'The henchmen of the Szim-sanatorium hanged their victim by his hair.'[43] An article quoted a witness who 'had seen in the cell that a man rolled about in his blood as the nails had been torn from his toes by Szim's executioners'.[44] The newspapers attempted to capture the attention of their readers. Shocking brief statements appeared on front-pages: 'Blood-curdling details on the horrors of the Szim-sanatorium,'[45] 'Lőrinc Szim's henchmen started their carefully chosen tortures at the evening peal of bells,' or 'Lőrinc Szim was Horthy's blood-handed henchman in Miskolc'.[46]

Latorczay-Szim and his defense lawyer attempted to rebut the accusations. Their tactic was directed against the charge of war crimes. Nevertheless, they did not challenge the thesis that the political crimes committed in 1919 and 1920 had been war crimes, but instead sought to prove that Latorczay-Szim had not actually carried out the actions attributed to him. The defendant did not plead guilty to the spreading of fascism. Denying this, he claimed that he had prevented the persecuted persons from being carried away by the authorities and that he had opposed the Germans and the Arrow Cross. However, he had not opposed the Russian army, which attempted to liberate the Hungarian people from German subjugation. Szim presented himself as a resistance fighter, who had kept the oath he had sworn to the Regent by not handing the barracks over to the Arrow Cross. He summed up his arguments in the following way:

> In the hardest and crucial period in the history of the Hungarian people, I was already advancing on the way as ordered by the laws of humanity and democratic ideals.

Basically, he was only a soldier, who had fought when the people demanded it, as in 1919 or during the Second World War.

According to the logic of the court, Latorczay-Szim, who was portrayed as a typical figure of the Horthy-regime, could not have prevented or reduced the devastation of the war. The acquittal of the defendant would have meant that the Horthy-regime had survived the war, and this was impossible to countenance. If the reason for the war was the Horthy-regime, then Latorczay-Szim could only be a war criminal. In order to justify this interpretation, the People's Tribunal tried to prove that the defendant was not a resistance fighter.

> According to the defendant's own presentation, he, as a resistance fighter, gained no significant merits that could be adduced as considerable mitigating circumstance. He did not suffer any legal disadvantages by the Arrow Cross rule, except for having been wounded, which would have been inconceivable if his resistance had been of great value. His injury was instead the consequence of the misunderstanding of the situation.

Such perception denied that Szim had actually resisted the Arrow Cross. In another statement, however, the court argued that it was theoretically impossible for a Horthy-officer to resist. 'The Hungarian people have nothing to do with the fact that these two beasts of prey: the Arrow Cross and the Horthy henchmen were wrangling over the bones.'[47] The People's Tribunal at this point demonstrated an attitude which was similar to that of certain inquisitors during witch trials; all kinds of behavior of the defendant could prove his or her guilt.[48]

Secondly, the sentence proved that Szim had led the life of a counterrevolutionary. In spite of the fact that he fought in the Hungarian Red Army, he had 'secretly' prepared himself for the coming of the counterrevolutionary regime. The prosecutor articulated this narrative in the following way:

> The defendant displayed a unity of desire and decision in the summer of 1919. The defendant started his activity before his capture, namely, he surrendered the company he commanded into

> the hands of the Czechs. He pursued this in captivity in Bohemia, when he organized people for the white terror. When he arrived home, it was a natural outcome that he, as a white terrorist officer, was put at the head of this commando...

The sentence accepted this interpretation as true and argued the following:

> His counter-revolutionary aspirations had already manifested themselves during the existence of the Soviet Republic. He had been the commander of one of the companies of the Hungarian Red Army, of the Red Army, which had defended Hungarian territories against the surrounding states that would subsequently organize themselves into the little *entente* in the spring and summer of 1919. The defendant believed that he could serve the so-called "national idea" manifested in the damned "thought of Szeged", which would later direct our foreign policy towards the national disaster with its extreme irredentism, by surrendering together with his troops to the Czech army and, thus, he himself poured murderous machine-gun fire onto his own soldiers who were fighting against the Czechs around Miskolc.
>
> It is obvious that he owed his honorable position to the full confidence of Horthy and his clique, who appreciated his merits in leading the counter-revolution to victory. He obtained the post of the commander of the so-called department of military investigation – since he was the ardent supporter of the 'white terror' which was the ground of the counter-revolution – which was created to terrorize and ravage the counties of Borsod, Gömör, Abaúj, Zemplén and Heves.[49]

Biographical records played a role similar to that of certain rituals in tribal societies where ambiguous identities were fixed.[50] The biography is a means of maintaining an identity that has already been formed. Life narratives reflect and reveal the character and essence of their bearers. These stories are able to demonstrate that the attitudes that caused the present behavior of a person were already present in his or her past. In mental hospitals, the case records play this role.[51] Prisons construct the essential character of the convict, the *criminal* through an observance and recording of his or her life-story. Penal institutions are convinced that the personality of the criminal can be identified with his or her crime, since malicious acts are the result of the past lives of the individual: crimes are born in life-stories.[52] Legal proceedings aim to achieve true knowledge about the past by connecting past acts to individuals. These institutions perceived the defendants as well-defined entities whose personal deeds formed a coherent unity with the personality of the culprit. The courts detected the connection between the past of the accused and his or her crime, as well as the expectations of his or her future. The legal procedure was interested in locating the origins of the crime within the criminal, be it the result of an instinct, the unconscious, the environment or family heritage. Crime was regarded as a consequence of the specific character of the individual, the way of life, or the thinking of the criminal. In reality, the trials themselves shaped the subjects of the committed crimes in order to establish the most appropriate and effective punishment for the criminals.[53]

If the defendant aspired to lead the system to victory, which was the reason for the war catastrophe, then the statement that he was a war-criminal seemed to be logical for the People's Tribunal.

> Thus, in this light, the defendant's acts met the criteria of war crimes. The connection to war is not excluded by the longer period passed between the time of committing the acts and the actual breaking out of the war.

Regarding the above-described narrative, Latorczay-Szim did not merely symbolize the Horthy-regime as a social and political system, but symbolized its history from its beginning to its inevitable end. To the court, his life narrative represented the history of the downfall: his destiny shed light on the fate of a whole social system. Latorczay's actual person represented the historical continuity between white terror and the war catastrophe, while his figure brought an abstract process to life. By staging him in the court, a particular historical narrative could be justified. He was the commander of 'a commando called the Department of Military Investigation; actions like these are ranked among the first phenomena of the reaction in Hungary, and, as such, they prevailed in the series of events which led necessarily to Hungary's drifting into the war and later to the fatal downfall.'[54] Thereby, a retrospective view of the happenings of 1919 made it possible to create a historical interpretation based upon individual actions. This fact provided the People's Tribunal with the proper conditions to fulfill its duty and to make statements that could be accepted as a sentence. Lawful sentences justify individuals and their personal deeds, whereas legal proceedings deal with individual activities. Consequently, utterances are not valid sentences unless they meet these requirements. A trial is a place where it is not sufficient to say certain things in order for them to be accepted: the conditions have to be appropriate and the participants have to follow the expected procedural routine.[55] In this way, the People's Tribunal successfully performed the act of sentencing people. As a valid sentence, however, or as an accepted truth, it verified an abstract historical representation the only evidence of which was the biography of the defendant constructed by legal means.[56] Consequently, the trials of war criminals did not prove the representation of an abstract historical process - the continuity of the events of 1919 and 1944 - based upon comprehensive research, but rendered them tangible through the construction of individual personalities.

3

Post-war political trials seemed to prove the Soviet-type of teleological narrative about the inevitable victory of communism by generating actual life courses that were directly tangible in the courtroom. Thus, it is hardly surprising that this peculiar mode of historical representation began to dominate communist interpretations of the recent past. The first published history textbook for the eighth class of the primary schools in 1948 began the history of the counter-revolutionary regime by focusing upon the brutal persecution of communists by 'Horthy's gangs':

> The counter-revolutionary hordes were authorized to massacre anyone labeled as 'communist conspirator', without a legal sentence in the street. The officers' commandos situated in hotels Gellért and Britannia and in various barracks terrified the capital. The situation was the same in the whole country. In Kecskemét, about one hundred persons were caught and killed in the Orgovány woods under the direction of Iván Héjjas. The real masters of the country were the bloodthirsty Prónay-, Ostenburg- and other detachments.[57]

The authors were convinced that the nature of violence reflected the fascist essence of the system. The textbook claimed that, in December 1919, 'The fascist terror continued to collect its victims'. The second edition of the schoolbook in 1950 stated that 1919 meant the birth of a system that was inherently against the people, since Horthy's group aimed at 'restoring the rule of the great land-owners and capitalists, diminishing the achievements of the revolution and taking bloody revenge on the Hungarian people'.[58] The historical interpretations emphasized the foundation of the putative fascist regime in Hungary.

Apart from highlighting the fact that Hungary had been the first fascist dictatorship, scholarly attempts to understand the counter-revolution provided more sophisticated explanations for the foundations of fascism. In 1951, in a book on the white terror, two young historians argued that the system of brutal oppression had been formed as a result of the resistance of the Hungarian people. The authors pointed out that, once they had experienced the benefits of a socialist regime, the Hungarian workers would no longer tolerate the restoration of capitalism. The combination of the techniques of suppression was the crucial factor in the genesis of Hungarian fascism.[59] The emphasis on violence and oppression is hardly astonishing. For communist scholars, the history of the inter-war regime was a genuine indictment that could be represented most adequately by following the pattern of the post-war trials of war criminals. The form of historical narrative did, in reality, include legal texts. Thereby, communist historians used a type of historical narrative the accepted truth of which was based upon no historical proof. Built upon legal authority and vested with the political authority of partisanship, communist historiography could claim the truth of these representations without the verification of historical narratives. Soviet-type historiography thus shifted the authority of historical representations from its regular basis of independent research and the interpretation of evidence towards political devotion and partisanship. Thus, the sovietization of history domesticated a pattern of historiographical authority that preceded the formation of modern historical scholarship. The modernization of historical studies took place as a result of the rejection of historical interpretations as articulated by traditional institutions of authority, such as the Church and the Prince, and the endowment of organizations, such as universities, which possessed the potential to define the criteria of proper scholarship.[60]

In 1953, the first volume of a series of source publications was published by Dezső Nemes, a research fellow in the Institute for Party History. The title of the book was *The Coming to Power and the Reign of Terror of the Counter-revolution in Hungary*.[61] The editor contributed to the volume with a lengthy study entitled *For the History of the Bloodthirsty Counter-revolution*. The author re-articulated the standardized opinions on the violent nature of the counter-revolution as a proof of its fascist essence and the inevitability of the foundation of the fascist dictatorship. Besides this, he elaborated a complex historical explanation concerning the necessary participation of the putative Hungarian fascist system in the war. Nemes argued that, although the social democrat government that succeeded the dictatorship of the proletariat on 1 August 1919 had advanced the restoration of capitalism, the bourgeoisie had not trusted it. According to the article, the 'capitalist classes' preferred a counter-revolutionary dictatorship in order to secure their interests. The author concluded that it was logical that the massacres committed by Horthy's troops against the communists had increased confidence in his person on the part of the imperialists. They perceived the activity of the 'robber and murderer detachments' as the policy of the 'strong hand' that was needed to restore capitalism.

> The counter-revolution gave power to the most bloodthirsty beasts of capitalism, to the most bloodthirsty representatives of the great capitalists and landlords. The Hungarian great capitalists and landlords, however, supported the coming to power of precisely these representatives, which was not only acknowledged by the *entente* imperialists, but was also endorsed by them. Horthy's army gained the trust of the industrialists by the bestial terror directed against the workers.[62]

The Party historian pointed out that the Horthy-regime had lived up to the expectations of the capitalist class that had been its sponsor. Nemes emphasized that the governments always acted on behalf of the capitalists. They reduced wages and tolerated a high level of unemployment, inflation and speculation. Nevertheless, the policy of unrestrained exploitation could only be maintained by means of sheer terror because of the desperate resistance of the workers. The author demonstrated the intensity of discontent by describing various strikes by miners and referring to the high membership of the trade unions. As a result, according to the study, the reign of terror came to an end: the massacre was the means designed to restore and maintain capitalist power after the communist experience. The terrorist regime developed logically, since the old means of suppression could no longer fulfill their task. Consequently, they argued, the counter-revolutionary regime employed a wide variety of measures in order to establish a profound system of oppression. The various governments introduced summary jurisdiction, political prisons, internment camps and frequent executions. The communist historian claimed that the fascist dictatorship had been established as the only possible tool to eliminate communism and thereby preserve capitalism.

Nemes presented his evidence to prove that fascism had inevitably led to war. Firstly, the exploitation of the workers had resulted in privation and serious economic hardships. Although the profit of capitalists rose, productivity declined. The author stressed that, in this situation, capitalism could only be saved by foreign loans. Nevertheless, repayments could be achieved through even more ruthless exploitation. Since the territory of exploitation had been narrowed, the Hungarian capitalist class had begun to search for new areas. The communist historian concluded that this inevitably resulted in a policy of revision and war. Secondly, foreign loans raised the dependency of the country on foreign capital, mainly on German economic and political interests. Thus, the 'adventure politics' of war of the counter-revolutionary regime had inevitably led to the destruction of the Horthy-regime.

> Eventually, during the 1930s, and especially at the time of the Second World War, Horthy and his fellows "successfully" transformed the country into Hitler's colony and the monopoly territory for the expansion of the German imperialist great capital, and resulted in Hungary's participation in the anti-Soviet imperialist war of robbery. They pushed the country into a new catastrophic war of robbery, which destroyed the Horthy-regime. Its fall was as shameful and disgraceful as its coming into existence.[63]

The constructed continuity between 1919 and 1944 made it possible to represent the Second World War as the world-wide collision of fascism and communism. Party historians emphasized the details of white terror and the persecutions against communists. They also claimed that the Nazi system had been the direct consequence of 1919. Thus, the white terror of 1919 overshadowed the memory of the genocide of the 1940s: the horrors of the counter-revolution eclipsed the abyss of the Hitlerite extermination. 1919, as a prelude, expelled the Jews and other victims from the narrative: it was claimed that the real victims of the death camps of fascism had been the communists. Thereby, it became possible to suggest that the only purpose of the Nazis had been the elimination of communists and that all anti-communist regimes were actually fascist. Party historians constructed a rigid interpretation of history that consisted exclusively of two factors: fascism and communism. All events of the past could be comprehended with the help of this scheme. The communist narrative of the Second World War did not make a development similar to that of the West possible. In the West, from the end of the 1950s, and after the Eichmann-trial in particular, the memory of the war was inseparably linked to the Holocaust. Thus, the notion of fascism began to be used to educate Western European peoples from committing mass extermination once again. In the Soviet bloc, in contrast, the concept was exploited to justify communist rule.

The narrative of the necessary victory of communism proved to be fragile. The indictment-like form of communist historical interpretation had one further important consequence. In its form, it was a counter-history. Counter-history writing is a peculiar mode of historical representations: it aims at depriving the target group from its self-identity by constructing a counter-identity. Counter-histories reverse the positive self-assessment of the adversary in order to substitute it with a negative image.[64] From the perspective of the inevitable defeat, the history of the Horthy-regime became a counter-history, because a political and social structure that inescapably led to collapse could only be a bad system. Counter-histories, however, generally fail to produce the positive self-image of their supporters. They focus on the image of the adversary and construct the self-image in contrast with the image of the enemy group. In practice, this meant that communist historians hoped to prove the necessary victory of communism by demonstrating the inevitable fall of the Horthy-system. However, although they did manage to provide a relatively successful negative image of their predecessor, they failed to incorporate positive evidence of the inevitable glory of communism into the narrative. To base the history of inevitable victory solely upon the history of the inevitable fall foreshadowed its very own inevitable fall.

Conclusion

Crisis of the Soviet Model and De-Sovietization

E. A. Rees

From the early 1980s, the Soviet system in the USSR and Eastern Europe entered a period of crisis that led to its eventual collapse. This was a crisis which affected all aspects of the Soviet system, and one which had a dual character. Firstly, it reflected the internal contradictions in the Soviet model as a political regime which was integral to the preservation of the Soviet imperium, both within the USSR itself and in Eastern Europe. Secondly, it stemmed from the incapacity of the Soviet model to meet the challenges posed by the dramatic transformations, which were associated with the new technological revolution, that were experienced by all modern economic systems. Having barely adjusted to the consumer goods revolution, the communist economies were required to adapt themselves to the information technology revolution.

The East European countries were never as fully or as deeply sovietized as the USSR. These regimes developed their own combination of hard and soft controls. The non-state sector of the economy remained more in evidence, especially in Hungary and Poland, than in the USSR. Religion survived more vigorously in these states, except, of course, in Albania, the first state to declare itself fully atheist, whilst in Poland, the Catholic Church acted as a counterweight to the rule of the communist authorities. The GDR was a system in which surveillance, informing, police control co-existed with the elaborate development of consumer culture. In Hungary, the New Economic Mechanism, tolerated a degree of economic plurality, without challenging the Party's rule or the country's membership of the Warsaw Pact. In Czechoslovakia the suppression of the Prague Spring in 1968 by Soviet intervention demonstrated the limits to socialist liberalization. The foundation of *Solidarność* in Poland led to the institution of martial law in 1981, demarcating the limits to democratization under state socialism, and marking a watershed in the history of the Soviet *Imperia*.[1]

The crisis of the Soviet economies was marked by economic slowdown, and by the difficulties experienced in adapting the system of central planning to the needs of modern, increasingly complex economies. The Soviet system had demonstrated its enormous capacity for mobilizing resources for economic modernization, but the high costs and the inefficiencies of the system pointed to a fundamental weakness. The economic crisis of the 1980s was reflected in the mounting concern of the Soviet military regarding the growing technology gap between the USSR and the USA; the growing difficulties of sustaining the costs of the arms race, and the pressure of maintaining the expanded Soviet welfare state.[2] These difficulties were compounded by the inability of the Soviet economy to adapt to the needs of the new technological revolution, embodied in computers, information technology, laser technology, electronics, bio-technology, *etc.*, which were made worse by the US imposed boycott that denied the USSR access to foreign technology. Notwithstanding its achievements in pure science and its successes in space and military technology, the Soviet model was weak in industrial research and development, in technical innovation and in the diffusion of new technologies.

The shortcomings of the model in terms of economic performance were matched by a failure to accommodate political and intellectual dissent as part of the normal discourse of society. Under mature socialism, whilst some academic disciplines gained limited degrees of autonomy, elsewhere the strategies of censorship became more subtle, with more attempts to incorporate and enlist intellectuals and artists into serving the needs of the state.[3] In cinema, critical directors such as Yugoslavia's Dusan Makavejev's *Mysteries of the Organism* (1971), Hungary's Péter Bacsó's *The Witness* (1969) and Pál Gábor's *Angi Vera* (1978), and Poland's Andrzej Wajda's *Man of Marble* (1977) and *Man of Iron* (1981) produced their own distinctive insights into the nature of the new Soviet civilization and its discontents.

The crisis paradoxically coincided with the high point of Soviet international standing. In the 1970s and 1980s, the USSR extended its sphere of influence, with its ambition to sovietize Afghanistan, and the former Portuguese colonies in Africa.[4] By this time, the fundamental principles underpinning the Soviet economic model were being questioned domestically. The need for the socialist economic system to embrace the market was well-recognized, at a time when the capitalist economies were moving even more fundamentally away from state intervention towards marketization. The rapid development of the 'tiger' economies of South East Asia, demonstrated the potential of import substitution strategies as a vehicle for unprecedented economic growth. The rise of consumer culture and the huge expansion of the service sector fundamentally transformed attitudes and expectations. Simultaneously, the capitalist societies were undergoing fundamental restructuring; the disappearance of the traditional working class, the growth in employment of women, and the development of part-time work, and the growing role of migrant labor.

The crisis of the system of Soviet rule became acute from 1985 onwards. The departure of the generation of Soviet leaders schooled during the Stalin era opened up the possibility of change. This also reflected more profound social changes. The rise of generations for whom the experience of the Second World War and the reconstruction period were remote, and for whom the legitimacy of the regime was based upon a judgement of current, not past, performance, and for whom the moral and symbolic capital that had been accumulated in the past was now severely depleted.[5]

Under the leadership of Mikhail Gorbachev, the Soviet leadership began fundamentally to question the basic principles which had underpinned the regime since the late 1920s, seeking an alternative model both in the New Economic Policy of 1921-28, and in the ideas of Nikolai Bukharin.[6] The tension between the logic of political authoritarianism and the logic of modern technology systems which had existed throughout the communist period became more acute.[7] But the failings of the Soviet model also stemmed from systemic exhaustion, where radical change threatened the entire structure of the system, whilst the highly integrated aspects of its sub-systems – political, economic, social, and cultural – meant that radical change in one area carried repercussions for the whole.[8] Gorbachev's 'third way', between the Stalinist model of socialism and capitalism, proved a chimera. The belief that it was possible to combine political democracy with a state owned, planned economy, an option which was widely favored in the USSR and in Eastern Europe, proved unworkable.[9] The failure of Gorbachev's reform strategy was caused not only by economic mismanagement, but also by the incompatibility of the different sub-systems, an open, pluralistic political system combined with a state owned economy, which through his reforms he tried to construct.

The Soviet Union also failed in the struggle for cultural supremacy with the United States.[10] This reflected a failure to combine both hard and soft controls as part of the post-Stalinist regimes' attempts to gain a new stability, and to win legitimacy. Nevertheless, state repression proved extremely effective in containing dissent. Poland was the only country that produced a mass movement of opposition. However, economic failure weakened the authority of these regimes, and attempts at reform created a dynamic or regime implosion that acted as a further catalyst to demands for revolutionary change.[11]

A fundamental weakness of the communist regimes derived from their lack of legitimacy, which was reflected in the widespread skepticism and cynicism with which the political authorities were viewed. The restrictions imposed on individuals in terms of life chances, opportunities, and individual freedom nurtured alienation and frustration. The dominant attitude which this system fostered was one of conformity and political quiescence, reflected in orchestrated manifestations and ritualized elections. These restrictions were felt acutely by the more highly educated members of society. The system of state control also impinged directly upon the development of science, the arts, culture, and on the wider sphere of public communication. In this, the Soviet model misconceived the central aspects of modernity which depended on nurturing a culture of individualism and of greater social and cultural autonomy. The expansion of education, the development of mass communications, and growth of prosperity served to erode political deference and respect for established authority.

The sovietization project in Eastern Europe retained its imperial character effectively until 1988. The weak sense of allegiance that people felt towards their own governments, posed serious risks to any attempt at liberalization or democratization. Notwithstanding the efforts of the people's democracies to develop their own variants of the Soviet model, their innovations as regards economic management, the organization of a new consumer culture and new leisure activities were constrained by the structures and practices of the prevailing political and economic system. The attempts to construct a new basis of legitimation, through rituals and ideology, encountered the problem of cognitive dissonance, the gap between promise and reality. The coercive methods used in establishing and sustaining the Soviet model in these countries worked towards subverting their claim to sovereignty and legitimacy.

From 1988 onwards, the Soviet leadership attempted to reform the Soviet political and economic system, whilst the Eastern European regimes were obliged to undertake their own reappraisals. The impetus towards restructuring was accelerated when Gorbachev renounced the 'Brezhnev doctrine' and with it the guarantee provided by the USSR to the Eastern bloc regimes. In 1989, a wave of anti-communist revolutions swept through Eastern Europe, ushering in a new era of de-sovietization, combining political democratization, with moves towards economic privatization and marketization. The same drive towards capitalist restoration was accelerated in the newly independent states of the former Soviet Union after 1991.

The failure of the Soviet model reflected the irreconcilable tensions between preserving an authoritarian political system, whilst adapting to the needs of economic and technological change. This failure was dramatized by the rapid and successful adaptation by Western political systems to the needs of new economic and technological developments. This points to deeper flaws within the sovietization project, and the Soviet conception of modernity. The belief that modernization could be realized through the use of state power, exercised in an authoritarian manner to overcome opposition, and with little consultation with society and without effective mechanisms of control or accountability, demonstrated a narrow conception of modernity. The trade-off between the restriction of political rights against the provision of material benefits – housing, employment, education, *etc.*, – proved to be a trade-off that did not work. In restricting the scope for individual and group autonomy, by denying the creative development of a critical public opinion, one of the checks on the dangers of excessive and arbitrary government was removed, and a major source of impetus for creative innovation was cut off. In this way, the possibility of a realistic appraisal of the needs and expectations of society was overridden by the dictates of the ruling Party and its priorities.

The re-emergence of the public sphere in the countries of Eastern Europe in 1989 set off a dynamic series of changes, which occurred, as in earlier crises, with extraordinary rapidity. It involved a profound change in political language and rhetoric, with the democratization of political discourse. With a more informed debate came the re-birth of a real, informed public opinion. This was associated with a reappraisal of what was deemed public memory, with a re-evaluation of recent history. These changes served to undermine the claims of these regimes to moral authority.[12] With this went the assertion of a new sense of individual and group identity and new expectations as regards to what government was and how it should conduct itself, which further subverted their claims to legitimacy.

The weakness of the system of communist rule in Eastern Europe stemmed in part from the inherent rigidities of the system, and from the sustained and unresolved crisis of legitimacy. The strength and weakness of the communist regimes derived from their reliance on coercive force to ensure their survival. Their authority was challenged by the appeals to individual and group rights as articulated by vocal dissident minorities. Their position was also weakened by the growing gap in living standards between East and West, by the corrosive appeal of Western fashion and mass culture, and the erosion of respect for traditional authority. The ultimate factor in its disintegration was the basic questioning of the premises of the system of Soviet rule unleashed by Gorbachev after 1985, the repudiation of the 'Brezhnev doctrine' which signaled a retreat from Empire, allowing the East European states to decide their own fate.[13]

Notes

Introduction

[1] On the Soviet conception of modernity, see David Hoffman, *Stalinist Values: the Cultural Norms of Soviet Modernity, 1917-1941*, (Ithaca NY, Cornell University Press, 2003), pp. 7-10. For a more critical view, see Rene Fülöp-Miller, *The Mind and Face of Bolshevism: An Examination of Cultural Life*, (trans. F. Stint & D.F. Tait) (London, G.P.Putnam's Sons, 1926).

[2] A.V. Kvashonkin, 'Sovetizacija Zakavkaz'ja v perepiske bol'shevistskogo rukovodstva, 1920-1922 gg', *Cahiers du monde russe*, Vol. 38, Nos. 1-2, 1997; Richard Pipes (ed), *The Unknown Lenin: From the Secret Archives*, (New Haven - London, Yale University Press, 1996), pp. 92-3; See also: A.M. Selishchev, *Yazyk Revolyutsionnoi epokhi. Iz nablyudenii nad russkim yazykom poslednikh let (1917-1926), (Second edition,* Moscow, 1928). This work has references to 'Sovietize' (*sovetizirovat'*), p. 53, and 'Sovietization (*sovetizatsiya)*, pp. 53, 184, 188, and 'Bolshevization' (*bol'shevizirovat')* pp. 52-53.

[3] The speech was published by T.S. Bushuevoi in *Novy Mir*, 1994, No. 12. The document is dismissed as a forgery by S.Z. Sluch in *Otechestvennaya istoria*, 2004, No.1, but is defended as authentic by V.L. Doroshenko, I.V. Pavlov and R.Ch. Raak in *Voprosy istorii*, 2005, No.8. Bushuevoi's account is accepted by Albert Weeks, *Stalin's Other War: Soviet Grand Strategy 1939-1941*, (Lanham, MD, Rowman & Littlefield, 2003) pp. 171-3.

[4] Jurij Borys, *Sovietization of Ukraine 1917-1923*, (Edmonton, University of Alberta, 1980).

[5] Anthony Adamovich, *Opposition to Sovietization in Belorussian Literature 1917-1957*, (New York, Scarecrow Press, 1958).

[6] Richard G. Havannisian, *The Republic of Armenia, Vol. 4: Between Crescent and Sickle: Partition and Sovietization*, (Berkeley, University of California Press, 1996); Rex A. Wade (ed), *Documents of Soviet History; vol. 2 Triumph and Retreat, 1920-1922*, ch. 1, 37 'Sovietization of Armenia' 2 December 1920, p. 151; Kvashonkin, 'Sovetizacija Zakavkaz'ja'. Douglas T. Northrop, *Veiled Empire: Gender and Power in Stalinist Central Asia*, (Ithaca NY, Cornell University Press, 2004), pp. 58-66 & 347-9 (Sovietization of Uzbekistan), pp. 215-25 (Bolshevisation of Uzbek Communist Party); Francine Hirsch, *Empires of Nations: Ethnographic Knowledge and the Making of the Soviet Union*, (Ithaca NY, Cornell University Press, 2004); H.S. Dinerstein, 'The Sovietization of Uzbekistan: the first generation', in: *Harvard Slavic Studies*, Vol. 4, 1957, pp. 499-513.

[7] Olaf Mertelsman (ed), *The Sovietization of the Baltic States 1940-1956*, (Tartu, Kleio, 2003); Endel Kareda, *Techniques of Economic Sovietization: A Baltic Experience* (London, Boreos Publishing Co., 1947).

[8] Jan Gross, *Revolution from Abroad: The Soviet Conquest of Poland's Western Ukraine and Western Belorussia*, (Princeton - Oxford, Princeton University Press, 2002).

[9] John McCannon, *Red Arctic: Polar Exploration and the Myth of the North in the*

Soviet Union 1932-1939, (New York, Oxford University Press, 1998).

[10] Christel Lane, *The Rites of Rulers: Ritual in Industrial Society - the Soviet Case*, (Cambridge, Cambridge University Press, 1981). Karen Petrone, *Life Has Become More Joyous Comrades: Celebrations in the Time of Stalin*, (Bloomington IN, Indiana University Press, 2000).

[11] Richard Stites, *Revolutionary Dreams: Utopian Visions and Experimental Life in the Russian Revolution*, (Oxford, Oxford University Press, 1989).

[12] Osip Aronovich Pyatnitsky, *The Bolshevisation of the Communist Parties by Eradicating Social Democratic Traditions*, (London, Modern Books, 1932).

[13] Ronald Tiersky, *Ordinary Stalinism: Democratic Centralism and the Question of Communist Political Development*, (London, George Allen & Unwin, 1985).

[14] E.A. Rees, 'Politics, Administration and Decision-Making in the Soviet Union, 1917-1953', *The Yearbook of Administrative History*, edited by Erk Volkmar Heyen (Baden-Baden, Nomos Verlagsgesellschaft, 2004), pp. 259-290.

[15] A.J. Polan, *Lenin and the End of Politics*, (London, Methuen, 1984).

[16] Hans Günther (ed), *The Culture of the Stalin period*, (London, Macmillan, 1990).

[17] Sheila Fitzpatrick (ed), *Stalinism: New Directions*, (London, Routledge, 2000).

[18] W. Berelowitch, *La soviétisation de l'école russe 1917-1931*, (Paris, L'age d'homme, 1990).

[19] Melanie Ilič (ed), *Women in the Stalin Era*, (Basingstoke, Palgrave, 2001); Linda Edmondson (ed), *Gender in Russian History and Culture*, (Basingstoke, Palgrave, 2001).

[20] Hirsch, *Empires of Nations*; Farideh Heyat, *Career, Family and Faminity: Sovietization among Muslim Azeri Women*, (London, University of London, 1999).

[21] E.A. Rees, *Political Thought from Machiavelli to Stalin: Revolutionary Machiavellism*, (Basingstoke, Palgrave, 2004) especially, chs. 5, 6. For a somewhat different view of Soviet moral codes, see Hoffman, *Stalinist Values*.

[22] J. Arch Getty & Oleg V. Naumov, *The Road to Terror: Stalin and the Self-destruction of the Bolsheviks, 1932-1939*, (New Haven, Yale University Press, 1999); J. Arch Getty, 'Samokritika Rituals in the Stalinist Central Committee', *Russian Review*, vol. 58, no. 1, 1999, pp. 49-70.

[23] Stephen Kotkin, *Magnetic Mountain; Stalinism as a Civilization*, (Berkeley, University of California Press, 1995).

[24] Sheila Fitzpatrick, *Everyday Stalinism: Ordinary Life in Extraordinary Times*, (New York, Oxford University Press, 1999).

[25] Katerina Clark, *The Soviet Novel: History as Ritual*, (Bloomington IN, Indiana University Press, 2000). For the pictorial arts, see Max Hollein and Boris Groys (eds), *Dream Factory Communism: The Visual Culture of the Stalin Era*, (Frankfurt, Hatje Cantz Verlag, 2003).

[26] C. Vaughan James, *Soviet Socialist Realism: Origins and Theory*, (London, Macmillan, 1973).

[27] Richard Stites, *Russian Popular Culture: Entertainment and Society since 1900*, (Cambridge, Cambridge University Press, 1998).

[28] Mikhail Gellner, *A Cog and the Wheel: The Development of Homo Sovieticus*, (London, Overseas Publications Interchange, 1985).

[29] Alexander Zinoviev, *Homo Sovieticus*, (London, Paladin, 1986) translated by Charles Jansen.

[30] Alexei Kojevnikov, 'Rituals of Stalinist Culture at Work', *Russian Review*, Vol. 57, No. 1, 1998, pp. 25-52.

[31] Kendal E. Bailes, 'Alexei Gastev and the Soviet Controversy over Taylorism, 1918-1924', *Soviet Studies*, Vol. 24, No. 3, 1977, pp. 373-94; Z.A. Sochor, 'Soviet Taylorism Revisited', *Soviet Studies*, Vol. 33, No 2, 1981, pp. 246-64.

[32] Alan M. Ball, *Imagining America: Influence and Images in Twentieth-Century Russia*, (Boulder CO., Rowman & Littlefield, 2003).

[33] Mark B. Tauger, 'The People's Commissariat of Agriculture', in: E.A. Rees (ed), *Decision-making in the Stalinist Command Economy, 1932-37*, (Macmillan, Basingstoke, 1997), ch. 6.

[34] Julie Hessler, *A Social History of Soviet Trade: Trade Policy, Retail Practices and Consumption, 1917-1953*, (Princeton NJ - Oxford, Princeton University Press, 2002); Jukka Gronow, *Caviar with Champagne: Common Luxury and the Ideals of the Good Life in Stalin's Russia*, (Oxford, Berg, 2003).

[35] Kendal E. Bailes, *Technology and Society under Lenin and Stalin*, (Princeton, Princeton University Press, 1978).

[36] Włodzimierz Brus, 'Stalinism in the 'People's Democracies', in: Robert C. Tucker (ed), *Stalinism: Essays in Historical Interpretation*, (New York - London, W. W. Norton, 1977).

[37] Nicholas Timasheff, *The Great Retreat*, (New York, E.P. Dutton and Co. 1946).

[38] Moshe Lewin, *The Making of the Soviet System*, (London, Methuen, 1985). See, also, David Hoffman, *Peasant Metropolis: Social Identities in Moscow, 1929—41*, (London, Cornell University Press, 1994). This might be compared to the more positive assessment of acculturation of the new working class in: Kotkin, *Magnetic Mountain*.

[39] Nina Tumarkin, *The Living and the Dead: The Rise and the Fall of the Cult of World War II in Russia*, (New York, Basic Books, 1994).

[40] E.A. Rees, 'Stalin and Russian Nationalism', in: Geoffrey Hosking & Robert Service (eds), *Russian Nationalism: Past and Present*, (Basingstoke, Palgrave, 1998), pp.77-106.

[41] Catriona Kelly, *Refining Russia: Advice Literature, Polite Culture from Catherine to Yeltsin*, (Oxford, Oxford University Press, 2001).

[42] E.A. Osokina, *Ierarkhiya Potrebleniya: O zhizn lyudei v usloviyakh stalinskogo snabzheniya 1928-1935gg*, (Moscow, MGOY, 1993); E.A. Osokina, *Our Daily Bread, Socialist Distribution and the Art of Survival in Stalin's Russia, 1927-1941*, (trans and ed. by Kate Transchel & Greta Buchner) (Armonk NY, M.E. Sharpe, 2001).

[43] Kotkin, *Magnetic Mountain*.

[44] Bertrand Russell, *Bolshevism: Practice and Theory*, (New York, Simon and Schuster, 1964), p 6.

[45] Richard Rose, 'Modern Nations and the Study of Political Modernisation', in: Stein Rokkan (ed), *Comparative Research Across Cultures and Nations*, (Paris - The Hague, Mouton, 1968), pp. 181-208.

[46] Richard Felix Starr, *Poland 1944-1962: The Sovietization of a Captive People*, (Baton Rouge LA, Louisiana State University Press, 1962); Stanislaw Mikolajczyk, *The Pattern of Soviet Domination*, (London, Sampson Low, Marston and Co. Ltd., 1948) ch. xv; Anna A. Ayars, *The Sovietization of Poland's Judiciary System*, (1951); *The Sovietization of Culture in Poland*, (Mid European Research and Planning Centre, Paris, 1953); Stanley M. Max, *The United States, Great Britain and the Sovietization of Hungary 1945-1948*,

(New York, East European Monographs, No. 177, Columbia University Press, 1985); Róbert Gábor, *The Bolshevisation of the Hungarian Trade Union Movement 1945-1951,* (New York, National Committee for a Free Europe, 1952); Michael Behucke, 'Democratization or Sovietization? The Development of the Soviet Zone of Occupation in Germany 1945-1950 in the Light of Recent Findings', PhD dissertation, (San Diego CA, Pacific Western University, 1983); Alexandru Zub & Flavius Solomon (eds), *Sovietization in Romania and Czechoslovakia: History, Analogies, Consequences,* (Bucharest, Polirom, 2003).

[47] Bradley F. Abrams, *The Struggle for the Soul of the Nation: Czech Culture and the Rise of Communism,* (Lanham NY - Oxford, Rowman & Littlefield, 2004); Ivan Svitak, *The Unbearable Burden of History: The Sovietization of Czechoslovakia,* (Prague, Czechoslovak Academy of Science, 1990).

[48] Archie Brown (ed), *Political Cultures and Communist Studies,* (Basingstoke, Macmillan, 1984).

[49] Russell Grigor Suny & Terry Martin (eds), *A State of Nations: Empire and Nation Making in the Age of Lenin and Stalin,* (Oxford - New York, Oxford University Press, 2001); Karen Dawisha & Bruce Parrott (eds), *The End of Empire? The Transformation of the USSR in Comparative Perspective,* (Amonk NY, M.E. Sharpe, 1997).

[50] E.A. Rees (ed), *Centre-Local Relations in the Stalinist State, 1928-1941,* (Basingstoke, Palgrave, 2002), ch. 3, 8.

[51] Waldemar Gurian (ed), *Soviet Imperialism: Its Origins and Tactics: A Symposium,* (Indiana, Notre Dame, 1953).

[52] N.S. Khrushchev, *Khrushchev Remembers,* Introduction and commentary by Edward Crankshaw; translation by Strobe Talbott, (London, Deutsch, 1971), pp.143-149.

[53] Alexander Stephan (ed), *Americanization and Anti-Americanism: the German Encounter with American Culture after 1945,* (New York, Bergham Books, 2004); Mathias Kipping & One Bjarnar (eds), *The Americanisation of European Business: the Marshall Plan and the Transfer of US Management Model,* (London - New York, Routledge, 1998); Volker Rolf Berghahn, *The Americanisation of West German Industry 1945-1973,* (Leamington Spa - New York, Berg, 1986); *L'Americanisation en Europe au XX siécle - Amercanisation in 20th century Europe,* (Lille, Université Charles de Gaulle, 2002); Victoria de Grazia, *Irresistible Empire: America's Advance through Twentieth Century Europe,* (Cambridge MA, Belknap Press, 2005).

[54] Terry Martin, *The Affirmative Action Empire: Nations and Nationalism in the USSR 1923-1939,* (Ithaca NY, Cornell University Press, 2001).

[55] J. Pakulskii, 'Legitimacy and Mass Compliance: Reflections on Max Weber and Soviet Type Socities', *British Journal of Political Science,* Vol. 16, No. 1, 1986, pp. 35-56; G. Gill, 'Changing Patterns of Systemic Legitimation in the USSR', *Coexistence,* 23, 1986, pp. 247-66.

[56] Václav Havel, *The Power of the Powerless: Citizens against the State in Central and Eastern Europe,* Introduction by Steven Lukes, (London, Hutchinson, 1983); Czeslaw Milosz, *The Captive Mind,* (New York, Knopf, 1953).

[57] Stephen Lovell, *Summerfolk 1700-2000: A History of the Dacha,* (Ithaca NY, Cornell University Press, 2003).

[58] Jadwiga Korolewicz, Ireneusz Bialecki, Margaret Watson (ed), *Crisis and Transition: Polish Society in the 1980s,* (Oxford - New York, Berg, 1987).

[59] I borrow the term from Robert L. Hutchings, *Soviet-East European Relations: Consolidation and Conflict 1968-1980*, (Madison WI, University of Wisconsin Press, 1983), pp. 5-1.

[60] Claes Arvidsson & Lars Erik Blomqvist (eds), *Symbols of Power: The Aesthetics of Political Legitimacy in the Soviet Union and Eastern Europe*, (Stockholm, Almqvist & Wiksell, 1987).

[61] Mathew E. Lenoe, *Closer to the Masses: Stalinist Culture, Social Evolution and Soviet Newspapers*, (Cambridge MA, Harvard University Press, 2004).

[62] Balázs Apor, Jan C. Behrends, Polly Jones & E.A. Rees (eds), *The Leader Cult in Communist Dictatorships: Stalin and the Eastern Bloc*, (Basingstoke, Palgrave, 2004).

[63] P. Hanson, *The Consumer in the Soviet Economy*, (London, Macmillan, 1968).

[64] James Riordan (ed), *Soviet Youth Culture*, (Basingstoke, Macmillan, 1989).

[65] Hilda Scott, *Women and Socialism: Experiences from Eastern Europe*, (London, Allison & Busby, 1976); Alena Heitlinger, *Women and State Socialism: Sex Inequality in the Soviet Union and Czechoslovakia*, (London, Macmillan, 1979).

[66] Judy Batt, *Economic Reform and Political Change in Eastern Europe: A Comparison of the Czechoslovak and Hungarian Experiences*, (Basingstoke, Macmillan, 1988).

[67] David Lane, *The Socialist Industrial State: Towards a Political Sociology of State Socialism*, (London, Allen & Unwin, 1976); Raymond Aron, *Eighteen Lectures on Industrial Society*, (London, Weidenfeld & Nicholson, 1967).

[68] John Connelly, *Captive University: the Sovietization of East German, Czechoslovak and Polish Higher Education 1945-1956*, (North Carolina, Chapel Hill University, 2000); Joseph Bronars, *Higher Education in Poland: Some Aspects of Sovietization*, Dissertation abstract, (Washington, Catholic University of America Press, 1957); Office of the Military Government for Germany (United States), Sovietization of the Public School System in East Germany (1951).

[69] E.A. Dobrenko & Eric Naiman (eds), *The Landscape of Stalinism: the Art and Ideology of Soviet Space*, (Seattle, University of Washington Press, 2003); David Crowley & Susan E. Reid (eds), *Socialist Spaces: Sites of Everyday Life in the Eastern bloc*, (Oxford - New York, Berg, 2002); Neil Leach (ed), *Architecture and Revolution: Contemporary Perspectives on Central and Eastern Europe*, (London - New York, Routledge, 1999); David Harvey, *Spaces of Capital:Towards a Critical Geography*, (Edinburgh, Edinburgh University Press, 2001).

[70] Miklós Haraszti, *A Worker in a Worker's State: Piece Rates in Hungary*, Introduction by Heinrich Böll, translated by Michael Wright, (Harmondsworth, Penguin Books, 1977).

[71] Susan E. Reid & David Crowley (eds), *Style and Socialism: Modernity and Material Culture in Post-War Eastern Europe*, (Oxford Berg, 2000); Susan E. Reid (ed), *Design, Stalinism and the Thaw, Journal of Design History*, 10, no. 2. Special edition.

[72] Vera Dunham, *In Stalin's Time: Middle Class Values in Soviet Fiction*, (Cambridge, Cambridge University Press, 1976).

[73] Mark Landsman, *Dictatorship and Demand: The Politics of Consumerism in East*

Germany, (Cambridge MA., Harvard University Press, 2005); David F. Crew (ed), *Consuming Germany and the Cold War*, (Oxford - New York, Berg, 2003).

[74] James Riordan, *Sport in Soviet Society: Development of Sport and Physical Education in Russia and the USSR*, (Cambridge, Cambridge University Press, 1977); James Riordan & Arnd Krüger, *European Cultures of Sport: Examining the Nation and the Regions*, (Bristol - Portland OR, Intellect, 2003).

[75] Leslie Holmes, *The Policy Process in Communist State: Politics and Industrial Administration*, (Beverley Hills CA, Sage, 1981).

[76] Tamás Kolosi & Edmund Wnuk-Lipiński (eds), *Equality and Inequality under Socialism: Poland and Hungary Compared*, (London - Beverely Hills CA, Sage, 1983).

Chapter 1

[1] Transcarpathia was an exception, being sovietized only once, after the Second World War.

[2] I owe this observation to Professor Stephen Kotkin. David R. Maples, *Stalinism in the Ukraine in the 1940s*, (London, Macmillan, 1992). For a short and important treatment of the re-imposition of Soviet rule within pre-1939 as well as 1941 Soviet borders as Re-Sovietization, see Sanford R. Lieberman, 'The Re-Sovietization of Formerly Occupied Areas of the USSR during World War II', in: Sanford R. Lieberman, David E. Powell, Carol R. Saivetz & Sarah M. Terry (eds), *The Soviet Empire Reconsidered: Essays in Honor of Adam B. Ulam*, (Boulder CO, Westview Press, 1994), pp. 49-66.

[3] See, for example, the fascinating collection *Sowietyzacja i Rusyfikacja Północno-Wschodnich Ziem II Rzeczypospolitej (1939-1941). Studia i materiały*, (Białystok, Wydawnictwo Uniwersytetu w Białymstoku, 2003), edited by Michał Natowski & Daniel Boćkowski.

[4] See Olaf Mertelsmann (ed), *The Sovietization of the Baltic States, 1940-1956*, (Tartu, Kleio, 2003).

[5] The western historiography of sovietization also included the writings of émigré authors from all territories which underwent sovietization after autumn 1939. Olaf Mertelsmann, Introduction to Mertelsmann, *Sovietization*, p. 9 *et seq*. Nevertheless, it seems plausible to assert that, on the whole, western historiography as well as non-scholarly usage has tended to think of the satellites and not the territories annexed directly into the Soviet Union, when the term 'sovietization' was used.

[6] Importantly, with the end of the Soviet Union, these points of reference have also become accepted in important post-Soviet research in the Russian Federation. See, for example, Leonid Gibiansky's Introduction in Leonid Gibianskii (ed.), *U istokov 'sotsialisticheskovo sodruzhestva': SSSR i vostochnoievropeiskiie strany v 1944-1949 gg.*, (Moscow: Nauka, 1995), p. 7.

[7] This terminological sample is drawn from Vladimir Tismaneanu, *Stalinism for all Seasons: A Political History of Romanian Communism*, (Berkeley CA, University of California Press, 2003), p. 107; François Fejtö, *A History of the People's Democracies: Eastern Europe since Stalin*, (London, Pall Mall Press, 1969), p. 12; Charles Gati, *The Bloc that Failed: Soviet-East European Relations in Transition*, (Bloomington IN, Indiana University Press, 1990), p. 19; Robin Okey, *Eastern Europe 1740-1985: Feudalism to Communism*, 2nd edition, (Minneapolis MN, University of Minnesota Press, 1986), p. 181; Stefan Mękarski, *Sowietyzacja Kulturalna Polski*, (London, Instytut Bliskiego i

Środkowego Wschodu 'Reduta', 1949), p. 17.

[8] The term 'Bolshevization' (*Bolshevizatsiia*) originally seems to have been a positive Soviet self-description and meant the achievement of full 'Leninist' maturity by non-Soviet Communist parties in the inter-war period. *De facto* this was, of course, a euphemism for complete Comintern, i.e., Moscow control over them. V.K. Volkov, 'U istokov kontseptsii "sotsialisticheskovo lageria"', in: Gibianskii (ed.), *U istokov 'sotsialisticheskovo sodruzhestva'*, p. 14.

[9] For a good, very short outline of the history of the term 'Sovietization,' which, however, can replace a full treatment as little as this essay, see Mertelsmann, *Introduction*, p. 9 *et seq*.

[10] Lenin is on record speaking about a 'Sovietization' of Lithuania as early as 1920. Mertelsmann, *Introduction*, at 9.

[11] *Tolkovy slovar russkovo iazyka*, main editors, B.M. Volin & D.N. Ushakov, vol. 4 (Moscow, 1940), p. 342.

[12] *Slovar sovremennovo russkovo literaturnovo iazyka*, volume 14, edited by L.I. Balakhonova & L.A. Voinova, (Moscow, 1963), p. 78.

[13] *Slovar russkovo iazyka v cheterekh tomakh*, volume 4, 2nd edition, chief editor of the second edition A.P. Evgeneva, (Moscow, 1984), p. 175. In spring 1944, Stalin and Molotov used the term 'Sovietization' to deny any plans towards its realization. In a telegram to Tito, they assured the latter that they had no intention to 'sovietize' either Yugoslavia or Bulgaria. Vladimir Volkov, 'The Soviet Leadership and Southeastern Europe,' in: Norman Naimark & Leonid Gibianskii (eds), *The Establishment of Communist Regimes in Eastern Europe, 1944-1949*, (Boulder CO, Westview Press, 1997), p. 56.

[14] Mertelsmann, *Introduction*, p. 9.

[15] Norman Naimark, 'Introduction', in: Naimark & Gibianskii, *The Establishment of Communist Regimes*, p. 8 *et seq*.

[16] Michal Reiman, '"Sowjetisierung" und nationale Eigenart in Ostmittel - und Südosteuropa. Zu Problem und Forschungsstand,' in: Hans Lemberg (ed), *Sowjetisches Modell und Nationale Prägung. Kontinuität und Wandel in Ostmitteleuropa nah dem Zweiten Weltkrieg*, (Marburg - Lahn: Herder-Institut: 1991), p. 3.

[17] For a typical example of this argument and for repeated (unsurprising) Soviet assertions that the lessons of Stalin's 'Problems of Leninism' remained valid, see Anthony T. Bouscaren, *Imperial Communism*, (Westport, Connecticut, Greenwood Press, 1953), p. 3 *et seq*.

[18] For instance, for Piotr Vail and Aleksandr Genis, Soviet Socialism ended up in empire by perverse default and out of a bafflingly simplistically imagined absentmindedness. Piotr Vail & Aleksandr Genis, *60-e. Mir sovietskovo chelovieka*, (Moscow, Novoe literaturnoe obozrenie, 2001), p. 284 *et seq*., and p. 354 note 86.

[19] Francine Hirsch, 'Toward an Empire of Nations: Border-Making and the Formation of Soviet National Identities', *The Russian Review*, Vol. 59, No. 2, 2000, p. 201 *et seq*; Timofei Agarin, 'Demographic and Cultural Policies of the Soviet Union in Lithuania from 1944 to 1956: A Post-Colonial Perspective', in: Mertelsmann, *Sovietization*, p. 113. My emphasis.

[20] See, representatively for a growing literature also including many other contributors, Jörg Baberowski, *Der Feind ist überall. Stalinismus im Kaukasus*, (Munich: DVA, 2003); Francine Hirsch, *Empire of Nation: Ethnographic Knowledge and the Making of the Soviet Union*, (Ithaca NY, Cornell University Press, 2005); Yuri Slezkine,

'Imperialism as the Highest Stage of Socialism', *The Russian Review*, Vol. 59, No. 2, 2000, pp. 227-34; Terry Martin, *The Affirmative Action Empire: Nations and Nationalism in the Soviet Union, 1923-1939*, (Ithaca NY, Cornell University Press, 2001).

[21] Ewa M. Thompson, *Imperial Knowledge: Russian Literature and Colonialism*, (Westport, Connecticut, 2000). For a discussion of the relevance of post-colonial approaches to Soviet History and an overview of pertinent literature, see, also, Agarin, *Policies*, pp. 111-5.

[22] Thompson, *Imperial Knowledge*, at 163-5.

[23] Boris Groys, 'Russia and the West: The Quest for Russian National Identity,' *Studies in Soviet Thought*, Vol. 43, (1992), p. 197.

[24] Groys, 'Russia', p. 197 and *passim*.

[25] Martin Malia, *Russia under Western Eyes: From the Bronze Horseman to the Lenin Mausoleum*, (Cambridge MA, 1999).

[26] Malia, *Russia*, p. 269.

[27] Malia, *Russia*, pp. 314-356.

[28] David Brandenberger, *National Bolshevism: Stalinist Mass Culture and the Formation of Modern Russian National Identity, 1931-1956*, (Cambridge MA: Harvard University Press, 2002), pp. 95-112.

[29] David Joravsky, 'The Stalinist Mentality and the Higher Learning', *Slavic Review*, Vol. 42, No. 4, 1983, p. 580.

[30] Roman Szporluk, *Komunizm i natsionalizm. Karl Marks proty Fridrikh Lista* (Kyiv, 1998), p. 426.

[31] Gerd Koenen, *Utopie der Säuberung: Was war der Kommunismus?* (Berlin, Alexander Fest Verlag, 2002), p. 96 *et seq*.

[32] See Stephen Kotkin's discussion of Moshe Lewin's influential work. Kotkin, *Magnetic*, p. 378 *et seq*.

[33] Eric J. Hobsbawm, *The Age of Revolution, 1789-1848*, (New York: Weidenfeld & Nicolson, 1962), p. 217 cited in Roman Szporluk, 'The Imperial Legacy and the Soviet Nationalities Problem', in: *The Nationalities Factor in Soviet Politics and Society*, Lubomyr Hajda & Mark Beissinger (eds), (Boulder CO: Westview Press, 1990), p. 9.

[34] Szporluk, *Legacy*, p. 10.

[35] M. Bril, *Osvobozhdennaia zapadnaia Ukraina*, (Moscow, Politizdat, 1940), p. 3 *et seq*., and pp. 11-6.

[36] Lenin speaking at the 8th Party Congress quoted in Heorhy Kasianov, *Ukrainska intelihentsia 1920-kh – 30-kh pokiv. Sotsialny portret ta istorychna dolya*, (Kyiv, Hlobus – Vik, 1992), p. 13. 'Socialism building,' was, of course, the single most essential policy of Bolshevism in power.

[37] Lowell, *Reading Revolution*, p. 16.

[38] Catriona Kelly & Vadim Volkov, 'Directed Desires: Kulturnost' and Consumption', in: *Constructing Russian Culture in the Age of Revolution: 1881-1940*, Catriona Kelly & David Shepherd (eds), (Oxford: Oxford University Press, 1998), p. 295.

[39] Kelly & Volkov, *Desires*, p. 295.

[40] Volkov, Vadim, 'The Concept of Kultur'nost. Notes on the Stalinist Civilizing Process', in: Sheila Fitzpatrick, *Stalinism: New Directions*, (London - New York, Routledge, 2000), p. 215, and Michael David-Fox, 'The Fellow-Travellers Revisited: The 'Cultured West' through Soviet Eyes', *Journal of Modern History*, Vol. 75, No. 2, 2003, p. 309. As Michael David-Fox has shown, this 1930s career of 'kulturnost'' resembled

Stalin's adoption of Trostky's forced-industrialization schemes. Kulturnost's stress on the forms of *byt*, too, had been assisted by Trotsky's prior work, especially his 'immensely popular 1923 "Questions of Byt" link[ing] high standards of personal behavior with the acquisition of culture'. Michael David-Fox, *Revolution of the Mind: Higher Learning among the Bolsheviks, 1918-1929*, (Ithaca NY, Cornell University Press, 1997), p. 106.

[41] David-Fox, *Revolution*, p. 107 (my emphasis).

[42] For the 'survival' terminology for the eastern tribes, see Slezkine, *Mirrors*, p. 231.

[43] Cited in Kelly & Volkov, *Desires*, p. 297.

[44] *Bilshovik Ukrainy*, 1939, September (No. 9), 'Manifest pobidaiushchoho komunizmu', (by V. Berestniev), pp. 39-53.

[45] *Bilshovik Ukrainy*, 1939, September (No. 9), 'Pro sotsialistychny humanizm' (by V. Paukova), pp. 54-72.

[46] *Bilshovik Ukrainy*, 1939, October (No. 10), 'Vyzvoleni z panskoho iarma' (unsigned), pp. 5-16.

[47] *Bilshovik Ukrainy*, 1939, November (No. 11), 'The 22nd Anniversary of the Great socialist revolution in the Soviet Union' (unsigned), pp. 1-7.

[48] *Bilshovik Ukrainy*, 1940, January (No. 1), 'Stalin: The Great Friendship of the Peoples', (Nikita Khrushchev), p. 74 *et seq.*

[49] *Bilshovik Ukrainy*, 1940, May (No. 5), 'The 25th Congress of the Communist Party (Bolsheviks) of Ukraine', pp. 42-5.

[50] *Bilshovik Ukrainy*, 1940, September (No. 9), pp. 11-22.

[51] Derzhavnyi arkhiv L'vivs'koi oblasti (DALO)-P 3,1,4: p. 43 *et seq.*, 67 *et seq.*, and 72.

[52] DALO-P-3,1,78: pp. 118-122.

Thus, a bootmaker managed to avoid the draft because he made boots for the responsible official. Later, he was discovered to be an 'active *Banderovets*', *i.e.*, a member of the Ukrainian nationalist anti-soviet resistance. *ibid.*

[53] Tsentral'nyi derzhavnyi arkhiv hromads'kykh ob"ednan' Ukrainy (TsDAHOU) 1,70,799: p. 70.

[54] Generally, the treatment and abuse of Soviet veterans, especially those in need of temporary or permanent medical care was a topic of significant, if long repressed resonance. Tumarkin, *Living*, p. 98.

[55] I owe this aspect of *Bakir*'s nickname to Professor Arfon Rees. In German, the same toy would be called a '*Stehaufmännchen*'.

[56] DALO-P 3,2,186: pp. 97-9.

[57] There were several million foreign prisoners in the early post-war Soviet Union. They included not only prisoners of war but also deportation victims from a number of European countries. Prisoners of war, of course, also included non-Germans. The German contingent formed a large plurality, which is of obvious importance in view of the special symbolism attached to Germany traditionally. Soviet statistics showed that POWs as a whole presented a considerable share of the labor force in important sectors. In building material production, for instance, nearly a quarter; in heavy-industry construction about a fifth. Baran, *Istoriia*, p. 62 *et seq*. Thus, the opportunities for contact were significant.

[58] Much later, then KGB head Yuri Andropov wrote to Union Central Committee

head Leonid Brezhnev that a 1952 Stalin speech affirming the central importance of the intelligence services with classical brutality was a 'little Asiatic' in 'its form' but 'in essence' an eternal truth. cited in Yoram Gorlizki, and O. V. Khlevniuk, *Cold Peace: Stalin and the Soviet Ruling Circle, 1945-1953*, (Oxford, Oxford University Press, 2004), p. 171.

Chapter 2

[1] J. Kornai, *The Socialist System: The Political Economy of Communism*, (Princeton NJ, Princeton University Press 1992).

[2] V. Průcha, *Hospodárské dějíny Československa v 19.a 20. storoči*, (Bratislava, Pravda, 1974); A. Teichová, *The Czechoslovak Economy 1918-1980*, (London – New York, Routledge, 1988), pp. 134-140; see, also, A. Teichová, 'Czechoslovakia: the Halting Pace to Scale and Scope', and Y. Yudanov, 'USSR: Large Enterprises in the USSR- the functional disorder', in: A. Chandler, F. Amatori & T. Hikino (eds), *Big Business and the Wealth of Nations*, (Cambridge, Cambridge University Press, 1997). pp. 447-456 and p. 397.

[3] J. Zeitlin, 'Introduction', in: J. Zeitlin & G. Herrigel (eds), *Americanization and its Limits: Reworking US Technology and Management in Post-War Europe and Japan*, (Oxford, Oxford University Press, 2000), pp. 2-3.

[4] R. Boyer *et al.*, (eds), *Between Imitation and Innovation: The Transfer and Hybridization of Productive Models in the International Automobile Industry*, (Oxford, Oxford University Press, 1998), pp. 3-4.

[5] J. Laux, *The European Automobile Industry*, (New York, Twayne, 1992), pp. 132-4, and A.C. Sutton, *Western Technology and Soviet Economic Development, 1917-1945*, Vol. 3, (Stanford CA, Hoover Institution, 1968), pp. 191-203.

[6] Y. Cohen, 'The Soviet Fordson. Between the politics of Stalin and the Philosophy of Ford, 1924–1932', and B. Shpotov, 'Ford in Russia from 1909 to World War II', in: H. Bonin *et al.* (eds), *Ford of Europe 1967-2003, Ford 1903-2003: The European History*, (Paris, P.L.A.G.E., 2003), pp. 531-558 and pp. 525-9 respectively.

[7] J.J. Chanaron, 'Lada, Viability of Fordism', in: M. Freyssenet *et al.* (eds), *One Best Way: Trajectories and Industrial Models of the World's Automobile Producers*, (Oxford, Oxford University Press, 1998), pp. 440-462.

[8] Škoda Auto Archives henceforth Aša, records Automobilové Závody, národní podnik henceforth AZNP, 27, Zprávy ze studijní cesty čs. Automobilových závodů, 9/2/1951 – 9/4/1951.

[9] J. Berliner, *Factory and Manager in the USSR*, (Cambridge, Mass., Harvard University Press, 1957), p. 141, and D. Granik, *Il dirigente sovietico*, (Milan, Edizioni di Comunita, 1962), and D. Filtzer, *Soviet Workers and Late Stalinism*, (Cambridge, Cambridge University Press, 2002), p. 214.

[10] P. R. Gregory, *Restructuring the Soviet Economic Bureaucracy*, (Cambridge, Cambridge University Press, 1990), pp. 15-9; see, also, among others, Berliner, *Factory and Manager*; Filtzer, *Soviet Workers*, and Kornai, *The Socialist System*.

[11] Aša, AZNP, 27 and Berliner, *Factory and Manager*, p. 13.

[12] L. Siegelbaum, *Stakhanovism and the Politics of Productivity in USSR, 1935-1941*, (Cambridge, Cambridge University Press, 1988), p. 13, and F. Benvenuti, *Fuoco sui sabotatori. Stachanovismo e organizzazione industriale in URSS, 1934-1938*, (Roma, V.

Levi, 1988), pp. 13-24. In a more theoretical perspective, see M.R. Beissinger, *Scientific Management: Socialist Discipline and Soviet Power*, (Cambridge MA, Harvard University Press, 1988).

[13] L. Siegelbaum, 'Masters of the Shop Floor: Foremen and Soviet Industrialisation', in: N. Lampert & G. Rittersporn (eds), *Stalinism. Its Nature and Aftermath*, (Armonk NY, M.E. Sharpe, 1992), pp. 127-156.

[14] Filtzer, *Soviet Workers*, p. 233.

[15] I. Margolius & C. Miesl, *Škoda-Laurin and Klement*, (London, Osprey Automotive, 1992); P. Kozisek & J. Kralik, *L&K-Škoda*, (Prague, Motorpress: MILPO, 1997), and A. Teichová, *An Economic Background to Munich: International Business in Czechoslovakia, 1918-1938*, (London, Cambridge University Press, 1976), pp. 203-217.

[16] Aša, records Akciová Společnost pro Automobilový Průmysl henceforth ASAP, 93, Resumé Zprávy o studijní cestě gen.rady V. Klementa do Spojených Států, vykonané spolu s Ing. J. Hauserem v době od 8-7 do 5-11-1927 ku zjištění výrobních poměrů v automobilovém průmyslu americkém, Mladá Boleslav, 5-2-1928. See, also, V. Fava, 'Fears, Hopes and Automobiles: Visions of Fordism in Inter-war Czechoslovakia in Engineers' Travel Reports'. Paper presented at the AAASS National Conference Copley Hotel, Boston, 4-7 December 2004.

[17] Aša, records Automobilové Závody, národní podnik/henceforth AZNP/p. 4, A. Taub, A people's technology. A report to dr. Ing. F. Fabinger, General Director of KOVO, Prague, September 1946, p. 6; see, also, F. H. Žalud, *Přežili jsme. Zkušenosti z mého života 1919-1993, popsané pro má vnoučata a jejich generaci*, (Prague, Trilabit, 1996), p. 61, and V. Fava, 'Tecnici, ingegneri e fordismo. Škoda e Fiat nelle relazioni di viaggio in America', in: *Imprese e Storia*, Vol. 10, No. 22, 2000, pp. 201-49.

[18] See A. Teichová, 'For and Against the Marshall Plan in Czechoslovakia', in: R. Girault & M. Lévy-Leboyer (eds), *Le Plan Marshall et le relèvement économique de l'Europe*. Colloque tenu à Bercy les 21, 22, 23 mars 1991, (Paris, Comité pour l'histoire économique et financière de la France, Ministère de l'économie, des finances et du budget, 1993), p. 108.

[19] D. A. Hounshell, *From the American System to Mass Production 1800-1932*, (Baltimore, John Hopkins University Press, 1984).

[20] Aša, AZNP/P, 4, See, in particular, the travel reports of J. Frei, V. Matouš, V. Kremar, R. Kneschik & Z. Kejval.

[21] The First Five-Year Plan planned that car production would increase from 17,774 vehicles in 1948 to 33,000 in 1953; see Státní Ustřední Archiv henceforth SÚA, Hospodářská rada Ústrední Výbor KSČ henceforth HR, ÚV, KSČ, sv.44, A.J.306.

[22] 'Směry v naší a světové motorové technice', *Svět Motorů*, No. 52, 1949.

[23] SÚA, ČZAL, 86, Problematika výroby automobilů a motocyklů, (1949); 64, Program vývojového oddělení pro vozidla (1949); 83, Některá hospodářská porovnaní mezi USA a ČSR, (1949).

[24] SÚA, ČZAL, 64, Program vývojového oddělení.

[25] SÚA, ČZAL, 86, Problematika výroby automobilů.

[26] SÚA, ČZAL, 83, Výroba automobilů v ČSR v ramci spolupráce s SSSR a zeměmi lidových demokracií, (1950). K. Kaplan, *Českonslovensko a RHVP (1948-1953)*, Praha, 1995.

[27] SÚA, ČZAL, 86, Problematika výroby automobilů.

[28] SÚA, ČZAL, 83, Výroba automobilů v ČSR v ramci spolupráce s SSSR.

[29] SÚA, ČZAL, 64 Program vývojového oddělení.

[30] Kornai, *The Socialist System*, pp. 97-109.

[31] F. H. Žalud, *Přežili jsme*, p. 82.

[32] Aša, AZNP, 34, Rozvoj automobilového průmyslu v ČSR, 1970. See, also, T. Bauer & K. A. Soos, 'Inter-firm Relations and Technological Change in Eastern Europe - The Case of the Hungarian Motor Industry', *Acta Oeconomica*, Vol. 23, Nos. 3-4, pp. 285- 303.

[33] SÚA, ČZAL, 64, Program vývojového.

[34] SÚA, ČZAL, 83 and Aša, AZNP\P, URSS, 1950; A. Tůma, 'Motorisace Sovětského Svazu', *Svět Motorů*, No. 91, 1950, p. 643; Motorismus v Sovětském Svazu, *Svět Motorů*, No. 95, 1951, p. 786; Sovětský automobilní průmysl, *Svět Motorů*, No. 98, p. 870.

[35] SÚA, ČZAL, 27, (1951) Spolupráce SSSR, Československé závody na výrobu vozidel. Zprávy ze studijní cesty ČS. Automobilových závodů.

[36] K. Kaplan, *Sovětšti poradci v Československu. 1949-1956*, (Prague, Ustav pro soudobe̍ de◉jiny AV C◉R , 1993), pp. 42-66, and *Ibid*., Českonslovensko a RVHP, p.55.

[37] K. Kaplan, *The Overcoming of the Regime Crisis after Stalin's Death in Czechoslovakia, Poland and Hungary*, (Köln, Index e.V., 1986).

[38] Aša, AZNP, 7 and 34, Rozvoj automobilového průmyslu v ČSR (1970).

[39] M. Lewin, *Storia sociale dello stalinismo*, (Turin, G. Einaudi, 1985), pp. 272-294, and S. Fitzpatrick, *The Russian Revolution*, (Oxford, Oxford University Press, 1994), p.81.

[40] Aša, AZNP, 26, Seznam obráběcích strojů které potřebují Aznp, v MB pro 5 letý plán v roce 1949-1953, (1949).

[41] Aša, AZNP\P, URSS, 1950.

[42] Y. Cohen, 'Administration, politique et techniques: Réflexions sur la matérialité des pratiques administratives dans la Russie stalinienne (1922-1940)', *Cahiers du Monde Russe*, Vol. 44, Nos. 2-3, 2003, pp. 269-307 and *Ibid*., 'L'autorità della materia: alcuni aspetti dell' amministrazione dell'industria in Urss negli anni trenta', *Imprese e Storia*, No. 31, 2005, pp. 7-40.

[43] See, also, M. Burawoy & J. Lukacs, *The Radiant Past: Ideology and Reality in Hungary's Road to Capitalism?*, pp. 18-19, and *Ibid*., *The Politics of Production: Factory Regimes Under Capitalism and Socialism*, (London, Verso, 1985), pp. 157-208.

[44] Aša, AZNP, 1, (1953).

[45] Aša, AZNP, 11, (1953), Zavádění dispečerské služby v Automobilových závodech.

[46] Beissinger, *Scientific Management*, p. 145.

[47] Y. Cohen, *Administration, politique et techniques*, pp. 274-5.

[48] *Ibid*., p. 290.

[49] Aša, AZNP, 11, (1952).

[50] Aša, AZNP,11, (1953).

[51] Aša, AZNP, 11, (1953), 15, (1953).

[52] J. Pernes, *Snahy o překonaní politicko-hospodářské krize v Československu v roce 1953*, (Brno, Prius, 2000), and *Ibid*., 'Dělnické demonstace v Brně v roce 1951', *Soudobé Dějiny*, No. 1, 1996, pp. 23-41. See, also, O. Ulč, 'Pilsen: the Unknown Revolt', *Problems of Communism*, Vol. 15, No. 3, 1965, pp. 46-9, and M. Kramar, 'The Early Post-Stalin Succession Struggle and Upheavals in East Central Europe. Internal – External

Linkages in Soviet Policy Making (Part 1)', *Journal of Cold War Studies*, Vol. 1, No. 1, 1999, p. 21, and R. K. Evanson, 'Regime and Working Class in Czechoslovakia', 1948-1968, *Soviet Studies*, Vol.37, No. 2, 1985, pp. 248-69.

[53] Aša, AZNP, 1, (1953), Kritické připominky k práci ministerstva strojírenství, Authors: Závodní ráda skupiny ROH, AZNP, Mladá Boleslav.

[54] J. Stalin, *Questioni del Leninismo*, (Rome, Ed. Unità, 1945).

[55] SÚA, Ministerstvo automobilového průmyslu a zemědělských strojů, henceforth MAP, Uvod.

[56] Aša, AZNP, 8, Oborová Konference pro osobní automobily konaná dne 30-31 brzna 1956.

[57] SÚA, MAP, 200. Návrh perspektivního plánu oboru osobní automobily od roku 1956 do roku 1975; Aša, AZNP, 26, 1956, Vyhledové plánování. Osobní automobily v Mladá Boleslav, dne 27 února, Aša, AZNP, 34, III etapa plánu royvoje a specialisace pro osobní automobily 1955-1960.

[58] C. Boffito & L. Foa, *La crisi del modello sovietico in Cecoslovacchia*, (Turin, Einaudi, 1970), pp. 26-7.

Chapter 3

[1] See *Стратегическое ядерное вооружение России* [Strategic Nuclear Weapons of Russia] (Moscow, IzdAT, 1998), pp. 3–6; Mikhail Pervov, *Зенитное ракетное оружие противвоздушной обороны страны* [Anti-Aircraft Missile Weaponry of the Air Defence Forces of Russia] (Moscow, Aviarus-XXI, 2001), pp. 104–5; *Советская военная мощь от Сталина до Горбачева* [Soviet Military Power from Stalin to Gorbachev] (Moscow, Voennyi parad, 1999), pp. 150–61; *Рожденные атомной эрой. 12 Главное управление Министерства обороны Российской Федерации: опыт создания и развития* [Born in the nuclear era. The 12 main department of the Ministry of Defence of the Russian Federation: experience of creation and development] (Moscow, Chekhovskii poligraf. kombinat, 2002), pp. 44-87.

[2] See Jörg K. Hoensch, 'The Warsaw Pact and the Northern Member States', in: Robert W. Clawson & Lawrence S. Kaplan (eds), *The Warsaw Pact: Political Purpose & Military Means*, (Wilmington: Scholary Resources Inc., 1982), pp. 33–8; V.A. Zolotarev (ed), *История военной стратегии России* [History of the Military Strategy of Russia] (Moscow, Kuchkovo pole, 2000), p. 383; Andrej A. Gretschko, *Die Streitkräfte des Sowjetstaates*, (Berlin, Militärverlag der DDR, 1975), pp. 98–101; Anatoli Gribkow, *Der Warschauer Pakt. Geheimnisse und Hintergründe des östlichen Militärbündnisses*, (Berlin, Edition q, 1995), pp. 34–6.

[3] See *Die sowjetische Militärmacht. Geschichte, Technik, Strategie*, (Bayreuth, Gondrom Verlag, 1979), pp. 202–6; *Военачальники ракетных войск стратегического назначения. Сборник очерков* [Military Leaders of the Strategic Missile Forces. Collection of Sketches] (Moscow, TsIPK RVSN, 1997), pp. 8–10; Raymond L. Garthoff, *Soviet Strategy in the Nuclear Age*, (New York, Praeger, 1958), pp. 224–6.

[4] See *Ракетный щит отечества* [The Missile Shield of the Motherland] (Moscow, TsIPK RVSN, 1999), pp. 52-4; *Die Streitkräfte der UdSSR. Abriß ihrer Entwicklung von 1918 bis 1968*, (Berlin, Militärverlag der DDR, 1974) pp. 658–60; J.I. Korabljow, W.A. Anfilow & W.A. Mazulenko, *Kurzer Abriß der Geschichte der Streitkräfte der UdSSR von 1917 bis 1972*, (Berlin, Militärverlag der DDR, 1976), pp. 305–6.

[5] *Zeittafel zur Militärgeschichte der Deutschen Demokratischen Republik 1949 bis 1968*, (Berlin, Deutscher Militärverlag, 1969), p. 135.

[6] Speech of Nikita S. Khrushchev at the 4th Session of the Supreme Soviet. *Pravda*, 14 January 1960; Bernhard Bechler, 'Der Raketen-Kernwaffenkrieg – eine neue Qualität des bewaffneten Kampfes', *Militärwesen*, No. 5, 1962, pp. 658–60.

[7] See Rodion Malinovskii, *Die Strategie des Kernwaffenkrieges*, Moscow 1964, Bundesarchiv-Militärarchiv (Federal Military Archive) in Freiburg i. Br. (hereinafter referred to as: BA-MA), DVL-3/29942, p. 131 [Unauthorized German translation of a Soviet top secret handbook on nuclear warfare for the Chiefs of the Military Districts of the Soviet Union].

[8] See *Zur geschichtlichen Entwicklung und Rolle der Nationalen Volksarmee der Deutschen Demokratischen Republik* (Potsdam, Militärgeschichtliches Institut der DDR, 1974), pp. 185–6. Until the GDR ceased to exist, this outline of the history of the EGA was classified as secret information.

[9] Speech of the Soviet Minister of Defense, Marshal Rodion Ia. Malinovskii, on the XXII Congress of the CPSU. *Neues Deutschland*, 23 October 1961, No. 294.

[10] See Central Intelligence Agency, National Intelligence Estimate (NIE) 12–65, 'Eastern Europe and the Warsaw Pact', 26 August 1965, <http://www.isn.ethz.ch/php/documents/collection_7/ docs/nbb36_1.pdf> (21 April 2004).

[11] See Draft resolution of the PCC of the Warsaw Pact (bearing the following handwritten note 'confirmed 29 March 1961'), 19 March 1961, *Российский государственный архив экономики* (Russian State Archive for economics) in Moscow (hereinafter referred to as: RGAE), 4372/79/792, p. 96; Ross A. Johnson, Robert W. Dean & Alexander Alexiev, *Die Streitkräfte des Warschauer Pakts in Mitteleuropa: DDR, Polen und ČSSR*, (Stuttgart, Seewald Verlag, 1982), pp. 31–2; Wolfe, *Soviet Power and Europe*, pp. 150–2.

[12] See Vladislav M. Zubok & Hope M. Harrison, 'The Nuclear Education of Nikita Khrushchev', in: John Lewis Gaddis, Philip H. Gordon, Ernest R. May & Jonathan Rosenberg (eds), *Cold War Statesmen Confront the Bomb: Nuclear Diplomacy since 1945*, (Oxford, Oxford University Press, 1999), pp. 150–54.

[13] See *A Cardboard Castle? An inside History of the Warsaw Pact 1955-1991*, (ed) by Vojtech Mastny & Malcolm Byrne (Budapest - New York, Central European University Press, 2005), pp. 7-15; Frank Umbach, *Das rote Bündnis: Entwicklung und Zerfall des Warschauer Paktes 1955-1991*, (Berlin, Linksverlag, 2005), pp. 134-140.

[14] See Speech of Soviet Minister of Defense Marshal Rodion Ia. Malinovskii on the evaluation of a command post exercise by the GSFG and the EGA, October 1961, BA-MA, DVW-1/5203, pp. 56–8.

[15] Speech of the USSR Minister of Defense, Marshal Rodion Iakovlevich Malinovskii, on the evaluation of a command exercise by the GSSD and the NVA, May 1961, BA-MA, DVW-1/5203, p. 7.

[16] For more details on these Soviet missiles, see A.B. Shirokorad, *Энциклопедия отечественного ракетного оружияю 1817-2002 гг.* [Encylopedia of Russia's Rocket and Missile Armament 1817-2002] (Moscow, AST, 2003).

[17] See Note on the fulfillment of requirements of the armies of the Warsaw Pact countries for military hardware from 1961 to 1965, March 1961, RGAE, 4372/79/792, pp. 106–7.

[18] See Report from GOSPLAN to the Central Committee of the CPSU on the

expected fulfillment of production requirements for arms deliveries, 20 December 1961, RGAE, 4372/79/759, p. 36.

[19] See Draft text of speech by Deputy Chairman of GOSPLAN Mikhail V. Khrunichev for the meeting of the PCC 'On Arms Production Specialization in the Warsaw Pact Countries and Mutual Supply of Military Hardware', 27 March 1961, RGAE, 4372/79/792, pp. 84-5; Draft resolution of the PCC of the Warsaw Pact (bearing the handwritten note 'confirmed 29 March 1961'), 19 March 1961, RGAE, 4372/79/792, pp. 96-8.

[20] See Note on the fulfillment of the requirements of the armies of the Warsaw Pact countries for military hardware from 1961 to 1965, March 1961, RGAE, 4372/79/792/, pp. 106-7; *Zur geschichtlichen Entwicklung und Rolle der Nationalen Volksarmee*, p. 200.

[21] See *Istoriia voennoi strategii Rossii,* edited by V.A. Zolotareva (Moscow, Kuchkovo pole, 2000), pp. 402-08 - W.D. Sokolowski, *Militär-Strategie,* (Cologne, Markus-Verlag, 1965), pp. 275-97.

[22] See appendix to the draft resolution of the PCC of the Warsaw Pact – lists of arms deliveries for the member states, 1962–1965, March 1961, RGAE, 4372/79/792, pp. 24-65. For more detailed information on the R-11 and Luna nuclear weapon delivery systems, see Harald Nielsen, *Die DDR und die Kernwaffen: Die nukleare Rolle der Nationalen Volksarmee im Warschauer Pakt,* (Baden-Baden, Nomos-Verlagsgesellschaft, 1998).

[23] See record of discussions of the Joint High Command on 1-2 December 1960, December 1960, BA-MA, AZN 32594, pp. 59-71; Martin Kunze, 'Das nukleare Trägerpotential der Nationalen Volksarmee', in: Walter Jablonsky & Wolfgang Wünsche (eds), *Im Gleichschritt? Zur Geschichte der NVA,* (Berlin, Das Neue Berlin, 2001), pp. 201-8.

[24] According to the minutes of the Joint High Command meeting of 31 March 1961, the following combat troops of the EGA were under Warsaw Pact command in peacetime: 1 missile brigade (R-11), 4 motorized rifle divisions, 2 armored divisions, 3 training regiments, 2 artillery regiments, and 2 anti-aircraft regiments. The air force provided 2 air defense divisions, comprising a total of 5 anti-aircraft missile regiments and 6 fighter squadrons, and also 1 helicopter squadron, 1 signal regiment, and 8 ground support battalions. The entire combat naval resources of the Volksmarine [People's Navy], comprising 4 frigates, 18 corvettes, 12 missile patrol boats, 27 large torpedo boats, 45 small torpedo boats, 12 minelayers, 24 minesweepers, and 18 landing craft, plus 1 *Sopka* missile battery, were also under the command of the Joint High Command. Further security and supply units of the EGA were also included, such as reconnaissance, sapper, intelligence, signal, and transport troops. In total, already in peacetime there were 90,000 men under the command of the military leadership of the Warsaw Pact. Only the Ministry of National Defense, the training facilities, and the military district (*Wehrbezirk* and *Wehrbereich*) commands remained under the command of the GDR. For a defense situation at the beginning of the 1960s, a further three (mobilization) divisions and newly formed troop formations were to be placed under the command of the Joint High Command. The combat strength of the EGA forces was stated in the protocol in 1961 as at around 200,000 men. Another 40,000 to 50,000 men were to serve as territorial defense troops and would therefore have been under the command of

the Ministry of National Defense rather than the Warsaw Pact. See Breakdown of target strengths of the EGA prepared for the chief of staff of the Joint High Command, Army General Aleksei Innokentevich Antonov, 30 January 1962, BA-MA, AZN 32871, pp. 37-47. See, also, Heinrich Engelhardt, 'Das Mobilmachungssystem der NVA', in: Klaus Naumann (ed), *NVA: Anspruch und Wirklichkeit; nach ausgewählten Dokumenten,* (Hamburg - Berlin - Bonn, Mittler, 1996), pp. 301-16; Fritz Streletz, 'Der Nationale Verteidigungsrat der DDR und das Vereinigte Oberkommando des Warschauer Vertrages', in: Wolfgang Wünsche (ed), *Rührt euch! Zur Geschichte der NVA,* (Berlin, Edition Ost, 1998), pp. 130-73.

[25] See Martin Kunze, 'Das nukleare Trägerpotential der Nationalen Volksarmee', pp. 214–23.

[26] See letter from the Minister of National Defense, Army General Heinz Hoffmann, to the commander-in-chief of the Joint High Command, Marshal Andrei A. Grechko, 24 March 1961, BA-MA, AZN 32598, pp. 1-2.

[27] See Letter from Malinovskii, Riabikov, and Arkhipov for the CC of the CPSU, 6 July 1962, RGAE, 4372/80/298, p. 312.

[28] See Letter from Khrushchev to Kádár, January 1962, RGAE, 4372/80/298, p. 18.

[29] See Draft resolution of the USSR Council of Ministers on the delivery of an R-11 missile brigade to Hungary, January 1962, RGAE, 4372/80/298, pp. 8-12. The Soviet Union did not charge its alliance partners for any of the costs for the storage of warheads in the USSR. For details on the handing over and installation of nuclear warheads, see Nielsen, *Die DDR und die Kernwaffen,* pp. 115-35 and Martin Kunze, 'Das nukleare Trägerpotential der Nationalen Volksarmee', pp. 228-30. Here, too, an exception applied in the case of East Germany. The atomic warheads allocated to the EGA under the command of the Group of Soviet Forces in Germany (GSFG) were already located on East German territory. In the mid-1960s, East Germany had built two nuclear warhead depots for this purpose, handed over for the use by the GSFG on completion. The facilities near Stolzenhain and Himmelpfort were each capable of housing up to 120 nuclear warheads. Himmelpfort was to supply the 3rd Army of the EGA (Military District III), to be formed in the event of war, with atomic warheads, and the Stolzenhain depot was designed to supply the requirements of the 5th Army (Military District V) for nuclear weapons. See Manfred van Heerde, *Stahltür 01-2001: Kernsprengkopflager 5001 der Sowjetischen Streitkräfte in Deutschland* (Frankfurt/Oder, Stahltür, 2001); *Geheimes Atomwaffenlager in Deutschland,* production of the Galileo unit of the Pro Sieben television channel, 28 February 2002.

[30] See Study material for the Chiefs of Staff of the EGA: *Offensive Operations of a Combined-Arms Army in the Initial Period of a War,* 5 December 1958, BA-MA, DVW-1/4358, p. 95; Combat order for the 35th Army Corps of the EGA in the 'Nordwind' exercise, 28 June 1962, BA-MA, DVW-1/5195, pp. 338-41.

[31] See note No. 8 - approximate *per capita* defense expenditure in the Warsaw Pact, 1961, RGAE, 4372/79/792, p. 141.

[32] See note on the expenditure of Warsaw Pact countries on purchases of military hardware from the USSR, 1961, RGAE, 4372/79/792, p. 114.

[33] See note on arms deliveries to the Soviet Ministry of Defense between 1961-1963, 24 September 1962, RGAE, 4372/80/185, p. 279.

[34] See draft Armaments Production Plan in the USSR for 1963, no date, RGAE, 4372/80/183, pp. 1-13.

[35] See Günther Wagenlehner, 'Militärpolitik und Militärdoktrin der UdSSR', in: Hannes Adomeit, Hans-Herrmann Höhmann & Günther Wagenlehner (eds), *Die Sowjetunion als Militärmacht*, (Stuttgart - Berlin - Cologne - Mainz, Kohlhammer, 1987), p. 20.

Chapter 4

[1] A. O. Hirschmann, *Shifting Involvements: Private Interest and Public Action*, (Princeton, Princeton University Press, 1982).

[2] A. O. Hirschmann, 'Abwanderung, Widerspruch und das Schicksal der Deutschen Demokratischen Republik', *Leviathan*, Vol. 20, No. 3, 1992, pp. 330-58. For studies about life styles and consumption typologies, see, in particular, P. Betts, 'The Twilight of the idols: East German Memory and Material Culture', *The Journal of Modern History*, Vol. 72, No. 3, 2000, pp. 731-65; G. Castillo, 'Domesticating the Cold War: Household Consumption as Propaganda in Marshall Plan Germany', *Journal of Contemporary History*, Vol. 40, No. 2, pp. 261-88; I. Merkel, 'Konsumkultur in der DDR. Über das Scheitern der Gegenmoderne auf dem Schlachtfeld des Konsums', *Mitteilungen aus der Kulturwissenschaften Forschung*, No. 37, 1996, pp. 314-31; S. Reid., 'The Khrushchev Kitchen: Domesticating the Scientific-Technological Revolution', *Journal of Contemporary History*, Vol. 40, No. 2, pp. 289-316. On the connection between policy strategies, citizenship and consumption regimes, see M. Daunton & M. Hilton (eds), *The Politics of Consumption: Material Culture and Citizenship in Europe and America*, (Oxford - NewYork, Berg, 2001).

[3] For a more exhaustive description of forms of consumption incentive in the GDR of the 1950s, see I. Merkel, *Utopie und Bedürfnis*, (Cologne, Böhlau Verlag, 1999), p. 123. On the relationship between the industrial system and the distribution system, see R.G. Stokes, *Constructing Socialism*, (Baltimore - London, John Hopkins University Press, 2000).

[4] A. Kaminsky, '"Warenproduktion und Bedürfnisse in Übereinstimmung bringen." Markt- und Bedarfforschung als Quelle der DDR-Sozialgeschichte', *Deutschland Archiv*, Vol. 31, No. 4, 1998, pp. 579-93. Before the foundation of the *IfMF* 'socialist research of commerce' (*sozialistische Handelsforschung*) was carried out by the Institute for Retail Commerce (*Fachinstitut für den Binnen Handel*). The institute mostly studied the mechanisms of economic planning, and not the attitude of consumers.

[5] See I. Merkel, *Utopie*, p. 121. In the West, the Individual had a different value; see S. Kroen, *Der Aufstieg des Kundenbürgers*, in: M. Prinz (ed), *Der lange Wege in den Überfluss. Anfänge und Entwicklung der Konsumgesellschaft*, (Paderborn, Schöningh, 2003), pp. 519-550.

[6] After the fall of the Berlin wall, the institute continued its research activity as a private research institution. Information about the current activity of the institute is available at: http://www.imleipzig.de. In general, there is a rich tradition of social and market research in Germany. The most important scholar in the field is Michael Verhofen, father of German market research and founder of the *Gesellschaft für Marktforschung*, an institute for market survey, which was founded in the late 1950s. There is also a trend to research the politics of consumption of the socialist movement. The

Austrian Group for Economic Psychology Research (*Österreichische Wirtschaftspsychologische Forschungsstelle*) functioned in Vienna between 1927 and 1938. On the activity of the group, see H. Zeisel, *Die Wiener Schule der Motivforschung*, in: J. Langer (ed), *Geschichte der Österreichischen Soziologie*, (Wien, Verlag für Gesellschaftskritik, 1988), pp. 157-166. On the tradition of consumer research in Germany, see C. Conrad, 'Observer les consommateurs. Etudes de marché et histoire aux annèe 1930 aux annèe 1960', *Le Mouvement Social*, No. 206, 2004, pp. 17-40.

[7] Merkel, *Utopie*, p. 150.

[8] Kaminsky, 'Warenproduktion und Bedürfnisse', p. 43.

[9] See K. H. Selbmann & E. Scholz, 'Die Auswertung von Konsumentenbefragungen - eine wichtige Voraussetzung für begründete Bedarfsprognosen', in: *Mitteilungen des Institutes für Markforschung* (hereinafter, *MIfMF*), 2 (1965), pp. 14-8. See, also, W. Dlouhy, 'Erfahrungen aus einer Befragung', in: *MIfMF* 2 (1965), pp. 19-23. And H. Fischer, 'Die Konsumentenbefragung- eine Form der Einbeziehung der Bevölkerung in die Planung und Leitung der Volkswirtschaft', in: *MIfMF* 1 (1967), pp. 23-16.

[10] On the persuading quality of the distribution techniques of mass consumption, see, V. Packard, *The Hidden Persuaders*, (New York, D. McKay Co, 1957). On the relationship of the techniques of diffusion and political consent, see D. Riesman., *La folla solitaria*, (New York, Il Mulino, 1954).

[11] W. Koeppert, 'Unsere Aufgaben im Jahre 1966', in: *MIfMF* 1 (1966), pp. 1-5. See, also, W. Koeppert, '10 Jahre Forschungsarbeit im Dienste der Versorgung unserer Werktätigen', in: *MIfMF* Sonderheft (1967), pp. 1-5.

[12] The conceptual and practical aspects of territorialization are described, in: G. Deleuze, *Divenire Molteplice. Saggi su Nietzsche e Foucault*, (Verona, Ombre Corte, 1996). G. Deleuze & F. Guattari, *Antiedipo. Capitalismo e schizofrenia*, (Turin, Einaudi, 1996).

[13] See A. Steiner, *Von Plan zu Plan. Eine Wirtschaftsgeschichte der DDR*, (Munich, Dva, 2004). In particular, pp. 83-115.

[14] H. Fabiunke, 'Kauf- und Konsum-Motivforschung- ein wichtiges Aufgabengebiet unserer sozialistischen Konsumgütermarktforschung', in: *MIfMF*, 3 (1965), p. 13.

[15] *Ibid.*

[16] *Ibid.*, p. 14.

[17] *Ibid.*, p. 15. In 1964, research specialists started focusing on motivational market research. Their approach was based on studies on the motivations of consumers and the reasons of their behavior. The principal theorist of motivational research is Ernest Dichter. See E. Dichter, *La strategia del desiderio*, (Milan, Garzanti, 1963); E. Dichter, *Handbook of consumer motivations*, (New York, McGraw-Hill, 1964); E. Dichter, *Motivating human behavior*, (New York, McGraw-Hill, 1971).

[18] *Ibid.*, p. 17. Forms 'of the consumers imagery about dowry' were analysed in particular, (*Konsumentenvorstellungen zur Aussteuer*).

[19] See A. Steiner, *Von Plan zu Plan*, and A.Steiner, 'Dissolution of the Dictatorship over Needs? Consumer Behavior and Economic Reform in East Germany in the 1960s', in: S. Strasser, C. McGovern & M. Judt (eds), *Getting and Spending: European and American Consumer Societies in the Twentieth Century*, (Cambridge MA, Cambridge University Press, 1998), pp. 167-186; W. Hermann, *Aufbau und Fall einer Diktatur*, (Cologne, Bund-Verlag, 1996); T. Pirker, M.R. Lepsius, R. Weinert, & H.-H. Hertle, *Der*

Plan als Befehl und Fiktion. Wirtschaftführung in der DDR, (Opladen, VS Verlag für Sozialwissenschaften, 1995). For the reconstruction of the general political economy, see J. Kopstein., *The Politics of Economic Decline in East-Germany 1945-1989,* (Chapel Hill, University of North Carolina Press, 1997).

[20] Bundes Archiv -Berlin (since now: BArch), DL 102/6, Institut für Marktforschung, Die Marktforschung in der DDR, 8.12.67. p. 2.

[21] *Ibid.*

[22] *Ibid.*, p 5.

[23] *Ibid.*, p. 6.

[24] R. Dietrich, 'Zur Methodik der Ausarbeitung des Perspektivplanes der Entwicklung des Konsumgüterverbrauchs', in: *MIfMF* 1 (1967), pp. 16-22. On the relationship between objects, modernity, social and individual identity, see W. Rupper (ed), *Fahrrad, Auto, Fernsehschrank. Zur Kulturgeschichte der Alltagsdinge,* (Frankfurt aM, Fischer-TB, 1993); U. Becher, *Geschichte des modernes Lebensstils: Essen, Wohnen, Freizeit, Reisen,* (Munich, Beck, 1990); V. de Grazia., *The Sex of Things,* (Berkeley CA - London, University of California Press, 1996); J. Engelhardt. *Schwalbe, Duo, Kultmobil. Vom Acker auf den Boulevard,* (Berlin - Brandeburg, Bebra, 1995).

[25] I refer to the practice of opening state shops, where second-hand electric and other used goods were sold to meet the demand triggered by the gaps in production. Moreover, there were frequent references in the IfMF researchers as well as in the ministerial directives to the urgency of introducing collective and social consumption forms of particular services connected to certain goods (i.e. listening to radio or watching TV; washing machines and other domestic automatic tools). See: W. Horn, *Vernünftig leben- rationell verbrauchen,* in: *MIfMF*, 4 (1979), pp. 31-3. See, also: Marcello Anselmo, 'Il consumatore comandato: pratiche e immaginario della cultura del consume realsocialista: Berlino est e DDR', PhD thesis (European Univeristy Institute, Florence, 2007).

[26] BArch., DL 102/268, IfMF, *Die Anwendung der Motivforschung in der sozialistischen Konsumgütermarktforschung,* 1967, p. 1.

[27] Pierre Bourdieu's concept *habitus* was used in reference to the GDR by: I. Merkel, *Utopie*. See, also, I. Dietrich & D. Muehlberg, 'Proletarische Lebensweise als kulturelle Tradition des Sozialismus', *Weimarer Beiträge*, Vol. 26, No. 11, 1980; K. Maenicke-Gyongyosi & R. Rytlewski (eds), *Lebensstile und Kulturmuster in sozialistischen Gesellschaften,* (Cologne, Wissenschaft und Politik, 1990). See, also, I. Merkel, 'Arbeiter und Konsum im real existierenden Sozialismus', in: P.Hübner & K. Tenfelde, *Arbeiter in der SBZ-DDR,* (Essen, Klartext, 1999), pp. 527-53, and I. Merkel, 'Der Aufhaltsame Aufbruch in die Konsulgesellschaft', in: Idem (ed), *Wunderwirtschaft: DDR- Konsum Kultur in den 60er Jahren,* (Cologne, Böhlau, 1996), pp. 8-20.

[28] BArch., DL 102/268, IfMF, 'Die Anwendung der Motivforschung in der sozialistischen', p. 2.

[29] *Ibid.*, 10.

[30] BArch., DL 102/268, IfMF, 'Die Anwendung', p. 16.

[31] BArch., DL 102/268, IfMF, 'Die Anwendung', p. 14.

[32] On the practices of consumers, M. De Certeau, *L'invenzione del quotidiano,* (Rome, Edizioni Lavoro, 2001). See, in particular, pp. 63-80. See, also, M. De Certeau, L. Giard, & P. Mayol, *Practice of Everyday Life. Living and Cooking,* (Minneapolis - London, University of Minnesota Press, 1998).

[33] BArch., DL 102/268, p. 7.

[34] *Ibid.*

[35] *Ibid.*, p. 8.

[36] *Ibid.*, p. 10.

[37] *Ibid.*, p. 12.

[38] *Ibid.*, p. 14.

[39] *Ibid.*, p. 15.

[40] The social sign of goods was initially described by Marx, in his essay on the fetishistic feature of goods. See, also, W. Benjamin, *L'opera d'arte all'epoca della sua riproducibilità tecnica*, (Turin, Einaudi, 1972). On the semiotic power of consumption, see W.F. Haug, *Warenästhetik, Sexualität und Herrschaft*, (Munich, Fischer-TB., 1982).

[41] BArch., DL 102/268, p. 18.

[42] *Ibid.*, p. 20.

[43] *Ibid.*, p. 21.

[44] *Ibid.*

[45] *Ibid.*, p. 23.

[46] *Ibid.*, p. 25.

[47] *Ibid.*, p. 26.

[48] *Ibid.*, p. 30.

[49] *Ibid.*

[50] *Ibid.*

[51] *Ibid.*

[52] See, for example, AA.VV, *Alltagskultur der DDR. Begleitbuch zur Ausstellung: 'Tempolinsen und P2'*, (Berlin, be.bra, 1996).

[53] Some examples of the research results can be found in: H. Zappe, 'Der Wohnungsbau – ein wichtiger Einflussfaktor auf den Bedarf von Wohnraumöbeln', in: *MIfMF*, 2 (1967), pp. 5-10. See, also, W. Nieke, 'Systematische Untersuchungen der Verbrauchs- und Lebensgewohnheiten unserer Bevölkerung – ein Beitrag zur Realisierung des komplexen Wohnungsbauprogramms', in: *MIfMF*, 2 (1975), pp. 16-23.

[54] The research of the IfMF also included members of the agricultural cooperatives, artisans, self-employed workers, and occasionaly soldiers.

[55] W. Nieke, *Systematische Untersuchungen der Verbrauchs*, p. 15.

[56] In order to reconstruct the social atmosphere of the GDR, we have to consider the emergence of the socialist small bourgeoisie, which was described by George Orwell as the 'lower-upper-middle class.' See also E. Fromm, *Arbeiter und Angestellte am Vorabend des Drittes Reiches*, (Munich, Deutscher Taschenbuch Verlag, 1983). A keen observer of the cultural transformations caused by the emergence of consumption society is Sigfried Kracauer. See S. Kracauer, *Die Angestellten. Aus dem neuesten Deutschland*, (Frankfurt am Main, Frankfurter Societäts Druckerei, 1971). See, also, S. Kracauer, *The Mass Ornament: Weimar Essays*, (Cambridge MA, Harvard Univeristy Press, 1995). Idem, *The Salaried Masses: Duty and Distraction in Weimar Germany*, (London - NewYork, Verso, 1998).

[57] H. Zappe, 'Der Wohnungsbau – ein wichtiger Einflussfaktor auf den Bedarf von Wohnraumöbeln', in: *MIfMF*, 2 (1967), p. 7.

[58] P. Stockmann, 'Möbel und Meinungen', in: *MifMF*, 1 (1970), p. 16. The majority of the families concerned – younger families, in particular – declared that they had more space at their disposal if compared to the locations they had previously stayed

at. They thus assumed different consumption habits. For example, the possibility of having a separate room for children triggered an increasing demand for furniture for children.

[59] *Ibid.*

[60] *Ibid.*

[61] *Ibid.*, p. 15.

[62] *Ibid.*, p. 16.

[63] For a history of the fall of 'real socialism' in the GDR, see, for example, C. Maier, *Dissolution: The Crisis of Communism and the End of East Germany*, (N.J., Princeton University Press, 1997).

Chapter 5

[1] '"Camera Buff", [in] trying to avoid being Manichean, showed, for example, the reasoning of the people representing the Communist authorities in a more ambiguous and complex light than other films such as "Man of Marble" or Zanussi's films. Friends started calling him "The balladeer of communist tears". I think that Krzysztof pursed what he inwardly felt to be the truth or a way to the truth. But he was very sensitive to the fact that many people, some of them close friends, thought he had rather overstepped the limits.'

Agnieszka Holland interviewed in 2003 for the Artificial Eye DVD edition of 'Camera Buff' (2003). See, also, Annette Insdorf, *Double Lives, Second Chances: The Cinema of Krzysztof Kieślowski*, (New York, Miramax Books, 2000).

[2] Ryszard Kreyser, *Amatorski Klub Fotograficzny*, (Warsaw, 1978), pp. 99-106.

[3] Anon., 'Międzynarodowe spotkanie fotoamatorów', *Fotografia*, August 1955, pp. 12-13.

[4] Gerhard Henninger, 'Weg und Ziel der Amateurfotografie in Der Deutschen Demokratischen Republik', *Fotografie*, No. 8, 1960, p. 292.

[5] Alfred Ligocki, 'O realizme socjalistycznym w fotografie', *Fotografia*, August 1953, pp. 2-3 continued in *Fotografia*, September 1953, pp. 2-4.

[6] *Świat*, No. 200, 22 May 1955, p 24.

[7] Henninger (1960), 'Weg und Ziel'.

[8] The thoughts in this essay were stimulated by seeing *Entuzjaści z Amatorskich Klubów Filmowych*, a remarkable exhibition/archive of amateur films curated by Marysia Lewandowska and Neil Cummings at the *Centrum Sztuki Współczesnej* in Warsaw in the summer of 2004. The 300 films collected for this project will form an on-line 'open' archive of amateur film. See http://www.enthusiastsarchive.net/.

[9] Marx, *Capital*, III, (London, Penguin Books, 1997), p. 820.

[10] Article 59 of the Polish Constitution (1952) stated, 'Every citizen of the Peoples Republic of Poland has the right to rest.' The first clauses of this article guaranteed worker rights to rest and the second promised a shopping list of organised 'holidays, the development of tourism, sanatoria, sports associations, houses of culture, *świetlice*, parks and other forms of organised rest to provide the possibility for healthy and cultural rest for the mass of the urban and rural working classes'. See Paweł Sowiński, *Wakacje w Polsce Ludowej. Polityka władz i ruch turystyczny (1945-1989)*, (Warsaw, Trio, 2005). On leisure in East Germany, see David Childs, *East Germany*, (London, Praeger, 1969), p. 168.

[11] Polish leader between 1956 and 1970 Władysław Gomułka acquired a reputation for monkish asceticism. See Eleonora Salwa-Syzdek & Ryszard Strzelecki-Gomułka, *Między realizmem a utopią. Władysław Gomułka we wspomnieniach syna*, (Warsaw, Wydawn. Studio Emka, 2003).

[12] *Świat*, March 1953.

[13] See, for instance, Lynn Abrams, *Workers' Culture in Imperial Germany*, (London, Routledge, 1992); Peter Bailey, *Leisure and Class in Victorian England: Rational Recreation and the Contest for Control, 1830-1885*, (London, Routledge & Kegan Paul, 1978).

[14] Theodor Adorno & Max Horkheimer, *Dialectic of Enlightenment*, (London, Verso, 1979), p. 137.

[15] Walter Benjamin, 'The Author as Producer', in: Idem, *Understanding Brecht*, (London, NLB, 1977), p. 90.

[16] Anne White, *De-Stalinization and the House of Culture: Declining State Control over Leisure in the USSR, Poland and Hungary, 1953-89*, (London, Routledge, 1990), p. 35. See, also, Simone Hain & Stephan Stroux, *Die Salons der Sozialisten. Kulturhäuser in der DDR*, (Berlin, Ch. Links, 1996).

[17] White, *De-Stalinization*, p. 36

[18] C. Miłosz, *The Captive Mind*, [1953], (Harmondsworth, Penguin, 1980), pp. 197-8.

[19] W. Sokorski, 'O Właściwy stosunek do sztuki ludowej', *Polska Sztuka Ludowa*, 5 (1949).

[20] See David Bathrick, *The Powers of Speech. The Politics of Culture in the GDR*, (Lincoln, NE, University of Nebraska Press, 1995), pp. 109-128.

[21] White, *De-Stalinization*, p. 49 and p. 63.

[22] For a discussion of consumerism in Gomułka's Poland, see my 'Warsaw's Shops, Stalinism and the Thaw', in: S.E. Reid & David Crowley (eds), *Style and Socialism: Modernity and Material Culture in Post-war Eastern Europe*, (Oxford, Berg, 2000), pp. 25-47.

[23] Paweł Machcewicz 'Intellectuals and Mass Movements, Ideologies and Political Programs in Poland in 1956', in: György Péteri, (ed), *Intellectual Life and the First Crisis of State Socialism in East Central Europe, 1953-1956*, (Trondheim, Program on East European Cultures and Societies, 2001), p. 127.

[24] See Leszek Kołakowski's 'The Priest and the Jester', in: *Twórczość*, (1959) reproduced in; *Toward a Marxist Humanism*, trans. Jane Zielonko Peel (New York, Grove Press, 1969), p. 34.

[25] W. Stradomski, 'Rola i znaczenie amatorskiego ruchu filmego w rozwoju kultury', *Fotografia*, 1968 cited by Sebastian Cichocki, in: 'Czas wolny i czas uwolniony', in: Marysia Lewandowska & Neil Cummings, (eds), *Entuzjaści z Amatorskich Klubów Filmowych*, (Warsaw, Centrum Sztuki Współczesnej Zamek Ujazdowski 2004), pp. 82-3.

[26] It should be noted that whilst amateur photography exhibitions in East Germany were open to all Germans in the 1950s, the guidelines issued to participants placed an emphasis on kinds of imagery that would be exhibited. Images were to represent the 'revolutionary tradition' or the social conditions were particularly encouraged. See Karl Gernot Kuehn, *Caught: the Art of Photography in the German Democratic Republic*, (Berkeley, Univeristy of California Press, 1997), p. 29.

[27] *Ibid.*, p. 46.

[28] GS, 'Bildreporter contra Fotoamateur – Fotoamateur contra Bildreporter?'

Fotografie, No. 11, November 1960, pp. 409-11.

[29] Henninger (1960), 'Weg und Ziel'.

[30] Bertold Beiler, 'Die westliche Fotografie in der Sackgasse der spätbürgerlichen Philosophie', *Fotografie*, No. 7, July 1967, p. 243.

[31] Hermann Exner, 'Fotomontage – eine Volkskunst', *Fotografie*, No. 10, October, 1960, pp. 372-5 & 404; see, also, Peter H. Feist, 'Fotografische Entlarvungen', *Fotografie*, No. 9, September 1958, pp. 329-31 & 349.

[32] G.O. Walter, 'Otto Croy oder Der Mißbrauch der Fotogragfie', *Fotografie*, No. 12, December 1962, pp. 424-44.

[33] Kuehn, *Caught: the Art of Photography*, p. 57.

[34] Rudolf Wedler, 'Fotografierverbote', *Die Fotografie*, March 1962, pp. 82-3 & 96.

[35] *Ibid.*

[36] See Edwin Hoernle, 'The Working Man's Eye' in David Mellor, (ed), *Germany, the new photography, 1927-33: documents and essays*, (London, Arts Council of Great Britain, 1978), pp. 47-50.

[37] Wolfgang Hütt, 'Fotografie des Proletariats', *Fotografie*, No. 8, August 1960, pp. 290-1. See, also, Wolfgang Hütt, 'Gedanken zur Problematik einer Bildgeschichte der Fotografie', *Fotografie*, No. 5, May 1960, pp. 166-8.

[38] SED announcement made in October 1957 cited by Bathrick, *The Powers of Speech*, p. 110.

[39] See Oscar Fricke, 'The Dzerhinsky Commune: Birth of the Soviet 35 mm Camera Industry', *History of Photography*, Vol. 3, No. 2, 1979, pp. 135-55.

[40] Elena Barkhatova, 'Soviet Policy on Photography', in Diane Neumaier, (ed), *Beyond Memory: Soviet Nonconformist Photography and Photo-Related Works of Art*, (New Brunswick, NJ., Rutgers University Press, 2004), p. 48.

[41] Kodak published its own magazine in Poland in the 1930s, *Kodak Mowi (Kodak Speaks)*.

[42] Barkhatova, *'Soviet Policy'*, p. 57.

[43] *Dłubak i Grupa 55*, exhibition catalogue, Muzeum Sztuki (Łódż, 2003).

[44] See Witold Jedlicki, *Klub Krzywego Koła*, (Paris, Instytut Literacki, 1963).

[45] See Juliusz Garztecki, 'Człowiek z kamera. Marek Holzman czyli Protest', *Fotografia*, No. 4, April 1965, pp. 85-6.

[46] See, for instance, Urszula Czartoryska, 'Sztuka Johna Heartfielda', *Fotografia*, No. 4, April 1964, pp. 76-7; Heryk Latoś, 'Fotoreporterzy wielkiej socjalistycznej rewolucju październikowej', *Fotografia*, No. 10, October 1967, pp. 222-27.

[47] Zbigniew Dłubak, 'Walka z estetyzmem' [1956] cited in *Dłubak i Grupa 55*, exhibition catalogue, Muzeum Sztuki, (Łódż, 2003), at 40.

[48] Bohdan Łopieński, 'Niezwykły Amator', *Fotografia*, November 1963, pp. 272-274.

[49] For a recent discussion of the position of artists in different Eastern bloc settings, see Piotr Piotrowski, *Awangarda w cienu Jałty: Sztuka w Europie Środkowo-Wschodniej w latach 1945-1989*, (Poznań, Rebis, 2005).

[50] Ekaterina Degot 'The Copy is the Crime: Unofficial Art and the Appropriation of Official Photography', in: Diane Neumaier (ed), *Beyond Memory: Soviet Nonconformist Photography and Photo-related Works of Art*, (New Brunswick, NJ, Rutgers University Press, 2004), p. 113.

[51] *Ibid.*

[52] James C. Scott, *Domination and the Arts of Resistance: Hidden Transcripts*, (New Haven & London, Yale University Press, 1992), pp. 38-9.

[53] On the organization and political signification of such parades, see Paweł Sowiński, *Komunistyczne świeto. Obchody 1 maja w latach 1948-1954*, (Warsaw, Wydawn. Trio, 2000).

[54] See Judith Butler, *Bodies that Matter: The Discursive Limits of Sex*, (London, Routledge, 1993).

[55] Walter Benjamin 'The Work of Art in the Age of Mechanical Reproduction', in: Idem, *Illuminations*, (London, Fontana/Collins, 1977), pp. 238-9.

[56] Scott, *Domination.*, p. 18.

[57] Jerzy Jenas interviewed by Marysia Lewandowska in the publication accompanying the *Entuzjaści z Amatorskich Klubów Filmowych* exhibition, Centrum Sztuki Współczesnej, (Warsaw, 2004), p. 147.

[58] Stefan Skrzypek interviewed by Marysia Lewandowska in the publication accompanying the *Entuzjaści z Amatorskich Klubów Filmowych* exhibition, (Warsaw, 2004), p. 141.

[59] Franciszek Dzida interviewed in Marysia Lewandowska and Neil Cummings, *Entuzjaści*, p. 67.

Chapter 6

[1] Ute Gerhardt, 'Re-Education als Demokratisierung der Gesellschaft Deutschlands durch das amerikanische Besatzungsregime. Ein historischer Bericht', *Leviathan*, Vol. 27, No. 3, 1999, pp. 355-385.

[2] Johannes R. Becher, 'Bemerkungen zu unseren Kulturaufgaben', in: *Gesammelte Werke*, Vol. 16, Publizistik II. 1939-1945, (Berlin - Weimar, Aufbau Verlag, 1978), pp. 362-366.

[3] Wolfgang Schivelbusch, *Vor dem Vorhang. Das geistige Berlin 1945-1948*, (Munich - Vienna, Hanser, 1995).

[4] Alexandra Kollontai, *Die neue Moral und die Arbeiterklasse*, (Berlin, A. Seehof & Co., 1920), p. 79.

[5] Gabriele Scheidegger, *Perverses Abendland – barbarisches Russland*, (Zurich, Chronos, 1993).

[6] See the Nazi poster *Der rote Krieg* that contrasts the Soviet 'female comrade' with the German 'mother', at http://www.museum-karlshorst.de/html/museum/dakapitel2.shtml.

[7] These articles are from 1945. The license-holders were the political parties that were allowed to function by the Soviet Military Administration in the first post-war months. These newspapers include the *Deutsche Volkszeitung* (communist), *Das Volk* (social democrat), *Neue Zeit* (Christian democrat) and *Der Morgen* (liberal democrat). Because all newspapers were available in all four sectors of Berlin, I have also analysed the following West Berlin newspapers: *Der Tagesspiegel* (American sector), *Der Kurier* (French sector) and *Telegraf* (British sector). I have extended my material with *Berliner Zeitung*, founded by the Soviet military administration and later published by the all-Berlin Magistrat, and *Neues Deutschland*, which on 23 April 1946 became

the official newspaper of the Socialist Unity Party, the party that was to govern East Germany).

[8] Quoted in Richard Taylor, *Film Propaganda: Soviet Russia and Nazi Germany* (second, revised edition), (London, Croom Helm, New York, Barnes & Noble Books, 1998), p. 15.

[9] Willi Münzenberg in: *Film und Volk* (1929), quoted in: Babette Gross, *Willi Münzenberg. Eine politische Biographie,* (Leipzig, Forum, 1991), p. 264.

[10] Soviet war films rarely differentiated between documentaries and feature films. See Peter Kenez, 'Films of the Second World War' in: Anna Lawton (ed), *The Red Screen: Politics, Society, Art in Soviet Cinema,* (New York, Routledge, 1992), pp. 148-71.

[11] Oksana Bulgakowa, 'Russische Filme in Berlin', in: *Die ungewöhnlichen Abenteuer des Dr. Marbuse im Lande der Bolschewiki. Das Buch zur Filmreihe, Moskau – Berlin'. Freunde der deutschen Kinemathek e. V.,* (Berlin, 1995), pp. 81-89.

[12] Wolfgang Harkenthal, 'Russen wieder in Berlin. Die Anfänge von Sovexportfilm', in: Bulgakowa, 'Russische Filme', pp. 260-261.

[13] During the Khrushchev-period, the documentaries *Berlin* and *Stalingrad* were reworked and the role of Stalin and Zhukov was significantly reduced. See Oksana Bulgakowa: 'Krieg und Stil', in: Freunde der Deutschen Kinemathek e. V. (ed), *Der Krieg gegen die Sowjetunion im Spiegel von 36 Filmen. Eine Dokumentation,* (Berlin, 1991), p. 8.

[14] Graham Roberts, *Forward Soviet! History and Non-fiction Film in the USSR,* (London - New York, I.B. Tauris, 1999), p. 138.

[15] Quoted in Christiane Habicht, 'Hitlers letzter Wille: Die Zerstörung Berlins. Berlin in zwei Schnittfassungen', in: 'Berlin (UdSSR 1945)'; in: *Der Krieg gegen die Sowjetunion,* pp. 45-47.

[16] E. St., Berlin. 'Ein Filmdokument von den letzten Tagen des Krieges', *Das Volk* (Berlin), 22 July 1945. (The initials, for example, E. St., Li., Fl. K., *etc.*, were short names or anonymous names for the journalists writing in the newspapers.)

[17] *Ibid.*

[18] Kenez: 'Films of the Second World War', pp. 153-154.

[19] Rosemarie Knop, 'Stalingrad. Ein erschütternder Dokumentarfilm', *Deutsche Volkszeitung* (Berlin), 18 November 1945.

[20] Marval., 'Stalingrad. Das Dokument der Kriegswende', *Der Kurier* (Berlin), 19 November 1945.

[21] St., 'Das Heldenlied von Stalingrad', *Das Volk* (Berlin), 20 November 1945.

[22] Peter Kenez, *Cinema and Soviet Society from the Revolution to the Death of Stalin,* (London - New York, I.B. Tauris, 2001), p. 172.

[23] Bernhard Reich, *Im Wettlauf mit der Zeit. Erinnerungen aus fünf Jahrzehnten Theatergeschichte,* (Berlin, Henschelverlag, 1970), p. 94, quoted in: Karl Schlögel, *Berlin Ostbahnhof Europas. Russen und Deutsche in ihrem Jahrhundert,* (Berlin, Siedler, 1998), p. 126.

[24] The negative image of *Ivan the Terrible* was based on three facts: the misdeeds of the Russian armies in the Livonian War, the terror of the oprichniks, and finally, the murder of his own son in 1581. Andreas Kappeler, 'Deutsche Flugschriften über die Moskowiter Russen und Russland aus deutscher Sicht 9. - 17. Jahrhundert', in: Lew

Kopelew & Mechthild Keller (eds), *West-Östliche Spiegelungen,* (Munich, Fink, 1985) Reihe A - Vol. 1, pp. 174-82.

[25] David Gillespie, *Russian Cinema,* (Essex, Harlow, 2003), p. 63.

[26] Bernd Uhlenbruch, 'The Annexion of History: Eisenstein and the Ivan Grozny Cult of the 1940s', in: Hans Günther (ed), *The Culture of the Stalin Period,* (London, Macmillan, 1990), p. 274. On the re-interpretation of Ivan's role during the Stalin-era see: Maureen Perrie, *The Cult of Ivan the Terrible in Stalin's Russia,* (Basingstoke, Palgrave, 2001).

[27] Werner Fiedler, 'Das Wesen der sowjetrussischen Filmkunst', *Neue Zeit* (Berlin), 14 August 1945.

[28] Joan Neuberger, *Ivan the Terrible,* (London, I.B. Tauris, New York, 2003), pp. 1-4, 14.

[29] Gillespie, *Russian Cinema,* p. 63.

[30] D. F., 'Peter I', wenn man so will, ein Monstre-Film', *Telegraf* (Berlin), 06 December 1946.

[31] F. K., 'Peter I', *Neue Zeit* (Berlin), 5 December 1946.

[32] 'Peter I., zweiter Teil', *Neue Zeit* (Berlin), 20 December 1946.

[33] Friedrich Luft, 'Bewegte Leinwand. Zu den Filmen "Peter I" und "Verdacht"', *Der Tagesspiegel* (Berlin), 7 December 1946.

[34] Alfred Maderno, 'In der Waffenschmiede des Lebens', *Der Morgen,* (Berlin), 4 December 1946.

[35] 'Vorschau auf den Film "Peter der Große"', *Neues Deutschland* (Berlin), 1 November 1946.

[36] W. B., 'Bild aus der Geschichte', *Der Kurier* (Berlin), 13 December 1946.

[37] W. B., 'Stürmisches Kapitel', *Der Kurier* (Berlin), 18 December 1946.

[38] W. B., 'Bild aus der Geschichte', *Der Kurier* (Berlin), 13 December 1946.

[39] Alfred Maderno, 'In der Waffenschmiede des Lebens', *Der Morgen* (Berlin), 4 December 1946.

[40] Pavel S. Kogan, *Gor'kij,* (Moskva/Leningrad 1928), p. 7. On the change of the depiction of women in the Stalin-era, see Melanie Ilič, *Women in the Stalin-era,* (Basingstoke, Palgrave, 2001).

[41] Hans Günther, *Der sozialistische Übermensch. M. Gor'kij und der sowjetische Heldenmythos,* (Stuttgart -Weimar, J.B. Metzler, 1993), pp. 180-1.

[42] Richard Taylor, 'The Illusion of Happiness and the Happiness of Illusion: Grigorii Aleksandrov's "The Circus"', *The Slavonic and East European Review,* Vol. 74, No. 4, 1996.

[43] M., 'Gesetz der Menschlichkeit', *Deutsche Volkszeitung* (Berlin), 21 February 1946.

[44] St., 'Zirkus. Ein sowjetischer Unterhaltungsfilm', *Das Volk* (Berlin) 19 February 1946.

[45] Hans Günther, 'Das Massenlied als Ausdruck des Mutterarchetypus in der sowjetischen Kultur', *Wiener Slawistischer Almanach,* Sonderband, 44, 1997, pp. 337–55.

[46] St., Zirkus, 'Ein sowjetischer Unterhaltungsfilm', *Das Volk* (Berlin) 19 February 1946; in: Gesetz der Menschlichkeit, *Deutsche Volkszeitung* (Berlin) 21 February 1946.

[47] John Haynes, *New Soviet Man: Gender and Masculinity in Stalinist Soviet Cinema,* (Manchester - New York, Manchester University Press, 2003).

[48] Li., 'Die reiche Braut', *Das Volk* (Berlin), 13 April 1946.
[49] Fl. K., 'Die reiche Braut', *Neue Zeit* (Berlin), 13 April 1946.
[50] Li., 'Die Reiche Braut', *Das Volk* (Berlin), 13 April 1946.
[51] Ft, 'Liebe unter dem Rechenschieber', *Der Tagesspiegel* (Berlin), 11 April 1946.
[52] Fl. K., 'Die reiche Braut', *Neue Zeit* (Berlin), 13 April 1946.
[53] Gillespie, *Russian Cinema*, pp. 82-7.

Chapter 7

[1] On the role of mass demonstration in the USSR in the 1930s, see Karen Petrone, *Life Has Become More Joyous Comrades! Celebrations in the Time of Stalin,* (Bloomington, Indiana University Press, 2000); Malte Rolf, 'Working Towards the Centre: Leader Cults and Spatial Politics in Pre-war Stalinism', in: Balázs Apor, Jan C. Behrends, Polly Jones & E. A. Rees (eds.), *The Leader Cult in Communist Dictatorships: Stalin and the Eastern Bloc,* (Basingstoke, Palgrave, 2004), pp. 141-157. On the origins of Bolshevik rituals, see James von Geldern, *Bolshevik Festivals, 1917-1920,* (Berkeley, University of California Press, 1993).

[2] See Zákon č. 93/1951 Zb. zo dňa 2.novembra 1951 o štátnych sviatkoch, o dňoch pracovného pokoja a o pamätných a významných dňoch.

[3] Christel Lane, 'Legitimacy and Power in the Soviet Union through Socialist Ritual', *British Journal of Political Science,* Vol. 14, No. 2, 1984, p. 212.

[4] For more detail on the celebrations, see Roman Krakovsky, *Rituel du 1er mai en Tchécoslovaquie 1948-1989,* (Paris, Harmattan, 2004), p. 214.

[5] See G. R. F. Bursa, 'Political Changes of Names of Soviet Towns', *Slavonic and East European Review,* No. 63, 1985, pp. 161-93.

[6] Zpráva o priebehu osláv 1. mája 1956 v meste Žilina, MV SNF v Žiline, Archives of the Region of Žilina (ARZ), OAV NF Žilina, 102/1956.

[7] Zpráva o činnosti technickej komisie prvomájových osláv v Žiline v roku 1956, 21/05/1956, ARZ, OAV NF Žilina, 102/1956.

[8] Zpráva o priebehu osláv 1. mája 1956 v meste Žilina, MV SNF v Žiline, ARZ, OAV NF Žilina, 102/1956.

[9] 'Kupředu, světová armádo pracujících!', *Rudé právo,* 1 May 1957.

[10] Jana Ratajová, 'Pražské májové oslavy 1948-1989. Příspěvek k dějinám komunistické propagandy', *Kuděj. Časopis pro kulturní dějiny,* No. 1, 2000, p. 61.

[11] The censor hid the gaps in the procession with artificial banners and the heads of demonstrators superimposed. See the photo of the parade in 1950, before and after the censor's intervention. Czech National Archives (CNA), Centrální katalog FFKD, heslo 1. máje (1950), 40417/52 and 82472/55.

[12] For the distinction between sacred and sacralized space, see Christel Lane, *The Rites of Rulers: Ritual in Industrial Society - the Soviet Case,* (Cambridge, Cambridge University Press, 1981). See, also, her article 'Legitimacy and Power'.

[13] See, for example, CNA, Centrální katalog FFKD, heslo 1. máje (1947), 77707/54.

[14] In 1952, the portraits of Gottwald and Stalin remained on the front of the Museum despite the danger that they might fall down due to their bad condition. See Zápis z 8. schůze městské májové komise, 17 April 1952, CNA, ÚAV NF, 1953.

[15] In 1949, for example, Hotel Evropa, next to the gallery, was covered with the

banner: 'The Five year plan defends peace and the happy future of the workers in the entire world'. CNA, Centrální katalog FFKD, heslo 1. máje (1949), 78195/54.

[16] In 1950, for example, the orders were sent to the owners of the buildings at the end of March. *Schůze ústřední májové komise UAV NF*, 25 March 1950, CNA, ÚAV NF, 1950.

[17] For Sokol, see Jean-Philippe Saint-Martin, 'Les Sokols tchécoslovaques. Un symbole de l'identité slave entre les deux guerres', *Cahiers de l'histoire. Revue d'histoire critique*, No. 88, 2002, pp. 43-58.

[18] In 1976, the Berlin May Day parade abandoned Karl-Marx Allee and the platform was erected in front of the new Republic Palace. The innovation was not accepted and in 1977, the parade returned to Karl-Marx Allee. See Birgit Sauer, '"Es lebe des Erste Mai in der DDR!" Die politische Inszenierung eines Staatsfeiertages', in: H. D. Braun, C. Reinhold & H. A. Schwartz (eds), *Vergangene Zukunft – Mutationen eines Feiertages*, (Berlin, Transit, 1991), pp. 115-31.

[19] See Zuzana Beňušková. 'Prvomájové sprievody v Bratislave', in: L. Tarcalová (ed), *Slavnostní průvody* (Uherské Hradiště, Slovácké muzeum, 1994), pp. 103-10.

[20] The procession left the town centre in 1977.

[21] The conference 'The Monuments of the revolutionary labor movement in Prague' took place in Prague, on 6-7 March 1973, gathering 214 guests and 23 speakers from 10 East European countries. The papers were published in: Zdislav Buřival (ed), *Pražské památky revolučního dělnického hnutí* (Prague, 1973).

[22] See Buřival, *Pražské památky.*

[23] Ľubomír Lipták, 'Rošády na piedestáloch', in: Ľubomír Lipták, *Storočie dlhšie ako sto rokov*, (Bratislava, Kalligram, 1999), p. 339. The paper was first published in: *OS*, No. 11, 1998, pp. 29-34; *OS*, No. 12, 1998, pp. 31-6.

[24] Robert Rotenberg, 'May Day Parade in Prague and Vienna. A Comparison of Socialist Rituals', *Anthropological Quarterly*, Vol. 56, No. 2, 1983, p. 63.

[25] Hodnocení prvomájové manifestace na Letenské pláni v Praze v roce 1983, CAN, ÚV NF, 1983.

Chapter 8

[1] Insights into the structure of Soviet space and Soviet spatial politics is provided by Evgeny Dobrenko & Eric Naiman (eds), *The Landscape of Stalinism: The Art and Ideology of Soviet Space*, (Seattle - New York, University of Washington Press, 2003).

[2] Katerina Clark, 'Socialist Realism and the Sacralizing of Space', in: *The Landscape of Stalinism*, pp. 8-19.

[3] The image of the artist–creator is analyzed by Boris Groys, *The Total Art of Stalinism: Avant-garde, Aesthetic Dictatorship and Beyond*, (Princeton, Princeton University Press, 1992). The concept of the 'unmoved-mover' is applied to the Soviet context by Malte Rolf, 'Working Towards the Centre: Leader Cults and Spatial Politics in Prewar Stalinism', in: Balázs Apor, Jan C. Behrends, Polly Jones & E.A. Rees, *The Leader Cult in Communist Dictatorships: Stalin and the Eastern Bloc*, (Basingstoke, Palgrave, 2004), pp. 141-157. On the representation of Stalin as the sacred centre in paintings,

see Jan Plamper, 'The Spatial Poetics of the Personality Cult: Circles Around Stalin', in: Dobrenko & Naiman, *The Landscape of Stalinism*, pp. 20-45.

[4] This phenomenon also characterized the cult of saints. See Peter Brown, *The Cult of Saints: Its Rise and Function in Latin Christianity*, (Chicago, University of Chicago Press, 1981).

[5] János Pótó, *Az emlékeztetés helyei. Emlékművek és politika*, (Budapest, Osiris, 2003); Reuben Fowkes, 'The Role of Monumental Sculpture in the Construction of Socialist Space in Stalinist Hungary', in: David Crowley & Susan E. Reid, *Sites of Everyday Life in the Eastern Bloc*, (Oxford - New York, Berg, 2002), pp. 65-84.

[6] On the transformation of space in the Hungarian context, see Péter György, 'A mindennapok tükre, avagy a korstílus akarása', in: Péter György & Hedvig Turai (eds), *A művészet katonái. Sztálinizmus és kultúra*, (Budapest, Corvina, 1992), pp. 12-23. See, also, András Ferkai, 'A sztálinizmus építészetéről', in: *A művészet katonái*, pp. 24-33. See, also, the relevant chapters of Éva Standeisky *et al.*, *A fordulat évei 1947-1949. Politika, képzőművészet, építészet*, (Budapest, 1956-os Intézet, 1998).

[7] *Szabad Magyarország*, 4 March 1945.

[8] 'The poem is also praising only him, the work of art praises its master. / He created the world and the sky out of nothingness, / he gave subject to ambitious poets, he gave the voice for songs, / strength to the voice, he is the number one in the line of poets, / and he is the greatest of all.' László Benjámin, 'Mindennap győzelem' [Every day is a victory]. The poem was first published in an anthology of 'progressive' poets. *Hét évszázad magyar versei*, (Budapest, Szépirodalmi, 1951), p. 972. It was later re-published in the literary anthology compiled for Rákosi's 60th birthday in 1952. *Magyar Írók Rákosi Mátyásról*, (Budapest, Szépirodalmi, 1952).

[9] 'Because he gave strength to do things, / clean air to breathe, / sense to the growing, great days, / solid material for the workbench, / and he also gave fresh water, so that this anguished, bleeding Hungary, / could slake her thirst. / He is standing on the gleaming peaks of the country / and opens up the large gates of its history.' Tamás Aczél, 'Az Első szóról' [About the first word], *Magyar Írók Rákosi Mátyásról*, pp. 192-6.

[10] One example is the poem by Géza Képes about the Rákosi-trials in the inter-war period, that compares Rákosi to a granite-rock that withstands the 'strokes of the filthy tides', *i.e.*, the accusations of court. Géza Képes, 'A szabadság dala' in *Magyar Írók Rákosi Mátyásról*, pp. 177-81.

[11] 'He is our kind. He stands out among us, he is much taller than us, and is large enough to embrace all of us.' Lajos Mesterházi, 'Személyes segítség', *Magyar írók Rákosi Mátyásról*, p. 273.

[12] The Hungarian Communist Party (MKP) united with the Social-democratic Party in June 1948. The name of the new party became Hungarian Worker's Party (MDP).

[13] See Karen Petrone, *Life Has Become More Joyous, Comrades: Celebrations in the Time of Stalin*, (Bloomington, Indiana University Press, 2000). Christel Lane, *The Rites of Rulers: Ritual in Industrial Society – the Soviet Case*, (Cambridge, Cambridge University Press, 1981). See, also, Rolf, 'Working Towards the Centre'.

[14] On 20 August and 7 November, no official demonstrations were held; these

holidays were usually celebrated in the Opera, with the participation of the party élite, and distinguished foreign – mainly Soviet – guests.

[15] *Szabad Nép*, 3 May 1949.

[16] *Szabad Nép*, 6 April 1950.

[17] *Ibid.*

[18] *Szabad Nép*, 3 May 1949.

[19] *Szabad Nép*, 3 May 1950.

[20] *Szabad Nép*, 3 May 1951.

[21] On the spontaneity-consciousness dialectic, see Katerina Clark, *The Soviet Novel: History as Ritual*, (Chicago, University of Chicago Press, 1985).

[22] *Szabad Nép*, 3 May 1949.

[23] György Szücs, 'A képfelség elve', in: *A művészet katonái*, p. 53.

[24] For more on the effect of seeing the leader during mass demonstrations in the Soviet Union, and the constant disorder at festivities, see Petrone, *Life Has Become More Joyous, Comrades*, pp. 26-7, & pp. 40-3.

[25] Politikatörténeti Intézet Levéltára (PIL), 274. fond 21/68.

[26] PIL, 274. fond 21/69.

[27] Katalin Sinkó, 'A politika rítusai: emlékműállítás, szobordöntés', in: *A művészet katonái*, p. 55 & p. 69.

[28] 'We should make sure that the erroneous cult of personality does not prevail at the demonstrations of mass organizations, offices, or certain party organizations on the countryside.' Magyar Országos Levéltár (MOL), 276. fond 108/26.

[29] MOL, 276. fond 108/9.

[30] MOL 276. fond 108/2.

[31] *Ibid.*

[32] György Dózsa was the leader of a 16th century peasant revolt in Hungary. Sándor Petőfi was a poet and radical political figure, who played a crucial role in the revolutionary events on 15 March 1848 in Budapest. He most probably died on the battlefield after a lost battle in 1849. Mihály Táncsics was a political thinker and radical politician, also active in 1848. He was later turned into the forefather of the Hungarian working class movement by social democratic and communist ideologues. Lajos Kossuth is one of the most important figures of the Hungarian national pantheon. He was elected as governor at the time of the Hungarian War of Independence (1848-49), and became a cult figure after the fall of the uprising.

[33] MOL, 276. fond 108/46.

[34] Szücs, 'A képfelség elve', p. 55.

[35] The concept 'visual syntax' is used here in the same way Victoria Bonnel defined it, *i.e.*, 'the positioning of figures and objects in relation to each other and the environment'. V. Bonnel, *Iconography of Power*, p. 10.

[36] On the 'Lenin Corners', see Nina Tumarkin, *Lenin Lives! The Lenin Cult in Soviet Russia*, (Cambridge MA, Harvard University Press, 1997).

[37] The first proposal to set up 'Red Corners' in factories was submitted by the propaganda department on 8 November 1948. MOL, 276. fond 108/26.

[38] György Szücs, 'A képfelség elve', p. 132.

[39] Open Society Archives (OSA), 300/40/3/264.

[40] Tabor Valuch, 'A magyar művelődés 1948 után', in: László Kósa (ed), *Magyar művelődéstörténet*, (Budapest, Osiris, 2000), p. 489.

[41] Ákos Major, *Népbíráskodás – forradalmi törvényesség. Egy népbíró visszaemlékezései*, (Budapest, Minerva, 1988), pp. 441-3.

[42] Miklós Szabó, 'Hétköznapi sztálinizmus Magyarországon', *Századvég*, Nos. 6-7, 1988, p. 162. The ubiquity of Rákosi's portraits was described in a lively way, in: Tamás Aczél & Tibor Méray, *The Revolt of the Mind: A Case History of Intellectual Resistance behind the Iron Curtain*, (New York, Praeger, 1959), p. 162.

[43] Tamás Aczél, 'Sztálin szobra – a béke jelképe', *Szovjet Kultúra*, Vol. 4, No. 1, 1952, p. 6.

[44] The turning of Lenin's images into icons is analyzed by Tumarkin, *Lenin Lives!*

[45] Márta Gergely, *Az ígéret*. Műsorfüzet, Dolgozó Ifjúság Szövetsége – Úttörő Mozgalom, Budapest, 1952. March-April-May, pp. 71-73.

[46] The play is analyzed in detail by György Szücs, 'A képfelség elve', p. 46.

[47] Martin Mevius, *Agents of Moscow: The Hungarian Communist Party and the Origins of Socialist Patriotism 1941-1953*, (Oxford, Oxford University Press, 2005), p. 201, pp. 205-6, & p. 253.

[48] PIL 274. fond 5/28.

[49] *Szabad Nép*, 23 August 1947.

[50] A linguistic approach to the practice of name changes in Soviet-type regimes is provided by Szergej Tóth, 'Nyelvhasználat egy totalitárius rendszerben (Nyelvszociológiai megközelítés)', PhD dissertation (Eötvös Loránd Tudományegyetem, Budapest, 1999.)

[51] MOL, 276. fond 55/50.

[52] MOL, 276. fond 108/2. It first was discussed at the meeting of the Secretariat on 26 October 1949. MOL, 276. fond 54/68.

[53] MOL, 276. fond 108/19.

[54] MOL, 276. fond 54/58.

[55] *Szabad Nép*, 20 August 1949.

[56] *Szabad Nép*, 1 November 1949.

[57] The renamings for the leader's 60th birthday were decided by the Secretariat in August 1951. MOL, 276. fond 54/158.

[58] There were some variations in the names of kolkhozes: 'Rákosi', 'Mátyás Rákosi', 'Rákosi Csillaga' (Rákosi's star). OSA, 300/40/3/264

[59] On the friendship propaganda, see Jan C. Behrends, *Die erfundene Freundschaft: Propaganda für die Sowjetunion in Polen und in der DDR (1944-1957)*, (Cologne, Böhlau, 2006).

[60] In Hungary, proposals to name a place or a particular institution after a non-Hungarian leader were often suggested by the Central Committee's Department of Foreign Affairs (*Külügyi Osztály*).

[61] *Szabad Ifjúság*, 16 August 1952.

[62] OSA 300/40/3/264

[63] Árpád Pünkösti, *Rákosi a hatalomért,* (Budapest, Európa, 1992), pp. 22-3.

[64] MOL, 276. fond 65/343.

[65] In the Soviet context, Malte Rolf called the attempt of local party organs to gain the privilege of using the leader's name: the 'colonization of the leader's name'. Malte Rolf, 'The Leader's Many Bodies: Leader Cults and Mass Festivals in Voronezh, Novosibirsk, and Kemerovo in the 1930s', in: Klaus Heller & Jan Plamper (eds), *Personality Cults in Stalinism – Personenkulte im Stalinismus,* (Göttingen, V&R Unipress, 2004), pp. 197-206.

[66] MOL, 276. fond 65/343.

[67] Árpád Pünkösti, *Rákosi a csúcson, 1948-53,* (Budapest, Európa, 1996), p. 293.

[68] Mevius, *Agents of Moscow,* p. 103.

[69] Quoted in Pünkösti, *Rákosi a csúcson,* p. 429.

[70] MOL, 276. fond 55/44.

[71] Anders Åman, 'Symbols and Rituals in the People's Democracies During the Cold War', in: Claes Arvidsson & Lars Erik Blomquist (eds), *Symbols of Power: The Esthetics of Political Legitimation in the Soviet Union and Eastern Europe,* (Stockholm, Almqvist & Wiksell International, 1987), p. 52.

Chapter 9

[*] This paper is based on Petr Roubal, 'Politics of Gymnastics: Mass Gymnastic Displays under Communism in Central and Eastern Europe', *Body and Society,* Vol. 9, No. 2, 2003, p. 1-25.

[1] James Riordan, *Sport in Soviet Society,* (Cambridge, Cambridge University Press, 1977).

[2] On *Sokols,* see Jean-Philippe Saint-Martin, 'Les Sokols tchécoslovaques. Un symbole de l'identité slave entre les deux guerres', *Cahiers de l'histoire. Revue d'histoire critique,* No. 88, 2002, p. 43-58.

[3] Ulrich Bröckling, *Disziplin. Soziologie und Geschichte militärischer Gehorsamsproduktion,* (Munich, W. Fink, 1997); Tim Armstrong, *Modernism, Technology, and the Body: a Cultural Study,* (Cambridge, Cambridge University Press, 1998).

[4] Anson Rabinbach, 'The European Science of Work: The Economy of the Body at the End of Nineteenth Century', in: S. Kaplan & C. J. Koepp (eds), *Work in France: Representations, Meaning, Organisation, and Practice,* (Ithaca, Cornell University Press, 1986), pp. 475-513.

[5] Walter Benjamin, 'The Work of Art in the Age of Mechanical Reproduction', in: Walter Benjamin (ed.), *Illuminations,* (New York, Harcourt, Brace & World, 1968), p. 240.

[6] Friedrich Ludwig Jahn and Ernst Eiselen, *Deutsche Turnkunst,* (Berlin, 1816), p. 223 quoted in George L. Mosse, *The Image of Man: The Creation of Modern Masculinity,* (Oxford, Oxford University Press, 1996), p. 200.

[7] Claire E. Nolte, *The Sokol in the Czech Lands to 1914: Training for the Nation,* (New York, Palgrave, 2002), p. 2.

[8] George L. Mosse, *The Nationalization of the Masses. Political Symbolism and Mass Movements in Germany from the Napoleonic Wars through the Third Reich*, (New York, H. Fertig, 1975), p. 130.

[9] Jens Ljunggren, 'The Masculine Road through Modernity: Ling Gymnastics and Male Socialization in Nineteenth-Century Sweden', *The European Sports History Review*, No. 2, 2000, pp. 86-111.

[10] Mosse, *The Nationalization of the Masses*, p. 135.

[11] James von Geldern, *Bolshevik festivals, 1917-1920*, (Berkeley, University of California Press, 1993); Riordan, *Sport in Soviet Society*.

[12] Jiří Kössl, *Dějiny tělesné výchovy*, (Prague, Olympia, 1986), p. 159.

[13] Ernst H. Kantorowicz, *The King's Two Bodies: A Study in Mediaeval Political Theology*, (Princeton, Princeton University Press, 1957).

[14] Max Gluckman, *Rituals of Rebellion in South-East Africa*, (Manchester, Manchester University Press, 1954).

[15] Július Chvalný, *Czechoslovak Spartakiads*, (Prague, Orbis, 1980), p. 45.

[16] The report 'Zpráva Ústředního Štábu Československé spartakiády' [Report of the Czechoslovak Spartakiad Headquarters] 1975, 15 April 1974 speaks about 700 full time employees. In: Archiv Českého svazu tělesné výchovy (AČSTV), 1975 (unprocessed). This number does not include the organizers of the army displays, who had their own independent hierarchical structure, see: Hodnocení účasti ČSLA na provedení Třetí celostátní spartakiádě 1965. In: Vojensko-historický archiv (VHA), fond 780 (Spartakiáda 1965).

[17] Vladimír Macura, *Šťastný vek: Symboly, emblémy a mýty 1948 - 1989*, (Prague, Pražská imaginace, 1992), p. 70.

[18] Vilém Mucha, *První celostátní spartakiáda 1955 - věcí všecho pracujícího lidu Československa*, (Prague, SVTVS, 1955), p. 15.

[19] *Ibid.*

[20] Henning Eichberg, 'Stadium, Pyramid, Labyrinth: Eye and Body on the Move', in: John & Olof Moen Bale, *The Stadium and the City* (Staffordshire, Keele University Press, 1995), p. 336.

[21] Ladislav Serbus, Bohumil Kos & Jaroslav Mihule, *Historický vývoj a základy tělovýchovných vystoupení v ČSSR*, (Prague, SPN, 1962).

[22] *Ibid.*

[23] Minutes of the Party Committee for the Assistance to the 2nd All-State Spartakiad. 1. Schůze stranické komise pro pomoc II. celostátní spartakiádě [The meeting of the Party Committee for the Assistance to the 2nd All-State Spartakiad]. In: Státní ústřední archiv (SUA) - Archiv ÚV KSČ, fond 40, archival unit 322-325.

[24] The report 'Zpráva stravovacího odboru' [Report of the Provision Department], Sept. 17, 1985. In: SUA fond ÚV ČSTV (1956 – 1989), balík 268 – Odbor hromadných vystoupení.

[25] Závěrečné hodnocení Československé spartakiády 1975, Zpráva Pořadatelského odboru [The Final Evaluation of the 1975 Czechoslovak Spartakiad, Report of the Organizing Department]. In: Archiv České obce sokolské (AČOS), The 1975 Spartakiad (unprocessed).

[26] The 1955 secret report of the Ministry of Trade speaks about an increase of beer production in Prague region to 10.000 hectoliters of beer. SUA, Fond SVTVS box 46.

The report from the 1985 Spartakiad is more specific, claming that 6.000 hectoliters of beer were sold at the tribunes of the Strahov stadium. Such a level of consumption was bound to interfere with the perception of the ideological message of the ritual, as it represented more than 2 liters of beer per each of 250 thousands spectators, infants included. Zpráva stravovacího odboru [The Report of the Provision Department]. In: AČOS, The 1985 Spartakiad.

[27] Don Handelman, *Models and Mirrors: Towards an Anthropology of Public Events,* (Cambridge, Cambridge University Press, 1990), p. 49.

[28] Abner Cohen, 'Political Symbolism', *Annual Review of Anthropology,* Vol. 8, 1979, p. 87.

[29] John M. Hoberman, *Sport and Political Ideology,* (Austin, University of Texas Press, 1984), p. 53.

[30] *Ibid.,* p. 2.

[31] Jaroslav Marek, *Za socialistický systém tělesné výchovy,* (Prague, Olympia, 1978), p. 101.

[32] Macura, *Štastný vek.*

[33] For instance, *Rudé právo,* 2 July 1975.

[34] Chvalný, *Czechoslovak Spartakiads.*

[35] Otakar Mohyla, *Verše ze Strahova 1985,* (Prague, Olympia, 1985).

[36] Leni Riefenstahl, *Hinter den Kulissen des Reichsparteitag-Films: der Film ‚Triumph des Willens' wurde im Auftr. des Führers geschaffen,* (Munich, F. Eher Nachf., 1935), p. 92.

[37] Susan Sontag, *Under the Sign of Saturn,* (New York, Anchor Books, 1991), p. 91.

[38] Clifford Geertz, *Negara: The Theatre State in Nineteenth-Century Bali,* (Princeton, Princeton University Press, 1983).

[39] Marek Waic, *Sokol v české společnosti 1862-1938,* (Prague, Univerzita Karlova, 1996).

[40] The internal report of the Sport Union on the 1975 Spartakiad, Režie hromadných tělovýchovných vystoupení, Odbor hromadných vystoupení [The Staging of the Mass Gymnastic Displays, The Department of Mass Gymnastic Displays]. In: AČSTV, The 1975 Spartakiad. For the visual material regarding the Strahov Stadium see the photographic collection of the Tyrs Museum of Physical Education and Sport. For the technical information of the Strahov Stadium, see Gustav Kouřimský, *Spartakiádní Areál Strahov,* (Prague, Olympia, 1982), an internal publication for the use of Spartakiad organizers.

Chapter 10

[1] In the international arena, the USSR insisted on the annexation of eastern Poland. This was carried out as part of the agreements reached in the Hitler-Stalin-Pact of 1939. The post-war Polish borders were only finally settled after the treaties of Potsdam (1945), Görlitz (1950), and Warsaw (1970), respectively.

[2] 'Manifest Polskiego Komitetu Wyzwolenia Narodowego', in: *Wizja programowa Polski Ludowej:Dokumenty i materiały 1942-1948,* (Warsaw, 1979), pp. 182-191.

[3] For a comparative elaboration of my argument, see Jan C. Behrends, *Die*

erfundene Freundschaft: Propaganda für die Sowjetunion in Polen und in der DDR, (Cologne - Weimar - Vienna, Böhlau, 2006).

[4] William J. Chase, *Enemies within the Gates? The Comintern and the Stalinist Repression, 1934-1939,* (New Haven CT - London, Yale University Press, 2001), pp. 217-292.

[5] Jan Tomasz Gross, *Revolution from Abroad: The Soviet Conquest of Poland's Western Ukraine and Western Belorussia,* (Princeton NJ, Princeton University Press, 2002).

[6] For a Polish memoir of the Gulag, see Gustaw Herling, *A World Apart: A Memoir of the Gulag,* (London, Penguin Books, 2005). See, also, Jan Tomasz Gross *et al.* (ed): *W czterdzięstym nas matko na Sybir zesłali.... Polska a Rosja 1939-42,* (London, Aneks, 1983); Katherine R. Jolluck, *Exile and Identity: Polish Women in the Soviet Union During World War II,* (Pittsburgh, Pa., University of Pittsburgh Press, 2002); see, also, *Katyń: Dokumenty zbrodni, Volumes I and II,* (Warsaw, NDAP: Trio, 1998).

[7] See Dimitrovs remarks of 27 August 1941, in: Ivo Banac (ed), *The Diary of Georgi Dimitrov,* (New Haven CT, Yale University Press, 2003), pp. 191-192.

[8] For a detailed discussion of this stereotype, see Jan T. Gross, *Fear: Anti-Semitism in Poland after Auschwitz: An Essay in Historical Interpretation,* (Princeton NJ, Princeton University Press, 2006).

[9] 'Notatki Alfreda Lampego, August 1943', in: *Archiwum Ruchu Robotniczego, Band IX,* (Warsaw, Książka i Wiedza, 1984), pp. 25-35.

[10] On Polish-Russian relations in broad perspective, see Klaus Zernack, *Polen und Rußland: Zwei Wege in der europäischen Geschichte,* (Berlin, Propyläen Verlag, 1994).

[11] See Norman Davies, *White Eagle, Red Star: The Polish-Soviet War 1919-1920,* (London, St. Martin's Press, 1972).

[12] *Teczka Specjalna J. W. Stalina: Raporty NKWD z Polski 1944-1946,* (Warsaw, Oficyna Wydawnicza Rytm, 1998).

[13] See Izabella Main, *Trudne świętowanie: Konflikty wokoł obchodów świąt państwowych i kościelnych w Lublinie (1944-1989),* (Warsaw, Wydawn. Trio, 2004), pp. 33-72.

[14] Sprawozdanie za okres lipiec 1944r-luty 1945r, Archiwum Akt Nowych (AAN), Warsaw, KC PPR, Wydział Propagandy, 295/X-3, pp. 1-4.

[15] Okólnik w sprawie dnia 7-go listopada, rocznicy Wielkiej Socjalistycznej Rewolucji Rosji, 25.10.1944, Archiwum Państwowe w Lublinie, KW PPR, 1/V/16.

[16] GA RF, fond 5283 (VOKS), op. 178, d. 227 [no pages].

[17] 'Założenia statutu Towarzystwa Przyjaźni Polsko-Radzieckiej', in: *Polsko-radzieckie stosunki kulturalne 1944-1949: Dokumenty i materiały,* (Warsaw, Pan'stwowe Wydawn. Nauk., 1984), pp. 25-27.

[18] Sprawozdanie z działalności Tymczasowego Zarządu Głównego za okres od listopada 1944 r. do dnia sierpnia 1945 r., GA RF, fond 5283, op. 17, d. 228, p. 18.

[19] On the use of nationalism in Polish communism, see Marcin Zaremba, *Komunizm, legitymizacja, nacjonalizm. Nacjonalistyczna legitymizacja władzy komunistycznej w Polsce,* (Warsaw, Wydawn. Trio, 2001).

[20] This followed the Stalininst 'primordialism', the conception of nations as ethnic communities with deep historical roots. These individual nations were seen

as the pillars of the 'friendship of the peoples' in the USSR. See Terry Martin, *The Affirmative Action Empire: Nations and Nationalism in the Soviet Union 1923-1939*, (Ithaca NY, Cornell University Press, 2001), p. 442 *et seq*.

[21] *Statut Towarzystwa Przyjaźni Polsko-Radzieckiej*, (Warsaw, 1945), p. 3.

[22] On Roman Dmowski, his National Democracy and the rise of Polish nationalism, see Brian Porter, *When Nationalism Began to Hate: Imagining Modern Politics in Nineteenth-Century Poland*, (Oxford, Oxford University Press, 2002). On Soviet nationalism, see David Brandenberger, *National Bolshevism: Stalinist Mass Culture and the Formation of Modern Russian National Identity, 1931-1956*, (Cambridge MA, Harvard University Press, 2002); and on Stalin's idea of the nation, see Erik van Ree, *The Political Thought of Joseph Stalin: A Study in Twentieth Century Revolutionary Patriotism*, (London, RoutledgeCurzon, 2002).

[23] On 19th century pan-Slavism, see Hans Kohn, *Pan-Slavism: Its History and Ideology*, (New York, Vintage books, 1960), (2nd edition).

[24] Wiktor Kornatowski, *Podstawy polskiej polityki słowiańskiej. Rozwoj idea słowiańskiej a stosunki polsko-rosyjskie*, (Warsaw, Nakł. Tow. Przyjaźni Polsko-Radzieckiej, 1946); Henryk Batowski, *Współpraca Słowiańska. Zagadnienia polityczne, kulturalne i gospodarcze w przeszłości i teraźniejszości*, (Warsaw, Państowy Instytut Wydawniczy, 1946).

[25] Jan Karol Wende, *Polska a Związek Radziecki*, (Warsaw, Nakł. Stronnictwa Demokratycznego, 1945); Henryk Świątkowski, 'Zagadnienie współpracy słowiańskiej', *Przyjaźń*, Nr. 10, 1946, pp. 6-8.

[26] Rezolucja Komitetu Słowiańskiego w Polsce w sprawie programu działania, in: *Polsko-radzieckie stosunki kulturalne*, pp. 100-103.

[27] On Polish-Russian relations in the western territories of Poland, see Gregor Thum, *Die fremde Stadt: Breslau 1945*, (Berlin, Siedler, 2003), pp. 60-106.

[28] *Białostocczyzna 1944-1945 w dokumentach podziemia i oficialnych władz*, (Warsaw, Instytut Studiów Politycznych PAN, 1998).

[29] Archiwum Państwowe w Krakowie (APK), Wojewódzki Urząd Propagandy i Informacji, Nr. 5, pp. 157, 158, 161; 765, 767, 769; Nr. 14, pp. 27 *et seq*.; Nr. 42, p.49.

[30] Protokół posiedzenia KC PPR z dnia 27 kwietnia 1945 r., in *Protokoły posiedzeń sekretariatu KC PPR 1945-1946*, (Warsaw, In-t Studiów Politycznych PAN, 2001), pp. 22-31.

[31] On Gomułka, see Paweł Machcewicz, *Władysław Gomułka*, (Warsaw, Wydawnictwa Szkolne i Pedagogiczne, 1995).

[32] *Protokół obrad KC PPR w maju 1945 roku*, (Warsaw, Instytut Studiów Politycznych PAN, 1992); Gomułka's speech, pp. 7-16; quotations pp. 13-14.

[33] *Ibid*., pp. 19-25.

[34] 'Nowy rok przyjaźni', *Wolność*, 1 January 1946.

[35] 'Der Minister für die Wiedergewonnen Gebiete an die Marschälle der Sowjetunion Georgij Žukov und Konstantin Rokossovski und den Botschafter der UdSSR in Warschau Viktor Lebev über Konflikte der polnischen Administration mit der Roten Armee, 10 January 1946', in: Włodzimierz Borodziej & Hans Lemberg (eds), *'Unsere Heimat ist ein fremdes Land geworden...' Die Deutschen östlich von Oder und Neiße 1945-1950. Dokumente aus polnischen Archiven*, Vol. 1, (Marburg,

Herder Institut, 2000), pp. 204-206. The editors note that it cannot yet be proven that Gomułka actually sent the letter.

[36] This is also clear in the German and Yugoslav cases. Milovan Djilas learned this in 1945 when he complained personally to Stalin about Soviet abuses in Yugoslavia. See Milovan Djilas, *Gespräche mit Stalin,* (Frankfurt aM, Fischer, 1962), pp. 113 *et seq.*; Wolfgang Leonhard, *Die Revolution entläßt ihre Kinder,* (Cologne, Kiepenheuer & Witsch, 1990), pp. 461 *et seq.*

[37] Wojciech Mazowiecki, *Pierwsze starcie. Wydarzenia 3 Maja 1946,* (Warsaw, Wydawn. Nauk. PWN, 1998), pp. 83-112.

[38] *Ibid.*, p. 155.

[39] 'Kongres Tow. Przyjaźni Polsko-Radzieckiej', *Przyjaźń,* No. 5, 1946, p. 1.

[40] 'Manifest kongresu Tow. Przyjaźni Polsko-Radzieckiej', *Przyjaźń,* No. 5, 1946, pp. 12-14.; 'Historyczna manifestacja przyjaźni polsko-radzieckiej', *Wolność,* 3 June, 1946.

[41] *Jak zorganizować koło Towarzystwa Przyjaźni Polsko-Radzieckiej,* (Warsaw, 1946).

[42] Włodzimierz Brus, *Urojenia i rzeczywistość. Prawda o ZSRR,* (Łódź, Spółdzielnia Wydawnicza "Książka", 1946).

[43] Sprawozdanie Wydziału Propagandy i Prasy za m-c maj 1947 r., AAN, KC PPR, 295/X-3, pp. 35-42.

[44] Uchwała Sekretariatu KC PPR w sprawie propagandy Przyjaźni Polsko-Radzieckiej i działalności Towarzystwa Przyjaźni Polsko-Radzieckiej, October 1947, APK, KW PPR, Nr. 208, pp. 113-114.

[45] Instrukcja Nr. 48 w sprawie akcji przygotowawczej do 30 rocznicy Rewolucji Październikowej, 15 September 1947, APK, KW PPR, Nr. 208, pp. 46-48.

[46] T. Konar, 'Sprawa, o której trzeba zawsze pamiętać', *Przyjaźń,* No. 9, 1947, p. 27.

[47] Henryk Świątkowski, 'Cel i zadania miesiąca wymiany kulturalnej', *Przyjaźń,* No. 9, 1947, pp. 3-4.

[48] See David L. Hoffmann, *Stalinist Values: The Cultural Norms of Soviet Modernity,* (Ithaca, New York, Cornell University Press, 2003).

[49] *Podstawy działalności Towarzystwa Przyjaźni Polsko-Radzieckiej. Materiały i wytyczne dla działaczy i kół terenowych,* (Warsaw, 1947).

[50] W sprawie odchylenia prawicowego i nacjanalistycznego w kierownictwe partii, jego źródeł i sposobów jego przezwyciężenia, 15 August 1948, in: *Protokoły posiedzeń Biura Politycznego KC PPR, 1947-1948,* (Warsaw, Instytut Studiów Politycznych Polskiej Akademii Nauk, 2002), pp. 245-253.

[51] *Stalinowskim kursem. Posiedzenie Komitetu Centralnego Polskiej Partii Robotniczej. 31 sierpnia – 3 września 1948 r. Stenogram,* (Pułtusk, Wyższa Szkoła Humanistyczna, Warsaw, Naczelna Dyrekcja Archiwów Państwowych, 1998), Moczar's statement p. 398.

[52] Stanisław Wroński, 'Zalecenia Zjazdu', *Przyjaźń,* No. 11, 1948, pp. 20-21.

[53] On the Stalin-cult in Poland: Robert Kupiecki, *'Natchnienie milionów'. Kult Józefa Stalina w Polsce,* (Warsaw, Wydawn. Szkolne i Pedagogiczne, 1993); Jan C. Behrends, 'Exporting the Leader: The Stalin Cult in Poland and East Germany (1944/45-56)', in Balázs Apor *et al.* (eds), *The Leader Cult in Communist Dictatorships:*

Stalin and the Eastern Bloc, (Basingstoke, Palgrave, 2004), pp. 161-178.

[54] *Żołnierz wolności ludu wolności Polski. O Marszałku Konstantym Rokosowskim*, (Warsaw, Książka i Wiedza, 1949); *Marszałek Rokossowski na czele Wojska Polskiego*, (Warsaw, 1949); *Konstanty Rokossowski. Marszałek Polski*, (Warsaw, Wyd. mon "Prasa wojskowa", 1949).

[55] Needless to say, important aspects of Rokossowski's life like his real birthplace or his arrest during the Great Terror were not mentioned.

[56] Marszałek Rokossowski na czele Wojska Polskiego — to wzrost naszych sił obronnych — wzmocnienie bezpieczeństwa Polski, in *Przegląd Wydarzeń*, No. 15, 1949, pp. 13-23, quotation p. 15.

[57] Iz dnevnika zaveduyushchego otdelom stran narodnoy demokratii redakcii inostrannoy informacii TASS N. R. Pantjuchina. Zapis' besed na prieme v posol'stve Pol'shi v Mokskve o reakcii poliakov na naznachenie K.K. Rokossovskogo ministrom nacional'noy oborony Pol'shi, 31.1.-1.2.1950, in: *Sovetskii faktor v vostochnoy evrope, tom 2, 1949-1953*, (Moscow, Rosspen, 2002), pp. 255-256; Po mianowaniu Marszałka Rokossowskiego Ministrem Obrony Narodowej, Meldunki z terenu, AAN, KC PZPR, Wyd. Org., 237/VII-119, pp. 135-164.

[58] III Zjazd Towarzystwa Przyjaźni Polsko-Radzieckiej, *Przyjaźń*, No. 46, 1949, p. 3.

[59] On theses celebrations, see Behrends, 'Exporting the Leader', pp. 165 *et seq*.

[60] Idea wieczystej przyjaźni z narodami ZSRR fundamentem moralno-politycznej jedności Narodu Polskiego, *Przyjaźń*, No. 47, 1949, pp. 8-9.

[61] W każdej gromadzie koło TPP-R - oto nasze najbliższe zadania, *Przyjaźń*, No. 47, 1949, p. 13.

[62] On Stalin's biography, see David Brandenberger, 'Stalin as a Symbol: a Case Study of the Personality Cult and Its Construction', in: Sarah Davies & James Harris (eds), *Stalin: A New History*, (Cambridge, Cambridge University Press, 2005), pp. 249-270.

[63] To jest przyjaźń, która weszła nam w krew, która weszła w naszej kości, weszła w nasze dusze i serce..., *Przyjaźń*, No. 47, 1949, p. 15.

[64] On the post-war purge, see Hermann Weber & Ulrich Mählert (eds): *Terror: Stalinistische Parteisäuberungen 1936-1953*, (Paderborn, Schöningh, 2001).

[65] GA RF, fond 5283, op. 22, d. 183, pp. 58.

[66] Protokół Nr. 39 posiedzenia Biura Politycznego PZPR, 4 July 1950, in: *Centrum władzy. Protokoły posiedzeń kierownictwa PZPR. Wybór z lat 1949-1970*, (Warsaw, Instytut Studiów Politycznych PAN, 2000), pp. 54-55.

[67] Program miesiąca pogłębienia przyjaźni Polsko-Radzieckiej 14.X.-15.XI.1951 r., ATPPR, 5/17, [no pages].

[68] See Konrad Rokicki, 'Kłotpotliwy dar: Pałac Kultury i Nauki', in: Jerzy Kochanowski (ed), *Zbudować Warszawę piękną... O nowy krajobraz stolicy (1944-1956)*, (Warsaw, Wydawn. Trio, 2003), pp. 97-212.

[69] See Katherine Lebow, 'Socialist Leisure in Time and Space: Hooliganism and *bikinarstwo* in Nowa Huta, 1949-1956', in: Christiane Brenner *et al*. (eds), *Sozialgeschichtliche Kommunismusforschung. Tschechoslowakei, Polen, Ungarn, DDR, 1945-1968*, (Munich, Oldenbourg, 2005), pp. 527-542.

[70] Program Ramowy Miesiąca Pogłębienia Przyjaźni Polsko-Radzieckiej, 7.X.-

7.XI. 1949 r., AAN, ZSCh, Nr. 1741, pp. 1-16. See, also, Jestem czytelnikem 'Prawdy', *Przyjaźń*, No. 18, 1951, pp. 4-5.

[71] Maria Dąbrowska, *Tagebücher 1914-1965*, (Frankfurt aM, Suhrkamp, 1996), p. 259.

[72] See William Taubman, *Khrushchev: The Man and His Era*, (New York, Norton, 2003).

[73] Tony Kemp-Welch, 'Khrushchev's 'Secret Speech' and Polish Politics: The Spring of 1956', *Europe-Asia Studies*, Vol. 48, No. 2, 1996, pp. 181-207; Paweł Machcewicz, *Polski rok 1956*, (Warsaw, Oficyna Wydawn. Mówią Wieki, 1993).

[74] Henryk Dankowicz, 'O martwych drogach i wdzięcznych tematach,' *Przyjaźń*, No. 18, 1956, p. 3.

[75] Edmund Makowski, *Poznański czerwiec 1956. Pierwszy bunt społeczeństwa w PRL*, (Poznań, Wydawn. Poznańskie, 2001).

Chapter 11

[1] Stelian Tanase, *Elite si societate. Guvernarea Gheorghiu-Dej 1948-1965*, (Bucharest, Humanitas, 1998), pp. 82-84.

[2] Olivier Gillet, *Religion et Nationalisme. L'Ideologie de L'Eglise Orthodoxe Roumaine sous le Regime Communiste*, (Brussels, Editions de l'Universite de Bruxelles, 1997).

[3] See Cristian Vasile's critique of Olivier Gillet in Cristian Vasile, *Intre Vatican si Kremlin Biserica Greco-Catolica in timpul regimului comunist*, (Bucharest, Curtea Veche, 2003), p. 208.

[4] Tatiana A. Chumachenko's interpretation in Tatiana A. Chumachenko, *Church and State in Soviet Russia: Russian Orthodoxy from World War II to the Khrushchev years*, (New York, M.E. Sharpe, 2002).

[5] Bohdan R. Bociurkiw, 'Church – State Relations in the USSR', in: Max Hayward & William C. Fletcher (eds), *Religion and the Soviet State: A Dilemma of Power*, (New York - Washington - London, Frederik A. Praeger, Publishers, 1969), p. 83.

[6] Talal Asad, 'Religion, Nation-State, Secularism', in: Peter van der Veer & Hartmut Lehman (eds), *Nation and Religion: Perspectives on Europe and Asia*, (Princeton, Princeton University Press, 1999).

[7] Departamentul Culte, Direcția de Studii: Culte Neo-Protestante (Neo-Protestant denominations) file number 95, volume 13/a, 1953, p. 2, Arhivele Secretariatului de Stat pentru Culte, Bucharest, Romania.

[8] Jane Ellis, *The Russian Orthodox Church: A Contemporary History*, (Bloomington IN, Indiana University Press, 1988), pp. 253-256.

[9] Departamentul Culte, Direcția de Studii, *Monahismul ortodox in paralelă cu cel catolic în țara noastră*, file number 85, volume 11, 1948, p. 2, Arhivele Secretariatului de Stat pentru Culte, Bucharest, Romania.

[10] *Ibid.*, p. 3.

[11] The specialist considered the example of the Greek Catholic Church while drafting the proposal. Some of the documents testify to the attempt of the state to ban the Greek Catholic Church before the 'unification' of the Greek Catholics with the Orthodox Church. Departamentul Culte, Directia de Studii: *Referat privind unirea greco-catolicilor cu biserica ortodoxă română*, file number 80, volume 10, 1948, p. 141, Arhivele Secretariatului de Stat Pentru Culte, Bucharest, Romania.

[12] Departamentul Culte, Directia de Studii, *Monahismul ortodox in paralelă cu cel*

catolic in țara noastră, file number 85, volume 11, 1948, p. 4, Arhivele Secretariatului de Stat pentru Culte, Bucharest, Romania.

[13] One of the first measures that the state implemented decided on the restriction of the number of theology students.

[14] Departamentul Culte, Directia de Studii: *Extras din decizia nr 22562/1960 cu privire la reîntregirea salariilor preoților si diaconilor,* file number 85, volume 6, 1950, p. 1, Arhivele Secretariatului de Stat pentru Culte, Bucharest, Romania.

[15] The recognized neo-Protestants were: Baptists, Pentecostals, Evangelical Christians, and Seven Day Adventists.

[16] An estimated statistics of religious denominations: orthodox believers - 80 %;
Neo Protestant (all 4 of them)- up to 50,000 believers;
Traditional protestant - 5/6 %;
Roman Catholic 5/6 %;
Others 7/8 %.

[17] Cristian Vasile, *Biserica Ortodoxă Română în primul deceniu comunist,* (Bucharest, Curtea Veche, 2005), p. 52.

[18] Some aspects of the policy guideline give the impression that the specialists, who drafted the document, came from within the church and considered the institutional needs of the Orthodox Church while devising the proposal.

[19] Among these 'specialists', there were some who were involved in the fascist movement or who held positions before the Second World War. There were also specialists with a different ethnic background from that of the majority of the believers, such as German protestant in Hungarian protestant denominations, and the other way around.

[20] See Sheila Fitzpatrick, *The Cultural Front: Power and Culture in Revolutionary Russia,* (Ithaca - London, Cornell University Press, 1992).

[21] Stelian Tănase, *Clienții lu' tanti Varvara,* (Bucharest: Humanitas, 2005) and Vladimir Tismăneanu, *Stalinism for all Seasons: A Political History of Romanian Communism,* (Berkeley CA, University of California Press, 2003).

[22] Departamentul Culte, Directia de Studii: *Referate cu privire la reglementarea situatiei dintre cultul romano catolic si Statul român,* file number 86, volume 3, 1953, p. 5, Arhivele Secretariatului de Stat pentru Culte, Bucharest, Romania.

[23] Departamentul Culte, Direcția de Studii: *Ședința cu protopopii de pe raza episcopiei Buzău,* file number 77, volume 2, 1954, p. 72, Arhivele Secretariatului de Stat pentru Culte, Bucharest, Romania.

[24] Departamentul Culte, Direcția de Studii: *Notă a Împuternicitului asupra alegerilor eparhiale,* file number 85, volume 4, 1954, p. 462, Arhivele Secretariatului de Stat pentru Culte, Bucharest, Romania.

[25] For example, the Sibiu regional Empowered 'from the discussion he had with councillors in Sibiu [Metropolitan See] he found out that the delegates of the Metropolitan See at the conferences of priests and deans or inter-confessional conferences make special reports about what the Empowered talked about' Departamentul Culte, Direcția de Studii: *Notă a Împuternicitului,* file number 76, volume 1 bis, 1954, p. 12, Arhivele Secretariatului de Stat pentru Culte, Bucharest, Romania.

[26] One of the examples was the conflict between Archbishop Nicolae Colan of Cluj and his vicar, Sabin Truția, a former Greek Catholic priest, who was accused of collaborating with the regime by the administration of the Bishopric. In a report, the

local Empowered noted: 'Colan does not take into consideration any suggestion that vicar Truția makes in the meetings of the Eparchy council and answers with a short 'no father vicar'. Or another example: when he leaves for a hierarchical visit, instead of leaving his rightful *locum tenens* [in charge], he tells secretary Gosescu or the Eparchy inspector Buiu Ioan [to replace him] and thus while he is away vicar Trutia has no right to sign any official papers or take any official measures'. The Empowered advised the Department for Religious Denominations to force the Patriarchy to intervene and convince Archbishop Colan to allow Truția to function as a vicar. Departamentul Culte, Directia de Studii: *Diverse lucrări în legătură cu cazul Pr vicar Sabin Truția dela Episcopia ortodoxă Cluj,* file number 85, volume 14 a, 1954, p. 63, Arhivele Secretariatului de Stat pentru Culte, Bucharest, Romania.

[27] One note of a local Empowered exemplifies the brutality of the authorities. The document described the case of a certain pastor Lațis: 'Lațis does not have the character a pastor should as a leader of a denomination and does not keep to his words, one thing that the Stat functionaries noted during the orthodox celebration of saint Mary on August 15: *this Lațis was caught proselytising in Copalnic manastiur and thus the Miliția beat him up, but since he knew himself to be guilty he did not report this to anyone, not even the leadership of the denomination.* [emphasis in the original] Departamentul Culte, Directia de Studii: *Note – caracterizări de pastori,* file number 95, volume 2, 1953, p. 2, Arhivele Secretariatului de Stat pentru Culte, Bucharest, Romania.

[28] 'A phenomenon characteristic to neo-Protestant denominations is proselytism that in the case of Pentecostals is practiced with more intensity, which gives birth to inter-confessional tension. Thus, recently, in the region of Oradea their numbers grew by about 1100 members creating four new communities without asking the Department for Religious Denominations for permission as specified in the Law for Religious Denominations. Cases of proselyte activity, masked as gatherings of believers from several villages, were signalled in Timişoara, Bacău, Cluj and Bucureşti.' Departamentul Culte, Directia de Studii: *Note informative cu privire la manifestările si atitudinea unor credincioşi si deservenți,* file number 95, volume 13 a, 1953, p. 2, Arhivele Secretariatului de Stat pentru Culte, Bucharest, Romania.

[29] In early 1950s, the institution of the Empowered inside the Ministry for Religious Denominations numbered around 200 employees.

[30] As of the early 1950s, the state was confronted with the so called 'Greek Catholic problem'. The semi-failure of the unification with the Orthodox Church and the clear incapacity of the Orthodox Church to engulf Greek Catholics compelled the state to enforce the unification. Departamentul Culte, Direcția de Studii: *Problema reveniților greco-catolici,* file number 80, volume 1, 1954, p. 3, Arhivele Secretariatului de Stat pentru Culte, Bucharest, Romania.

Chapter 12

[1] *Ljudska pravica,* 14 July 1945, p. 1.

[2] Milovan Djilas, *Vlast* (London, Naša reč, 1983), p. 132; Stella Alexander, *Church and State in Yugoslavia since 1945,* (Cambridge, Cambridge University Press, 1979), p. 57.

[3] Josip Broz Tito, *Graditev nove Jugoslavije (I),* (Ljubljana, Cankarjeva založba, 1948), p. 30.

[4] Richard Pattee, *The Case of Cardinal Aloysius Stepinac,* (Milwaukee, The Bruce

Publishing Company, 1953), pp. 470-480, (Document LXX).

[5] Tito, *Graditev nove Jugoslavije (I)*, p. 234.

[6] *Slovenski poročevalec*, VI, 7 October 1945, p. 2.

[7] Arhiv Slovenije – The Archive of Slovenia (AS) 1799, 28/2. The problem of religious classes in schools, 18 April 1949, p. 1.

[8] AS 1589, Box 2, Session of the Politburo of the Central Committee of the Communist Party of Slovenia (CC CPS), 30 June 1950, p. 2.

[9] AS 223, Box 6, folder 554, Bishop's office in Ljubljana to the Presidency of the People's Republic of Slovenia, 20 November 1950; Bishop's office in Maribor to the Presidency of the People's Republic of Slovenia, 20 November 1950, 1 December 1950.

[10] AS 1589, Box 2, Session of the Politburo of the CC CPS, 20 December 1951, pp. 1-2.

[11] AS 537, Box 25, Session of the Executive Committee of the Liberation Front of Slovenia, 3 January 1952, p. 4.

[12] AS 1589, Box 1, The seventh plenum of the CC CPS, 26-27 January 1952, p. 12.

[13] *Slovenski poročevalec*, XIII, 7 March 1952, p. 3.

[14] *Slovenski poročevalec*, XIII, 13 April 1952, p. 4.

[15] *Slovenski poročevalec*, XIII, 24 April 1952, p. 4.

[16] AS 1589, Box 27, Notes of the meetings with chief editor of newspapers and with editors of the domestic political affairs' desks, 24 June 1952, p. 2.

[17] Janez Janžekovič, 'Izkustvena znanost, svetovni nazor, svoboda vesti', *Nova pot*, IV, Nos. 4-5-6, 1952, pp. 72-86.

[18] *Slovenski poročevalec*, XIII, 1 May 1952, p. 2.

[19] AS 1589, Box 1, The seventh plenum of the CC CPS, 26-27 January 1952, p. 8.

[20] AS 1211, Box 83, Annual Report 1955 - Roman Catholic Church in Slovenia, p. 10.

[21] AS 1931, A-13-0, Inv. 1558, Annual Report 1951, p. 25; AS 1931, A-13-0, Inv. 1559, Annual Report 1952, p. 19.

[22] Mateja Režek, 'Jurisdiction and Political Penal Repression in Yugoslavia in the Decade Following the Dispute with the Cominform (1948-1958)', *East Central Europe/ L'Europe du Centre-Est*, Vol. 29, part 1-2, 2002, pp. 84-85.

[23] AS 1589, Box 1, The seventh plenum of the CC CPS, 26-27 January 1952, p. 11.

[24] *Ibid.*, pp. 36-38.

[25] AS 1589, Box 2, Session of the Organising Secretariat of the Central Committee of the League of Communists of Slovenia, 15 October 1953, p. 6.

[26] AS 1589, Box 2, Session of the Politburo of the CC CPS, 20 November 1950, p. 2.

[27] AS 1211, Box 87, Memorandum of the CMD, pp. 7-8.

[28] AS 1211, Cyril-Metodius Association of Catholic Priests in Slovenia, 1968, pp. 5-7.

[29] AS 1211, Box 5, The fourth session of the Commission for Religious Questions by the Executive Council of the People's Assembly of the People's Republic of Slovenia, 8 January 1954, p. 1.

[30] AS 1211, Box 53, Analysis of the association of Catholic priests in the Socialist Republic of Croatia, p. 2.

[31] AS 1211, Box 83, Annual report 1955 - Roman Catholic Church in Slovenia, p. 2.

[32] AS 1529, Box 12, Material regarding the relationship between the Vatican or the

Catholic Church and FPRY, Copies and translations of texts - document 11: the report of Bishop Vovk about the status of CMD, sent to Monsignor Oddi in January 1951.

[33] AS 1529, Box 12, Material regarding the relationship between the Vatican or the Catholic Church and FPRY, Copies and translations of texts - document 12: the report of Bishop Vovk about his and Držečnik's conversations with Boris Kraigher on 10 November 1951, delivered to Monsignor Oddi.

[34] AS 537, Box 25, Session of the Executive Committee of the Liberation Front of Slovenia, 30 May 1951, pp. 24-25.

[35] Dragoljub R. Živojinović, *Vatikan, Katolička crkva i jugoslovenska vlast 1941-1958,* (Belgrade, Prosveta, 1994), p. 367.

[36] Josip Broz Tito, *Govori i članci (VII),* (Zagreb, Naprijed, 1959), p. 79.

[37] Alexander, *Church and State in Yugoslavia Since 1945,* pp. 138-139.

[38] AS 1529, Box 12, Material of the Federal Executive Council regarding the law on the legal status of religious communities, Letter from the Yugoslav Catholic Episcopate to Marshall Tito.

[39] AS 1529, Box 12, Material regarding relations between the Vatican or the Catholic Church and FPRY, Copies and translations of texts - document 15: the notes of Dr. Držečnik and Bishop Vovk about the conference in Zagreb.

[40] *Borba* (Zagreb), XVII, 18 December, 1952, pp. 1, 3.

[41] Darko Bekić, *Jugoslavijia u hladnom ratu: odnosi s velikim silama 1949-1955,* (Zagreb, Globus, 1988), pp. 448- 449; Živojinović, *Vatikan, Katolička crkva i jugoslovenska vlast,* p. 382; Alexander, *Church and State in Yugoslavia Since 1945,* p. 141; Pattee, *The Case of Cardinal Aloysius Stepinac,* p. 151.

[42] *Slovenian Report on Yugoslavia,* IV, 1953, No. 2, pp. 25-34.

[43] *Slovenski poročevalec,* XIII, 20 December 1952, pp. 1-3.

[44] AS 1211, Box 87, Memorandum of the CMD, p. 15.

[45] *Nova pot,* I, 1949, No. 2, p. 30.

[46] Edvard Kocbek, *Zbrano delo: Listina – prve objave,* (Ljubljana: DZS, 2000), p.127.

[47] AS 1529, Box 12, Material of the Federal Executive Council regarding the law on the legal status of religious communities, Comments of Belgrade archbishop Ujčić about the proposed law, p. 1.

[48] *Slovenski poročevalec,* XIV, 12 February 1953, p. 5.

[49] AS 1529, Box 12, Material of the Federal Executive Council regarding the law on the legal status of religious communities, Comments of Belgrade archbishop Ujčić about the proposed law, p. 1.

[50] AS 223 (The Cabinet of Boris Kraigher), 1953/I, Doc. 93/53; *Slovenski poročevalec,* XIV, 23 May 1953, p. 4.

[51] AS 1529, Box 12, Material of the Executive Council of Slovenia regarding the law on the legal status of religious communities, Notes about conversations of Boris Kraigher and the Slovenian ordinate, 17 April 1953.

[52] AS 1529, Box 12, Material of the Federal Executive Council regarding the law on the legal status of religious communities, Notes of the meetings of the provisional commission of the Federal Executive Council with representatives of the Catholic Church, 23-24 April 1953.

[53] AS 1529, Box 12, Material of the Executive Council of Slovenia regarding the law on the legal status of religious communities, Meeting of the Slovenian provisional commission for the normalization of relations with religious communities in Slovenia, 13 May 1953.

[54] Uradni list FLRJ (The Official Government Gazette of the FPRY), 1953, No. 22.

[55] *Slovenski poročevalec*, XIV, 23 May 1953, pp. 1-4.

[56] *Slovenian Report on Yugoslavia*, IV, 1953, No. 10, pp. 3- 10.

[57] Josip Broz Tito, *Borba za mir in mednarodno sodelovanje*, (VII) (Ljubljana: Cankarjeva založba, 1958), pp. 276-277.

[58] Tretji kongres ZKS (Ljubljana: Cankarjeva založba, 1954), pp. 360-361.

[59] AS 1521, Box 10/9, Clericalism – materials for the third congress of the League of Communists of Slovenia.

[60] Vjekoslav Cvrlje, *Vatikanska diplomacija: pokoncilski Vatikan u međunarodnim odnosima*, (Zagreb, Školska knjiga, 1992), pp. 117-119.

Chapter 13

[1] For a broader definition of *Geschichtskultur*, see Jörn Rüsen, *Historische Orientierung*, (Cologne, Böhlau, 1994), pp. 211-258.

[2] W. Pieck, G. Dimitrov & P. Togliatti, *Die Offensive des Faschismus und die Aufgaben der Kommunisten im Kampf für die Volksfront gegen Krieg und Faschismus*. Hrsg. v. Institut f. ML beim ZK der SED (Berlin (GR) 1960), pp. 161-178; W. Berthold, 'Marxistisch-leninistische Geschichtswissenschaft im Kampf gegen den Faschismus und für die antifaschistische Volksfront', *Beiträge zur Geschichte der Arbeiterbewegung*, 27, 1985, pp. 473-86; W. Berthold, 'Zur Geschichte der Geschichtswissenschaft der DDR. Vorgeschichte, Konfrontationen und Kooperationen', in: E. Schulin (ed), *Deutsche Geschichtswissenschaft nach dem Zweiten Weltkrieg (1945-65)*, (Munich, Oldenbourg, 1989), pp. 39-51.

[3] J. Barber, *Soviet Historians in Crisis, 1928-32*, (New York, Holmes & Meier, 1981); G.M. Enteen, *The Soviet Scholar-Bureaucrat: M. N. Pokrovskii and the Society of Marxist Historians*, (University Park, Pennsylvania State University Press, 1978).

[4] For the Nationalist aspect, see D. Brandenberger, *National Bolshevism: Stalinist Mass Culture and the Formation of Modern Russian National Identity, 1931-56*, (Cambridge MA - London, Harvard University Press, 2002); Martin Mevius, *Agents of Moscow: The Hungarian Communist Party and the Origins of Socialist Patriotism 1941-53*, (Oxford, Clarendon/Oxford University Press, 2005); for the aesthetic aspects which was true for literature as well as for historiography: see H. Günther, 'Education and Conversion: The Road to the New Man in the Totalitarian *Bildungsroman*', in: H. Günther (ed), *The Culture of the Stalin Period*, (London, Macmillan, 1990), pp. 193-209.

[5] *A Szovjetunió Kommunista (Bolsevik) pártjának története (Rövid tanfolyam)* [Short Course of the History of the Communist (Bolshevik) Party of the Soviet Union]. (Budapest, Szikra, 1949); for an understanding of the meaning of the *Kratkii Kurs* as an introduction of a new, official historical narrative, see V. Volkov, 'The Concept of 'Kulturnost': Notes on the Stalinist Civilizing Process', in: Sheila Fitzpatrick (ed), *Stalinism: New Directions*, (London – New York, Routledge, 2000), p. 227; another example of an extreme attempt to 'master' the 'Kratkii Kurs' is given in: L.H. Siegelbaum & A. Sokolov (eds), *Stalinism as a Way of Life. A Narrative in Documents*, (New Haven, London, Yale University Press, 2000), Doc. 75, pp. 214-215.

[6] W. Schulz, 'Die marxistisch-leninistische Geschichtswissenschaft', in: *Marxismus im Systemvergleich. Geschichte 2* (Frankfurt, New York, Herder & Herder, 1974), pp. 132-167; J. Kocka, 'Parteilichkeit in der DDR-marxistischen Geschichtswissenschaft',

in: R. Koselleck, W.J. Mommsen & J. Rüsen (eds), *Objektivität und Parteilichkeit. Theorie der Geschichte*, vol. 1. (Munich, Deutscher Taschenbuch Verlag, 1977), pp. 263-69.

[7] See: *Magyar Történész kongresszus 1953 Jún. 6-13*, (Budapest, Akadémiai Kiadó, 1954).

[8] *Ibid.*, p. 12.

[9] *A magyar nép története. Rövid áttekintés.* Written by Gusztáv Heckenast, Miklós Incze, Béla Karácsonyi, Lajos Lukács & György Spira, (3rd ed) [1st ed. 1951], (Budapest, Művelt Nép, 1953).

[10] József Révai, *Marx és az 1848-as magyar forradalom*, (Budapest, Szikra, 1953), p. 73.

[11] See Tibor Erényi, 'A nemzeti ünnep és a pártok', *Századok*, Vol. 132, No. 2, 1998, pp. 477-88, and 481.

[12] Andics taught classes on 1848 at the Lenin School of the Komintern, where later Dimitrov, Pieck and others also gave lectures. Katalin Petrák, *Magyarok a Szovjetunióban 1922-45*, (Budapest, Napvilág, 2000), p. 202.

[13] Erzsébet Andics, 'Az egyházi reakció 1848-49-ben', in: Aladár Mód (ed), *Forradalom és szabadságharc 1848-1849* (Budapest, Szikra, 1948), pp. 317-413.

[14] In a document of the communist controlled Tudományos Tanács (Scientific Council), Ember was called a 'szimpatizáns' of the party. See Politikatörténeti Intézet Levéltára 276. f./68 cs./77 ő.e., p. 23.

[15] Győző Ember, 'Magyar parasztmozgalmak 1848-ban', in: *Forradalom és szabadságharc*, p. 265.

[16] General Windischgrätz became commander-in-chief of the Austrian army in October 1848. He was involved in the coup to replace Ferdinand V with Franz Joseph on the throne later that year, and he was also the leader of the subsequent Austrian military campaign against Hungary. The series of bitter military defeats in early April 1849 led to his abdication on 12 April.

[17] *Szabad Nép*, 30 May, 1948. Quoted in András Gerő, *Az államosított forradalom: 1818 centenáriuma*, (Budapest, Új Mandátum, 1998), pp. 240-1.

[18] *Századok*, Vol. 82, 1948, p. 388.

[19] Magyar Országos Levéltár (hereafter: MOL) 276 f./68 cs./74 ő.e., p. 21. (Révai's papers).

[20] MOL 276 f./68 cs./76 ő.e.

[21] Jenő Berláz, 'A Századok 1948. évi eredeti kötetérôl ...', *Századok*, Vol. 123, Nos. 3-4, 1989, pp. 238-40.

[22] The history of the 'Tudományos Tanács' has been studied by: György Péteri, *Academia and State Socialism: Essays on the Political History of Academic Life in Post-1945 Hungary and Eastern Europe*, (Highland Lakes NJ, Atlantic Research and Publications, Inc., 1998); Tibor Huszár, *A hatalom rejtett dimenziói. Magyar Tudományos Tanács 1948-49*, (Budapest, Akadémiai Kiadó, 1995); Sándor Kónya, *A magyar tudományos tanács (1948-49)*, (Budapest, Magyar Tudományos Akadémia Könyvtárának Közleményei, 1998).

[23] Ferenc Glatz, 'A nemzetállam zsákutcája', in his *Történetírás korszakváltásban*, (Budapest, Gondolat, 1990), p. 345.

[24] Contrary to this view, Martin Mevius stresses the efforts of the Communist Party to make as much use as possible of 'patriotic' history and ideas which were not very different from nationalism. See Martin Mevius, *Agents of Moscow: The Hungarian*

Communist Party and the Origins of Socialist Patriotism 1941-53, (Oxford, Oxford University Press, 2005).

[25] Hans Günther, *Der Helden- und Feindmythos in der totalitären Kultur*, (Tübingen, Slavisches Seminar der Univ., 1994), p. 9.

[26] Georg von Rauch, 'Das sowjetische und sowjetzonale Geschichtsbild', in: *Schicksalsfragen der Gegenwart. Handbuch politisch-historischer Bildung*. Hrsg. v. Bundesministerium f. Verteidigung, Erster Band & Max Niemeyer, (Tübingen, 1957), p. 322-48, especially p. 328.

[27] Boris Groys, *Gesamtkunstwerk Stalin: Die gespaltene Kultur in der Sowjetunion*, (Munich – Vienna, C. Hanser, 1988/1996), p. 47; Boris Groys, 'Socialist Realism and the Russian Avant-Garde', in: *The Culture of the Stalin Period*, pp. 122-48, and p. 144.

[28] Siegfried Lokatis, 'Geschichtswerkstatt Zensur', in: Martin Sabrow (ed), *Geschichte als Herrschaftsdiskurs. Der Umgang mit der Vergangenheit in der DDR*, (Cologne, Böhlau, 2000), pp. 175-226.

[29] Gwidon Zalejko, 'Soviet Historiography as a "Normal Science"', in: Jerzy Topolski (ed.), *Historiography between Modernism and Postmodernism: Contributions to the Methodology of the Historical Research*. Poznań Studies in the Philosophy of the Science and the Humanities, Vol. 41, 1994, pp. 179-190, at 190. The 'second reality' of sovietized East German historians is analysed in: M. Sabrow, 'Dictatorship as Discourse: Cultural Perspectives on SED legitimacy', in: K.H. Jarausch (ed.), *Dictatorship as Experience: Towards a Socio-cultural History of the GDR*, (New York - Oxford, Berghahn Books, 1999), pp. 195-211.

[30] Magyar Tudományos Akadémia Levéltára, 86. dob., Jegyzőkönyv a Magyar Történész Kongr. A SzU-ból és a népi dem. Országokból érkezett delegációk, 1953 jun. 13-án a MMI-ben tartott közös értekezletéről.

Chapter 14

[1] It is still doubtful if and to what extent are we to use the terms 'Marxist' and 'Stalinist' while referring to intellectual or cultural phenomena of the Stalinist period. Georg G. Iggers points at differences between 'Western Marxism' and the official Marxist philosophy of the international Communist parties. On the other hand Leszek Kołakowski claims that Stalinism is a form of Marxism. I do follow this last path and use 'Stalinist' as an equivalent of 'Marxist'. See Georg G. Iggers, *Historiography in the Twentieth Century: From Scientific Objectivity to the Postmodern Challenge*, (Hanover – London, New England, Wesleyan Univ. Press, 1997), p. 78; Leszek Kołakowski, *Główne nurty marksizmu*, (Poznań, Zysk i Spółka, 2000), Vol. 3, pp. 111-26.

[2] Wanda Moszczeńska, 'Stosunek do dorobku dawnej historiografii polskiej', in: *Pierwsza Konferencja Metodologiczna Historyków Polskich*, Vol. I, (Warsaw, PWN, 1953), p. 91.

[3] Konrad Jarausch & Matthias Middell, 'Einleitung. Die DDR als Geschichte: Verurteilung, Nostalgie oder Historisierung?', in: Konrad Jarausch & Matthias Middell (eds), *Nach dem Erdbeben. (Re-) Konstruktion ostdeutscher Geschichte und Geschichtswissenschaft*, (Leipzig, Leipziger Universitäts-Verlag, 1994); Stefan Ebenfeld, *Geschichte nach Plan? Die Instrumentalisierung der Geschichtswissenschaft in der DDR am Beispiel des Museums für Deutsche Geschichte in Berlin (1950 bis 1955)*, (Marburg: Tectum, 2001); Ralph Jessen, *Akademische Elite und kommunistische Diktatur. Die*

ostdeutsche Hochschullehrschaft der Ulbricht-Ära, (Göttingen: Vanderhoeck & Ruprecht, 1999); Ilko-Sascha Kowalczuk, 'Die Durchsetzung des Marxismus-Leninismus in der Geschichtswissenschaft der DDR (1945-1961)', in: Martin Sabrow & Peter Walther (eds), *Historische Forschung und sozialistische Diktatur. Beiträge zur Geschichtswissenschaft der DDR,* (Leipzig, Leipziger Universitäts-Verlag, 1995); Ilko-Sascha Kowalczuk, 'Die Historiker der DDR und der 17. Juni 1953', *Geschichte in Wissenschaft und Unterricht,* Vol. 44, 1993.

[4] Jindřich Schwippel, 'ČAVU a ČSAV: otázky kontinuity a diskontinuity I', in: Jiří Pokorný & Jan Novotný (eds), *Česká akademie věd a umění 1891-1991. Sborník příspěvků k 100. výročí zahajení činnosti,* (Prague: HÚ AV ČR 1993); Alena Míšková, 'ČAVU a ČSAV: otázky kontinuity a diskontinuity II. (Vytvoření sboru členů ČSAV a jeho vztah k členské základně ČAVU a KČSN)', *ibid.*; Rafał Stobiecki, 'Between Continuity and Discontinuity: A Few Comments on the Post-war Development of Polish Historical Research', *Zeitschrift für Ostmitteleuropa-Forschung,* Vol. 50, No. 2, 2001, pp. 214-29.

[5] Konrad Jarausch, 'Historische Texte der DDR aus der Perspektive des linguistic turn', in: Georg Iggers, Konrad Jarausch, Matthias Middell & Martin Sabrow (eds), *Die DDR-Geschichtswissenschaft als Forschungsproblem,* (Munich, Oldenbourg, 1998); Konrad Jarausch & Martin Sabrow, 'Das Konzept der "historischen Meistererzählung" als Maßstab eines deutsch-deutsches Historiographievergleichs', in: Max Kerner, Peter Droste, Angelika Ivens & Cornelia Kompe (eds), 43. *Deutscher Historikertag Aachen 2000. Skriptheft 2 Eine Welt – eine Geschichte?,* (Munich, Oldenbourg, 2003); Matthias Middell, 'Historische Meistererzählung und Institutionalisierung in der Geschichtswissenschaft', *ibid.*; Martin Sabrow, 'Bauformen einer erneuerten nationalen Meistererzählung in der DDR: das "Lehrbuch der deutschen Geschichte"', *ibid.*; Konrad Jarausch & Martin Sabrow (eds), *Die historische Meistererzählung. Deutungslinien der deutschen Nationalgeschichte nach 1945,* (Göttingen, Vanderhoeck & Ruprecht, 2002).

[6] Martin Sabrow, *Das Diktat des Konsenses. Geschichtswissenschaft in der DDR 1949-1969,* (Munich, Oldenbourg, 2001).

[7] See Marcin Zaremba, *Komunizm, legitymizacja, nacjonalizm. Nacjonalistyczna legitymizacja władzy komunistycznej w Polsce,* (Warsaw, Trio, 2001), p. 398.

[8] For the thorough interpretation of Czechoslovak Marxist historiography, see Maciej Górny, 'Past in the Future. National Tradition and Czechoslovak Marxist Historiography', *European Review of History-Revue européenne d'Histoire,* Vol. 10, No. 1, 2003, pp. 103-14

[9] Vormärz is the time period that preceded the revolution(s) in March 1848 in the territories under Habsburg rule.

[10] Hans Kohn, *Pan-Slavism: Its History and Ideology,* (Notre Dame IN, University of Notre Dame Press, 1953), p. 238.

[11] See Celina Bobińska on 1st Congress of Polish Science, *Kwartalnik Historyczny* 1951, LVIII, p. 404.

[12] *Ibid.*, pp. 24-25.

[13] Kuczynski described these events in his book: *Frost nach dem Tauwetter. Mein Historikerstreit,* (Berlin, Elefanten Press, 1993).

[14] Ernst Engelberg, 'Politik und Geschichtsschreibung. Die historische Stellung und Aufgabe der Geschichtswissenschaft in der DDR', *Zeitschrift für Geschichtswissenschaft* Vol. 6, 1958, p. 482.

[15] Gerhard Schilfert, 'Leopold von Ranke', in: Joachim Streisand (ed), *Die deutsche Geschichtswissenschaft vom Beginn des 19. Jahrhunderts bis zum Reichseinigung von oben,* (Berlin, Akademie-Verlag), 1963, p. 269.

[16] Leo Stern, *Gegenwartsaufgaben der deutschen Geschichtsforschung,* (Berlin, Rütten & Loening, 1952), p. 29; Hans Schleier, *Sybel und Treitschke. Antidemokratismus und Militarismus im historisch – politischen Denken großbourgeoiser Geschichtsideologen,* (Berlin, Akademie-Verlag, 1965), p. 161.

[17] *Ibid.,* p. 228.

[18] *Ibid.,* p. 230.

[19] Andrzej Poppe, 'U źródeł postępowej historiografii szlacheckiego rewolucjonizmu: Zorian Dołęga Chodakowski (1784-1825)', *Kwartalnik Historyczny,* 1955, LXII.

[20] Josef Macůrek, *Úvahy o mé vědecké činnosti a vědeckých pracích,* (Brno, Matice Moravská, 1998), p. 79.

[21] Josef Hanzal, 'Čeští historici před únorem 1948', *Český Časopis Historický,* 91, 1993, p. 283.

[22] See Josef Macek, František Graus & Ján Tibenský (eds), *Přehled československých dějin,* Vol. II part 1, (Prague, ČSAV, 1959), pp. 10-11.

[23] Josef Kočí, 'Revoluce v Čechách roku 1848', *Československý Časopis Historický,* 2, 1954, p. 511.

[24] Bedřich Šindelář, 'František Palacký a dělnická třída', *Časopis Matice Moravské,* 76, 1952, p. 35.

[25] Vladimír Mináč, 'Tu żyje naród', in: Rudolf Chmel (ed), *Kwestia słowacka w XX wieku,* transl.: Piotr Godlewski, Zofia Jurczak-Trojan & Maryla Papierz, (Gliwice, Agora, 2002), p. 376.

[26] Karol Goláň, *Štúrovské pokolenie (Výber z diela),* František Bokes, (ed), (Bratislava, SAV, 1964), p. 367.

[27] *Ibid.,* p. 371.

[28] Július Mésároš, 'Štúrov boj za oslobodenie slovenského roľníctva spod jarma feudalizmu', in: *Ľudovít Štúr – život a dielo 1815-1856. Sborník materiálov z konference Historického ústavu Sloveskej akadémie vied,* (Bratislava, SAV, 1956), pp. 152-153.

[29] Almost every aspect of his rich personality was analyzed by authors of the volume: *Ľudovít Štúr – život a dielo 1815-1856. Sborník materiálov z konference Historického ústavu Sloveskej akadémie vied,* (Bratislava, SAV 1956).

[30] See Karol Goláň, *Štúrovské pokolenie (Výber z diela),* edited by František Bokes, (Bratislava, SAV, 1964), p. 376.

[31] 'Veľke jubileum', *Historický Časopis Slovenskej Akadémie Vied,* 4, 1956, p. 4.

[32] Vladimír Matula, 'K niektorým otázkam slovenského národného hnutia štyridsiatych rokov XIX stor', *Historický Časopis Slovenskej Akadémie Vied,* 2, 1954, pp. 375-405.

[33] Karol Goláň, 'Ľudovít Štúr a slovenské národné hnutie v štyridsiatych rokoch XIX. Storočia', *Historický Časopis Slovenskej Akadémie Vied,* 3, 1955, p. 91.

[34] (JT) [Ján Tibenský], 'Konferencia slovenských historikov o tézach slovenských dejín', *Historický Časopis Slovenskej Akadémie Vied,* 3, 1955, pp. 300-301.

[35] Ľudovít Holotík (ed), *Dejiny Slovenska (tézy),* (Bratislava, SAV, 1955), p. 115.

[36] 'Veľke jubileum', *Historický Časopis Slovenskej Akadémie Vied,* 4, 1956, p. 4.

[37] Július Mésároš, 'Boj Ľudovíta Štúra proti feudalizmu', *Historický Časopis Slov-*

enskej Akadémie Vied', 4, 1956, pp. 6-19.

[38] 'Vedecké zasednutie v Moskve venované stému výročiu smrti Ľudovíta Štúra', *Historický Časopis Slovenskej Akadémie Vied*, 4, 1956, p. 8.

[39] Vladimír Matula, 'Štúr a slovanstvo', in: *Ľudovít Štúr--život a dielo*, pp. 386-387.

[40] Josef Macek, František Graus & Ján Tibenský (eds), *Přehled československých dějin (Maketa)*, (Prague, ČSAV, 1956), Vol. I, p. 769.

[41] Vladimír Matula, 'Vyvrcholenie štúrovskej koncepcie myšlienky slovanskej vzájomnosti v štúrovom diele "Slovanstvo a svet budúcnosti"', *Historický Časopis Slovenskej Akadémie Vied*, 8, 1960, p. 376.

[42] Vladimír Mináč, 'Tu żyje naród', in: Rudolf Chmel (ed), *Kwestia słowacka w XX wieku*, transl.: Piotr Godlewski, Zofia Jurczak-Trojan & Maryla Papierz, (Gliwice, Agora, 2002), p. 383.

[43] Ľudovít Holotík, 'Desať rokov Historického ústavu Slovenskej akadémie vied', *Historický Časopis Slovenskej Akadémie Vied*, 11, 1963, p. 601.

[44] Richard Marsina, 'Slovenská historiografia 1945-1990', *Historický Časopis Slovenskej Akadémie Vied*, 57, 1991, p. 372.

[45] I refer to the conclusions of one of the best Polish historians – persecuted in the 1950s – Henryk Wereszycki, who in 1957 reviewed the Polish Marxist handbook in history. He paid attention to the pessimism characterizing the book and especially the section on the history of the 19th century. In his opinion, the overwhelming majority of Polish insurrections and political movements were treated by the Marxists as 'not progressive enough'. In fact, only the movements of the lower classes were defined as progressive, and that was a condition no Polish insurrection could fulfill. The pessimism of the authors was also of a methodological kind. Wereszycki questioned the sense of years of hard work of the generations of Polish historians, if Marx and Engels had already known everything and the only conclusion a Marxist historian was able to achieve is that Marx and Engels were right. See Henryk Wereszycki, *Pesymizm błędnych tez, 'Kwartalnik Historyczny'* 1957, LXIV.

[46] Lutz Raphael, *Geschichtswissenschaft im Zeitalter der Extreme. Theorien, Methoden, Tendenzen von 1900 bis zur Gegenwart*, (Munich, Beck, 2003), pp. 58-59.

[47] Jan Herman Brinks, *Die DDR-Geschichtswissenschaft auf dem Weg zur deutschen Einheit. Luther, Friedrich II und Bismarck als Paradigmen politischen Wandels*, (Frankfurt aM - New York, Campus, 1992), p. 309.

Chapter 15

[1] Elek Karsai & Ervin Pamlényi, *Fehérterror*, (Budapest, Publisher unknown, 1951), pp. 71-2.

[2] On the first five decades of Soviet historiography, see Konstantin F. Shteppa, *Russian Historians and the Soviet State*, (New Brunswick, Rutgers University Press, 1962). On early Soviet historical scholarship, see John Barber, *Soviet Historians in Crisis, 1928-1932*, (New York, Holmes & Meier, 1981). An intriguing recent work is David Brandenberger, *National Bolshevism: Stalinist Mass Culture and the Formation of Modern Russian National Identity, 1931-1956*, (Cambridge MA - London, Harvard University Press, 2002).

[3] On the system of the People's Tribunals in Hungary, see Tibor Lukács, *A magyar népbírósági jog és a népbíróságok*, (Budapest, Közgazdasági és Jogi Könyvkiadó, Zrínyi

Katonai Kiadó, 1979); Tibor Zinner, 'Adalékok az antifasiszta számonkéréshez és a népi demokrácia védelméhez különös tekintettel a budapesti népbíróságra', in: *Budapest Főváros Levéltára Közleményei '84,* (1985), pp. 137-69. Idem, 'Háborús bűnösök perei. Internálások, kitelepítések és igazoló eljárások 1945-1949', *Történelmi Szemle,* Vol. 28, No. 1, 1985, pp. 118-40; Sándor Szakács & Tibor Zinner, *A háború "megváltozott természete",* (Budapest, Genius Gold, 1997), pp. 182-93; Károly Szerencsés, *"Az ítélet: halál",* (Budapest, Kairosz, 2002), pp. 29-53. On the armistice, see Mihály Korom, *Magyarország Ideiglenes Nemzeti Kormánya és a fegyverszünet,* (Budapest, Akadémiai Kiadó, 1981). The best comprehensive work on the history of the legal system is Mária Palasik, *A jogállamiság megteremtésének kísérlete és kudarca Magyarországon, 1944-1949,* (Budapest, Napvilág, 2000), esp. pp. 41-5.

[4] Borsod-Abaúj-Zemplén Megyei Levéltár Mezőcsáti Fióklevéltára (The Mezőcsát Section of the Archives of Borsod-Abaúj-Zemplén County, hereafter: BAZ ML) Records of the People's Prosecution 1038/1949. On Latorczay's role in the war, see Péter Bokor, 'Egy ezredes két halála', *Élet és Irodalom,* 14 May 1982, pp. 3-4. and 'Egy lázadás története', *Magyar Hírlap,* 15 October 1993, p. 8.

[5] The Act on the People's Tribunals is in: *Magyar Törvénytár. 1943-1945. évi törvénycikkek,* (Budapest, Franklin Társulat, 1946), p. 93.

[6] BAZ ML.

[7] Ibid.

[8] Ibid.

[9] Ibid.

[10] In Roman times, Christians were frequently accused of sacrificing children and of drinking their blood during their ceremonies. This was the main motif for their horrible persecution in Lyon in the second century. Murdering and sacrificing children repeatedly appeared also against heretics: in the eighth century against the Paulicians, in the twelfth century against the Cathars, and in the fourteenth century against the Waldensians. The motif of baking babies was among the accusations against the Knights Templars, while witches were considered to be experts in child killing. See Norman Cohn, *Europe's Inner Demons,* (London, Pimlico, 1993) and Klaniczay Gábor, 'Az orgiavádak nyomában' in: Idem, *A civilizáció peremén,* (Budapest, Magvető, 1990), pp. 194-208.

[11] BAZ ML, the indictment.

[12] *Szabad Magyarország,* 28 September 1947.

[13] BAZ ML.

[14] Ibid.

[15] Ibid. On the investigation of military organisations, see Dr. Vargyai Gyula, *Katonai közigazgatás és kormányzói jogkör (1919-1921),* (Budapest, Közgazdasági és Jogi Könyvkiadó, 1971), pp. 104-46.

[16] BAZ ML.

[17] *Felvidéki Népszava,* 17 March 1948.

[18] *Szabad Magyarország,* 7 April 1948.

[19] *Szabad Magyarország,* 29 May 1947.

[20] *Szabad Magyarország,* 7 April 1948.

[21] *Felvidéki Népszava,* 7 April 1948.

[22] BAZ ML.

[23] Ibid.

[24] Ibid.

[25] Michael André Bernstein, *Foregone Conclusions*, (Berkeley LA – London, University of California Press, 1994), p. 16.

[26] BAZ ML.

[27] See László Karsai, 'The People's Courts and Revolutionary Justice in Hungary, 1945-46', in: István Deák, Jan T. Gross & Tony Judt (eds), *The Politics of Retribution: World War II and Its Aftermath*, (Princeton: Princeton University Press, 2000), pp. 233-51; László Varga, '"Forradalmi törvényesség": Jogszolgáltatás 1945 után Magyarországon', *Beszélő*, Vol. 4, No. 11, 1999, pp. 57-73.

[28] The Decree on the People's Tribunals. No. M. E. 81/1945, p. 6.

[29] See *The Politics of Retribution*; Henry Rousso, *The Vichy Syndrome: History and Memory in France since 1944*, (Cambridge MA, Harvard University Press, 1991); Pieter Lagrou, *The Legacy of Nazi Occupation: Patriotic Memory and National Recovery in Western Europe, 1945-1965*, (Cambridge, Cambridge University Press, 2000). For forgetting the Second World War, see Tony Judt, 'The Past is Another Country: Myth and Memory in Postwar Europe', in *The Politics of Retribution*, pp. 293-324. The German case is in Alf Lüdtke, 'Coming to Terms with the Past: Illusions of Remembering, Ways of Forgetting Nazism in West Germany', *Journal of Modern History*, Vol. 65, No. 3, 1993, pp. 542-572, and Bernhard Giesen, 'National Identity as Trauma: The German Case', in: Bo Stråth (ed), *Myth and Memory in the Construction of Community*, (Brussels, Pieter Lang, 2000), pp. 240-7. On Sweden in the same volume, see Bo Stråth, 'Poverty, Neutrality and Welfare: Three key Concepts in the Modern Foundation Myth of Sweden', pp. 393-4. For the Hungarian case, see István Rév, 'Miért győzhetett oly elviselhetetlenül könnyen a kommunizmus Magyarországon?', *Rubicon*, Vol. 4, No. 7, 1989, pp. 4-6.

[30] Michel Foucault, 'Truth and Juridicial Forms' in: Idem, *Power*, (New York, New Press, 2000), pp. 46-7; Patrick Nerhot, *Law, Writing, Meaning: An Essay in Legal Hermeneutics*, (Edinburgh, Edinburgh University Press, 1992), pp. 24-109. See Carlo Ginzburg, *The Judge and The Historian*, (London - New York, Verso, 1999), pp. 12-14.

[31] BAZ ML.

[32] *Szabad Magyarország*, 7 April, 1948.

[33] *Felvidéki Népszava*, 7 April 1948.

[34] *Felvidéki Népszava*, 7April 1948.

[35] Ibid.

[36] BAZ ML.

[37] Roland Barthes created the concept of 'reality effect' to signify these apparently unimportant particulars in narratives. See his 'The Reality Effect' in Idem, *The Rustle of Language*, (Oxford, Basil Blackwell, 1986), pp. 141-8.

[38] *Szabad Magyarország*, 24 March 1948.

[39] *Szabad Magyarország*, 25 March 1948.

[40] *Felvidéki Népszava*, 18 February 1948.

[41] *Szabad Magyarország*, 23 March 1948.

[42] *Felvidéki Népszava*, 23 March 1948.

[43] *Szabad Magyarország*, 21 March 1948.

[44] *Felvidéki Népszava*, 24 March 1948.

[45] *Szabad Magyarország*, 20 March 1948.

[46] *Felvidéki Népszava*, 17 March 1948.

[47] BAZ ML.

[48] The way in which Szim's wounds demonstrated his war crimes was the same way in which the inquisitors condemned the suspected witches on the basis of the literature of demonology that clearly prescribed identities. If the defendant 'were to confess, she was guilty; if she remained silent, even under torture, she did so by virtue of an enchantment (the so-called *maleficium taciturnitatis*); if she denied being a witch, then she lied, seduced by the Devil, the father of lies'. Ginzburg, *The Judge and The Historian*, p. 103.

[49] BAZ ML.

[50] During these rites, entities that cannot be categorized without doubts are usually imposed to occupy one prescribed position in the taxonomy, or are simply eliminated through a ceremonial meal. Anthropological data testify to the way in which a system of categories attempts to deal with ambiguity or anomaly. A well-ordered structure of classifications tries to encompass all the phenomena of the surrounding world, whereas an ambiguous or anomalous event entails a challenge to it due to the invitation of more than one interpretation. The experience that does not conform to the previously set system is ordinarily considered 'impure' or dangerous. In other words, an indefinable event spoils the pattern and causes pollution. In order to dissolve the confusion the maintainers of the structure may choose to control the danger physically and to aim at excluding any plurality of meaning by settling for one or the other interpretation. For example, a monstrous childbirth may threaten the cultural order of a society. The Nuer cope with this anomaly by secluding the possibility of manifold interpretations. They treat the children as baby hippopotamuses born to humans accidentally and drive them back to their proper place among animals: the river. Mary Douglas, *Purity and Danger*, (London, Routledge, 1966), pp. 37-40, 49-53 & 94-5.

[51] Erving Goffman, *Asylums: Essays on the Social Situation of Mental Patients and Other Inmates*, (London, Penguin, 1991), pp. 155-6, pp. 375-7, & p. 87.

[52] Foucault, *Discipline and Punish*, (New York, Vintage, 1979), pp. 251-2. On biography as evidence, see István Rév, 'In Mendacio Veritas', *Representations*, Vol. 35, 1991, pp. 1-20.

[53] Foucault, *Discipline and Punish*, pp. 17-22, 99-101, 189-94. Foucault, 'Truth and Juridicial Forms', pp. 56-7, & 83-4.

[54] BAZ ML.

[55] See John L. Austin, *How to Do Things with Words*, (Oxford, Clarendon Press, 1975), pp. 14-5.

[56] Mark J. Osiel also claimed that the formation of collective memory in court is unintentional. The author also expresses doubts concerning the success of history writing in legal proceedings. 'Ever Again: Legal Remembrance of Administrative Massacre', *University of Pennsylvania Law Review*, Vol. 144, No. 2, 1995, pp. 463-74. For a comprehensive view on the structure of retrospective justice, see Stanley Cohen, 'State Crimes of Previous Regimes: Knowledge, Accountability, and the Policing of the Past', *Law and Social Inquiry*, Vol. 20, No. 1, 1995, pp. 7-50.

[57] *Történelem VIII*, (Budapest, Publisher unknown, 1948), pp. 64-5.

[58] *Történelem VIII*, (Budapest, Publisher unknown, 1950), p. 186.

[59] Karsai - Pamlényi, *Fehérterror*, note 1 *supra*.

[60] On the institutional segments of the modernization of history, see Gerard Noiriel, *Sur la "crise" de l'histoire*, (Paris, Éditions Belin, 1996).

[61] Dezső Nemes (ed), *Iratok az ellenforradalom történetéhez*. Vol. 1. *Az ellenforradalom hatalomrajutása és rémuralma Magyarországon 1919-1921*, (Budapest, Szikra, 1953).

[62] Dezső Nemes, 'A vérengző ellenforradalom történetéhez', in: *Iratok*, pp. 7-144.

[63] Nemes, 'A vérengző ellenforradalom', p. 108.

[64] Amos Funkenstein, 'History, Counterhistory, and Narrative', in: Saul Friedlander (ed), *Probing the Limits of Representation*, (Cambridge MA – London, Harvard University Press, 1992), pp. 66-81.

Conclusion

[1] Seweryn Bialer, 'Poland and the Soviet Imperium', *Foreign Affairs*, America and the World 1980.

[2] Jan Adams (ed), *Economic Reform and Welfare System in the USSR, Poland and Hungary*, (London, Macmillan, 1991).

[3] Miklós Haraszti, *The Velvet Prison: Artists under Socialism*, (New York, Noonday Press, 1987).

[4] S.B. Majrooh & S.M.Y. Elmi, *The Sovietization of Afghanistan 1979-1989*, (Peshanar, Manohar Books, 1986); A. Rasul Amin, 'A General Reflection on the Stealthy Sovietization of Afghanistan', *Central Asian Survey*, Vol. 3, No. 1, 1984, pp. 58-61 (1985).

[5] Moshe Lewin, *The Gorbachev Phenomenon: A Historical Interpretation*, (London, Hutchinson Radius, 1989).

[6] Marshall L. Goldman, *Gorbachev's Challenge: Economic Reform in the Age of High Technology*, (New York - London, W.W. Norton, 1987); Alec Nove, *The Economics of Feasible Socialism*, (London, Allen and Unwin, 1983). For reflections on the economic reasons for the collapse of the communist economic system, see János Kornai, *The Socialist System: The Political Economy of Communism*, (Oxford, Oxford University Press, 1992).

[7] Loren R. Graham, *The Ghost of the Executed Engineer: Technology and the Fall of the Soviet Union*, (Cambridge MA - London, Harvard University Press, 1993).

8 E.A. Rees, 'Systemic Exhaustion and Political Collapse: Explaining the demise of Soviet Communism', (Unpublished paper presented to the Conference on the Demise of Communism, Gramsci Institute Rome, May 2001).

[9] L. Gordon & A. Nazimova, 'Perestroika in Historical Perspective: Possible Scenarios', *Government and Opposition*, Vol. 25, No. 1, 1990, pp 3-15. See, also, E.A. Rees (ed), *The Soviet Communist Party in Disarray: The* XXVIII *Congress of the Communist Party of the Soviet Union*, (Basingstoke, Macmillan, 1992), Introduction.

[10] David Caute, *The Dancer Defects: The Struggle for Cultural Supremacy during the Cold War*, (Oxford, Oxford University Press, 2003).

[11] Piotr Pykel, 'The Final Stage: A Comparative Study of the Transition from Communist Rule to Democratic Government in Poland and Czechoslovakia', Ph.D thesis, (European University Institute, Florence, 2004).

[12] Stanley Cohen, *State of Denial: Knowing about Atrocities and Suffering*, (Cambridge MA, Polity Press, 2001).

[13] Raymond Pearson, *The Rise and Fall of the Soviet Empire*, (New York, St. Martin's Press, 1998); John L. H. Keep, *Last of the Empires: A History of the Soviet Union 1945-1991*, (Oxford, Oxford University Press, 1996); Ryszard Kapuscinski, *Imperium*, (London, Granta, 1998)..

Contributors

Dr. Tarik Cyril Amar Academic Director of the Center for Urban History of East Central Europe in Lviv, Ukraine.

Dr. Marcello Anselmo recently received his PhD from the European University Institute, Florence.

Dr. Balázs Apor Lecturer, Kodolányi János University College and University of Debrecen.

Dr. Péter Apor Research Fellow at the Central European University, Budapest.

Dr. Jan C. Behrends Research Fellow at the Wissenschaftzentrum Berlin für Sozialforschung.

Dr. David Crowley Deputy Head of Department, Royal College of Art, London.

Dr. Valentina Fava Max Weber Fellow, European University Institute, Florence.

Maciej Górny Research Fellow, Center for Historical Research of the Polish Academy of Sciences in Berlin.

Dr. Árpád von Klimó Privatdozent, Research Fellow at the Zentrum für Zeithistorische Forschung, Potsdam.

Roman Krakovsky PhD candidate, Sorbonne University Paris, Lecturer at Institut d'études politiques, Paris; Sorbonne University, Paris; and Comenius University, Bratislava.

Sibylle Mohrmann Researcher, Department of European Ethnology, Humboldt University, Berlin.

Professor Arfon Rees Professor of Eastern European History, European University Institute, Florence.

Dr. Mateja Režek Research Assistant, Institute for Contemporary History, Ljubljana.

Dr. Petr Roubal Lecturer East and Central European Studies, Charles University, Prague.

Anna Maria Şincan PhD candidate, Central European University, Budapest.

Dr. Matthias Uhl Research Fellow, Deutsches Historisches Institut, Moscow

Index

www.ingramcontent.com/pod-product-compliance
Lightning Source LLC
LaVergne TN
LVHW050925080826
845145LV00001B/216

* 9 7 8 0 9 8 0 0 8 1 4 6 6 *